D1550538

SIENA

View of Siena from the Public Gardens

(S. Domenico at the left, the Cathedral at the right)

SIENA

THE STORY OF A MEDIÆVAL COMMUNE

BY

FERDINAND SCHEVILL

WITH ILLUSTRATIONS AND MAPS

NEW YORK
CHARLES SCRIBNER'S SONS
MDCCCCIX

PREFACE

THE persistent interest manifested by the public in the story of the Italian communes will, I hope, make an apology for the present book on Siena unnecessary. The method which I have pursued, however, as well as my general purpose, require a brief explanatory statement.

Though availing myself, to the best of my ability, of the work of my many predecessors in this field, I have constantly striven to arrive at an independent view of every circumstance of Sienese history by a personal study of the sources, both printed and unprinted. But while my critical method was as severe as I could make it, during the labors of composition I kept in mind a prospective audience, composed, not of a small group of specialists, but of that larger body of men and women who constitute a spiritual brotherhood by reason of their common interest in the treasure of the past. My book addresses itself frankly to the general reader. A considerable and flourishing group of historical students would have that important, though alas! often mythological, member of the commonwealth wholly ignored, on the ground of his being as incapable of raising himself to the level of the high concerns of scholarship as he is unworthy to receive its benefits. I venture to differ with this opinion, and make bold to affirm my belief that scholarship practised as the secret cult of a few initiates, amidst the jealous and watchful exclusion of the public, may indeed succeed in preserving its principles from contamination, but must pay for the immunity obtained with the failure of the social and educational purposes which are its noblest justification.

Whoever is not fundamentally hostile to the popularizing function of scholarship which I have just expounded will not quarrel with my system of notes and references. Having the general reader in view, I considered it highly important not to confuse or irritate him with the distracting rumble of a vast accompanying apparatus. I determined on a minimum in this respect—a minimum to be determined by two, as I thought, simple and intelligible criteria. In the first place, I was resolved that my references should be complete enough to enable the scholar to possess himself, in a general way, of my equipment and to test the accuracy of my procedure, and further, I wished to supply the general reader, who might desire to enlarge his information on any matter touched upon in the text, with a convenient list of references. The carrying of this plan to its logical conclusion seemed to call for a catalogue of all the printed works mentioned in the footnotes. This catalogue will be found at the end of the book in the form of an appendix. Of course it lays no claim to being a complete bibliography of the subject.

It remains to say a word as to the plan and contents of my book. I have not written a political history of Siena. To be sure, I have dealt with the political evolution of the commune, but only as one, though an important, phase of the larger problem of its civilization. On this point, on the civilization of Siena, I have concentrated all my efforts. Starting with the simple fact that this town of southern Tuscany, in the period of its freedom, erected for its comfort and delight a diversified, engaging, and wholly distinctive house of life, I determined to illuminate this attractive edifice from as large a number of angles as possible. As soon as my object had thus clearly defined itself, I could not fail to discover that a topical treatment of the material was better suited to my ends than a strictly chronological one. The latter system would have required the steady following of a score of paths, coupled with the perpetual retention in my hands of a hundred interwoven threads. I preferred the plan of following through a series of selected threads in the order in which I took them up, and of meeting the requirements of unity by an occasional chapter weaving my constituent elements into a connected whole. By isolating for examination the nobles, the clergy, the merchants, and the other classes of the commonwealth, by following separately the developments of public and private life, by reviewing the achievements of the various arts, I have, as it were, delivered to my reader the small colored cubes, which of their own accord should fall into suitable relations, achieving the end I had in view—as complete a mosaic of Sienese culture as was possible within the compass of a single volume.

But even should I have attained this purpose, I should not feel that I had reached my ultimate goal, unless I had succeeded in still another matter far more difficult and subtle, and had brought out clearly and convincingly that the achievements of Sienese civilization are nothing but the successive emanations of a town personality, which, though unseen and intangible, was and remains more real than its surviving monuments of brick and stone. The Siena of the Middle Age, in spite of its narrow limits, was a nation, and had a distinctive soul as certainly as any nation which plays a rôle on the political stage of our own day. Shy as a swallow this imperishable personality still flits over the hills among the silvery olives, or in the purple dusk wanders like a stray wind among the narrow streets. As the one gift utterly worth giving, I would fain hope that I had disclosed to the reader something of the charm and diffused fragrance of this local spirit, integral and indestructible part of the eternal spirit of truth and beauty; failing in this, I have failed in the most essential part of my task, and must consider myself to be making a poor return for the generous hospitality of which, during many years and at various seasons, I have been the grateful recipient. For

Siena still has the large heart which, according to an old inscription on Porta Camollia, swings as wide open to the stranger as the gate whereby he enters: *cor magis tibi Sena pandit.* Not to have stamped upon a book dealing with the City of the Virgin a likeness, in some degree, at least worthy of its past and present, is to invite the oblivion which is the wage of incapacity.

CONTENTS

LIST OF ILLUSTRATIONS

xi

SIENA

SIENA

CHAPTER I

THE ORIGIN OF MEDIÆVAL SIENA

THE province of central Italy, known as Tuscany in our day, has a broken and richly diversified physical character, due to its position between the mountains and the sea. The Arno is its chief artery. Rising among the bare crags of the upper Apennines, it drops by gradual stages from the mountains to the foot-hills, and, holding a general westerly direction, makes its way through a plain, growing ever broader, greener, and more smiling, to the Mediterranean Sea. In its proud progress it receives, now at its right hand, now at its left, innumerable tributaries. The northern affluents flow, like it, from the Apennines, which sweep seaward at this point, marching with the river and raising a lofty barrier between Tuscany and the Lombard plain; the southern streams, on the other hand, come from the Tuscan upland, across which the high central Apennines look out upon the open sea.

Within this Tuscan upland, defined by the soaring Apennines, the city-bearing Arno, and the blue Mediterranean, befell the human circumstances which will engage our attention in this book. Though small in area, it is a region fair to look upon, being a broken

1

plateau of many valleys cut by many streams, which, as a glance at the map will show, run in the main in two directions—to the north and to the west. The northward-flowing waters feel their way in thread-like streams, capable, however, of sudden, torrential expansion, to the Arno, while the westward rivers cut a difficult and circuitous path through frowning barriers of wood and rock to the sea. Northward the rivers flow and westward, a point of capital importance, for on the irregular central ridge dividing the streams lies the town of Siena, clearly designed by the place it occupies to be the ruler of the region. Rising almost under its walls the Elsa River finds its way after a capricious journey into the Arno, while a network of small streams, all tributary to the rapid Ombrone, carries the memory of the fair queen of the upland to the Mediterranean.

If beauty of situation determined the importance of a city, Siena would have been second to none in Italy. But, unfortunately, the unrivalled site imposed a number of permanent material drawbacks. One alone of these, the lack of water, constituted no less than a calamity; for at their sources among the hills the Elsa and the Ombrone are mere brooks, not only unsuited to navigation but incapable even of yielding a liberal supply of drinking water for man and beast. Was it conceivable that Siena should ever overcome this fundamental disability? Was it at all likely that a town suffering from scarcity of water and deprived of what in early times was always the safest means of communication with the surrounding territory, a generous water-course, should ever become a great directive agent of civilization? No, its action would necessarily be limited, its world would be hardly more than the dependent district which the citizen, gazing from the ramparts, saw lying at his feet. The story of Siena, set high and dry among the hills, could never be the tale of a world-centre, such as Venice, or Milan, or Florence, bestriding each, like a colossus, one of the great and convenient highways of the Italian peninsula.

And yet, within its narrow provincial limits the destiny and fortunes of Siena might rise to inspiring and memorable heights. Any visitor of the town has still brought vividly home to his attention that, in compensation for its lack of navigable streams and its relative remoteness from the crowded lines of trade, it is endowed with a lavish sum of minor natural advantages. The fair ridge upon which it lies enjoys an admirable climate, secure from the extremes of heat and cold; the air, washing the middle levels between the sea and the Apennines, is splendidly bracing and salubrious; and although the countryside is broken and uneven, being trenched in all directions by numerous torrential brooks, the soil is generally fertile, bearing all the products of the temperate zone and excellently adapted on the steep hillsides for the cultivation of the vine and olive. Here, then, was from of old a sufficient promise of riches, the necessary foundation for every higher civilization. But the civilization itself would have to be the work of the people, the men and women of Siena. Would Siena ever reap, to match her material opportunities, that nobler harvest, the harvest of the mind, the harvest of the soul? To this, the human issue, every question in history in the end comes back, wherefore we may assert that as Siena produced a worthy or a negligible race of men, it would be remembered or forgotten among the cities of the world. And because its success in this field, in the mediæval period at least, was great, because in some respects it was even astonishing, I need offer no apology for calling the attention of a later time to the ruling city of the Tuscan uplands. It is mediæval Siena which is our concern in this book, but because this mediæval city was founded on an earlier past, I may be permitted to glance rapidly, by way of introduction to our subject, at some of its antecedent phases.

ETRUSCAN SIENA

At the time when we get our first certain information about Tuscany it was called, in the Latin tongue, Etruria, and was inhabited by a people known to their Latin neighbors as Etruscans. The Roman writers, through whom the Etruscans were introduced to history, recount the vigorous resistance which they offered to the encroachments of the ambitious republic in the Tiber valley. We hear of their great cities, perched high on hills, like eagles' nests, and called by names which prove that they were the authentic ancestors of Volterra, Chiusi, Fiesole, Arezzo, and many other still existing settlements. In the third century before Christ the Romans, after a long struggle, completed the conquest of Etruria (280 B.C.), and the cities, referred to by the Roman writers as centres of opulence, became allies (*socii*) of Rome and lost their independence. Therewith the process of their Latinization set in, but had hardly gone very far when the towns were ruined and the country turned into a desert by the long civil struggle which preceded the downfall of the republic. Julius Cæsar, and, after him, Augustus, the great restorer, gave their best efforts to the recovery of Italy from the awful harrying of the civil wars, and by means of colonies planted throughout the peninsula, in desolated towns, or on new sites, set flowing once more the arrested currents of life. Naturally the Roman colonies produced a Roman civilization. In Etruria such natives as the wars had spared were absorbed by the conquerors, and presently adopted the Roman speech, dress, and manners. Etruria forgot that it had been Etruscan and proudly called itself Latin. To all intents and purposes the transformation was effected in the lifetime of Augustus.

The Etruscan people, which thus dropped out of history at the moment when the republic assumed the purple and became an empire, has exercised a strong and persistent fascination on the historian, the philologist, and the student of art. Who were they? whence came they? with what race or races known to history were they connected by blood and speech? Some five thousand inscriptions in their tongue, which might clear up the mystery, have been collected in various repositories, but they remain dumb, as no philologist has penetrated the secret of their language. The only thing which may be reasonably deduced from these literary remains is that the Etruscans were not related to the Italic peoples who occupied the country to the south and east of them, nor to the Celts, who, having forced their way across the Alps and seized the valley of the Po, bounded them on the north. Far more

responsive to the inquirer than the unread inscriptions
of this strange people are their other archæological
remains. No race of men ever gave more loving care
to the disposal of its dead, and none, judging by existing
fragments of city walls, delighted in such gigantic
masonry. Courses of stone still visible at Fiesole,
Cortona, Volterra, and elsewhere, fill the mind with
amazement at the vanished folk who could build on this
colossal scale. Even more suggestive is the revelation
afforded by the uncovered burial places. Sometimes
in the flanks of hills, sometimes under the shelter of a
crumbling citadel, have been found, frequently hol-
lowed out of the living rock, underground streets and
cities of the dead; and throughout the region humbler
vaults with rows of burial urns have been turned up
by a chance thrust of the peasant's spade. As the
Etruscan custom was to lay with the dead in their last
resting-places common objects of daily use, and often,
as well, precious utensils and ornaments, such as vases,
ear-rings, bracelets, scarabs, and mirrors, the uncovered
graves have put us in possession of a body of material
attesting a high degree of craftsmanship and a developed
sense of the beautiful, and bearing profoundly upon the
origin and character of this mysterious people. The
derivation of many of their remains from the Hellenic
world, whether directly by exchange or indirectly by
local imitation, appears at a glance. What, therefore,
in view of this association, was the exact share of the
native genius in these exquisite evidences of culture?
This and a hundred related questions lie beyond our
scope. For our purposes it must suffice definitely to
assure ourselves that the Etruscans were a people of

no mean ability, who, even before the period of their contact with the Romans, had reached a notable level of civilization.

In the days of Etruscan power, when Chiusi and Volterra were defending their independence against the Roman republic to the south, was there an Etruscan settlement at Siena? The Roman records make no mention of it, and yet we know now by irrefutable evidence that such a settlement existed: no vigorous centre of commerce or of war, but a modest group of habitations around an arx or citadel, whither the farming population of the neighborhood could retire on the approach of danger. The citadel, it must be admitted, is largely an inference based on the analogy of other settlements planted by this people; but the fact of men of Etruscan blood having lived in considerable numbers on the Sienese ridges is established beyond challenge by the discovery of numerous burial places, some within the walls of the present town, others within a radius of a few miles.* Their uniformly small scale is a suggestive index of the size of this original Siena. Professor Rossi, a leading local antiquarian, carefully weighing the evidence, ventures to formulate a number of propositions which constitute a chain of reasonable probabilities. He affirms that an Etruscan town, the name of which in Latin transliteration was Saena, existed; that it was small, perhaps dependent on Volterra, and that its arx was located on the highest point of the present town, still known, after hundreds of years, and

* The reader wishing to inform himself on the details of these finds may turn to an article by Pietro Rossi in the "Conferenze," published by the Commissione Senese di Storia Patria (1895).

possibly in memory of its ancient dignity, as Castel
Vecchio, that is, the old citadel. All this does not set a
very definite image before the mind, but in establishing
the certain fact of the settlement and making probable
an arx upon the height, it renders a kindly service to the
imagination by associating the present town with the
dawn of recorded time, and by spinning a thread,
slender but secure, between the twentieth-century
chafferers of street and market and the mysterious
Etruscans, who, out of their graves, still speak to us of
great achievements.

ROMAN SIENA

We reach a more solid footing when we pass from
Etruscan to Roman times. Professor Rossi,* who again
serves as our chief guide, has indicated the probable
stages of a growing intimacy between our upland hamlet
and the conquering republic of Rome. Putting such
conjectures to one side as too intangible, let us fix our
attention on the time when Rome adopted the policy of
planting colonies throughout Italy. She followed this
course, as already mentioned, in consequence of the
depopulation and ruin wrought in Etruria and elsewhere
by the terrible civil wars which preceded the downfall
of the republic. As early as the time of Sulla, Etruria,
and possibly Saena, began to receive Roman colonists,

---

* In the "Conferenze" of 1897 (Published by the Commissione Senese di
Storia Patria). It may seem advisable to explain briefly why I take no account of the many legendary tales touching the origin of Siena. The
simple fact is that most of them carry the stamp of a late invention on their
face, and have little poetic and less historical value. The reader desiring to
inform himself on the subject may consult Rondoni, "Tradizioni popolari
e leggende di un Comune medioevale."

but, however that may be, it is certain that Augustus
is the real Latin rebuilder of the ruined Etruscan town.
Following his victory over Antony, he inaugurated,
probably in the year 30 B.C., the Roman period of
Sienese history.

Our shadowy settlement, which we can barely discern
against the dusk of time, and which we must imagine
smitten with the blight befalling all things Etruscan,
now revived as a Roman colony, bearing the name
Saena Julia.   The evidence on this point, furnished by
inscriptions as well as by the ancient writers, is entirely
conclusive.   In truth the town begins now to become,
if not an individuality with sharply marked characteristics, at least an indisputable historic fact.   Pliny
names it in his Natural History,* so does Ptolemy
in his Geography,† and Tacitus ‡ tells an amusing
story of how a Roman senator passing through Siena
aroused the displeasure of the mob, who, not content
with hustling and cuffing him, mortally wounded his
dignity by drawing about him in a circle and setting up
the customary lamentations over the dead.   Inscriptions, too, containing references to Siena, and found,
some within Sienese territory, some as far away as remote Britain, throw a faint light into the prevailing
gloom of the period.§   From these various sources we
can gain a reasonably distinct picture of the town,
governed, like the other colonies, in imitation of Rome,
by magistrates and senate (*curia*, *ordo*), and composed
of a hierarchy of official classes, resting on the broad

---

* Pliny, III.   † Ptolemy, III, 1.
  ‡ The incident belongs to the time of Vespasian (70 A.D.).   "Historiae,"
IV, 45,
  § On Roman inscriptions, see "Bull. Senese," Vol. II, 74 *ff.*; IV, 136 *ff.*

foundation of the people or plebs. Professor Rossi, guided by a few remaining indications in existing wall or line of street, makes the interesting attempt to draw the axes and fix the gates of the Roman town; but without the help of systematic excavations, which for the present are out of the question, such archæological inquiries will hardly pass out of the realm of speculation. For the present-day visitor of Siena the suggestion of a Roman past is constantly renewed by the symbol, encountered at every turning, of the she-wolf with the twins. Its use as the heraldic emblem of the town has been proved for the thirteenth century,* but may have been general much earlier, and in any case shows a rooted popular conviction that Siena was sprung from the City of the Seven Hills. Avoiding all debatable ground we may assert that Saena Julia flourished for some centuries; that, a small mirror of Rome, it boasted its forum, its temples, and its baths;† and that having shared, within the scope of a decidedly provincial settlement, the greatness of the empire, it began presently to be involved in its decay.

Before the decay ended in the cataclysm of the Barbarian invasions, which involved Siena in a common ruin with the rest of the peninsula, an event occurred of immense consequence for the coming ages: the Roman world adopted Christianity. The general circumstances under which the twilight of the pagan gods set in and the old temples were deserted for the new altars are well known, but few historical data exist which enable

* Rossi, "Conferenze," p. 22.
† For additional notices on archæological remains, see "Bull. Senese," Vol. VI., 103 ff., and Bargagli-Petrucci, "Le Fonti di Siena," Vol. I, chap. 1.

us to see how the great change was effected in the
provinces, and none of an absolutely authoritative
character tell us how Christ's kingdom was established
in Siena. Fact failing, we have legend. In the Middle
Age the story passed from mouth to mouth how, during
the persecution of the emperor Diocletian, a noble
Roman youth, Ansanus by name, escaping from the
capital, sought refuge in Siena, preached, was appre-
hended, and, after working a few miracles of—it must
be confessed—a disappointingly unoriginal character,
suffered death by the sword. A few miles beyond the
eastern gate, on a spur over the river Arbia, and
contiguous to the famous battle-field of Montaperti,
stands, and has stood for many hundred years, a chapel
supposed to mark the spot where the Sienese protomartyr gave up his life. The spur goes by the name
of Dofana. It is not improbable, nay, it is quite
credible, that there is some historic foundation to the
story of Ansanus, for the memory of so significant an
event as the conversion of the city to Christianity was
sure to have lived on; and even if the uncontrolled
fancy of the people is likely to have embellished the
occurrences connected with the coming of the new faith
with the usual exuberant detail, we must admit that concealed beneath the mass of irrelevancies may lie a kernel
of truth. The depth of popular conviction, the spot
of martyrdom, definitely designated as early as the
seventh century, and, finally, the ancient character of
the office of Sant' Ansano read in the Sienese churches,*
lend his ghostly personality an almost irrefutable basis

* The office in its received form dates from the year 1213, and is published
in the "Ordo officiorum ecclesiæ senensis," Bologna, 1766, p. 273.

of fact.   Very probably Christianity first filtered in thin
streams into Siena as into the rest of Italy through
the agency of Greek merchants and travellers, but, in
the early fourth century, we may assert with some
confidence the new faith was through the preaching
of a Roman, Ansanus by name, established for the first
time on a popular foundation destined to broaden and
deepen and to become in the end the substructure of an
entirely new civilization.

Throughout the fourth century the Barbarians at the
boundaries of the empire had been showing increasing
signs of restlessness.   In the fifth century their pressure
on the border posts became irresistible, and the end of
the struggle was foreshadowed as early as 410 A.D.,
when Alaric, chief of the West Goths, seized and plundered Rome.   The story is told of how for years he had
heard an aerial voice which lured him with the whispered words, *Penetrabis ad urbem*, until, in spite of long
inner resistance, he was forced to do its bidding.   In
a letter of St. Jerome we catch the reverberation which
this amazing event produced in the Mediterranean
world; from afar, in his cell at Bethlehem, where the
news reached him and laid him prostrate with grief,
he raised the despairing cry, *Quid salvum est si
Roma perit?* *   Italy now became the prize of the Teu-
tonic invaders, but it is still too often thoughtlessly
repeated that a hitherto flourishing country was by this
occupation first made acquainted with misery.   True,
the conquerors poured over the Alps in successive
waves; they brought not peace but war, and doubtless,
therefore, desolation followed in their path; but, before

---

* Hodgkin, "Italy and Her Invaders," Book I, Chs. 16 and 17.

The Abbey Church of Sant' Antimo

Interior view

it was possible for them—a rude and ill-disciplined savage host—to break into the garden of civilization, the inhabitants of that garden must have sunk into all but complete decay. The history of the later empire is the history of a prolonged sick-bed. Wherever the cover is lifted the eye meets the same evidence of incurable disease. A central government hardened into a selfish bureaucracy, its financial agents an organized band of spoliators, the local administration corrupt and in dissolution, the army unpaid and mutinous—these are some of the signs which declared with sound of brass that the empire was sick, sick beyond recovery. If the invasions brought the plundering of cities, rich with the accumulated treasure of the ages; if they brought the harrying of fields and the slaughter of their tillers, they did no more than to effect, in swift, dramatic form, a catastrophe which, in the absence of human violence, would have been wrought just as completely by the slow-grinding mills of time.

The successful raid in the year 410 of Alaric, king of the West Goths, was the prelude to similar expeditions. Plunderers came and went, like a summer storm or a spring flood, leaving no permanent mark on the peninsula. But with the Herulian Odoacer, and, more emphatically still, with Theodoric, king of the East Goths, the Barbarians adopted a new policy of permanent settlement. The East Goths made themselves at home in Italy and held fast to its choicest lands from their coming under their great king to their overthrow by the armies of Justinian, that is, for a period of about half a century (489–553). For a short interval after the fall of the East Goths, Italy was again a part of the empire, an empire, however, no longer Latin, but purely Greek and ruled from Constantinople (554-68). Then came the invasion of a new German folk, the Lombards (568), and the piecemeal conquest of the peninsula from the stubbornly resisting emperor. In the end the Lombards came to dominate the whole north and centre, incorporating these regions in their kingdom of Lombardy. As their destructive rule, while completing the wreckage of the old culture, inaugurated the Italian Middle Age, we must give some little attention to it if we would understand the rise of mediæval Siena.

However, before taking up the Lombard conquest in detail, we may pause to raise the epitaph over Saena Julia. What was its history during the long period of inner decay which preceded the coming of the northern tribes? How did it fare at the hands of West Goths, Vandals, East Goths, Lombards? No writer has deigned to tell us how the great circumstance of Rome's overthrow affected the provincial town at the headwaters of the Elsa and the Ombrone. The darkness lying over these many centuries of local history is impenetrable. All that we may say, judging by the consequences, is that Roman Siena perished from the face of the earth. Did it die of that moral dry-rot which ate out the vitals of Rome? Or was it at some quiet dawn surrounded by the forces of Alaric, Ricimer, or some other plunderer bound for Rome, taken before the watchman could sound the alarm, and left at nightfall a heap of smoking ruins? The completeness with which the Roman colony vanished, leaving hardly a course of masonry behind which can be definitely identified as Roman, proves at least that it was over-taken with disaster. By the time of the coming of the Lombards it could hardly have been more than an aggregation of hovels, an inconsiderable market-place for the ravaged and depopulated uplands. But as with these same Lombards new germs of life appear everywhere throughout Italy, so with them begins a new period of the history of Siena. As early as the eighth century, while the Lombard kingdom was at its height, we get news of her, news which tells us in no uncertain terms, that life is again stirring in the desolate land, and that the third, the Italian Siena, is slowly taking shape.

ITALIAN OR MEDIÆVAL SIENA

The quality about the risen Siena of the eighth century, communicating itself immediately and with clearness in the few notices of the time, is, that the *milieu* of the town is no longer Roman, but mediæval and Lombard. For this reason we must, if we would understand the beginnings of Siena's third and trium-phant epoch—the epoch with which this book is to deal —possess ourselves, at least in outline, of the political and administrative history of the Lombard kingdom.

When, in the spring of the year 568, the Lombards under their king Alboin crossed the Julian Alps, they had no difficulty in effecting a foothold in the valley of the Po. The emperor at Constantinople was repre-sented in his province of Italy by an official called an exarch, whose seat was at Ravenna. The exarch made little resistance, and the Italian natives, calling them-selves, as members of the empire, Romans, though

really a mixture of many races, reduced under the long
Latin rule to a common type, were too unmanned and
broken by the interminable succession of previous
invasions and recent pestilence and famine to render
their ruler any effective help. Moreover, this latest multitude "which the populous North poured from her
frozen loins," was, if we are to believe contemporary
evidence, the most terrible of all the Barbarian hosts
which fate had let loose upon poor Italy. Their fierce
manners and savage aspect, unrelieved by any softening
influences of civilization, struck a cold fear through the
hearts of the effete Romans. Especially did the delicate, clean-shaven natives single out for notice and
aversion the savage masses of hair and beard adorning
their enemies, characteristic features to which this
rugged folk owes its name of Langobards, that is,
Longbeards. They soon dominated the north with the
exception of Venetia, the Ravennese, and Genoa, maritime districts which were not reducible without a fleet,
and presently pushed southward over the Apennines
through Tuscany to Spoleto and Benevento. In the
south, too, the maritime districts with their strong ports
of Bari, Tarento, Otranto, and Naples, withstood the
onset of the strangers, who had neither ships nor any
knowledge of the sea. Likewise, Rome, energetically
defended by its spiritual rulers—above all, by the great
Pope Gregory—maintained its independence.

The equilibrium thus established between invaders
and defenders determined the history of Italy throughout the two centuries of the Lombard dominion. The
fragments of the empire north and south, ruled by the
exarch at Ravenna and held together to a certain extent

by the spiritual prestige of the pope, resisted with all
their might the further progress of the Lombards, who
for their part, possessed approximately of two-thirds of
the peninsula, were naturally desirous to disembarrass
themselves entirely of their struggling enemies and to
complete their conquest.   In the long run the scales
inclined in favor of the Lombards.   Every new sovereign continued to push out his boundaries by making
some small acquisition from the emperor and his
exarch, until it became plain that the unity of Italy
under Lombard auspices was inevitable.   Disconsolate
over the impending peril, the pope made appeal after
appeal to the great folk of the Franks across the Alps
to come to his assistance.   But we are anticipating.
For the present we note with interest that Tuscany
was part of the Lombard kingdom almost from the
first, having been occupied as early as the year 570,
in the days of Alboin.

The rule of the conquerors, especially in its early
stages, was of the most primitive order.   Paul, son of
Warnefrid, a literary Lombard of the eighth century,
has told us almost everything we know about it.*   He
relates that his forbears, on their first coming into Italy,
ruthlessly murdered the great Roman landowners, and
made the rest of the inhabitants tributary by exacting
a payment of one-third of the produce of the fields.
They came for booty and its division must have been
their main, if not their only, concern.   Inevitably, however, and almost from the first day, the need would make
itself felt for some kind of government.   Without a
trace of reverence for the Roman name the Barbarians

* In his Historia Langobardorum.   Paul died about the year 795.

began to organize their administration along lines which
appealed to their greed of possession and which were not
too remote from their experience. Then it was that the
distinctive features of the Roman administration, in so
far as any had survived the storms of the last generations, were swept into oblivion. The leading features
of that system were, it is generally agreed, the municipal
senate or curia, which performed the service of a local
government, and the Roman law, which bound all the
parts of the wide empire together under a common
system of justice. It used to be maintained that Roman
curia and Roman law disappeared indeed from sight
in the Lombard period, but somehow eked out a hunted
and subterranean existence until, after many years,
they experienced a glorious rebirth in the Italian communes of the twelfth century.* These communes,
according to this view, mark not only the happy appearance of political liberty in the world after the intolerable
anarchy of feudal times, but specifically denote the
rebirth of the Roman municipal constitution, which,
never destroyed, had merely dropped into a long winter's

* I touch here upon the famous controversy inaugurated by Savigny,
who in his "Geschichte des Römischen Rechts im Mittelalter" urged that
the Roman system never perished, and taken up by Hegel, who in his
"Städteverfassung von Italien" expounded the contrary view. A fair
recapitulation of the respective arguments will be found in Hodgkin, "Italy
and Her Invaders," Vol. VI, chap. 13. I should add that the question of the
Roman municipal institutions is now generally separated from the question
of the Roman law. The persistence of the latter in the church and, with
limited application, among the laity, as personal law, is no longer doubted.
Further, the opinion is coming to prevail that certain minor administrative
officers of Roman origin, such, for instance, as had to do with the repair of
fountains, the maintenance of roads and bridges, survived, at least in many
places. What interest could the Lombards have had in sweeping them
away? They fastened their grip upon those elements of the administration
which ensured them the political control of the country, such as justice, taxes,
and the army.

sleep.   We may now safely declare this opinion chimer-
ical.   The Lombards were enemies; they were complete masters of the situation; they knew no compromise.   There is no evidence that they suffered any
government but that which they authorized, and which
they could comprehend and utilize for their selfish
purposes.   But there is evidence that the awful times
were beginning to work their own remedy by means of
certain voluntary associations not contemplated in the
official Lombard arrangements.

The growth of voluntary associations, involving the
gradual recovery by the down-trodden Italians of self-
government, at first, of course, on a very modest basis,
may be presented in the following general terms.   The
monarchy of Alboin did after a while, with the cessation
of plunder, bring comparative peace, peace brought new
life, and life in its busy, irrepressible fashion led to new
forms of social organization.   In the Lombard period
we may see how men deprived of the fruits of civilization,
separated violently from the institutions on which they
had leaned, thrust back almost into the state of nature,
take their first timid steps toward social regroup-
ing along entirely simple and natural lines.   In these
humble measures, assuming the form of agreements
among neighbors for adjusting quarrels, for repairing
roads and water conduits, and for other matters of immediate interest to a small circle, scholars are now
agreed to seek for the germs of the great free communes,
which shed their incomparable light over the later
Middle Age.   An idle quarrel this, the general reader
may be tempted to interpose.   As long as the cities
achieved their freedom and used it for some noble end,

what can it matter if they owed it entirely to themselves or received it as a heritage from imperial Rome? But surely it is not pedantry, it is an instinctive sympathy with youth and force, which gives us pleasure in the knowledge that the Italian liberty of the Middle Age was not a successful copy or revival of extinct Roman forms, but a healthy, spontaneous, and original product, cultivated through silent or almost silent centuries from a seed sown at a time when to outward seeming the end of the world was at hand. I have broached a great question here, though I am not able to follow it further at this point. It is impossible to write about any Italian commune without giving attention to the controversy, as old as the modern science of history, concerning the origin of the town liberties. I have indicated broadly the direction and implication of the most recent studies in the field. In a later chapter, when the specific question of the liberties of Siena is before us, I shall return to this issue, which is possessed, as a long line of brilliant names testifies, of the most persistent fascination. For the present I shall take up the thread of the Lombard administration.

The power of the Lombard king depended largely on his character and personal equipment. When he was a man of force and daring he made his will felt to the uttermost corners of his realm; when he was weak or a child, the agents who represented him in the provinces became practically independent. These representatives were of two kinds, dukes and gastalds, the dignity of duke being the higher distinction and conferring a semi-independent position. A gastald was more definitely the appointee of the king, sent out on the king's business

and removable at the will of his master. Duke and
gastald alike made their homes in the cities, not because
they preferred them to the country—a thing unlikely in
view of the keen passion of the German peoples generally for the open air—but because experience would
teach that the cities were the convenient and necessary
centres of administration for a given district. In
Tuscany gastalds prevailed, an indication that the
king kept his hand more firmly on this province; and
indeed rebellion, so constant and distressing a phenomenon of Lombard history, seems to have been relatively
infrequent within the boundaries of Tuscany. In the
early eighth century Siena had a gastald of the name of
Taipert, during whose rule we get our first lively glimpse
of the town since the cloud of darkness which descended
upon it in the later stages of imperial Rome. No Tuscan
city of the time introduces itself to our attention with an
incident of equally bold relief. At the hand of authentic documents * we can recover the details of a most
passionate situation.

Following the terrible decay and anarchy associated
with the migrations, Siena must have begun slowly to
feel the effects of the comparative security of Lombard
rule, for in the seventh century we get news of her as
the seat both of a bishop and of a royal gastald. A
bishop, Maurus by name, exercised episcopal authority
in Siena about 650 A.D. Perhaps he was the first of
the episcopal line, more likely he marked the restoration
of a diocese, which, established in the fourth century
in the first flush of the Christian triumph, had in the

* All the documents bearing on the case will be found in Pasqui, "Documenti per la Storia della Città di Arezzo."   Florence, Vieusseux, 1899.

following period of confusion suffered shipwreck. At any rate, the territory over which Maurus held spiritual sway was very small and the dioceses of his neighbors pressed upon him most uncomfortably, especially to the east where the bishop of Arezzo held the territory almost up to the city wall. Perplexing as this was in view of the fact that the dominion of the gastald, the bishop's temporal counterpart, embraced all the region immediately about the city, it was rendered positively distressing by the circumstance that the bishop of Arezzo became thereby lord of the tomb where lay the bones of the Sienese apostle, Sant' Ansano. Bishop Maurus tried to extend his authority eastward on the plea that the diocese ought to be coextensive with the civil district ruled by the gastald. All his efforts remained futile. The case, involving the beloved saint, appealed not only to the clergy, but to gastald and people as well. However, the Aretine prelate was in possession and would not retire in spite of the growing resentment of the Sienese. Then suddenly, as might have been foreseen, came an armed clash. In the year 711 the bishop of Arezzo, Lupertianus, came, in performance of his duties, to the Dofana region where the body of Ansano lay. That was all the provocation which the Sienese needed. Did they suspect that Lupertianus had come to carry away secretly to Arezzo for permanent safe-keeping the precious relics of the saint? At any rate they poured out of the town, led by the gastald, Taipert, and his judge, Godipert. Their going might mean mischief and the bishop, as a man of peace, wisely stayed at home. We can fancy him restlessly pacing his room, climbing the tower perhaps to scan the bare chalk hills to the east, whither the angry crowd had poured to assert the Sienese citizenship of their saint. Let the Aretine chronicler * tell the story as he found it recorded in *"vetustissimis thomis."*

"Lupertianus, bishop of Arezzo, was staying with his servants in the church of S. Maria in Pacina, quietly attending to those things which pertain to a bishop in his diocese. At that time the city of Siena was ruled by Aripert, king of the Lombards, and in it dwelt a royal judge, Godipert by name. He, coming with Taipert, the gastald, to the church where Lupertianus, bishop of Arezzo, was, without showing the bishop the least respect, began to hurl injuries at the bishop's men, and to insult them, and to vex them with legal proceedings (*per placita fatigare*). The which the Aretines attending the bishop supported for some time, until, flaming up, they fell upon and killed Godipert, the Sienese judge. Wherefore the whole people of Siena (*universus senensis populus*) became enraged against Bishop Lupertianus and put him to flight; and they obliged Adeodatus, bishop of Siena, who was the cousin of the aforesaid Godipert, the judge whom the Aretines had slain, to hold that parish whether he would or no for one year; and there outrageously and against the canons of our church he consecrated three altars and two priests."

The routed bishop of Arezzo made frantic appeals for justice in all directions, and presently the pope at Rome as well as the Lombard king interposed to quell the disturbance. The case, as submitted to judgment, involved, in addition to the spot of Ansano's martyrdom, all the parishes of the Sienese political territory—eighteen, to be exact, with three monasteries—which were

* The chronicler is Gerardus, head of the cathedral chapter of Arezzo. He wrote his narrative about 1056 from ancient records, and his facts, in spite of his being a partisan, have every appearance of veracity. See Pasqui, p. 23, note 2.

incorporated with the diocese of Arezzo. The first sentence of the authenticity of which we may be sure was delivered in the court of the major-domo of King Liutprand—the successor to Aripert—in August, 714, and the verdict was in all respects favorable to the complainant. But neither Bishop Adeodatus nor the Sienese would rest content. They caused the case to be reopened, a mountain of evidence was collected, and only after a bench of neutral bishops had declared against the Sienese pretensions and King Liutprand had confirmed the finding (October 14, 715) did they at last desist. But even so not for long. Their beloved saint, their pride as a growing commonwealth were at stake, and every time an opportunity offered they returned to the attack. The case became one of the famous law-suits of mediæval history, dragging its interminable convolutions through five hundred years. Not till 1224 did the matter come to a definitive close with a new solemn sentence by the Roman pontiff in favor of Arezzo.

Although the quarrel has some slight interest on its own account, it merits our attention chiefly by reason of the light which it throws on the reborn city. For Siena was reborn! The issue of the eighteen parishes, in its origin nothing but a technical question between two bishops, took a lively and even warlike turn, for the single reason that the town was aglow with youthful vigor. Siena wanted her saint, a characteristic mediæval desire; but more than that, she wanted no foreign bishop on her political territory. Nor did she handle the case with polite calm through the official channels of bishop and gastald. It developed into a clash at arms for no

Picture of a Monk of S. Galgano
From a Book-cover in the Archivio di Stato

other reason than that the people insisted on playing
a part in the affair.   We have the assurance that it was
the "universus populus senensis" which encouraged
Godipert in his nagging of the bishop's followers, and
then, when Godipert was slain, set upon the Aretines
and their bishop and drove them home with bruised
limbs.   This was no longer the inert human mass
which once let itself be plundered and slaughtered
without resistance by the Barbarian hordes.   Indubitably life was stirring here, not a thin stream of official
life, which is nothing, but broad currents of strong
volition filling the whole people and giving evidence that
a new race was in the process of formation.   And what
a stream of light the little riot with its murdered judge
and routed bishop throws on the traditional view, still
repeated in many books, that the communal liberty of
the Italian towns was born suddenly and without warning about 1100 A.D., and that its origin was a mystery
past finding out!   Perhaps historians have in the past
confined their investigations too narrowly to evidences
of political institutions, forgetful that before liberty can
express itself in the laws, its dominion must be established in the mind and spirit.   Centuries were to pass
before Siena boasted a free, popular government in
full working order, but of this much we may be sure as
early as the eighth century—Siena and her territory
were indeed unfree, being governed in things temporal
by a royal gastald, and in things spiritual by a bishop;
but the people were no longer a multitude of despicable Romans, but alive, moved by ambition, capable
of action, in short, a factor to be reckoned with.

Letting our glance travel beyond the hills of Siena we

become aware presently that elsewhere in Tuscany, in Lombardy as well, nay, north and south in the peninsula, the signs were increasing of a similar popular resurrection. All Italy was coming back to life. Since Alaric had heard the voice which lured him on to Rome three hundred years had passed. If the successive hordes of conquerors who poured across the Alps repel us with their coarseness, brutality, and greed, viewed as men they rise infinitely above the Roman natives, too abject to raise a finger in their own defence. The invaders, without regular supplies, with rude weapons and poor military discipline, numbered at best a few tens of thousands; the unresisting natives rose into the millions. If moral judgments ever have a place in history, we may assert that the unmanned, cringing Romans deserved their subjection to the plundering Herulians, Goths, and Lombards. But among the numerous Germanic invasions, only the Lombard conquest, as we have seen, led to anything like a successful occupation of the soil. It was in the full elation of triumph that the victors set up their rule over the vanquished. They exploited their victims with cold and calculating indifference, but they were thrown into daily association with them, and although they had and planned to keep their own courts, customs, dress, and speech, they found themselves presently exposed to the operation of the common physical law that the greater mass draws the smaller into its orbit. The Lombards had not been a hundred years in Italy before they replaced the Arian Christianity, to which they had been converted during their wanderings in the valley of the Danube, with the Catholic faith championed by the pope and practised by their neighbors; by slow degrees they absorbed increasing elements of the Roman manners, dress, and language. A superior civilization with its arts and inventions, perhaps even more by means of its comforts and cheap delights, exercises a subtle and far-reaching dominion over the simple minds of a Barbarian people. But the question has another side, for, if the Lombards became involved in a gradual process of Romanization, the natives themselves were, to a certain extent, Germanized. To say positively that the Lombards breathed into the exhausted people of the peninsula the spirit of liberty which afterward immortalized itself in the free communes, would be rash, but we can hardly doubt that their successful use of force taught their victims a valuable lesson and brought force once more into repute as the true foundation of society.

In the days of King Liutprand, before whose throne the bishops of Arezzo and Siena brought their quarrel, the Lombards were still conscious of a racial difference between themselves and the natives, but the assimilation of conquerors and conquered must have made immense strides, as the very incident upon which we have lingered proves. The leading persons in Siena were of Lombard blood. We have, in order to convince ourselves, only to examine the names of the officials mentioned in the old legal documents—Taipert, Godipert, Warnefrid, Willerat, and so forth. The Bishop Adeodatus himself with his artificial name of Given-by-God suggests a Lombard origin, which, as was not uncommon, he hid under a Latin pseudonym intended to convey an impression of conspicuous Christian zeal. But if the governing class was still largely Lombard, the old hostil-

ity between it and the people must have subsided, for
in the issue, affecting, through the precious body of
Ansano, the welfare of the whole community, rulers and
ruled acted as one man. In the spirited conduct of
that affair there is not the slightest sign of a division into
Lombards and Romans; to all appearances the old
enemies have fused to form the new race of modern
Italians, which from the eighth century rises into view
with all those characteristics destined to bring the
peninsula to the front once more as the torch-bearer of
civilization.

CHAPTER II

THE FEUDAL AGE AND THE EMERGENCE OF THE FREE COMMUNE

THE thick veil, which hangs over Siena and is lifted a moment by the documents recounting the conflict between the episcopal sees, presently descends anew. Our glimpse disclosed the picture, not only of a people active and even aggressive in its own interest, but of a coöperation between rulers and ruled, affording a clear indication of the advanced state of the fusion of Lombards and Romans into the new Italian race. This fusion was conducted under the auspices of the Lombard state, which, although still of a rudimentary character with the power distributed among dukes, gastalds, and other local agents, was sufficiently centralized to enforce a fair degree of order throughout its dominion. If the Lombards could have completed the conquest of the coast districts, thus uniting Italy under their rule, the peninsula would have met other and happier fortunes than it did. Italian unity, established as early as the eighth century, would, in the course of a few generations, have become so deeply rooted in popular sentiment that the chances of breaking it by assault from without would have been slight. But it was decreed that Italy was not to enjoy the blessing which a strong Lombard state would have brought, and, as every student knows, the Lombard failure resulted from the existence on the peninsula of a rival state, the papacy.

The bishop of Rome, already at the time of the coming of the Lombards the acknowledged spiritual leader of the West, did not have to be a political genius to divine the great and golden future of his office, if only he could secure freedom of movement for himself and immunity from subjection to a temporal sovereign. This is why he became the centre of resistance to the Lombard conquest, and this, too, explains why, when the Lombard kings, following a natural movement of expansion, were at last on the point of possessing themselves of Rome, he made a passionate appeal for help to the Franks. He would have turned preferably to the Greek emperor at Constantinople, as more distant and therefore less dangerous, but that potentate's decline had, by the eighth century, reached the point where he could hardly maintain himself in his immediate dominions. The powerful kingdom of the Franks was the pope's only visible resource. Pippin, and after him his famous son, Charlemagne, came at the papal bidding, and by the year 774 the last Lombard king was a prisoner and his state the prize of a Germanic rival. Charles won a new crown and presently mounted the utmost pinnacle by assuming, on Christmas day of the year 800, the title of Roman emperor.

I am not here narrating the political history of Italy, except in so far as knowledge of it is indispensable for our understanding of the development of Siena. Now the significant feature stamped upon Italian history by the ruin of the Lombard state is the complete decentralization of political power. How did this result come

about? The answer is simple. The empire of the
Franks, overwhelmingly powerful under Charles, presently went to pieces. Italy thereupon became the object
of fierce contention among its dukes and princes, and
the easy victim of any enterprising foreign sovereign
who could lead an army across the Alps. These simple
facts define the political problem of Italy for the whole
mediæval period and for the modern period as well
down to very recent times. What is the significance of
their long persistence? Fancy a state handed over to
innumerable local agents who are perfectly free to
follow their own bent, except for the more or less
theoretic restraint exercised by a usually absent sovereign. The inevitable consequence will be that the local
agents will drop such deep roots, that they will grow
so strong and jealous of their independence that their
subjection to a national ruler will be rendered well-
nigh impossible. Now of all the petty sovereigns of
the peninsula there was none to compare in point of
energy, resources, and venerability with the pope.
What he willed could not be easily resisted, and what he
willed with regard to Italy was, that she should not be
united because her union would put an end to his
temporal sovereignty. One thousand years of papal
history show that the pontiff was ever ready to defeat
the national hopes, and when, hardly a generation
ago, these hopes were at last realized, the consummation was effected in the face of the open hostility
and secret machinations of the successor of Saint
Peter. Even so, now that the union is some forty
years old and enjoys the good-will of all the world,
the pope alone sulks in his palace, a voluntary prisoner,

and declares himself irreconcilably opposed to the national triumph.

But if the fall of the Lombard state gave life—and long life, as it proved to be—to the temporal aspirations of the papacy, it had another consequence more immediately affecting our town of Siena, in that Italy was now feudalized. Of course the feudal germ was planted in the Lombard state, as well as in every other Germanic conquest of the West, but the reach and vigor of Italian feudalism, a reach and vigor suggesting the riotous luxury of a tropical jungle, would have been impossible without the failure of the central and national authority.

Following the death of the great Charles, the Lombard crown—called interchangeably from this time the Italian crown—was permanently weakened. Bandied about for a time among the Italian magnates, each unwilling to concede it to the other, it was at last seized by a capable and vigorous foreigner, King Otto I of Germany (961). Henceforth Italy was an adjunct of Germany, but the German king, bearing the title also of emperor after the ceremony of his coronation by the pope, was usually so weak and far away that he could not keep his provincial agents, dukes, counts, gastalds, or whatever their title, from making themselves more and more independent. To counteract their influence he tried to create a rival for them in the bishops, whom he made civil functionaries by the system called immunities. An imperial diploma or charter of immunities gave the bishop certain sovereign rights, such as the exercise of justice on the episcopal domains and the collection thereon of the taxes and services due to the state. In some cases the king went even farther, and raised the bishop to the post of duke or count; that is, he made him his civil representative throughout a province. The less real the royal power was the more readily the sovereign purchased a temporary support by the gratuitous distribution of privileges. The result was only too inevitable. With the king impotent and generally beyond the Alps, Italian history became a wild scramble for place and power among lords, big and little, lay and spiritual.

For this scramble, characteristic of every society loosely joined and uncontrolled from above, feudalism is the fine and somewhat misleading name. For feudalism in its essence was anarchy. Theoretically the national cohesion was maintained by a system of services due to the king from his dukes and counts, and to them in their turn from their knights; but as these services were rendered only on compulsion, and the compulsion, in Italy at least, was irregular, the practical effect of feudalism was the breaking up of the country into hundreds of larger or smaller lordships, engaged in unscrupulous rivalry and exercising each one an actual power, the measure of which was furnished by the success and failure of each new combination of forces. To this substance of Italian history in the feudal centuries no one should be blinded by the superficial prominence of pope and emperor. These sovereigns, as international potentates, occupied an exalted position; they had constantly to be reckoned with, especially when they brought to bear upon their office a clear intelligence and an enterprising temper; but they were so far from controlling the situation that the only

practical course open to them for political purposes was
to ally themselves with one or another of the many
local factions.   In the Middle Age the pope, and more
conspicuously still, the emperor, was a partisan.   Of
course occasional great emperors, like Henry III, or
Frederick I, rose above purely factional considerations;
but in general the imperial position was weak, false,
and precarious.   The continued feebleness of the nomi-
nal head of the peninsula bears out the assertion that a
strong state and a feudal state are irreconcilable terms,
and that feudalism itself was an extreme form of decentralization.

Under these conditions with every lord frowning
challenge on his fellow from his stronghold among the
hills, with the whole country a seething caldron of
confusion, the only chance for the cities was to help
themselves.   Their existence was founded on labor.
But in the permanent state of petty war confirmed by
feudalism, of what good to any one was labor, with its
fruits exposed to instant confiscation by a crew of lawless freebooters?   The cities could help themselves only
by withdrawing from the vicious circle of feudalism, and
enforcing, by virtue of an independent civic organization, peace, the peace wherein all men may work.   I
have said that in the feudal age the substance of Italian
history was the scramble for power among the great and
small vassals of an impotent, or almost impotent, emperor;
but, as the period advanced, the situation was modified
in the most significant fashion by the gradual emergence
of the cities with their independent aims and programmes.
Here, in fact, lies the vital interest in the Middle Age.
At the first glance the situation only complicated itself

when the cities asked for an independent position in the Italian polity. The struggle was already going on in several planes: pope and emperor towered above the counts, bishops, and other great vassals, who in turn dominated a class of smaller landholders, and now, aspiring to be treated as a separate political element,the cities raised their heads. Among these cities was Siena. Every step taken by her citizens toward a position of ultimate independence would involve consideration: first, of emperor and pope, temporal and spiritual overlords respectively of this and every other Tuscan town; second, of the feudal lords, great and small, possessed of the countryside up to the very walls, engaging in guerilla war as in a sport, and levying way-tolls at every ford and under the shadow of every frowning castle. These general factors must be constantly borne in mind as we follow the history of Siena in the feudal age.

The documentary evidence concerning Siena during the period following the fall of the Lombard state is slight. The feudal darkness descended upon the land, and the few records of the time, which have reached us, speak chiefly of the doings of the great. We hear of lords and princes who harry one another's possessions, of prelates who meet in solemn conclave to consider the welfare of the church, of kings who pass with hosts and banners down the peninsula to be crowned at Rome; laboriously we piece together the starched, official tale of a society, composed apparently merely of an upper class, resting on an undistinguished and negligible mass of common people. As to the life in Siena and in the other Tuscan towns, we are left largely to our fancy, aided by occasional indications, usually of a chance character. Nevertheless, on close scrutiny, the early political fortunes of these towns become, in a general way, discernible. To begin with it is clear that they possess no very definite individuality, correspond in the main to a single type, and experience a common development. Florence and Siena, Pisa and Lucca, so different afterward in their lusty manhood, are alike, if not as pea and pea, at least as children at a christening. For the historian a considerable advantage of these early resemblances is that any bit of information gleaned for one town may be used, with due reserve, to throw light upon the condition of every other.

We know that in the Carolingian epoch the gastald of Siena, representative of the Lombard king, was replaced by a Frankish count. That was merely a change of title; the count continued to preside in court, maintain order, collect the royal fees and rents, to play, in a word, the part of local government. The territory of his jurisdiction was called the *comitatus* (*contado*, county) and comprised the city of his residence and its neighborhood. The comitatus originally may have been clearly staked off, but with the growing confusion of the times, the boundary became uncertain and caused grave disputes with the representatives of the neighboring counties. A similar uncertainty prevailed occasionally with regard to the exact extent of the dioceses. *Comitatus* and *episcopatus*—the dominions respectively of the civil and the spiritual lord—commonly corresponded throughout the kingdom of Italy; but, it would not have been the feudal age, if there had been no exceptions to the rule. Siena, for instance, it may be remembered, learned to her sorrow that certain parishes, lying within her comitatus, were none the less outside the diocese of her bishop. Yet here, also, the two administrative units of state and church coincided in a general way. As the Sienese county is an object of great interest to us, we shall be doing well to familiarize ourselves with its boundaries.

In approximate terms the county of Siena was bounded on the west by the headwaters of the Elsa, on the east by the swamp of the Chiana, and on the south by the courses of the Orcia and the Merse. The Chianti hills, the sunny terraces of which have for centuries grown the rarest wine of Italy, and which draw a close arc around the city to the north, were, to the sorrow of Siena, embraced within the comitatus of Florence. Orcia and Merse themselves, forcing a difficult path through a region of savage cliff and forest before they empty their waters into the Ombrone, were, strictly speaking, beyond the Sienese pale. A small territory, this, and from the economic point of view an average territory without conspicuous resources, but capable, perhaps, in the hands of energetic men, of calling the world's attention to itself.

As the count in this primitive society was not only the leader of the armed host, but also the civil and criminal judge, we hear of him most frequently in connection with sentences delivered in his court. In the work of justice he was regularly assisted by a number of freemen, chosen by the people on account of their knowledge of the law and called *scabini*. As the Franks established in Italy their system of personal law, by which every man according to his nationality had the right to be tried by the Lombard, Frank, or Roman code, the scabini acquired at least a superficial acquaintance with all these systems. In measure as society became less barbarous, and the legal threads binding man to man grew more numerous, only men with special training could serve as scabini. Naturally, therefore, the time came when the scabini were transformed into a professional class of notaries and judges. This formative group, the lawyer element, we may note in passing, had afterward—long after the Frank period with which we are just now concerned—an important share in organizing the free commune, for it was this class that was entrusted with the work of giving the constitutions of the communes a legal shape. By throwing their influence on that occasion on the side of the Roman law, which could not but appeal powerfully to professional men by reason of its evidences of system and culture, the trained lawyers effected the withdrawal of the ruder Germanic practices and penalties in favor of a new local code, which every town worked out for itself on general Roman principles. A little reflection will show that this revival of a defunct system and its complete triumph were inevitable in a country saturated, like Italy, with Roman memories, but we should not fail to note that it offers no proof of the uninterrupted domination of the whole Roman administrative system.

But I have anticipated, led on by the interest attaching to the evolution of the system of justice in the Italian towns. I desire now to return to the history of

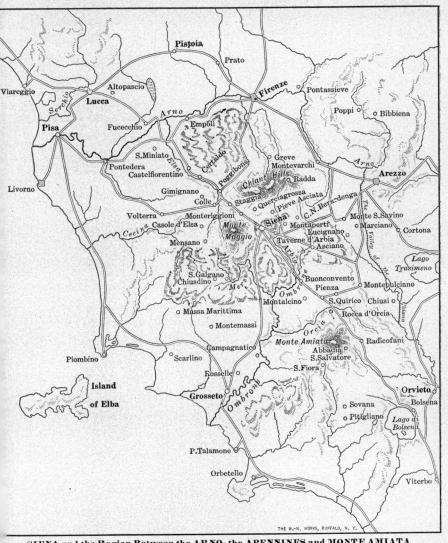

SIENA and the Region Between the ARNO, the APENNINES and MONTE AMIATA

the count's territory, the comitatus. If, in the days of Charlemagne, the comitatus was the fundamental administrative unit of the empire, effectively governed by the count, the ninth century had not yet declined to its setting, when we find the comitatus threatened with disaster. The confusion and paralysis which descended on the head of the state naturally spread to all the members. I have already spoken of this confusion under the name of the feudalization of society. Having glanced at the fate of the sovereign under the centrifugal tendencies of feudalism, we have now an opportunity to observe what havoc this movement worked with the constituent elements of the kingdom, the counties. As the ninth century passed into the tenth, certainly one of the most desolate of all the desolate stretches of the journey of our race since the time of Christ, the symptoms multiplied which indicated that the comitatus would become the prey of selfish interests. This fact becomes intelligible only, if we keep before our mind the picture of the feudal king, weak, beset with enemies, often absent, as often squandering his spurt of energy upon a rival, the puppet of a faction, and perforce ill-informed about the affairs of the counties and incapable of attending to them. Under these circumstances the count could forget his public mission and think chiefly of making as excellent provision as possible for himself and his family. What was to hinder his seizing suitable portions of the public domain in the sure expectation that the hour would come, the hour of need, when his sovereign would pay for a momentary support by legalizing the usurpation?

We gather dimly—the records are few and indefinite
—that it was in some such way as this that the Sienese
territory passed into the hands of a number of great
feudal families. In the eleventh and twelfth centuries
we find them encircling the town like a besieging host.
Not only do they profess, in sign of their origin, the
Lombard, or more frequently still, the Frank law, but
they bear the title of counts. In this connection we
should remember that in the early Middle Age the
title count was never a merely honorary distinction, but
always designated an official engaged on the king's
business. But if the successive families of counts came
to Siena to govern in the name of the king, they stayed
to enjoy the domains to which, by some means or other,
they managed to secure the enfeoffment. Only in this
way can we account for the great family of the Soarzi
to the west of the city on the slopes of Monte Maggio
and at the headwaters of the Elsa, and for the still
greater family of the Scialenghi or Cacciaconti to the
east, settled in many branches through the region of the
eighteen baptisteries disputed between Arezzo and
Siena. In the neighborhood of the Cacciaconti we
find also the Forteguerri and the Manenti, the latter
descendants, it would seem, of counts of Orvieto, while
directly south of the city, almost touching the walls,
the Ardengheschi had their castles and estates. Completing the circuit of the town we discover among the
inhospitable hills to the south and west, beyond what
was strictly Sienese territory, the clans of the Aldobrandeschi and the Pannochieschi, claiming authority
over vast solitudes of wood and marsh. If the measures
by which these families secured their great fiefs from the

empire are not entirely clear, we are at least sure that they prospered at the expense of the public lands and of the comitatus. To all intents they had succeeded in cutting their holdings out of the Sienese and the neighboring counties, in order to rule them as sovereign under the emperor on the basis of a charter of privileges and immunities.

If we have here one of the chief factors which diminished the imperial prerogatives and disintegrated the imperial administration of Tuscany, we face another when we follow the development of the church. Bishops and monasteries vied with the lay lords in importunate demands upon the emperor for special favors and immunities. By means of gifts distributed in those pious days with liberal hand, the church was waxing constantly richer, but, left unprotected by the disorganized civil government, it had to suffer its treasures to be seized and its territories to be invaded by a lawless baronage. Under the circumstances the bishops and abbots, the natural guardians of the possessions of the church, were forced to provide for their own defense, and not unnaturally appealed to the emperor to improve their position by the grant of a charter which conferred on them the highest temporal authority in their dominions. Dovetailed, therefore, among the great nobles of the countryside, we find the great prelates, hardly less numerous and powerful than their lay rivals. South of Siena, toward Monte Amiata, lay the monastery of Sant' Antimo; as early as the year 952 its abbot was endowed with the temporalities,* and, in the words of Dante, joined the sword to the shepherd's crook. As

* "Bull. Sen." IV, 72–74.

for the great Benedictine abbey on the slopes of Monte Amiata, San Salvatore, which fills a large page in the history of Siena, each new emperor tried to outdo his predecessor in magnanimous concessions to it.* What a lord abbot successfully demanded could not be reasonably denied to a lord bishop. The Aretine prelate, for example, neighbor and rival of him of Siena, acquired an extensive immunity as early as the year 843,† and similar concessions can be proved for other dioceses of the neighborhood. When we turn to Siena we discover that the episcopal archives ‡ have been neglected by the chapter and dissipated by time, and that the earliest imperial diploma which has been preserved bears the date 1055, but the concessions which fairly rained upon all the bishops of the immediate neighborhood, generations and centuries before 1055, make it more than probable that the bishop of Siena, too, began at a very early time to acquire a political foothold in his dominions by means of special privileges from the sovereign. In fact, the very phrasing of the document of 1055 makes it probable that it is largely a recapitulation of previous grants.

This important diploma was issued from the chancellery of the Emperor Henry III and, if relatively late, contains at least an enumeration of ample concessions to the beneficiary. It is worth reproducing in part, in order to enable us to see at first hand how the bishop

---

* The original documents are preserved in the Archivio di Stato of Siena in the section called *Diplomatico*. For a brief description of them, see Lisini's Inventario, "Bull. Sen." XIII, 230 *ff*. and 487 *ff*.

† Pasqui, "Documenti per la Storia della Città di Arezzo," No. 33.

‡ On the archives see Lusini, "Bull. Sen." II, 145.

Before the Fortress of Montalcino

became a temporal lord, on a level with the proudest
members of the king's baronage.

"In the name of the Holy and Indivisible Trinity, We, Henry,
by the favor of God Roman Emperor . . . concede, give, and
confirm to the Sienese church all the possessions which it has
legally acquired or shall acquire in the future, that is, *Castellum
Vetus* and these lands and manors (a long list follows, some of
which can be still identified to the south of the town).   All these
lands with their appurtenances we concede, granting to the bishop
judicial authority over the possessions of the church and the residents thereon, and the right to conduct a wager of battle after the
established forms.   Further, we desire and command that the
bishop shall have a right to the public services resting upon the
afore-named possessions of his church (*facere munitiones*) without
interference from any archbishop, bishop, duke, margrave, count,
viscount, or any other person of our realm. . . . In witness whereof, etc." *

It is plain that this document makes the bishop a
temporal ruler.   However, the question immediately
arises, what is the exact meaning of the concession
specified as Castellum Vetus?   Under that name was
known the highest hill of the city, site of the original
Etruscan settlement.   Some writers have maintained
that the part is here put for the whole, and that the
grant to the bishop of Castellum Vetus was tantamount
to declaring him ruler of all Siena.   To the unbiased
reader that must look like a very improbable interpretation.   As we know of the bishop that he originally
resided on the hill of Castellum Vetus, we may assume
that he had landed possessions there; and it is at least
entirely reasonable to maintain that the privilege of

* Pecci, "Storia del Vescovado di Siena," p. 120.

Henry III sought primarily to endow him with political rights within and immediately about his private
property. In any case that is all the document actually says. If the exact area embraced by so loose a
term as Castellum Vetus is not entirely clear, there
remains no doubt that the bishop received, in addition,
sovereign rights over lands constituting a considerable territory to the south of the city between the
Arbia and the Merse. Over all this region he is declared to be temporal lord with the power to collect
dues and to pronounce judgment, and he is even authorized to conduct a wager of battle, always a sign
in those times of high criminal and civil jurisdiction.
True, neither this nor any other privilege ever gave
the bishop the title and authority of a count of the
empire, although an assertion to this effect has often
been made,* but it did eliminate the imperial count
from a considerable section of the county of Siena,
and this fact, taken in connection with his elimination from the estates of the larger monasteries, and
from the compact possessions of the Soarzi, Cacciaconti,
and other lay lords, gives us a vivid indication of the
sorry decline of the once powerful local administrator
and of the imperial prerogatives which he represented.
As late as the twelfth century, in the time of the
Hohenstaufen, we hear of counts of Siena, whom the
Emperor Barbarossa, or his son Henry, sent to this region to stand guard over the remnant of the imperial
authority, but, hardly finding breathing-space among
the powers whose usurpations overspread the land, he

---

* For instance, Rondoni, "Sena Vetus," p. 8. No existing document
designates the Sienese bishop as count of the territory.

lived a pale, unnoticed existence and presently faded away.*

Among these general conditions were cast the first steps of the free commune of Siena. That they were timid and uncertain needs no explanation when we remember that we are dealing with the period of infancy. I have already said that it is absurd to seek for the exact birthyear of the commune, or to maintain categorically that it was born on such and such an occasion, as, for example, when the magistracy of the consuls assumed the political direction of the city. The consuls, to be sure, are the declaration *urbi et orbi* that the town will henceforth look to itself and manage its own affairs, but long before there were consuls—centuries before, in fact—the citizens had begun to provide for their most pressing interests by their own efforts. The history of the free commune is really the history of burgher self-help in the midst of the distressing conditions of the feudal age. When to make a journey over land, or rather when to step over your threshold was to take your life into your hands, it would have been strange indeed if men had not learned that the individual, if he would survive, must multiply himself, as it were, by free association with others in the same precarious position. These first beginnings of communal freedom in voluntary groups, formed for the most primitive social ends, long escaped the attention of historians. The pomp of kings, the clash of mailed warriors, the anathemas of

* As to the evidence concerning the existence of Sienese counts as late as the twelfth century, see Muratori, "Antiquitates Italicæ," IV, 577. A list of ten counts, from approximately 1145 to 1200, shows that although the comitatus had been distributed among private interests, a remnant of the imperial administration stubbornly persisted.

popes, created a rich and many-colored panorama,
through our delight in which we forgot the lowly masses
with their unromantic doings in field and shop. But
within a generation all this has changed and the earnest
effort of many scholars to lift the veil from the lives of
those who were not knights and ladies, and rode to hunt,
and banqueted in halls, has led us to revise, in good
part, our whole view of the Middle Age. Unfortunately
our first-hand information of the submerged masses is
fragmentary and deficient. The chroniclers of the
time, monks, for the most part, of small outlook and
encased in class prejudice, had no eyes for what went on
among the common people; and the manor and parish
records, which might tell us much of the administrative
activities of the inhabitants, have reached us only in
occasional survivals. In the case of Siena, in particular,
the remains are very scanty. However, the history of
early voluntary associations has been carefully pieced
together for more favored regions, and, as it is becoming
constantly more apparent that a primitive sort of self-
help was a feature common to all Italy, we are justified
in predicating an analogous development for Siena.*

* The most effective, if not the original, impetus to the investigation of
voluntary associations was given by Davidsohn in an article entitled, "Entstehung des Konsulats" ("Zeitschrift fuer Geschichtswissenschaft," Band VI,
1891, p. 22 ff). An Italian translation, "Origine del Consolato," will be
found in the "Archivio Stor. It.," Serie V, tomo 9, 1892. To these early
investigations Davidsohn has made considerable additions by an article in
the "Historische Vierteljahresschrift," 1900, pp. 1–26, and by a remarkable
chapter (the eighth) in his "Geschichte von Florenz." His thesis is, that in
measure as these voluntary associations familiarized the people once more
with self-government, they expanded by a perfectly natural process into the
consulate and the free commune. Within the last generation scholars have
made special studies of a great number of towns and villages, and in every
case their results have confirmed Davidsohn's views. It is out of the question
to enumerate all these studies here. Suffice it to name two, separated geo-

In order to bring out with all the clearness possible
the origin of the self-governing movement, let us take
our start from the conditions prevailing in the Lombard
and Frank periods, when the gastald, and after him the
count, was the governor of the city and its territory.
Even in this early period, when the royal official was
more or less absolute in his district, he neither did nor
could attend to all the affairs of the dwellers of town and
country. The church, for one thing, charged itself
with the spiritual interests of the population. Possessed
of a strength and vigor which enabled it to withstand
the assaults of the migrations and mock at the floods
which rose and swirled about its foundations, it had
come to enjoy a respect which raised it in common eyes
far above the state. Secular administrations came and
went, but the ecclesiastical administration, with its unit,
the parish, braved every storm. While insisting on the
special importance of the parish, we should note that the
organization of the church in Italy has some additional
features, with which it is necessary to become familiar.
In the countryside a number of parishes together constituted a larger administrative division, the *plebs* or *pieve*,
of which the distinguishing feature was the baptistery
with its font of holy water, where the whole population,
subject to the plebs, partook of the first Christian rite.
In the town all the inhabitants enclosed within the walls
were regarded as constituting a single plebs and were
attached to a single baptismal font. Travelers in Italy

graphically by almost the whole length of the peninsula. Lothar von Heinemann, "Zur Entstehung der Stadtverfassung in Italien," 1896, has examined
the self-governing activities of the people of Gaeta in the kingdom of Naples,
and Sella in the "Arch. St. It.," Serie V, tomo 36, 1905, has done the same
for certain districts of Piedmont.

will remember that in Florence, Pisa, Siena, and elsewhere, the baptistery stands to this day as a separate
building in the heart of the town, and very likely it has
happened that even as they gazed at these wonderful
structures, thrilling with their beauty and antiquity, new-
born babes were brought in by nurses and god-parents
to be received into the Christian fold. *Il mio bel San
Giovanni* raised something like a sob in the bosom of
the exiled Dante, and surely no one can stand beneath
its brave cupola without seeing with his mind's eye an
interminable procession of Florentine childhood, reaching back and growing fainter, until it loses itself in the
dim days of the Lombards. A walled city, then, such
as Florence or Siena, constituted, ecclesiastically speaking, a plebs, which, to meet the necessities of worship,
was divided into parishes, called *populi*. This swift
scrutiny of the organization of the Italian church has,
I hope, made clear that its main administrative divisions
were diocese, plebs (pieve, baptistery) and parish.*

Now these divisions, familiar to peasant and cobbler,
and rooted in the affections through daily association,
imposed themselves, to a certain extent, on the secular
administration. There is reason to think that the plebs
became an administrative and judicial subdivision of
the comitatus, and that a judge, or some other delegate
of the count, exercised jurisdiction there. At any rate
the inhabitants of a plebs, and more conspicuously still,
the small group of neighbors associated in a parish, came
to look upon themselves as forming a practical social

---

* Siena to-day contains sixteen parishes, or populi, within the walls.
Probably that number corresponds to the original number in the days of the
republic. See Cappelletti, "Le Chiese d'Italia," Vol. XVII, p. 531.

La Rocca di Tintinnano or La Rocca d'Orcia

unit. The simple country folk, who loved their parish church as the familiar centre where as infants they had been baptized, where as youths and maidens they had received confirmation, and in whose holy precincts they expected to be buried, would linger after mass or evensong, and, seated under the elm spreading its shade before the door, would discuss their common interests as defined by paths, roads, pasture, cattle, and streams. In the case of a town the neighbors of street and parish would find themselves no less absorbed by questions touching cisterns, fountains, public hygiene, and the maintenance and the repair of the church. Trusty men, elected from the parish associates, looked into the various neighborhood issues submitted to them, and presently might even be called upon to act as judges and settle a quarrel between fellow-parishioners involved in a dispute. Everywhere, in hundreds and thousands of small centres, in town and country alike, this modest, almost invisible self-activity sprang into being, accelerated by the decay of the central power; and because it was sound at heart, and provided for the most immediate and primal needs of society, it was destined not only to survive, but to grow and crowd the dominant system of misrule, called feudalism, from its seat.

In the course of time the neighborhood assemblies tended to become permanent and regular, and to draw increasingly important subjects within the range of their discussion. Such would be, especially for the villages of the countryside, the regulation of the tie binding them to their feudal lord, perched above them in his castle. By the eleventh century we find elected representatives, called *boni homines*, signing contracts with feudal landowners, sitting in judgment over their fellows much like a regular court, and meeting with other boni homines to discuss the common business of contiguous parishes and even of larger geographical districts. In the cities, where men lived more closely together and were pressingly dependent on each other's coöperation, the need for common action was even more urgent than in the country. Proceeding from particular interests to more general ones, the neighbors finally took up the great matter of self-defence. Only as the inhabitants of a town learned from their feudal masters the invaluable lesson of force and took measures to man their walls and gates at the approach of danger, did they give the final and conclusive proof concerning their ability to support the responsibilities of self-government. The attention to questions of defence and war would of necessity involve the whole town, and is, wherever we encounter it, a sure indication that the coöperation among the original groups had reached a relatively advanced stage.

For many generations of that submerged epoch of the mediæval period to which we refer currently as the Dark Age, there was, therefore, some limited form of self-government, of which the boni homines, entrusted with the business of the parish, or of some limited social or agricultural group, are the symbol. They have hardly begun to represent the interests of the larger unit, the town, when we find them adopting a name indicative of their new honor—they call themselves consuls. The appearance of the name is a certain sign of an enlarged and improved organization, but it does not mean, as used to be maintained, that the citizens now first experimented in self-government. On the contrary, we should now be amply convinced that extensive self-governing activities characterized all the Italian towns long before we hear of consuls. And just as the consular officials are by no means synchronous with the beginnings of democracy, so a town provided with such dignitaries has not necessarily renounced allegiance to the emperor and his agents, and entered into all the rights of sovereignty and independence. All through the twelfth and thirteenth centuries when we know definitely that the Tuscan communes were governed by consuls or some other elected authority, when, furthermore, they showed every mark of a vigorous self-consciousness, they did not conceive themselves as entirely emancipated from the authority of the empire. Self-government and independence—these were indeed the twin objects of every town beginning to disentangle itself from the feudal net; but we must accustom ourselves to think of both of them as reached by very devious paths, and after a process like the annual coming of the spring, which for long weeks advances and recedes and again advances, until the young season, bringing fresh and ever fresh battalions to the front, drives old winter into hopeless flight.

The first reference to a governing body of consuls in the city of Siena belongs to the year 1125.* In the previous year (1124) we have a reference to boni homines who, in representation of their city, accompanied the bishop of Siena, Gualfredo, to Rome, in order to help plead

---

* Pasqui, "Documenti," etc., p. 573. The reference occurs in a deposition made by witnesses summoned in 1177 in the course of the interminable Siena-Arezzo conflict.

the cause of their diocese when that zealous prelate reopened the interminable feud with Arezzo over the eighteen baptisteries. These two notices suggest the connection, amounting almost to identity, between boni homines and consuls. Very probably the boni homines of the city parishes or other minor groups, with the growth of common interests, had been for some time meeting together to take advice, and very probably the full assembly of boni homines had been found too cumbersome for the satisfactory dispatch of business. On the election of an executive committee of boni homines, involving for the first time the representation of the whole town, the higher dignity of the new body was recognized by the adoption of the title, about which still hung the glamor of the Roman republic—the title of consuls. Everywhere in Tuscany the consuls came forward about the same time. For Pisa and Lucca they can be proved shortly after 1080;* in the case of Florence the first reference to the new magistracy belongs to the year 1138;† and as regards Siena, we first hear of consuls, as already stated, in 1125. But where there are consuls there is a commune, for when the constituent groups came together to give themselves a common set of officials they recognized also that they had created a new practical unity. And let the reader note that this new unity, the commune, is not identical with the town or city. Town and city are geographical expressions, but the commune denotes a political entity, to the privileges of which the citizen body

---

* See Henry's Privileges of 1081, Muratori, "Antiq. It.," IV, 20, and Ficker, "Forschungen," IV, no. 81.

† Davidsohn, "Geschichte," I, 345.

taken as a whole need not be, and very generally was not, admitted.

The general appearance of the consulship among the Tuscan towns about the year 1100 would tend to show that, in spite of an infinite variation in detail among them, they all presented an essential identity in social structure and political experience. In attempting now to take a closer view of the new office, let us keep before our minds the unfamiliarity of the age with political thought and action. Must it not fill a modern man with surprise that no town exhibited a sense of having done anything meritorious in providing itself with an elected magistracy, and that none showed the least tendency to magnify its courage with a ringing Declaration of Rights? Such ideas and methods characterize a struggle for freedom conducted by a people who have achieved political consciousness. In the Middle Age self-government was never evoked, as has been frequently the case in our own day, by political theory, but was a groping, practical growth, nursed among small groups and made necessary by the barbarous incompetence of the official government. On this account the consuls did not for a long time pass out of the realm of experiment. One year they were elected to represent the commune, another not—the single groups being evidently content on occasion to fall back on the older, though less manageable, institution of the boni homines. Everywhere it was the same, but everywhere, too, experience would teach the advantage for the town of an uninterrupted central direction of affairs secured by the permanent establishment of the new magistracy. Under these circumstances, toward the middle of the twelfth century, the consulship began to function more regularly,* and about the same time, also, the elaboration of the new government in the direction of political effectiveness had made considerable progress. With the consuls came to be associated a council, representing more or less numerous groups of citizens and acting as an advisory body—the nucleus, it will be seen, of a future legislature; and, further, with a view to protecting the citizens against possible illegalities on the part of the chief magistracy, there was drawn up, at first in rude and summary form, a document defining its functions. This received the name of *breve consulum*, and on it the consuls, on assuming their duties, took the oath of office. Growing from year to year as the result of accumulated political experience, it became the celebrated communal constitution of the Age of the Republics. In the early days we hear very generally, too, of the meeting of the whole people, the *parlamentum*, called for the purpose of laying important matters of state before the general body of citizens, but it does not appear that the parlamentum anywhere became an effective instrument of control or acquired other than a theoretical claim to power and sovereignty. To the development of these and similar institutions which gradually took shape to serve the needs of the new republic of Siena I shall later devote a separate chapter. At present it behooves us to attend the consuls in their first efforts to direct the destiny of the city.

* In Siena, as late as 1151, we encounter instead of consuls or boni homines, a single executive, one Scudacollus. The fact is a further support of the theory of the elastic nature of the early republican institutions. For Scudacollus see Ficker, "Forschungen," IV, no. 120.

The chief concern of the new magistracy was to
live. Strictly speaking it was a rebel magistracy, for
it represented the self-governing attempt of a community which legally was governed by the emperor
and his delegate, the count. The count of Siena, as
we have seen, had long since, by reason of the emperor's
weakness, the feudal usurpations, and the ecclesiastical
immunities, become a negligible factor, but, as it happened, about the middle of the same century which
saw the rise of the consuls, a really great emperor,
Frederick I of the House of Hohenstaufen, called
Barbarossa, came to the throne in Germany, and
undertook to revive all the obsolete imperial rights in
his fair dominion beyond the Alps. To general
mediæval history belong Frederick's heroic attempt and
failure to turn back the wheel of time and bring the
cities under the old subjection. In Lombardy, especially,
where, owing to geographical conditions, urban life
was more developed than in Tuscany, they met heroism
with heroism, and after a great victory at Legnano
(1176) forced the emperor to confirm their right to
elect their own officials and to conduct their own affairs.
The peace document, a notable milestone in the history
of democracy, was signed at Constance in southern
Germany, in the year 1183. The Tuscan cities played
only a secondary part in the struggle, and did not receive
the benefits of the peace, but they had with characteristic agility used the embarrassment of the emperor to
strengthen their position. When Frederick, therefore,
toward the end of his reign, and being now an old man,
whose red beard had long since turned white, paid a
visit to Tuscany, he found the cities not only governing

themselves by the consular régime, but possessed by
conquest each one of its comitatus or a large part of it.
The fiery emperor did not hesitate to show his displeasure at this situation, took measures which raised
the spectre of a Tuscan war, counterpart of the late
struggle in Lombardy, and then, satisfied with the
vigorous affirmation of his rights, relented, offering a
compromise. A picture of his fortunes in Tuscany at
this critical junction is furnished by a review of his
relations to Siena. Let us examine them as briefly as
possible.

In the year 1179 the emperor's Italian legate, the
Archbishop Christian of Mainz, had been captured by
some private enemies and imprisoned at Montefiascone,
pending the payment of an immense ransom. In
return for a contribution to this end the Sienese received
from the prisoner a charter,* recognizing not only the
consuls but their rule over such districts in the comitatus
as they had already annexed by the defeat of the feudal
barons. As usual the concession did not hinder the
application of the law of might, as soon as the tables
were turned. When, in 1185, Frederick paid the visit
to Tuscany already referred to, he attempted as before in
Lombardy, to save the feudal system with its hierarchy
of nobles, by destroying the usurped power of the cities.
Siena resisted this diminution of her authority, yielding
only after a siege conducted by the emperor's son,
King Henry. In a reconciliation, so-called, of June,
1186, the Sienese threw themselves abjectly at their
sovereign's feet.† Pleased with the effect produced,
the young king gave back to the town some of its cus-

* Muratori, "Antiq. It.," IV, 575.   † *Ibid.*, IV, 467.

tomary rights, solemnly confirming them in a parchment over his signature.*

"In the name of the Holy and Indivisible Trinity, We, Henry VI., by divine favor, king of the Romans . . . make known to all the faithful of the empire, present as well as future, that in view of the merits of our trusty subjects, the citizens of Siena, we grant them (*universitati ipsorum*) the free election of their consuls. However, the consuls shall receive the investiture annually from our hand or that of our most glorious father, Frederick, emperor of the Romans, or that of our successors, without any charge or exaction. . . . In addition we grant them full jurisdiction in the city of Siena, and outside the city, in the comitatus, over the men belonging to the bishop of Siena or to any Sienese resident at the time this document is drawn up, saving the right of appeal in cases amounting to more than twenty pounds. Also, we grant to the Sienese people the fodrum † of these same men . . . All nobles outside the city and all other men throughout the Sienese comitatus, except those noted above, with all jurisdiction over them, their fodrum and services in general, we retain in our power. Also, we concede to the Sienese the privilege of coining money in the city of Siena. . . . In witness whereof" [Follows a long list of witnesses, the seal of King Henry, and the date, October, 1186].

The full importance of this document will appear in the light of a rapid recapitulation. The consular régime had now been in existence for many years, being proved for 1125, and reaching back, with high probability, to an earlier date. Moreover, long before the appearance of consuls, there had been self-government of one sort or another, beginning with simple parish

---

* *Ibid.*, IV, 469.

† The fodrum was an important service, consisting usually of provisions paid by the barons to the emperor when he was on a journey.

matters and increasing steadily in scope. Although the
providing for local interests of a purely administrative
nature was sanctioned by a long and uninterrupted usage,
and was tolerated, if not expressly endorsed, by the central feudal power, the seizure of the political direction by
the citizens, or any group of citizens, as indicated by
the election of consuls, was indisputably a usurpation.
Luckily for Siena similar usurpations were universal
in Italy, and fell, furthermore, at the auspicious moment
when the empire was engaged in a struggle for its very
life with the church. The result of multiform embar-
rassments was that the successive emperors, however
deeply they may have resented the illegal procedure of
the cities, had to move cautiously. Pisa, without whose
money and ships the imperial action in southern and
central Italy would have been paralyzed, as early as
1081 won a privilege from Henry IV, by which it
became practically an independent republic.* In the
same year Lucca received a patent conferring extensive
prerogatives.† A hundred years later, in consequence
of their victory at Legnano (1176), the Lombard communes acquired a sweeping sanction of the liberties
which they had long ago seized as a natural and inde-
feasible right. Siena, generally on the side of the emperor against the church, had coaxed favors from
several sovereigns in payment for her loyalty, but, as
far as appears from surviving records, had never
enforced the legalization of the consulship. However,
the emperors and their agents had not refused to deal
with the elected representatives of the city, thereby

* Muratori, "Antiq. It.," IV, 19.
† Ficker, "Forschungen," IV, no. 81.

accepting and honoring them in fact, if not in law.* Under the circumstances the status of Siena was both ambiguous and uncomfortable. The emperors, however grateful to the town for its services against the pope and other enemies, conceded to it as little as possible in the hope that the time might come when they would be strong enough to reintegrate the feudal rule; and the citizens, for their part, although anxious to legalize a revolutionary magistracy, found a limited satisfaction in not being hindered in the exercise of self-government. In the year 1186 the contradictory position of emperor and townsmen led to a war in which the victory remained, as we have seen, with the feudal lord. King Henry could, therefore, dictate a settlement. His initial measure was to declare null and void the "submissions," by which the lusty city authorities had forced their yoke upon the nobles of the country. These nobles he took under his protection, declaring them subject only to himself. But, although he thus set back the development of the city, he made up for his action, in part at least, by a charter recognizing the consular rule within the walls and, beyond their circuit, over the territory of the bishop and of other Sienese residents. The consuls were to be freely elected according to local custom, but were to be fitted into the framework of feudalism—a framework which Henry's position as a feudal chief obliged him to maintain—by being enfeoffed with the city by their suzerain. However much the citizens may have mourned the many

* For the dealings with Siena of Rainald of Köln, Frederick's plenipotentiary in Italy in the period 1164–67, see Davidsohn, "Geschichte von Florenz," p. 498. Rainald's favors look very much like an express recognition of the republican régime.

reductions of authority stated or implied in the charter of 1186, they had good reason to rejoice that their self-government now had a firm footing in law. In the shelter of the imperial privilege the free institutions of the town, still in a rudimentary form, could be elaborated with greater dispatch and security.

It is perfectly plain that the fundamental considera-tion with Henry, in issuing his diploma, was to preserve the country nobility in its immediate dependence on the empire. For this purpose he made a concession to the city in the matter of self-government, but at the same time he declared firmly that from the nobles and imperial fiefs in general the townsmen must keep their grasping tentacles. From his point of view his policy is perfectly intelligible. If things went on in the future as they had been going on in the past, each city would presently be paramount in its contado, the feudal nobility would be reduced at best to a class of citizen-landholders, and the emperor would find the services due to him usurped by the towns, his income gone, and himself in effect crowded out of his kingdom of Italy. The citizens, on the other hand, were as imperatively driven to persist in their course, for, with the comitatus and its highways in the hands of the nobility, what assurance did they have that they could pursue the trade by which they pros-pered? They might bend a humble knee before their suzerain coming at the head of an irresistible army, but, as they held life dear, they would have to strive openly and secretly to bind the countryside to their interests with hoops of steel. This terri-torial struggle was, therefore, the necessary concomitant of the struggle for political recognition which we have just followed.

As a matter of fact all the towns had no sooner taken their first steps on the road to self-government than they began to realize their parallel aim of controlling the neighborhood. The whole twelfth century of Sienese history is filled with wars conducted for this end, and about the same time we first hear of consuls, we hear also of the first "submissions" made to the city. In 1137 the Soarzi surrendered a fourth part of Monte-castelli and other dominions to Siena;* in 1138 Count Manente ceded to the bishop and people one-sixth of the castle of Radicofani, on the border toward Rome;† in 1145 the abbot of San Salvatore on Monte Amiata followed the example of Count Manente and yielded certain rights of his own in Radicofani;‡ in July, 1151, Count Paltonerius of the Forteguerra family gave up San Giovanni d'Asso, a fortified place to the east;§ in 1157 the Ardengheschi sold the hill of Orgia, just beyond the southern gate, after the Sienese had taken and burned the castle there;‖ and in 1168 Count Ildebrandino Cacciaguerra lost the important little town of Asciano.¶ These are a few items selected at random from an almost interminable record of triumphs, of which the Sienese archive preserves the moving memory. In spite of varying terms of submission all the treaties affirm alike the purpose of drawing the baronage within the radius of the city's influence. As this was the feudal age, the

* Archivio di Stato, "Caleffo vecchio," c. 4t.
† Ibid., "Caleffo vecchio," c. 21t.
‡ Muratori, "Antiq. It.," IV, 567.
§ Archivio di Stato, "Caleffo vecchio," c. 21.
‖ Ibid., c. 17.   ¶ Ibid., c. 7t, 8

conquered nobles had imposed upon them also a ceremony of submission, some of the details of which we may learn from the legal documents. From the parchment of 1157, for instance, we learn that the Counts Ardengheschi were obliged to appear in person before the people of Siena assembled in parliament in front of the episcopal church, and to confirm their renunciation of Orgia with an oath. The notary invited to give the surrender the necessary legal form, affirmed the appearance of the counts in language devoid of every human touch, but our imagination readily revives the stirring scene. The present wonderful cathedral with its façade gay as a parti-colored carpet did not yet exist; in its place stood a smaller and a ruder church, dedicated, like its successor, to the Virgin and approached by a flight of steps from the open square in front. On this square, on that February day duly noted in the document, are crowded the citizens of high and low degree, gesticulating, chattering, exulting in the fall of their enemies. At last the counts appear upon the stone terrace before the church to take the oath. Silence falls upon the close-pressed throng until the decisive word is spoken, and then, a shout! The accumulated hate of generations finds vent in that spontaneous cry.*

* As it may interest the reader to note the kind of terms on which defeated noblemen usually surrendered their sovereignty and became citizens, I add the document by which four counts of the Cacciaconti family acknowledged their subjection to Siena:

"In the name of the Lord, Amen. We, Cacciacomes, Cacciaguerra, Guido, son of Cacciacomes, and Rainaldus, son of Ildebrandinus, swear on the Holy Gospels, that henceforth and forever we shall be Sienese citizens, and shall preserve and protect every person of the city of Siena and of its suburbs and their goods. . . . And we, Cacciacomes, Cacciaguerra, and Rainaldus promise to reside within the walls of Siena for three continuous

In all the earlier documents preserved in the Sienese
archive the submission, on the part of the conquered
nobleman, is made not only to the people but also to the
bishop, and sometimes to the bishop alone.   This was
an empty formula, which should mislead no one into
the belief that the bishop was the ruler of the city, or
even in the slightest way the special beneficiary of the
victories of the citizens.   The bishop had indeed long
been a great lay lord, as is amply proved by the diploma
of 1055, but with the rise of the commune he found himself in much the same position as the other lords, and
by degrees which escape our attention yielded his
temporal sovereignty to the vigorous commonwealth.
Signs that his yielding was not altogether graceful are
not lacking, for we hear of one bishop, Ranieri by name,
who in the struggle between Barbarossa and Pope
Alexander leaned too openly toward the church and was
driven out of the city by a popular uprising.   He died
in exile (1170) "expulsus a scismaticis"—a not uncommon fate in those days of political and ecclesiastical
revolution.*   But if the Sienese were thus occasionally
in conflict with their bishop as a power commanding a
considerable political influence, they had no serious

months in time of peace as well as in time of war.   (Guido, son of Cacciacomes, makes the same promise for two months.)   And we swear we will give
ear and attend to the commands of the Sienese consuls as well as to the commands of the court officials (*consules placiti*) who will summon us in matters
of justice.   And we shall retain the privileges enumerated in various chapters
of the *breve consulum* (*i. e.* the Sienese constitution). . . . And we shall offer
every year to the cathedral church of Siena, on the festival of Our Lady of
August, one candle of six pounds (for our possession of) Monte Santa Maria,
and one of eight pounds for Chiusure (and so forth for six other places
specified).   Done at Siena. . . . February, 1197."—Muratori, "Antiq. It.,"
IV, 583.
   * For the narrative of Bishop Ranieri's conflict with Siena see an article by
Davidsohn, "Bull. Sen.," V, 63 *ff*.

quarrel with him as spiritual head of the state. On the contrary they looked upon the great prelate with sincere veneration, and when they ordered the notaries to formulate the surrender of towns and castles as made to him, they did so in the prudent calculation that their conquests, essentially illegal, might seem less offensive by being draped with the authority of the church.* In consequence the imperial power, which the illusory phrasing planned to conciliate, had no sooner begun to wane than the citizens dispensed with their stalking-horse. By 1186 the position of the townsmen had become so firmly established that not only was the fiction of the bishop's supremacy entirely dropped in the documents of submission, but in the imperial char-ter of that year the sovereignty of Siena over the episcopal territories was expressly recognized. It certainly de-serves to be noted as a sign of the advancing organiza-tion of the state, that by the year 1186 the church of Siena was, as regards its landed possessions, already subordinated to the civil power.

The breakdown of the empire in Tuscany, delayed as far as human power could delay it by Frederick Barbarossa, came with suddenness and completeness in the year 1197. In that year Henry VI, the energetic and unscrupulous successor of Frederick, died in Sicily, leaving as his heir a boy in swaddling-clothes. No sooner did this news reach the north than the Tuscan cities rose in revolt. They met at San Genesio, beneath that lofty San Miniato, which was the centre of the imperial administration for the Tuscan province, and

* The Florentines, among others, followed a similar practice. See for their procedure Santini, "Contado e Politica Esteriore del secolo XII," p. 44.

formed a league planned to secure them against any future tyranny of the empire. Now the best security of a free condition was the subjection of the neighboring lords, mainstays of the imperial power, who would have been reduced to obedience long ago and definitely, but for the frequent interposition in their favor of the emperor. With Henry's death came the great opportunity: the cities formed their spontaneous union, and proceeded straightway to realize its main object, to wit, that each city should put itself in possession of its contado. During the following years while the empire was almost annihilated through the convulsions attending a disputed succession, the Sienese reduced, either to direct submission or to dependence through the less humiliating form of an alliance, all the great families which still defied their authority. In the year 1197 the sharp sword of the townsmen once more smote the Cacciaconti, who now definitely became Sienese citizens;* in the year 1202 the Counts Ardengheschi agreed to pay an annual hearth-tax of twenty-six denari for each family resident in their many lands;† in the same year the Counts of Sarteano signed an offensive alliance directed against Montepulciano;‡ finally, in the year 1203, the Aldobrandeschi, the greatest of all the feudal families and destined to loom terrible on the horizon for another century and a half, signed a treaty of friendship, the first, if inconsiderable, step in the long process of their subjection.§

As minor towns in the neighborhood were not less

* See foot-note, p. 62.
† Malavolti, p. 41, della Prima Parte.   ‡ *Ibid.*
§ Archivio di Stato, Section *Diplomatico.* Date Jan. 4, 1202 (old style).

offensive to the pride and ambition of Siena than the great lords, this same occasion, when the empire was in abeyance and the Tuscan towns were bound together by a general convention, was used to bring into subjection all neighboring places which might become the basis of military or commercial action against the regional metropolis. In pursuit of this policy, Montalcino, crowning a magnificent conical hill to the south, fell, not without stubborn resistance, into Sienese hands (1202).* Thereupon the townsmen girded their loins for a still more hardy enterprise, the capture and subjection of Montepulciano, which lifted its towers and battlements not far to the east of Montalcino. But now appeared prominently a new difficulty, which had long cast its shadow before. The attempt to seize Montepulciano was furiously resented by the Florentines, even though they were in formal alliance with the Sienese. Not content with enjoying their own comitatus, the ambitious dwellers of the Arno valley were already aspiring to control a vaster region, if not to dominate all Tuscany. They resolved at all hazards to check the expansion of Siena, and determined by guile, and when guile failed by war, to keep the Sienese out of that hilltown to their east, dominating the Chiana valley and opening a gate to all central Italy. Thus the two cities lately allied for a common end against the emperor, at the beginning of the new century turned upon each other with unexampled bitterness. The whole thirteenth century resounds with this struggle, in which each seeks aid wherever it can, from Tuscan city neighbors, from feudal nobles, from pope and emperor.

* Malavolti, p. 41, della Prima Parte.

Pisa, Lucca, Arezzo, Pistoia, all figure in the conflict; its object, the supremacy in Tuscany.

The century which we have been considering, the century of the great Hohenstaufen emperors Frederick I and Henry VI, did not close without a significant change in the chief magistracy of Siena. The other towns went through a similar evolution, approximately at the same time. Did the consuls, whose number varied from three to six, prove, as a plural executive, incapable of that quick decision demanded by the needs of the hour? Very likely with the increasing complication of society, with friction among the urban classes, and with foreign war, a certain cumbersomeness would appear in this magistracy, and would create a preference for a single head. Single executives, I have already said, were from time to time intercalated in the succession of consuls almost from the first. The idea made headway, and with the advent of the thirteenth century, almost all the cities replaced their consuls with a single ruler, called *potestà*. The first potestà * of Siena came from Lucca in the year 1199; in the next year a native, Filippo d'Orlando Malavolti, filled the office. But the young republic looked with marked distrust upon a native ruler, fearful lest he use his position to push the material interests of his family, or, still worse, to perpetuate his power with the help of some faction and crown himself the city's tyrant. In consequence, and as security against this dire eventuality, a decision was made after a period of fluctuation in favor of a foreign potestà on the ground that he would be un-

* See for a full list of the Sienese potestà "Miscellanea Storica Sanese," IV, 186 *ff.*

acquainted with the factions of the city and presumably
willing to maintain an independent position among
them. His term of office in the beginning lasted
usually one year and he was handsomely housed and
remunerated.

It is impossible to see the replacement of the consuls
by the potestà in any other light than that of an advance
in political organization. However, it was a change
merely at the top. The foundations upon which the
government rested did not suffer change, and these
foundations, although they comprised, in a broad sense,
the whole people of Siena, were, closely considered,
essentially aristocratic. Let us see what that means:
The consular constitution was undoubtedly due to the
democratic impulse of the new centres of life, the towns,
but the free associations, the union of which gave birth to
the commune, were composed of, or at least were directed
and controlled by, a relatively small class of wealthy
members. These alone enjoyed full citizen rights in
the commune. This needs to be said expressly in
rectification of the common tendency to overstate the
case of the young democracy of Italy. And yet that
that democracy would be limited in its early stages must
appear the moment we reflect that the upper class alone
possessed the material resources and commanded the
experience of life required to make the best of the new
opportunities which offered with the revival of commercial intercourse among the nations. And that brings
us to the question as to what elements of society composed the ruling class in the first phase of the free commune. The answer varies, within certain limits, for
the different towns of Tuscany; but for Siena, which is

our immediate concern, we may affirm that the upper class of the consular era consisted of a group of lesser feudal lords, who, possessed of fiefs near the city, dwelt within the walls and were therefore citizens, and that allied and practically identical with them was a group of burghers who had prospered in trade, notably in the lucrative business of money barter. This upper group of the well-to-do was variously designated as nobles, magnates, and *grandi*. No effort was made to distinguish socially between those rich by virtue of land and those rich by commerce, or to place one kind of riches above another. In fact such a distinction would have been impossible owing to the circumstance that the Sienese gentry engaged in commerce without a touch of the usual aristocratic contempt for trade, and that the successful bankers preferably invested their funds in agricultural property. From the ranks exclusively of these leading citizens were chosen the consuls in the early days of self-government, with the result that to the prestige which the dominant class enjoyed by reason of its wealth was added the further prestige associated with political prerogative.

As soon as the development of industry and commerce succeeded in awakening new strata of the citizen body to mental and economic activity, it became improbable that the favored political position of the oligarchy could be maintained. Then with the blood running red in their arteries the masses would be certain to make an effort to break down the monopoly of the upper class. The thirteenth century had hardly begun when the people opened the combat. In the year 1212 a Sienese chronicle reports a struggle (the

first of which we have definite information) between
grandi and *popolo*. It is the inauguration of the chapter
of domestic revolution, a long and dreary story, and
destined not to be closed until Siena herself ended her
life as an independent state. The chronicler reports
under the year 1212: "St. Francis of Assisi of the
Order of the Brothers Minor came to Siena; and there
was great enmity between people and nobles, and he
made peace and union among them."* No more
than that: a class struggle, which St. Francis, the good
brown brother, exercising his inspired ministry of peace
on earth, composed. Slight though the information
be, it is pleasant to have the assurance that that kindli-
est of spirits once entered in very flesh the gate, paced
the narrow streets, and laid his inexorable benediction
on the turbulent factions. Did he favor the claims of
the people against the grandi? We cannot tell, but this
we know—the brief entry is precise—that with the
thirteenth century began a struggle for a wider participation of the people in the government of the city.

The year 1200 marks a convenient mile-stone in the
history of Siena where we may pause a moment to look
backward and forward. The empire, moving plainly
to its setting, was no longer able to count greatly in
Tuscany either for good or for ill; the bishop, once a
ruler of great sway, had been reduced, as far as his
territories were concerned, to citizenship; the feudal
nobles, if not annihilated, had all felt the rod of the
burgher on their backs. These triumphs of the twelfth
century declared that Siena had broken her feudal

---

* Muratori, "Scriptores," XV, Cronica Senese, ad annum, note 4. See
for confirmation of St. Francis's visit to Siena, the "Fioretti," chap. XI.

shackles and had embarked upon a career of independence. But as the old difficulties vanished from the path of the republic, fresh ones rose to take their place. In the new century Siena would have to face Florence to decide the question of supremacy in Tuscany; she would have to solve the domestic struggle between oligarchs and democrats. And greater than either of these issues, if we consider well, she would have to meet the problem, sole measure of every community's true worth, the problem of building a noble mansion for herself upon her hills and finding a human mind and soul to house therein.

CHAPTER III

THE SIENESE CHURCH

WHAT we have heard so far of the bishop, head of the Sienese church, does not differentiate him particularly from any other feudal lord: he quarrels with his neighbor of Arezzo for five hundred years, renewing ever and again, and in a spirit grotesquely unchristian, the attempt to possess himself of the eighteen baptisteries, and he goes on accumulating immunities until, by the diploma of Henry III (1055), he acquires, in addition to the usual jurisdiction over the clergy in his diocese, the political dominion over territories constituting a considerable section of the city and county of Siena. To be sure, in the twelfth century, his temporal authority waned, being gradually absorbed by the rising commune, but did he for that reason become an unimportant figure in the state? Not in the least, for we must not fail to see that if the bishop, being the child of his time, was infected with the feudal spirit and tried to secure as wide a secular dominion as possible, his authority with his diocesans and his good name in the world did not depend on his military and financial resources, but rested, in the final analysis, on immaterial claims: his authority was spiritual. Thus it had been at the beginning when the church was the bride of poverty, and thus and not otherwise it still was in the twelfth and thirteenth cen-

turies, after a stream of pious donations, both long and
deep, and the grant of the tithe by the state together
with freedom from taxation, had transformed it into the
wealthiest corporation of the age.   But even had its
riches disappeared, or had they been appropriated by
some such act of force as that by which Siena and the
other rising communes deprived their respective bishops
of political jurisdiction, the life of the church, its real
life, would hardly have been threatened.   For the
church was an idea, the most powerful and universally
distributed idea of the Middle Age, and as long as that
idea retained its vigor, any catastrophe, if we can conceive of such, which at some dusk should have obliterated its material existence, its shrines, its houses, its
rents, would have been followed the next morning by a
rain of donations reëstablishing it in its integrity
undiminished by a jot or tittle.   We call the mediæval
period currently the Age of Faith.   There is much
mistaken information disseminated in books and sermons about the quality of this faith and the loveliness
of its works—and of these misconceptions we shall hear
anon—but the mediæval period is the Age of Faith
unmistakably in the sense that all men accepted the
church as the divinely appointed instrument of salvation, and believed that the seven sacraments, administered by bishop and clergy, were the seven converging
roads to heaven.   With such faith abroad, burning in
every heart, the church was indeed founded upon a rock.

To the awe and reverence inspired by the church on
the score of its service in saving souls, other elements,
almost from the first, contributed.   When society went
to pieces under the hammer-blows of the Barbarians, the

church alone of Roman institutions resisted dissolution and became a rallying-point of the cowed and
broken population; and when, in the course of time,
men began again to take heart and interest themselves
in the conduct of their own affairs, we have seen that
it was the parish church, the familiar symbol of the
bond of neighborhood, which served as the focus for
all the community interests, religious, social, and political. As it was possible to assert that the free commune
with its consuls, its governing boards, and its parlamentum, represented the evolution of the parish meeting, so we may with the same assurance affirm that the
palazzo pubblico or city hall was the direct descendant
of the parish church. And since the new city-state
leaned in its infancy so largely on the older and firmer
ecclesiastical organization, we ought not to be surprised
to discover that this early dependence left its mark in
the form of an enduring intimacy between the old
associates. Here is the feature of the mediæval period
that more than any other remains incomprehensible
to the modern mind. Church and state, far from holding aloof from each other and drawing a definite
trench between their activities, were fused to such an
extent that the state concerned itself without contradiction with certain affairs of the church, and the church
without contradiction with certain affairs of the state.
In fact it never occurred to any one that the functions
of church and state could be entirely separated, since
the coöperation of both was necessary for the preservation of society. Nevertheless, as the democratic principles gathered vigor and the views of men concerning the
function of the civil power were enlarged and clarified, we

The House of Saint Catherine

may notice a tendency to reduce the share of the clergy in the business of society, and to emphasize the supremacy of the state over all the affairs of its members.

These views of a modified clerical domination were reflected in all the constitutions of the young Italian republics, and with no little force in the earliest draft of the Sienese constitution which has come down to us, belonging to the year 1262. As this document affords a very clear picture of the relations of church and state within the frame of the commune, we cannot do better than to take our stand upon the information which it supplies. If some reader is tempted to object that the year 1262 is a relatively advanced period in the evolution of the commune, he may rest assured that the condition of the church in that year was not substantially different from what it had been during the previous century, for since 1186 at the latest—the year when Henry VI issued his charter of liberties—the territories of the church had been a part of the political dominion of the city and the church itself reduced to some kind of dependence on the young commonwealth. The Sienese constitution devotes innumerable articles to the affairs of the church and the clergy, plainly indicating thereby the large place which religion filled in the public life of the time.* Among these articles is a solemn declaration to the effect that Catholicism is the sole religion of the state and that its injunctions must be satisfied by every citizen of high or low degree under penalties which, according to our present code, are not only severe but even atrocious. The articles further declare that the

---

* "Il Constituto di Siena dell' anno 1262." Edited by Zdekauer. See Distinctio I, "De Fide Catholica."

state will protect all the possessions of the church and suppport its enterprises, as, for instance, its building operations, with generous contributions; but, in exchange for these benefits, the document affirms in resonant tones that the state expects obedience from the church and its members in all matters recognized to be strictly temporal. Of course with the long established independence of the church in matters spiritual the state did not pretend to interfere. Reducing the varied information afforded by the Sienese constitution to general terms, we may assert that, in spite of certain losses which the church sustained by being detached from the imperial system and assimilated to the commune, it remained under the new régime a powerful, self-directive polity.

Throughout the history of Siena as a free commune there obtained, therefore, the idea of a partnership between two coördinated governments, the one supreme in matters temporal, the other in matters spiritual. A Sienese citizen as possessed of membership in both gladly paid equal allegiance to them, and rejoiced in the success and greatness of the church no less than in the success and greatness of the state. His patriotism took this double direction without any sense of contradiction, and, happily for him, without occasion for feeling any contradiction as long as the world rested content in a single absorbing and satisfying faith. It is this patriotic feeling toward the church that explains why, when the bishop of Siena raised a technical issue with his neighbor of Arezzo, the citizens of Siena took a hand in the quarrel and in that dim scuffle of the year 711 drove the Aretines into flight; and again it is the patriotism of the

Sienese which accounts for the fact that their bishop
would not be silenced by an endless succession of royal,
imperial, and papal sentences, but, prompted by the
pride and ambition of his spiritual subjects, constantly
renewed his suit.

If we have become convinced that the love of the
church among the mediæval communes was, to a large
extent, a manifestation of local patriotism, we are
prepared to understand the peculiarly intimate relation
which bound the residents of Siena to the saints of their
home.   The saints dwelt indeed in heaven, garmented
in light and intoning songs of praise around the throne,
but also in a mysterious way they were present in Siena
and took brotherly cognizance of the ills of those who
brought them gifts and called upon them from their
hearts.   This nearness to the divine powers stirred the
soul to its depths and produced all those exquisite
manifestations of religious fervor in which mediæval
Siena abounded.   Above all it produced the inspiring
ceremonies, national in the truest sense of the word,
associated with the worship of the Virgin Mary.   To
her was dedicated the cathedral, seat of the bishop; and
just as the cathedral bound all the shrines and churches
of the Sienese dominion into a concordant whole, so,
regardless of parish obligations to other saints, the
Virgin laid her mild injunction on every heart.   Her
annual festival was a day of joy and thanksgiving,
officially proclaimed by the state and celebrated spon-
taneously by the whole population.   It fell on the
15th of August, the day of her assumption to the side of
her Son.   To evoke that wonderful festival is not only
to set before our eyes in material form the strange fusion

achieved by the mediæval mind of the life terrestrial and
the life spiritual, but also to realize one of those gay and
colored spectacles for which the modern world has no
equivalent, and which are like the moving page of some
blithe and exquisite romance.

A general animation became apparent in the city as
the middle of August drew near. The town crier,
sounding his trumpet before him, passed through the
streets announcing the programme for the festival;
at the same time he made proclamation concerning the
great fair of three days,* which, with characteristic
prudence and in keeping with the homely character of the
celebration, the government did not hesitate to associate
with the season of thanksgiving. On the eve of the
looked-for day fell the opening public act. All the
citizens from the age of eighteen to seventy, forming in
procession according to parishes and under the leadership of the parish priests, marched to the cathedral.
For the greater glory of Our Lady each celebrant carried
in his hand a lighted taper, and before the citizens went
the magistracy, attended by the *carroccio* or car of state,
upon which were conspicuous the official offering of
candle and banner. Thus before sundown of August
14th, Siena had renewed its vows to the goddess of its
choice and love. But the next day came a procession
of another kind, one which swelled the hearts of the old
burghers with patriotic felicity. The castles, villages,
towns, and monasteries, conquered outright or subdued
under the euphemistic name of an alliance, knocked,
as it were, at the gate of the city, and in the person of
the proprietors or of elected delegates proceeded in

* "Il Constituto di Siena dell' anno 1262," I, 195.

solemn state to the duomo to repeat the oath of allegiance to the victorious commune. A scene more
splendid and, at the same time, more feudal cannot be
imagined. The free town was a perpetual protest
against the feudal system, but when the problem presented itself as to how the shattered elements of feudalism were to be organized under the new sovereignty,
the city leaders chose a solution which proved that they
could not emancipate themselves from the domination
of current legal forms. They simply assumed toward
the nobles and corporations of the county the familiar
position of suzerain. The morning of the fifteenth,
therefore, saw the procession of Sienese vassals march
to perform an annual act of homage. In that procession
were the proud descendants of the ancient counts of
the city, mitred abbots or their mandataries, the representatives of villages and towns; and in their hands
they bore, in honor of the Virgin, each one a lighted
candle. Through dense and exultant crowds they made
their way up the marble steps of the cathedral until they
stood within the portal, before the desk of a secretary
of the commune. To the humble scrivener, seated
before a solemn ledger, they consigned their offerings,
all destined for the service of the Supreme Lady and
consisting of candle-wax, or banners of brocade, or
money, according to the articles of submission.*

Meanwhile the fair had begun in the great central
square called the Campo, at first merely an ordinary,
undistinguished, provincial piazza, but gradually trans-

---

* See for the official order of the day, "Il Constituto di Siena dell' anno
1262," Distinctio V, 36, 37. Also, Toti, "Atti di votazione della città di
Siena," pp. 10–16.

formed by the erection of public and private buildings into one of the most beautiful and most unique squares of Italy. Wooden booths in rows filled the wide space and their displays of delicates, oriental spices, armor, and goods of all kinds were intended to attract not only the peasants of the neighborhood but also foreign traders from Arezzo, Florence, and more distant parts. Mimes, acrobats, and musicians, the whole tribe of bohemians embraced under the more or less opprobrious epithet of *homines curtis*, flooded the city, reciting ballads, turning somersaults, and engaging in merry-making, each after his kind. To satisfy a very prevalent taste the government even authorized the erection of a gambling booth, around which, according to abundant evidence, always pressed an eager throng. At the same time the bells rang to worship, and into the open churches poured great crowds, drawn as much by the desire to see the flaming candles and decorations of the altar as to make offer to heaven of a contrite heart. Throughout the day the Virgin and the host of saints were conceived to hover close at hand, almost within reach of ear and eye, pleased with all the ways of their people. Thus on the 15th of August Siena mixed heaven and earth, achieving a national holiday that had all the elements of joy, sincerity, and poetry.

This festival, repeated year after year and rousing with each return the emotions of an excitable people to a state of religious exaltation, led at last to one of the most moving and picturesque episodes of the Italian Middle Age. It was the year 1260. The Florentines, supported by almost all the other towns of Tuscany, had acquired the upper hand in the province, and now led

an army against Siena, wounded and at bay, to deliver
the death blow. We shall have much to say of that
memorable campaign when we take up the many wars
between the two neighboring cities.   Here I wish merely
to detach from the struggle a wonderful, culminating
episode in the worship of Mary. We have seen how
that worship lay imbedded in the mystic longings, as
well as in the daily thoughts and cares of the whole
population. It sank roots which drank at the well of
tears. Love of home, yearning for heaven, right living
and forgiveness—the name of Mary signified all that.
And now the Florentines were at the gate and the day
of doom seemed at hand. Is it wonderful that this
people, thoroughly convinced of the power of their
patroness to save as well as to destroy, should have given
themselves into her hands utterly and without reserve?
An old chronicle * records the story in words of which
no translation, be it regretfully confessed, can render the
subtle flavor. After telling us how in their black hour
the city council made one of their number, the excellent
Buonaguida Lucari, head or syndic, it proceeds:

"And whilst this election was in progress, our spiritual father,
my lord the bishop, caused the bell to ring to summon his clergy.
And he made to come together all the clergy of Siena, priests, and
canons, and friars, and all the religious, to the duomo, and being

---

* This famous chronicle exists in several MSS. of the first half of the fifteenth century. It is generally held that they are all transcriptions or
versions of a much earlier original.   The Sienese antiquary, Porri, has earned
our gratitude by publishing one of the manuscripts in his "Miscellanea
Storica Senese," 1844, under the title, "La Sconfitta di Montaperti, secondo
il MS. di Niccolò di Giovanni di Francesco Ventura."   The above vigorous
and skilful translation is from the "History of Siena" of Langton Douglas,
p. 84 ff. Mr. Douglas, in addition to Porri, has made use of an unpublished
MS. in the Ambrosian Library of Milan.

assembled there he made a short sermon to them, admonishing them and comforting them, and bidding them pray to God and His Most Holy Mother, the Virgin Mary, and to all the saints . . . for the people of the city; . . . that as he had spared the city of Nineveh because of its fasting and repentance, so it would please Him to free Siena from the fury and pride of these knaves of Florentines. And so he ordained that every one should make bare his feet, and should go devoutly in procession through the duomo, singing with a loud voice and invoking ceaselessly the pity of God.

"And whilst my lord the bishop with all the religious and clergy were thus going in procession singing their litanies and prayers, God did put it into the mind of the syndic, that is to say of Buonaguida Lucari, to rise, and say in a voice so loud that he was heard by the citizens who were outside the church in the piazza of S. Cristofano: 'My lords of Siena, and my dear fellow citizens, we have already commended ourselves to King Manfred, now it appears to me, that we ought in all sincerity to give ourselves, our goods and our persons, the city and the contado, to the Queen of life eternal, that is to say, to our Lady Mother, the Virgin Mary. To make this offering, let it be your pleasure to bear me company.'

"And no sooner had he said these words than this Buonaguida stripped himself to his shirt. And, being barefooted and bare-headed, he took his leathern girdle and fastened it round his neck with a slip-knot. And in this guise, at the head of the procession of the citizens, he set out towards the duomo. And behind him went all the people; and whomsoever they met by the way went with them, each man being shoeless and without cloak or hat. . . . And as they went they ceased not to cry 'Mary Virgin, succor us in our great need, and deliver us out of the claws of these lions, and from these haughty men who seek to devour us.' And all the people prayed, 'Oh, Madonna, most holy Queen of Heaven, we miserable sinners entreat your mercy.'

"And upon their arrival at the duomo, my lord the bishop was going in procession through the church, and was at that moment at the high altar, before our gracious Lady, the Virgin Mary. And he began to sing the 'Te Deum Laudamus' in a loud voice.

"It was just then that the people reached the door of the church,

and commenced to cry out 'Misericordia, Misericordia!' with many
tears. At that plaint so dolorous and piteous, my lord the bishop
and all the clergy turned round, and went to meet Buonaguida.
And when they were come together, all kneeled down, and Buonaguida prostrated himself to the earth. Whereupon my lord the
bishop raised him up and gave him the kiss of peace. And then
all the citizens went one to another and kissed one another on
the mouth. And this was done at the entering to the choir of
the duomo.

"And taking one another by the hand, my lord the bishop and
Buonaguida went up to the altar of our Mother, the Virgin Mary,
and there they kneeled down with great lamentation and bitter
tears. And this venerable citizen, Buonaguida, lay all prostrate
on the ground, and so did all the people, with much weeping and
many sighs. And so they remained for a quarter of an hour.
Then Buonaguida raised himself to his feet in front of our Mother,
the Virgin Mary, and uttered many wise and prudent words.
And amongst others he spake these following: 'Oh, Virgin,
glorious Queen of Heaven, Mother of sinners! I, a wretched
sinner, give, grant, and yield to thee, this city and contado of
Siena, and I pray thee, sweetest Mother, that it may please thee
to accept it, notwithstanding our great frailty and our many sins.
Regard not our offences, but guard, defend, and deliver us, I beseech thee, from the hands of these perfidious dogs of Florentines,
and from whomsoever may wish to oppress, to harass, or to ruin us.'

"These words having been said, my lord the bishop went up
into the pulpit and preached a very beautiful sermon, admonishing
the people with good examples, and praying and commanding them
to embrace one another, and to forgive one another all trespasses,
to confess and to communicate. . . . And he charged them that
they should go with him and with all the clergy and religious in
procession.

"And in this procession before all the rest went that carved
crucifix which is in the duomo, and immediately after it followed
many clergy. Then came a red standard, behind which walked
my lord the bishop. He was barefoot, and by his side was
Buonaguida in his shirt, with his girdle around his neck. Then

followed all the canons of the cathedral, all without shoes and bareheaded, and as they went they sang psalms and hymns very devoutly. After them passed along all the women, shoeless and bareheaded, and a part of them with hair dishevelled, ever commending themselves to God and to the most holy Mother, the Virgin Mary. And so they went in procession to S. Cristofano, and into the Campo, and returned to the duomo. And they commenced to make peace one with another. And he that had received the greatest injury went to seek out his brother to make peace with him, and to pardon him, and to kiss him. And soon concord was made. . . ."

Which befell on the 2d of September, 1260; and the next day the Sienese marched out of the city with unfurled banners and in the furious battle of Montaperti swept the Florentines off the field like chaff. Seeing that their exaltation gave them irresistible strength they were not far wrong in ascribing their victory to the Virgin. More than ever Siena was henceforth her city, the Sienese her sons. That presentation of the keys in the duomo was an act unconsciously moulded by the prevailing feudal ideas. By virtue of it Queen Mary became sovereign and liege, ruling *amœna Sena* as her earthly fief. The very coins henceforth recounted the new glory, for from the time of the dedication they appeared, bearing in addition to the ancient legend, *Sena Vetus*, the proud words, *Civitas Virginis*.

The gate out of which the Sienese marched to strike the enemy opened upon the country to the east, and was and is still called *Porta Santo Viene* (The Saint Comes). And thereby hangs the tale of another procession which deserves a word in this record of the cordial relation of a mediæval people and its saints. Older than Montaperti by one hundred and fifty years, the story introduces

Fonte Branda

us once more to the Sienese protomartyr, Sant' Ansano, and to the church at Dofana, which possessed his body and had from the early eighth century been the occasion of furious litigation between the bishops of Arezzo and Siena. In the year 1108 the body of the saint, a priceless relic, which had lain undisturbed for eight hundred years, was exhumed. The bishop of Arezzo and his followers, full of distrust against their neighbors, were for carrying it away with them, but yielding either to reason or to force, agreed to a division.* Accordingly the head was apportioned to Arezzo, the trunk to Siena. On February 6, 1108, occurred a remarkable scene.† The Sienese clergy accompanied by many people went to Dofana to bring back the martyred saint, now a heap of dust without a skull, to the city which he had given his life to save. As the procession, moving to the accompaniment of solemn chants, drew near the gate the waiting people rushed forth unable to restrain their jubilation. Cries of *"Il santo viene! Il santo viene!"* rent the air, and from that day the gate by which Ansano had gone forth to death and had returned triumphant, after biding his time for eight centuries, has been called from the auspicious event.‡

* A spirited account, contemporary or almost contemporary, and curiously distorted by Sienese bias, may be found in Pecci, "Storia del Vescovado di Siena," p. 145 *ff.*

† Date and fact supplied by "Annales Senenses," Monumenta Ger. Hist., Scriptores, XIX.

‡ The Porta Santo Viene is now interchangably called Porta dei Pispini from the name of a neighboring fountain. In connection with the older name I may note that doubt has recently been thrown, not on the above procession, which is an indisputable fact, nor on the name of the gate, which is no less certain, but on the origin of that name. It has been pointed out that Santo Viene may be a popular corruption of Sant' Eugenio, a monastery close by, from which the gate in remote days may conceivably have been named. See Bargagli-Petrucci, "Le Fonti di Siena," I, p. 319.

But to return to the proffer of the city to the Virgin
on that dark September day when the army of the
Florentines lay outside the city. The reader will
recall that the procession of citizens, chanting and crying
mercy, wound from the duomo to S. Cristofano and
back again. The duomo was on the southern hill of
the city, while the church of San Cristofano lay to the
north on the way to Porta Camollia. Note these two
terminals, for they are an affirmation of the dependence
of the young state upon the church, a dependence
which must have been great indeed, since Siena, although by the year 1260 a commonwealth of considerable importance and long past the period of apprentice-
ship, did not yet have a separate edifice to house her
civil government. True, the first steps looking to the
creation of permanent municipal offices had been taken,
for we hear of a mint and a general salt-store existing
on the Campo, but the potestà still had his private
residence in some house which he rented from a citizen,
and conducted court in the church of San Pellegrino.
In San Pellegrino, too, were installed the administrative
offices of the commune, known as La Biccherna, while
the city council, called the Council of the Bell, came
together in the church of San Cristofano. In 1260 this
last edifice fulfilled in some sort the functions of a city
hall. That is the reason why the penitential procession,
making the round of the city, swung between it and the
cathedral. The great palazzo pubblico, which in our
own days dominates the central piazza and constitutes
the chief monument of Sienese civic pride, was not begun
till the end of the thirteenth century. So long did it
take for the mediæval mind to learn to differentiate

between civil and ecclesiastical functions and to recognize the necessity of an entirely separate physical organism for the state! Again I may point out that we must always keep present before us the essential crudity of the society of this early republican period and its total unfamiliarity with that political theory and practice which give our proceedings so much more precision and firmness. Nothing is so certain as that the town government, in process of slow formation for hundreds of years, took each forward step only under the pressure of the new practical necessities attending the commercial expansion of the city. Therefore the churches, being the only spacious edifices which a mediæval city boasted, were quite good enough for secular matters until the accumulation of business and the more elaborate organization of the government demanded offices of special construction.

The Sienese church, such as we have found it, was undoubtedly alert and vigorous with red blood coursing in its veins. In spite of abuses which cropped up from time to time, it maintained an effective organization of parishes and baptisteries, by which its spiritual comfort was made accessible to the poorest beggar of the town and to the lowliest charcoal burner of the mountains. But it could not, even when served by a devoted priesthood, satisfy the extraordinary religious fervor of the Middle Age. Everywhere in Europe the passion for sanctity gave birth to a special institution, by means of which men, withdrawing from the world and its lusts, could surrender themselves to a life of prayer and meditation. As early as the Apostolic Age an element of Oriental asceticism appeared in the Christian religion, and in the course of time this element created a suitable expression of its ideal in the monastery.

Naturally the monastic fervor did not fail to reach Siena, over whose territory it deposited its monuments with a lavish hand. Leaning from the rampart outside the gate of San Marco a large red mass rises into view. It is the monastery of Sant' Eugenio, called by the Sienese with a pleasant familiarity *Il Monistero,* as if it were the only one of its kind. It was secularized in the eighteenth century when, after a thousand years of not unhonorable service, the ample cloisters and dormitories were turned without objectionable alterations into a country residence. Il Monistero is the first monastic foundation of this neighborhood, owing its existence to a pious gift made in the year 730 by a Lombard gastald—*Magnificus Warnefrid Gastaldius Civitatis Senensis.** The monks under their abbot governed themselves by the Benedictine rule, the usual constitution adopted by all early monasteries. South of Il Monistero, some twenty miles as the crow flies, and not far from Montalcino, may still be seen the fine ruin of a church marking the site of another Benedictine foundation, the abbey of Sant' Antimo. Its origin, too, falls probably in the eighth century, for, by the ninth, it was well-to-do and had acquired ample immunities from the emperors. Still it was overshadowed in importance by the great Benedictine house of San Salvatore, which stood on the slopes of Monte Amiata, and which constituted one of the greatest feudal patrimonies of all Italy. San Salvatore, likewise, dates from that

---

* The interesting deed was published by Pecci, "Storia del Vescovado di Siena," p. 44.

age of monastic fervor, the eighth century, received gifts from many noblemen, coaxed immunities from emperors and popes, quarrelled constantly with its greedy and powerful neighbors, the family of the Aldobrandeschi, declined, was plundered, and rose again— what a story if our day had leisure to write and read such tales! Such are some of the oldest monastic foundations of the neighborhood of Siena. That they have been permitted to decay or been quietly surrendered to unhallowed uses sufficiently defines the attitude of our time to the ascetic ideal of the Middle Age, but should not hinder us from doing justice to the period when their abbots owned rich estates and enjoyed equal consideration in the land with the great barons.

The foundations I have named are of a very venerable antiquity, owing their rise to the first great wave of monastic enthusiasm which passed over Europe. No sooner had the force of the first wave spent itself than it was followed by another and still another; in fact, monastic revivals were a common phenomenon of a period which conceived them to be the highest expression of its faith. Numerous were the foundations by which Siena marked its participation in all these movements. At the height of her power scores of greater and smaller homes dotted her territory within and without her walls.* I can do no more here than add to the list of original settlements the names of some of the more famous and enduring establishments of the later periods. In the valley of the Merse may still be seen the wonder-

---

* For a partial list of such places, mostly vanished and forgotten, see the "Constituto dell' anno 1262," Distinctio I. Falletti-Fossati in his "Costumi Senesi," p. 115, reckons that in 1310 there were twenty-eight convents within the city alone, with over six hundred inmates.

ful ruin of the abbey of San Galgano, founded in the
twelfth century in the days of the Cistercian reform.
Outside the gate of Fonte Branda, in the deep solitude
of one of the few magnificent forests which still adorn
modern Italy, lies the Augustinian monastery of Lecceto; and at the opposite point of the compass, to the
east of the town, lies, not buried in an enchanted wood,
but high on a summit, commanding a wide view over
rolling hills and valleys, the Certosa of Pontignano. In
the naves and cloisters of San Galgano, Lecceto, and
Pontignano the footsteps of the monks have long since
ceased to sound, but, though fallen from their estate, they
still speak with the compelling power of beauty of a time
which entertained other hopes than ours and dreamed
other dreams.

Within the city proper the monastic wave of the thirteenth century, which was the most fervid of all and
which directed its energy particularly upon the towns,
could not but have a large effect. I am speaking of the
movement named of the begging friars and associated
with the two towering figures of St. Francis and St.
Dominic. Missionaries and brothers of these two
orders got a foothold very early in Siena and, favored
by the piety of the citizens, began the creation of those
two edifices which, not without additions and changes
imposed by the succeeding generations, still dominate
respectively the east and west hills of the town.

But Siena boasts a nobler product of the Christian
spirit than its many monasteries of the city and contado,
nobler because sprung from a more unselfish desire to
render service to mankind. I am referring to the famous hospital, which, erected opposite the cathedral

steps and called from that circumstance Santa Maria della Scala, still flourishes, accumulating new vigor with each century and multiplying its benefactions to the poor and heavy laden. Such an institution, keeping pace with advancing time, reaffirms our faith in the enduring power of the Christian ideal.

Santa Maria della Scala, recognized in the days of the Italian republics as the greatest hospital of Tuscany, grew from a small seed, being in its origin nothing but a house of rest for pilgrims. Its founders were the canons of the cathedral church, whose bounties enabled it to take shape, probably in the eleventh century, for the first documentary reference to it is of the year 1090.* Its scope was soon extended, till it embraced many forms of charity, and constituted, besides satisfying its original function, a hospital in our modern sense, a home for foundlings, an orphan asylum, and a poor house.† The service of the institution was performed by a company of volunteers, men and women, who took no religious vows, but wore a special garment with the insignia of the hospital and regarded themselves as a lay brotherhood under rules framed and voted by themselves. These rules, enforcing a very rigorous discipline inspired by the monastic ideal, have been luckily preserved for us in several redactions.‡ Besides giving the

---

* See Banchi, "Statuti Senesi," Vol. III, Introduzione, p. 7.

† Of the scale on which the hospital was established in all its services, the following inscription, touching the waifs of the year 1298 and still legible on the wall toward the piazza del duomo, gives a graphic impression: Hec domus facta est pro gittatellis in anno domini M.CC.LXXXXVIII in quo tempore sunt in numero CCC. gitetelli et plus.

‡ The earliest redaction, of the year 1305, has been published by L. Banchi, "Statuti Volgari de lo Spedale di S. Maria Vergine di Siena scritti l'anno MCCCV."

conditions under which the brothers and sisters were
received, and precisely regulating such matters as
prayer, food, and drink, they inform us that the company was governed by a rector, elected in a general
session. This privilege of naming their own ruler the
brothers had not obtained without a struggle. In fact,
almost from the first they were involved in a severe
quarrel over the control of the institution with their
patrons, the canons of the cathedral. Laymen though
they were, and, therefore, in that age an inferior social
order, they had seen the property of the hospital grow
by the free gifts of themselves and their fellow-citizens,
and chafed at the leading-strings of their superiors.
The conflict was at last carried to the highest ecclesiastical tribunal, to the pope at Rome, and by sentence of
the year 1194,* the brothers were practically freed from
canonical interference. Henceforth the great hospital
of Santa Maria della Scala was in all respects a lay
institution, operated by the brothers and enjoying the
official support of the state, an expressive witness of the
successful and inevitable emancipation of society from
the church.†

The Catholic church, which in the Dark Age, following the invasions, held disorganized society together
by means of its parish organization, which served as a

---

* Muratori, "Antiq It.," IV., 585.
† To the above brief historical account there is a curious legendary corol-
lary. We are told that legends have a valuable historical kernel; that may
be true in general, but the story recounted admirably by Banchi ("Statuti
Senesi," Vol. III, Introduzione, 17–28) of how the brothers of the hospital,
needing a saint and founder, discovered, or rather literally manufactured one,
proves that some legends, at least, are cut out of whole cloth. The hospital
was founded, as we have seen, by the canons. The brothers, hostile to the
canons, would have preferred a lay origin. A wish warmly entertained is
readily converted into a fact. The brothers spread the news—not till the

staff to the young republics in the days of their youth, which fostered the spirit revealed in the monasteries of city and country and in such institutions of charity as the hospital of Santa Maria della Scala, was in the main a vast power for good.   And yet it was constantly threatened with the sloth and corruption attending success. The inheritor of wealth and a secured position is always in danger of falling asleep, like the giant Fafner, over his treasure, to grumble like him when forcibly aroused: "ich lieg' und besitze; lass mich schlafen." Out of this indolence the church had to be shaken at frequent intervals by the elemental force of a popular revival. I have spoken of the many monastic movements, each of which earnestly tried to bring to the front the ascetic aspect of the Christian ideal. Much wilder agitations than these, originating generally in a protest against the hollowness of official forms of worship and ending in religious ecstasy, attended the evolution of society throughout the Middle Age. Every student of religion has heard of the flagellants, bands of whom, stripped to the skin and lashing their macerated bodies, passed again and again up and down the highways of the peninsula, chanting songs strange and terrible as the howling of eastern dervishes. If the church was inclined to resent all demands for

---

fourteenth century—of a pious cobbler, who began the hospital enterprise from his own means hundreds of years before; presently they named him Sutore or Sorore (Latin sutor—cobbler); in the course of another generation they found his body, miraculously preserved *dinanzi l'altare de' Pizzicaioli* (A. D. 1492); and, finally, the whole amusing fabrication had an official stamp set on it by one of those lying lives of the saints put forth with barefaced impudence in that unloveliest period of Italian history, the Counter-Reformation. Since then for the good *popolano* of Siena the fame of the cobbler, Sorore, rests upon a foundation of stone.

change raised by unofficial bodies, as constituting an interference with its authority and a threat against its peace, it generally took the wise course toward all these movements of letting them alone. The hysterical ones would soon spend their force and perish; the more durable might, with a little manipulation, be adopted and dominated. To the adopted class belong the movements associated with the Cistercians, Dominicans, Franciscans, and many other monastic societies. All these organizations, springing from religious enthusiasm and fed in part, at least, by the popular indignation against the vices and human insufficiencies of the clergy, were thus comfortably fitted into Rome's elastic system.

All this can leave no room for doubt that, by the side of the established service of the Lord and His saints, solemnly conducted by the church and supplemented by the monasteries, there existed in the Middle Age an intense personal search for the fruits of the spirit, the continuation of the original evangelical passion. Some of the most exquisite as well as some of the most ferocious phenomena of the religious activity of the period are the outflow of this individual attitude toward the problems of the life eternal. Among all the republics of Italy none was more rich in representatives of personal sanctity than Siena. Pier Pettignano, Saint Catherine, San Bernardino—these are only the more prominent names in the list of her impassioned visionaries. To the variety of religious experience for which they stand I shall give attention in another place, convinced that no other study will bring us nearer to the heart of this fascinating people.

CHAPTER IV

THE BURGHERS

THE past contains the record of many cities whose mere name suffices to set our imagination on fire. Athens, Rome, Venice, Florence—all these gave birth to a wonderful civilization, which survived their political power, long since crumbled to dust, and of which the succeeding generations of men have been the often unmindful beneficiaries. With regard to one and all of these cities it is hardly necessary to recall to the reader that their immortal achievements in the arts rested upon a solid material basis, created by the fruitful and closely interwoven activities of a busy population of peasants, artisans, and merchants. Whoever, therefore, would penetrate to the sources of the culture of the Athenians, the Romans, the Venetians, and the Florentines must seek to inform himself in each case about such fundamental problems as the productivity of the soil, the forms of urban labor, the opportunities of commerce; in a word, he must master the conditions surrounding the homely, ineluctable, ever-renewed struggle for bread and those many things of which bread is the universal symbol. And if such an economic review opens an avenue to the understanding of the lordly cities of the past, it must be of equal service in interpreting the cultural significance of that secondary group of towns, of which Siena is a conspicuous member. As an approach to my chief end in this book, the Sienese civilization, I purpose in this chapter to examine the economic basis upon which the City of the Virgin reared the remarkable edifice of her political power and artistic achievement.

The Italian cities of the Middle Age owed the first flush of their material prosperity to the stirring of the stagnant pools of life effected by that world movement called the crusades. The quickened pulse-beat of the great city-centres presently produced an accelerated political development, of which we have the proof in the courageous republicanism of the twelfth century, signalized by the universal emergence of the consulship and the heroic resistance to Frederick Barbarossa. So closely related are all the fields of human endeavor that an expansive movement in one of them is certain to affect advantageously all the others. Thus the more compact political organization in its turn reacted favorably on trade and industry, with the result that an international commerce sprang into being, which spun ever-increasing threads of intercourse around the countries of the Mediterranean and Atlantic. In this commercial renascence Siena participated according to the measure of her opportunities and resources.

When in the twelfth and, with gathering momentum, in the thirteenth century, commerce revived in western Europe, it employed as its most convenient instrument, the fair, and preferably, for the purposes of general or international exchange, the fairs of Champagne in eastern France. These French fairs were world-marts, and presented themselves to view in all the color and picturesqueness of the Middle Age. In the period of their prosperity the long process, by which the diverse peoples of Europe have been more or less reduced to a common type, had hardly begun. In dialect and dress, in food and drink, in the forms of social intercourse, every man reflected the peculiarities of the immediate small group into which he was born. A Florentine knew a Genoese at a glance by the cut of his beard or cloak; that fur cap signified a Pole; that greasy curl a Jew from York or Bruges. A score of tongues, a hundred dialects, resounded along the streets of temporary booths erected to serve the convenience of exchange. The county of Champagne saw annually no less than six of these international gatherings. While they owed their popularity in the first instance to the central position of Champagne in Europe, they further recommended themselves to the traders by the circumstance that they succeeded one another in such a way as to extend practically throughout the year. They thus assumed the character of a permanent international money market and produce exchange, and became the most convenient instrument at hand for regulating the supply and demand of many necessities. Each of the six fairs lasted from one and a half to two and a half months. When Lagny fair, with which the year began, was over, the town of Bar-sur-Aube set up its booths, with Provins and Troyes following in the summer and autumn, nay, following with two fairs apiece to complete the full round of six.

The procedure in connection with any one of these fairs did not differ greatly from the order of exercises usual in all the others. Each gathering was, in accordance with mediæval sentiment, inaugurated on or near one of the great holidays of the church, the occasion being emphasized by a formal act of worship, such as in the Middle Age was inseparable alike from the business and pleasure of the people. The first week passed amidst the noise and confusion attending the erection of the wooden booths and the installation of the merchants from far and near, to be followed presently by an animated barter in all known varieties of merchandise, among which figured, as leading articles, the cloth of Flanders, the leather of Spain, and the pepper and spices of the Orient. When the sale and purchase of the goods had been effected, the work of the bankers and money-changers began, a work the risks and worry of which will not fail to appeal to us if we recall the many coinage systems in use and the as yet helpless infancy of capital and credit. Such, briefly, were the fairs of Champagne.*

In these merchant gatherings, Italians, usually designated as Lombards, or with scant international courtesy, on account of their sharp bargains, as Lombard dogs, occupied a conspicuous place. Especially toward the end of each fair, when, as we have seen, the banking began, did they step forward with the air of polite and accommodating middlemen; and among them, from the beginning of the thirteenth century,† were prominent many adventurous citizens of Siena. For the second half of that same century we have orig-

---

* On the fairs of Champagne and the general commercial activity of the Sienese in the thirteenth century, see the following: Paoli, "Siena alle Fiere di Sciampagna"; Paoli and Piccolomini, "Lettere Volgari"; Zdekauer, "Documenti Senesi riguardanti le Fiere di Champagne" ("Studi Senesi nel circolo Giuridico," XII, 337); "Il Monte dei Paschi," Vol. I; Patetta, "Caorsini Senesi in Inghilterra," "Bull. Sen.," IV, 311 ff.

† See Paoli, "Fiere di Sciampagna," p. 69. The earliest date is 1216.

Saint Catherine

By Andrea Vanni (in the Church of San Domenico)

inal material of a unique kind, being a number of
letters of Sienese merchants in the Tuscan idiom, recording the transactions of Champagne with accuracy and
fulness.* Although these documents, owing to their
antiquity, constitute an important contribution to the
general history of mediæval commerce, the student of
Siena is interested in them chiefly because they furnish
a clear, direct, and wholly intelligible picture of the
activity on which the early prosperity of the town was
founded.

What economic facts do those letters communicate?
To begin with, we make out that it was customary,
toward the middle of the thirteenth century, for a number of enterprising Sienese citizens to form a partnership
and dispatch one or more of their number to Champagne
to turn the subscribed capital to account. As almost
all the great Sienese families with whom we shall be
dealing, the Salimbeni, the Tolomei, the Buonsignori,
the Malavolti, the Cacciaconti, and many more, figure
in this correspondence, we may affirm that the great
fortunes of Siena were made in trade and were fed from
the French tap-root. While the chief activity of one and
all of the companies was the traffic in money, the chief
aim, in the frank language of one of the letters, was
guadagniernne grosamente, that is to say, big profits.†
And the opportunities must be acknowedged to have
been golden. Armed with great purses of thick leather
the Sienese volunteered their deft services in effecting
an exchange between the different moneys that flowed
together at the fair, or in extending a loan, on good

* The "Lettere Volgari" referred to above.
† Paoli, "Lettere," p. 75.

security, to some unlucky fellow-mortal hard pressed for cash. Engaged thus in exchange and loans they did the business of an ambulatory bank. Their interest charge on loans was rarely less than twenty per cent. per annum, and might be sixty, per cent. and more. The monstrous height of this rate is less a sign of Italian greed than of the scarcity of metal in the Middle Age. It stands to reason that persons in need of money would not have paid such a preposterous interest if coin had been plentiful and the lending companies numerous.

The inevitable consequence of the growing international relations of trade and finance was the gradual appearance of improved banking devices, and in this connection it is noteworthy that the ruler who, in the thirteenth century, supplied the main impetus toward this development was the pope. A universal power, he had financial relations with all the world, due to the general offering called Peter's Pence, to the impost which he was empowered to lay on ecclesiastical property in connection with a crusade, and to the payments which he required of newly appointed bishops in return for the papal confirmation. From all the corners of Europe flowed toward Rome sums of money, the collection and transmission of which gradually trained a capable and enterprising school of financiers. With this administrative service the pope naturally entrusted his own countrymen, the Italians, and preferably the Italian merchants, because of their familiarity with foreign moneys and markets. The experience thus gained in the pope's business, added to the knowledge acquired in the pursuit of their personal affairs, largely explains why these Mediterranean traders took the lead in banking and kept it against the whole world for many generations.

However, the Italian merchants, enjoying not only the rich harvest of their own enterprise in Champagne and elsewhere, but also the vast financial advantages resulting from collecting and accumulating the pope's moneys, were by no means an object of general affection. From the beginning of the world the dealer in money, the capitalist, has excited envy and hatred; and for reasons, sometimes paltry, sometimes grave and convincing, the Italian agents of the pope brought down upon their heads the aversion of the various peoples among whom they operated. A lively echo of the English feeling toward them comes to us from the chronicle of that vigorous enemy of the Roman curia, Matthew Paris.* In the reign of Henry III (1216-65) the pope— often enough with the consent of the king, who stipulated for a share in the profits—wrested huge sums from the fat English prelates, making use, of course, in his hateful and often tyrannical game, of his Italian servants. The indignant Matthew abominates them as the pest of his country, designating them sometimes as *Lombardiæ canes*, sometimes as Caorsini. This latter term, literally meaning men of Cahors in France, was opprobriously applied in the Middle Age to money-lenders and usurers in general. Now it is a fact certain to stir our interest that, among "the Lombard dogs" and Caorsini so cordially detested by the patriotic Matthew, were also merchants from Siena. In the capacity of papal collectors they overran the land, and if we give credence to Matthew, covered both themselves and their master

* Mon. Germ. Hist., Scriptores, Vol. XXVIII.

with dishonor. The unchristian greed of the papal
curia may be admitted without further argument, but
the hard practices of the merchants deserve a brief
elucidation. As the bishops and abbots, whom the
Italians fleeced on the pope's orders, had no ready cash,
they were obliged to borrow from the collectors themselves and at an offensive and usurious rate of interest.
In this way the foreign agents, without any doubt whatever, ruined many men and committed many iniquities,
but in partial excuse of them it may be urged that the
whole business world was as yet inchoate and disorganized, and that there were few or no acknowledged
rules of commercial conduct and honor. Nothing
illustrates this state of affairs so well as the ludicrous
mediæval attitude toward usury.

Usury in the Middle Age was interest—interest high
or low, fair or unfair, and was strictly forbidden by the
church.* Councils and fathers had taken the matter
up and had never hesitated to declare all money lending
for profit as contrary to the gospels and, therefore,
monstrous. In the year 1179 the Lateran Council
held under the presidency of Pope Alexander III, re-
issued a number of earlier prescriptions against usury
in a more definite form, and Alexander's declarations
were afterward often republished by his successors.
Owing to the ascendancy of the church in all the affairs
of life an echo of the papal fulminations may be found
in the legislation of almost all the states and cities of
Europe. Wherever in the Middle Age we encounter

* Among the numerous books on the subject of usury I refer the reader
to W. J. Ashley, "Introduction to English Economic History and Theory,"
I, chapter III.

an expression of principle, usury, broadly defined as interest, was tabooed and forbidden.

However, what, in contrast to doctrine and law, were the facts? We have already had a hint of them in connection with our exposition of the development of Mediterranean commerce, and must have assured ourselves that money-lending flourished as a necessary adjunct to trade. We may go further back than the Middle Age and easily convince ourselves that money-lending has existed in the world since the remote day when one man, by saving, laid up a store of value which another desired to put to use. In view of so ancient and immemorial a practice how did the mediæval period come to develop its peculiar position? The answer is found in the special religious and economic conditions of the era. With the fall of the Roman Empire civilization went to pieces, and capital and business enterprise alike disappeared from society. In the petty world of the Barbarian kingdoms the views of the church on trade and interest acquired an indisputable ascendancy, enforced by the circumstance that they sprang from a high-minded, though ascetic, interpretation of Christ's message. As a result the little borrowing and lending, for which there was occasion in a primitive society, was gladly left, with its stigma of corruption and illegality, to the outcast race of the Jews. But when the West again summoned its energies, and trade, stimulated by the crusades, expanded in volume, it was unlikely that the Christians would permit the profitable banking field to be monopolized by the dingy folk of the ghetto. Laws or no laws, they could not resist the temptation of gain, and in the period of the fairs of

Champagne we have seen that Christian money lenders, and, above all, Italians, leaped to the front. To Italians, accordingly, it was given to organize in the course of the following generations the traffic in money as a serviceable and necessary adjunct of business; Italians, too, gradually succeeded in giving the despised calling a respectable standing in society. For a long time, however, church and state combined to maintain their theoretical prohibitions, and, under cover of them, frequently pounced on money-lenders, subjecting them to outrageous extortions. In all Europe there was hardly a prince, lay or spiritual, who did not periodically arrest Jews, and if possible, Italians, on the ground of an illicit trade, to set them free again in return for a surrender of their money-bags or such a percentage thereof as sufficed to establish a presumption of innocence in a mind open to financial persuasions. A moral justification for this bare procedure might seem to have been furnished by the hatred with which the mass of the people looked upon the usurious, blood-sucking practices of the capitalists. But these practices, if common sense had prevailed, might have been regulated by drawing a sharp line, after our modern fashion, between usury and interest, and permitting one while prohibiting the other. Only this the church, sworn to its ideals, would never consent to do, and the civil governments, with singular shortsightedness, long delayed taking the initiative. It was the grave risk, associated with the money traffic under a system alternating between sufferance and confiscation, which partially explains the appalling interest charge usual in that age. Safety, secured by the legalization, under proper restrictions, of the operations of finance, would have been attended by a large decline in the interest rate. Thus the vacuous idealism of the church— vacuous and even cynical, for the pope and the prelacy were among the leading figures of the money market both as clients and as silent partners of the merchant companies—long delayed the cure of a most crying evil.

It is not without pleasure that the historian of Siena observes the little hill-town to have been among the earliest cities to enter a protest against the intransigent position of the church. As early as the thirteenth century, as is proved by the Constitution of the year 1262, the government of the republic, though clamorously professing obedience to the church in all things, authorized usury, provided the usurer be not in other respects a man of ill repute and suspicious religious opinions.* Probably such legislation as this put banking operations on a sounder basis in Siena than was usual in Italy, and especially north of the Alps. Nevertheless, while the church stood her ground some peril dogged the steps of the usurers, as is proved by a curious denunciation which has come down to us from the records of a papal inquisitor, sent to ferret out heresies in Tuscany. To this inquisitor it was reported that a Sienese notary, Ser Pietro by name, not only practised usury, but "stubbornly asserted that to lend money to people was not a sin, and that the brothers and religious who said otherwise *nesciunt quid loquantur:*" they do not know what they are talking about! † We thank Ser Pietro for

* "Il Constituto di Siena dell 'anno 1262." Dist. II, 151; with comment thereon by Sanesi, "Bull. Sen.," VI, p. 507.

† Ser Pietro lived during the first half of the fourteenth century. See Sanesi, "Bull. Sen.," VI, 497 *ff.*

sending us out of his tomb a breath of common sense on
a matter distastefully redolent of unctuous and insincere
professions.   At the same time we are pleased to gather
from the document that the bold heretic, being at the
time of the denunciation against him already dead, was
as safe as a grave could make him from the clutches of
the all-powerful tribunal.   Conceivably the Sienese
state, in view of its partial authorization of money-
lending, would have interfered to protect its subject
against the ecclesiastical police, but we can hardly
flatter ourselves that it would have prevailed in the
struggle.   At any rate, with or without the approval of
the church, the state remained true to its convictions
about the legitimacy of financial operations, and in the
year 1339 gave the final sanction to its views by authoriz-
ing every one to engage in money-lending who registered
in a special ledger, *nel libro detto usuraio di Biccherna*,
an act of entry equivalent to the purchase of a license.*

Returning once more to the fairs of Champagne, we
find, on looking into the procedure at these international
gatherings in connection with the sale and purchase of
goods, that drafts, letters of credit, and other similar
devices of a perfected capitalistic régime had only just
made a beginning, and that settlements were preferably
effected directly between traders and with actual coin.
Not until toward the year 1300 did the draft become a
universal instrument of business.   During the preceding
one hundred years experiments looking forward to its
perfection were frequent, and undoubtedly our Sienese
bankers, and even more certainly their Florentine rivals,
counted for something in giving this admirable device

* Muratori, XV. "Cronica Sanese."   Ad annum 1339.

for universalizing trade its final form.* Still, with
or without the draft, minted money, as the most convenient means of hoarding wealth, would be an important staple of commerce, and it is curious to see how
the Tuscans by their superior adaptability, as well as by
their superior cunning, drove a thriving business in this
article. The standard coin of the Champagne fair was
the *provisino*, a small silver penny (denarius or denier)
from the mint of the local magnate, the count of Champagne and Provins; 12 pennies made a shilling (solidus),
and 240 pennies constituted a pound or *libra*. The
Tuscans, and prominently among them alas! our
Sienese, learned that by coining a provisino of their own,
part silver and part copper, they could enter the Champagne market, capture from the unsuspecting traders
the native money with its greater intrinsic value, and by
sending it home for recoinage, clear a handsome profit.†
Undoubtedly one of the ambiguous features of the early
money traffic, and sure in the long run to be its own
undoing! Experience declares that the debasing of the
currency once begun knows no end, while the confusion
of prices caused by a fluctuating standard of value puts
an insufferable burden on commerce. Presently only
the cheaper or Tuscan kind of provisino held the market, with a still cheaper preparing to drive out the hybrid
rival. The king of France, not to be outdone, followed
the insidious example set by the Transalpine merchants,
and shamefully debased the standard royal coin, the
silver penny or denier from the mint of Tours. The
wily Italians had killed the goose that laid the golden

* Schaube, "Anfänge der Tratte." Zeitschrift für Handelsrecht, XLIII,
pp. 1–51.　　　　　† "Il Monti dei Paschi," Vol. I, p. 20 *ff*.

eggs! With no reliable standard in circulation the whole business world was subjected to great annoyance and loss. In this crisis an ingenious people stepped forward, a people whom Pope Boniface VIII. once declared to have been added by a special act of divine grace as a fifth element to a world effectively complete with four. In the year 1252 the Florentines* abandoned the silver basis, rendered unreliable by a flood of debased silver coins, and, first of mediæval nations, went over to the gold standard: they issued the gold florin, very carefully coined and almost 100 per cent. fine. Commerce welcomed the new standard as a godsend, and soon the florin had made its way into every market of the world. The establishment of an honest currency was an act of enlightened self-interest, designating more plainly than words the supreme seat of Tuscan intelligence. Most certainly we are justified in holding that the financial wisdom symbolized by the florin contributed in no small measure toward securing the ultimate primacy in Tuscany to the city of the Red Lily.†

If in sketching the activity of the Sienese in Champagne I have dwelt chiefly on its sordid and disorganized

---

* For description of the florin see Villani, "Croniche," Book VI, chap. 53. For its value (fine) as well as that of other current coins, see Schneider, "Die finanziellen Beziehungen der florentinischen Bankiers zur Kirche," p. 74.

† The stages of Florentine financial ascendency may be briefly given as follows: In the early Middle Age the silver penny was the standard coin, and of silver pennies there were many varieties (of Tours, of Pisa, of Siena, etc.). In 1234 the Florentines took the step of issuing a much more valuable coin, a silver *solidus* (1 solidus =12 pennies). The popularity of this coin induced them to adopt (1252) the still bolder measure of issuing a gold florin, which contained in small volume the value of 20 silver solidi and 240 silver pennies. See Davidsohn, "Geschichte von Florenz," II¹, pp. 213, 411.

phases, I would not convey the impression that this
French trade did not have a very romantic side. The
truth is that, if it had not touched the love of life and
challenged the spirit of adventure lurking in the human
breast, it would never have been followed with persistence. Prizes beckoned, supreme prizes as the world
counts, but they were to be had only at the risk of a
journey down a long lane of perils. The Sienese companies of the Salimbeni, the Tolomei, and the rest were
the thirteenth century prototypes of the gentlemen-
adventurers of Elizabeth's day; and the fairs of Champagne were the Gold Coasts and Golcondas which they
sought with high hearts and faces lifted to the dawn.
A distinguished scholar has drawn a vivacious picture
of the dangers besetting in those anarchic days the
journey across Apennines and Alps, which we children
of these piping times of peace can see only in the happy
light of a vacation outing.

"When all was ready and the rolls and bales were loaded on
the pack-asses, the company proceeded in long caravans and by
short stages across valleys and mountains over perilous paths and
ways, where from time to time thieves, and lords and castle-owners
worse than thieves, burst forth to steal, or to impose exactions;
and with one and the other it was necessary now to use the sword
and now to compound with dues and presents, as seemed best.
Then came the journey from fair to fair through distant and
often inhospitable countries, always in the midst of the greatest
risks and dangers. The dues, imposts, and exactions of every
sort to be paid on passing through villages and cities are not to be
enumerated. If the barons of France agreed to let the companies
of Italian merchants impoverish their subjects with commercial
bargains and even more with money-lending, it was certainly not
for nothing; for they did not fail to draw profit from the situation

in their turn.   The agents of the companies were obliged, in order to curry favor, to keep their purses open, since without a discreet liberality neither life nor substance was secure."*

What a tale of oppressions almost inconceivable to us of another and a milder period!   But the hard school of life had at least the advantage of developing suppleness and decision, and of giving the manhood of these trading adventurers something of the fine temper of steel.   Without this training, we may boldly assert, there could never have been an Italian Renaissance, which, with its arts and letters, is nothing but a later and a nobler phase of the same passion of adventure which drove the merchants to seek new opportunities across inhospitable lands and seas.

I have already spoken of the association of the Sienese merchant companies with the Roman curia in the capacity of collectors of papal taxes, and I have made it plain that this was one of the main sources of Sienese prosperity.   In fact, toward the middle of the thirteenth century a large percentage of the papal moneys flowed through Sienese hands.   In the narrow *via del rè* may still be found an interesting reminiscence of this early fiscal bond between Siena and the capital of Christendom.   On an ancient house front can be read an inscription informing the passer-by that Angelieri Solafica, *campsor Domini Papæ Gregorii IX*, built this residence A. D. 1234.†   This Angelieri, who is memorable as the grandfather of the famous poet, Cecco Angelieri, was in all probability one of the very Caorsini who bled England in the days of Henry III and excited

* Signor Menzozzi in "Il Monti dei Paschi," Vol. I, 54.
† For fac-simile of this inscription see "Il Monte dei Paschi," I, 14.

The Duomo Nuovo

the savage protest of Matthew Paris. But if Matthew
was displeased, Gregory declared himself well served,
as Angelieri's fine house sufficiently shows, and Gregory's successors continued for some time to employ the
Sienese companies in their affairs. But the honor was
invested with perils. For one thing, rival cities, like
Florence, never ceased playing upon the pope's suspicions, and, further, the complicated politics of Italy
required powers of quick resolution and deep deception
which the Sienese did not command. An inevitable
crisis resulted when, toward the middle of the thirteenth
century, the struggle which the papacy had long been
waging with the Empire came to a head. Obeying their
impetuous temper, the Sienese plunged headlong into this
conflict on the imperial or Ghibelline side. Cool-headed
Florence upheld the Guelph or papal cause with loud
deeds and still louder protestations. As a reward, more
and more of the Roman banking business was turned
toward the Arno city. Worse followed. In November,
1260,* on the heels of the great victory of Montaperti,
which for a brief moment delivered all Tuscany into the
hands of the Sienese and their Ghibelline allies, the pope
smote them with his interdict. Throughout the Middle
Age ambitious pontiffs used this weapon, and the even
sharper one of excommunication, most unscrupulously
for political ends. The confusion produced among the
Sienese merchants abroad by the papal enmity was
immense. Andrea Tolomei, writing from Troyes in
1262 to his associates, is full of lamentations on the

---

* Paoli, "Fiere di Sciampagna," p. 84. The interdict was not removed
till 1266. Consult with regard to the effects of the papal displeasure Davidsohn, "Geschichte von Florenz," II¹, p. 532.

subject; many debtors refuse to pay "per lo fato de lo schumunichamento," and the abbess of the Mount of Provins alleges as a further reason that "maiestro Mille"—apparently the papal nuncio—"forbade her to pay." In fact, the good Andrea is on the point of losing faith in human nature: "if the pope should dispatch the order that all the Sienese were to be seized in person and goods, as it is rumored he plans to do, I believe that his order would be obeyed, for there are many wicked people here, who take pleasure in robbing their neighbor; and they will rob him if they can, and urge the pope as a pretext."* Many of the banking companies, among them the very house of the Tolomei, which, according to the above letter, found itself in a painful situation, soon made peace with the papacy, privately, of course, and behind the back of the municipality. By and by, too, the interdict and its attending excommunications were withdrawn. Although it is true that the pope never ceased to employ certain of his Sienese servants, even while their city was under the ban, the fact remains that the Florentines, with their reputation of tried Guelph fidelity, steadily improved their hold on the papal finances at the expense of their neighbors.

Certainly the pope did not cease his relations with the greatest of all the Sienese merchant houses, the Buonsignori. The history of this house is a mirror of the commercial fortunes of Siena in the thirteenth century. Founded in the year 1209, it rose to be the foremost company of Europe under the name of the Magna Tavola. La grande table was a name to conjure with at the French fairs. As the century advanced the

* "Lettere Volgari," pp. 45–47.

society established agents in all parts of the world, engaging in banking on a scale which suggests a great international credit institution of our own days. In the year 1289, on the occasion of a reorganization, its capital amounted to the sum, huge for those days, of 35,000 gold florins, while among its clients we find popes, emperors, kings, barons, merchants, and cities.* It weathered many storms, which broke over it in the form of royal confiscations and papal anathemas, until in 1298, when seemingly at its zenith, it was overtaken by disaster. There was a panic, accompanied by a run of the depositors, and the proud institution went to the wall —an accident, the patriotic historian Tommasi † would have us believe, due to a quarrel among the partners and the envy of rivals, but if an accident, it was ominously coincident with the decline of Sienese and the rise of Florentine banking prestige.

We have seen that the Sienese merchant companies were financial institutions doing business in exchange and loans. But they also dealt, though in a subsidiary way, in general merchandise. That valuable literary jetsam, the Lettere Volgari already referred to, reveals that the companies sold wax, pepper, and spices at the French fairs, and carried back Flemish cloth to Siena. Many articles besides,‡ such as shoes, stockings, belts, ploughs, cuirasses and helmets, found their way to the markets of the town, showing clearly a certain backwardness in its industrial development. Truth to tell, Siena was not and never became a great manufacturing

* "Il Monte dei Paschi," I, p. 41.
† "Dell' Historie di Siena," Lib. VII, p. 141.
‡ Zdekauer, "La Vita Privata nel Dugento," p. 46.

centre. But this much the thirteenth century with its
world-wide stimulation of urban life accomplished: it
brought the desire for industrial activity and organization and with it that characteristic institution of the
Middle Age, the guild. Naturally the merchants,
whose rise preceded the coming of industries to Siena,
led the way in the formation of a general society planned
to protect their common interests. We hear of a Sienese
merchant guild as early as the year 1192. But the
crafts were not slow to follow suit, and presently the
masons, carpenters, inn-keepers, barbers, butchers,
millers, and the other classes of workmen and artisans
were organized as *arti*, with the usual apparatus of
constitution, officers, regulations, prohibitions, and
fines.* Under these conditions the general social and
economic aspect of Sienese life was much like that of
any other mediæval town.

While the presence in Siena of merchant and craft
guilds implies life and organized power, it does not
prove the existence of great industrial establishments.
The manufacture which in those days was the greatest
source of prosperity in Europe was woolen cloth. It
conferred the same sort of preëminence as coal and iron
give to-day. Cloth created the wealth of Flanders; her
flocks of sheep were the riches of England; Florence,
just girding her loins for her victorious race, owed her
material greatness to the excellence of her cloth. The
Sienese, too, made an effort to acclimate the cloth industry, but their wool guild never really throve because

---

* "Il Monte dei Paschi," Vol. I, 15, *note*. Very likely such characteristic
expressions of the mediæval spirit of association as the guilds go far back
of the twelfth century; no Sienese document, however, recording the fact,
has come down to us.

of the great number of adverse conditions with which it
had to battle. For one thing, the wool crop of the out-
lying district was never large or of high grade, and most
important, in fact decisive, was the grievous dearth of
water. Never have men since cities have a history
struggled so hard against a decree of nature, or so persistently hoped against hope, pinning their faith in the
last resort to a miracle. With admirable patience the
burghers brought water from afar by means of cunning,
subterranean conduits which still exist, arousing the
admiration of modern engineers.* Nevertheless the
supply obtained was insufficient. When that picturesque upland region, where Siena has her seat, failed to
reveal, even to close scrutiny, any further spring capable
of being tapped for city uses, the townsmen encouraged
one another to believe in a hidden river underneath their
feet. They even knew its name, the Diana; borings
were invited at public expense, and sensitive ears in the
still hours of the night plainly heard the rush of its
waters. Readers of the Divine Poet have laughed
merrily over his contemptuous fling at the *gente vana*
who hugged such illusions to their breast,† but for the
lover of this people the curious aberration has the deep
pathos inseparable from the spectacle of hopes heroically pursued in the face of the unchangeable decrees of
nature.

No, the *arte della lana*, though it took root, never
acquired commanding proportions; in fact, the industrial guilds, taken as a whole, did not prosper compared
with neighboring Florence. Doubtless the absence of

* On the water supply see the meritorious work by F. Bargagli-Petrucci,
"Le Fonti di Siena."   † Dante, "Purgatorio," XIII, 153.

water, and the relative poverty of the neighborhood in such raw products of industry as wool, copper, and iron, are a sufficient explanation of the situation, but the mistaken zeal of the municipality and the rigorous statutes of the guilds themselves count for something in the result. Among many excellent regulations which concerned themselves with obtaining for the consumer a full measure and an honest product, were to be found others which, by paralyzing the free activities of the workers, must have caused grave harm. Thus the statutes of the wool guild required * that only one piece of cloth be woven at a time, that it be neither longer nor shorter than a certain standard, and that only native wool be put on the looms; and all guilds alike pursued a selfishly exclusive policy, imposing a heavy tax on all candidates for admission, and positively forbidding the exercise of their respective occupations to all but guild members in good standing. Add minute regulations regarding the hours and quantity of labor and the observation of so many church festivals that about one hundred and thirty days of the calendar year were devoted to an enforced rest,† and we get some idea of the mischievousness of that spirit of over-regulation which characterized both the guilds and the government. However, we can hardly pretend that Siena

* "Statuti Senesi," II, p. XXI. Banchi, the editor, writes indeed of the wool guild of the Radicondoli, but what he says holds of the wool guild of Siena as well, as may be seen by consulting the "Statuto dell' arte della Lana" in Vol. I of the same publication.

† "Statuti Senesi," I, p. 311, gives the list: "queste sono le feste che pare al Comune dell' Arte de la Lana che sieno da guardare," seventy-eight in all, which, with fifty-two Sundays, brings the total to one hundred and thirty. It is, however, not likely that the suspension of work on all these feast-days was complete.

suffered more in this respect than her neighbors, for the guild system was universal and the petty and chaotic economic views, upon which it rested, enjoyed a general currency in the Middle Age.

The final and conclusive proof of the industrial weakness of Siena is furnished by the fact that the craft guilds never played a political *rôle* of any importance. The city became in due time a democracy, much more of a democracy, indeed, than Florence, where the *arti* simply and without ceremony took possession of the government and admitted to citizenship only through the door of their organizations. In Siena the guilds were not strong enough to seize the power, and when popular rule came, the political franchise was distributed without any regard to the guild connection. The closer we examine the situation the more firmly we become convinced that the only really powerful guild was that of the merchants, and the only occupation, largely remunerative, that of trade. The merchants, therefore, not only had a political *rôle* assured to them,* but they alone, through their companies, were responsible for lifting Siena above the plane of a provincial market, and for bringing her into contact with the general political and economic forces of Italy. For this reason I return once more to her commercial fortunes. Here is the root of her vitality, and here, too, the key to the most stirring phase of her political destiny.

What I have said of the unenlightened views which were entertained in the Middle Age with regard to industry, and which, while turning every occupation into

* The political power exercised by the merchants will be treated in chapter VII.

a monopoly, almost buried it under a mountain of
regulations, should prepare our minds for a wealth of
unfavorable conditions weighing also upon commerce.
Many of these had their origin in the undeveloped state
of society and in the relative infrequency of intercourse
even among neighbors. The crusades, we are aware,
greatly stirred and accelerated the sluggish stream of
mediæval trade, but, even after the crusades, a Tuscan
town, steeped in the current feudal concepts, long continued to see in a neighbor merely an enemy, to be put
down if possible, in any case to be hated while breath
came and went. The foreign trader who entered the
gates of Siena was watched with suspicion, and, in accordance with the prevailing legal theory, was looked
upon as gathered into a single personality with the city
of his origin. He was a Florentine or Pisan as the case
might be, with the rights of a Florentine or Pisan, which
in the rude, formative days would mean none at all.
Only treaties, for which the time ripened but slowly,
could give him a standing in the eyes of the Sienese law.
In case, therefore, a visiting trader delayed payment of a
debt, or defaulted, the courts gave the native creditor
the right to indemnify himself by the seizure of the goods
of any of the debtor's fellow citizens who happened to
be at hand. In the view of the rhadamanthine judge,
the individual merchant's fault implicated the whole
foreign society to which the individual belonged.
This barbarous practice with regard to international
trade was known as the system of *rappresaglie* or
reprisals. The havoc which it wrought may be left to
the imagination. No sooner did the courts render a
verdict than all the countrymen of the defaulting

merchant, taking what they could gather in their arms, fled precipitately, leaving the bulk of their goods as loot in the hands of the creditor. The rival city, insulted in the person of its routed merchants, hardly awaited their return before it visited a similar fate on the traders of the offending party. Here was commercial war, which might at any moment be transferred to the grim decision of the field. Men would have to see the patent folly of such action and learn to look upon one another with more fraternal eyes before their intercourse could be put upon a higher plane. From the beginning of the thirteenth century—doubtless a timid commencement was made before that time—the documents permit us to see how the Tuscan cities strove to replace the institution of reprisals, worthy of Mohawks and Hurons, with commercial treaties, planned to eliminate violence and to give international trade that security without which it could not live. During the century lying between 1200 and 1300 tentative agreements gradually crystallized into durable instruments of peace.* The judicial action with regard to a debtor was limited to the guilty person, and one man's fault or misfortune did not apply the shears to every thread which trade and civilization had spun between two communes. Treaties in the place of violence and rude self-help—such is the road that has been travelled by men in Italy and throughout the world in order to secure the fruits of civilization. The

* See on reprisals Del Vecchio and Casanova, "Le Rappresaglie nei Comuni medioevali"; also Arias, "I Trattati Commerciali della Republica Fiorentina." Parte seconda takes up the *rappresaglie* and their gradual amelioration. See especially "Documenti," p. 371 *ff*. As early as 1213 a Bolognese document puts forth the principle *a cui dato, a colui richiesto*, which principle, the result probably of the revival of Roman law, gradually crept into all trade agreements.

effect of treaty arrangements among the Tuscan communes was to replace cruelty, injustice, and brute force
with a peaceful procedure advantageous and honorable
for everybody concerned. Not that trade in Tuscany
became entirely free and unrestricted, since for financial
reasons, if there had been no others, the cities were
obliged to levy customs duties at the gates; but if trade
did not become free as the air, it liberated itself from
the most barbarous disabilities and became as secure as
cities in a divided nation without a central head could
make it. Thus commerce will be seen to have been a
potent agent of civilization; but as civilization means
peace, and as peace stimulates the exchange of goods,
trade steadily produced more trade until commercial
considerations became the leading preoccupation of
Siena and all her Italian sisters.

From what we have seen of the association of Siena,
with the papacy on the one hand, and with the fairs of
Champagne on the other, we are prepared to assert
that the all-important highway which Sienese trade
would struggle to keep open and make sure was the road
from Rome over Siena into France. That was the
famous *via francigena* or *via francesa*. On the north-
bound journey from Siena it debouched from the Elsa
into the Arno valley not far beyond Poggibonsi, and on the
southbound journey the last town in Sienese territory
which it touched was San Quirico, flanked on right and
left by the far-seen hill-towns of Montalcino and Montepulciano. We have learned in an earlier chapter how
a natural patriotism impelled the young republic to
possess itself of its county or contado, though it had to
ride roughshod over a thousand difficulties; we may

now learn how that patriotism was steadily blown upon by the merchant class, whose self-interest was completely identical with the political passions of the multitude. But to hold the via francesa, or rather that small part of it which passed through strictly Sienese territory was not easy, for the Florentines claimed Poggibonsi and guarded it as the apple of their eye, while in the region of San Quirico, Siena met the combined opposition of the city of Orvieto, of the great feudal clan of the Aldobrandeschi, and of course, of Florence, only too ready to support her rival's enemies any and everywhere. In consequence, we may note that if we have seen trade grow more humane by reason of the gradual abandonment of reprisals, the political relations between Florence and Siena did not therefore in the least improve, because with the quantitative growth of trade the points of friction between the two towns became more numerous. It is a melancholy fact that trade, which I have just celebrated, and with undoubted justice, as the mother of civilization, is at the same time the most fruitful source, known to history, of envy, war, and every form of mischief. Florence and Siena were impelled by reasons of trade, each to bring the other under its law, and as Florence was the stronger and more aggressive power, she was sure to carry the conflict straight to the via francesa, because only in this way could she attend effectively to the clipping of her neighbor's wings.

It is therefore clear that, to follow the directions of Sienese trade under the natural law of expansion, is to touch the regions where the commune encountered the greatest resistance and engaged in its most critical battles. The via francesa, effecting an approach to the markets north and south of Siena, was all-important, but this one avenue was not likely to exhaust the desire of ambitious merchants. Having crossed the Alps and acquired a world-wide outlook in England and the Champagne, they would not fail to be impressed with the importance of the sea as a universal highway. The whole history of Florence, whose merchants were possessed of a conspicuous intelligence, is a struggle to get to the Mediterranean, and Siena, although the approach was difficult, was moved by the same desire. Westward across scarped hills, following the general direction of the unnavigable Ombrone, lay the town of Grosseto, before which coiled, like some vast, torpid monster of the sea, the sullen and fever-ridden swamps of the Maremma. On the sea-edge of this deadly bog hung a few fever-wasted settlements, such as Orbetello, Port' Ecole, and Talamone, and one or the other of these, preferably Talamone, it was the patriotic dream of the Sienese to turn into a seaport, thus opening an unimpeded communication with the outer world. The plan involved as a preliminary step the seizure of Grosseto.

The story of that acquisition is a typical chapter in the expansion of the town which boasted the favor of the Virgin. Grosseto was a dependency of the feudal house, so often referred to, the Aldobrandeschi; in measure as its fortunes waxed, chiefly by reason of the salt stores of the neighborhood, it aspired to emulate the consular movement common to all Italy and win political independence from its feudal lords. Siena, therefore, on casting a covetous eye in that direction, would have to deal with both the Aldobrandeschi and the growing commune, impertinently looking forward to a career of sovereignty. With the patience of a beast of the thicket the city, whose emblem was the wolf, lay in wait for its prey. By various means the Aldobrandeschi were eliminated from the situation; at the same time, through apparently harmless commercial treaties,* Grosseto was gradually drawn into the Sienese orbit; and, finally, in the ripeness of time, the grim wolf leaped upon its victim. The capture occurred in the year 1224, and is inscribed in red letters in the calendar of the republic.†

Thus, gradually, was Grosseto won, but like Montalcino, Montepulciano, and the other places of the contado, which had to bend the neck to receive the Sienese yoke, it proved a restive captive. The annals of the next one hundred years are full of revolts and attempted

* The first treaty is of the year 1151. See Repetti, "Dizionario Geografico," under Grosseto.

† A patriotic son has left an engaging description of the triumphant expedition of his fellow-citizens against Grosseto:

"No one ever saw a more beautiful army. The shields, the cuirasses, and the tents lent a lustre to all the country round about so that it seemed another paradise. Arrived near the walls of the hostile city the potestà, full of anxiety for the safety of his people, ordered fortifications to be built; before they were ready an accidental skirmish took place. Unable to recall his men, and seeing them assaulted by the defenders from the walls with an incessant shower of arrows, stones, beams, and every kind of weapon, he put himself spiritedly at their head and fought with death-defying courage for the honor of his city. In such manner, with the aid of God, he won a wonderful victory, entering the city with his host and carrying away captive all the men whom he found, to the eternal glory of Siena and to the increase of her strength and power, which henceforth extended as far as the sea." And another chronicler adds: "Grosseto was stormed on the day of Saint Mary of September (the eighth). And the host which went there numbered 3,100 men between foot and horse. And on their return, for joy of the victory gained, there was a great festival with a bonfire, and all the shops around the Campo were shut up." Banchi, "Il Memoriale delle offese fatte," etc. "Arch. Stor. It.," Serie terza, XXII, pp. 226–27.

revolts, but regardless of cost and effort Siena held fast
to her prize in the conviction that Grosseto was a necessary stage in the march to the Mediterranean, which
spread its blue waters not six miles distant from the
walls of the recalcitrant little town.   However, Grosseto, though it dominated a part of the Tuscan littoral,
was not itself a port.   Hence the seaward ambition of
Siena found its natural culmination in the acquisition,
in the year 1303, of the small haven of Talamone, also
originally a possession of the great Maremma counts.
From the Aldobrandeschi it had passed into the hands
of the abbot of San Salvatore of Monte Amiata, and
from him, a man of peace, often in need of ready money,
the prudent republic obtained its cession for a round
sum.   The purchase was much remarked in the Italian
world and aroused the ever ready envy of Florence.
The greatest of all Florentines, however, took a purely
ironical view of the incident.   In a biting passage *
Dante treats the idea of Siena becoming vicariously,
through Talamone, a seaport, as on a level with that
other fancy of the light-headed, self-deluded subjects of
the Virgin, touching the hidden river, called Diana.
Time, the incorruptible judge of our dreams as well as
of our deeds, has confirmed the correctness of the poet's
view.   Talamone, sand-choked and fever-ridden, came
to nothing, and Grosseto itself accordingly lost something of its early hopeful look of being a great bargain;
but as long as the Sienese entertained the ambition of
becoming an Italian power and transcending the obsta-
cles of nature, they naturally linked Grosseto and Talamone in a common prayer.

*"Purgatorio," XIII, 152.

Interior view of the Cathedral

Such is the material story of the doughty burghers
who made mediæval Siena—a story revealing at every
stage the exercise of moral qualities which in their sum
compose the picture of an impressive manhood.   Our
backward view of the prolonged struggle of the citizens
closes on the sad reflection that all their efforts did not
suffice to produce the hoped-for result of commercial and
political greatness.   For a moment in the thirteenth
century, from the heights of Montaperti, Siena had a
glimpse of the Promised Land, but the vision faded away
and the town was thrust back behind provincial bars.
Durable victories are not won upon the battlefield.
The gifts of the Sienese of one kind and another, especially their artistic gifts, were as great as could be found
anywhere in Tuscany; their failure, if we weigh the
facts judicially, was due to shortcomings neither of
mind nor heart, but must be laid, primarily at least, to
the door of certain physical conditions, such as the town's
situation high among the hills, the dearth of water, the
difficult communications, and the poverty of the neighborhood in such articles as might serve as the basis of
a great industry.   Without native manufactures with
which to trade on the world's markets, Sienese commerce, though it began so promisingly, was doomed to
failure in the long run.   On the other hand, none of the
drawbacks of Siena obtained in the rich and noble Arno
valley, from the heart of which the towers of Florence
rose.   Therefore a sketch of the struggle and failure of
Siena in the field of production and exchange becomes
an involuntary apostrophe to the greatness of the city
of the Lily.   Invisible hands point to her as the predes-
tined economic capital of Tuscany.   How with un-

wavering persistence and with steady flame of passion she used her natural and economic advantages to cap them with a political triumph, it shall be the object of a later chapter to make clear.

CHAPTER V

THE LAWS AND INSTITUTIONS

IN speaking, in a previous chapter, of the rise of the commune, I tried to bring out the fact that many generations before it arrived at its splendid young manhood in the age of the consuls, it had been engaged in silent, groping, and uncertain development among the older and overshadowing feudal institutions. Then when it rose into view sufficiently to permit a closer examination, we noticed that it had indeed an apparent democratic basis, in so far as it rested upon the meeting of the townsmen in the public square, the so-called *parlamentum*, but at the same time we became assured that the practical political power was in the hands of a body of consuls, appointed from a small group of noble families. I now purpose to examine more at leisure what the consular government was and what it became. We are agreed that the consular era marked the happy revival of self-government in the midst of feudal brutality, but we should not fail to see that all the details of self-government, such as a suitable executive, a legislative assembly in touch with the people, and an effective administrative service, remained to be worked out with infinite trouble amidst the usual perils of revolutionary explosions. As we take up the story of laborious internal organization, let us remember that such work furnishes a conspicuous test of the character and temper of a people.

Throughout the twelfth century the work went bravely on, a movement out of chaos and darkness into cosmos and light. In order to measure its full significance we must start with a clear perception of the loose and accidental character of the earliest institutions of the commune. To illustrate what I have in mind by means of the consuls, I note again that we hear of consuls of Siena for the first time in the year 1125, though it is very likely that they were in existence before that date. Now the consuls of the early twelfth century were not a settled magistracy, the forms of which were precisely defined by a series of statutes, but, in accordance with the haphazard character of the first measures of the young commune, they bore rather the aspect of a temporary committee, appointed to perform a particular public service. Such occasional committees discharged every variety of public business in the early days, and were called, in Sienese usage, *balìe*. When the particular affair for which a *balìa* was appointed, had been attended to, the balìa was again dismissed. But much business, as soon as men give themselves a government, being constant or at least recurrent, the balìa tended to establish itself, that is, the temporary committee showed an inclination to be converted into a permanent magistracy. This movement was hardly well under way when the advantage appeared of defining as precisely as possible the functions of the new officials in a document which might serve as a guide to their conduct, and upon which they might be required to take the oath of office. This document received the name of *breve*.

Such is the genesis of the consulship: originally only a temporary committee or balìa, it developed a breve, which grew, by additions, into a formal body of statutes regulating the city executive. And on this order was the genesis of every other communal institution. Of course the new commonwealth required a department of justice to further peace and order among the citizens. The earliest town courts were tentative creations, that is, balìe. Hence they were dissolved and again established until, under the pressure of social necessity, they became fixed and permanent. At the same time, beginning with a few regulations laid down in a breve, they gradually came to rest upon an elaborate corpus of statutes and enactments. Administrative committees, appointed to look after the revenues, the walls, the fountains, and other public services, were not lacking from very early times, and though clothed at first, like the consuls and the courts, with a provisional character, they would tend, like them, to become permanent magistracies, carefully regulated by means of brevi.

Presently among so many and diverse beginnings the need made itself felt of adjustment and unification. There were now many offices of more or less accidental origin, and each office had in its breve an effective constitution, but there was no general constitution of the commune. By throwing the brevi together and carrying through a dovetailing of their articles and powers that desideratum could be attained without great effort. It is by such contributions from many streams that Siena acquired a constitution, a composite instrument of which we hear for the first time in the year 1179.*

* Zdekauer, "Il Constituto . . . dell' anno 1262," Introduction, p. XIV.

Doubtless it is older than that, just as it is highly probable that there were consuls before 1125. The date of
the constitution is of little importance compared with the
understanding of the process by which it came to be.
Just as the stable magistracy developed by logical stages
from the ephemeral balìa, so the constitution has its
roots in the several brevi defining the various offices.

The fashioning of a written constitution marks the
passage from political unconsciousness to consciousness,
from unsettled youth to disciplined manhood. What
the constitution of Siena was, and, more particularly,
what the institutions were with which it adorned the
state, we shall examine presently at the hand of the
remarkable copy of the year 1262, which is preserved in
the Sienese archive and has been edited in exemplary
fashion by Professor Zdekauer.* However, before I
take it up, I wish to examine the local class and party
struggle, without which we can not possibly put ourselves in touch with the true spirit of Sienese public
life nor catch the individual profile of each municipal
office.

(A) THE SOCIAL MOVEMENT

With the birth of the commune the theoretical sovereignty of the Italian cities is, by most writers, declared
to have been transferred to the people assembled in
public meeting, that is, to the institution called parla-

---

* "Il Constituto del Comune di Siena dell' anno 1262." This work is an
inexhaustible storehouse of fact, bearing upon every phase of thirteenth-cent-
ury life. Two broad avenues of approach to it have been driven by the
editor in two studies, the first offered as an Introduction to the Constitution,
the second, a published lecture to be found among the "Conferenze" issued
by the Commissione Senese di Storia Patria for 1897. The present chapter
is greatly indebted to these lucid studies.

mentum. Without quarreling with the theory we may rest assured that the practical authority, in Siena at least, rested elsewhere. The people, assembled in the square before the cathedral at the bidding of the magistrates, participated in a general way in politics by having treaties communicated to them and by receiving the submissions of conquered noblemen, but they did not govern. That privilege was exercised exclusively by a small circle of ancient and well-to-do families, from among whom the consuls were regularly elected. The consular régime was therefore essentially an oligarchy. Such a system was possible because the upper class had mainly created and defended the commune, and because, possessed of wealth, vigor, and superior intelligence, it found no difficulty in dominating the noisy and disorganized parliament. The consuls presently surrounded themselves with a council, called the Council of the Bell, which, being of more practicable size than the parliament, handled the business of the city with dispatch and made the general assembly of the citizens more superfluous than ever. Naturally the Council of the Bell marched under the same aristocratic banner as the consuls. The rule of the people would be carried from theory into the realm of reality only when the masses had acquired sufficient economic independence and political ambition to organize as a popular party for the express purpose of capturing the offices. I pointed out in another place * that in the year 1212 there was, according to the chronicler, "great enmity between people and nobles," an unmistakable revolutionary disturbance; in the next year (1213) we have our first refer-

* Chapter II, p. 70.

ence to the existence of a popular party, a *societas populi senensis.** This body was probably the common army of Siena organized for political purposes. In this connection it is important to recollect that, all through the twelfth century, the army, composed of the whole citizen body, was in existence, that it was mobilized for a particular end, usually the overthrow of a neighboring castle, and that, the campaign over, it was again dissolved. While the upper class constituted the knights or *milites*, who rode on horseback, the citizen mass made up the *pedites* or foot-soldiers. Together they marched out of the gates when the war banner was unfurled, but just as the milites in that display outshone the pedites, so they towered above their humble neighbors in political influence. Nevertheless, though docile at first, the people would soon feel the power which was theirs by reason of their numbers, and would strive to turn it to advantage. Slowly the common longing of dumb thousands would create a leader, and from his efforts would result an organization, which we may designate as the political counterpart of the ancient military union of the people.

By some such process the societas populi senensis of 1213 must have come into being, but since, in the absence of documents, we are not justified in pressing the matter of origin, let us content ourselves in fixing the significance of the accomplished fact. Undeniably the phenomenon means that by the beginning of the thirteenth century the masses had reached a conscious political purpose and had organized into a party aiming at control. Therefore a struggle followed, a struggle

* Zdekauer, "Il Constituto," etc. Introduction, p. XLIII.

between the new elements calling themselves the people (*il popolo*) and the upper class in possession, referred to variously as *magnati, grandi*, and *cives majores*. My task is to show how, moving onward inch by inch under an irresistible momentum, the people gradually displaced the oligarchs from every post of influence, until at last, by a general decree, characteristic of a resentful and exultant victory, they excluded the former rulers from all participation in public life.

In the conflict between oligarchs and masses, thus inaugurated with the thirteenth century, the replacement of the consuls as chief executive by the potestà is of little consequence. It is prudent to dispose of this incident before plunging deeper into the social struggle. In the year 1199, for the usual multiple executive was substituted a single man, plainly a step in the direction of greater concentration of power. For some years after 1199 there was an uncertain practice in Siena with regard to the chief executive, until, beginning with the year 1211, we have regularly the *potestas foretaneus*, the foreign potestà, installed for one year. The men of the Council who called him belonged to or sympathized with the dominant caste; they gravitated naturally toward a person of their own social level, preferably from Bologna, Modena, or some other town as far removed as possible from the interests and passions of Siena; and, after he came, they constituted themselves his advisers, or rather, from more than one point of view, his lords and keepers. His entrance upon the scene marked no immediate displacement of political power, although it is clear that the crowding of the local nobles out of the highest dignity in the town must have made room for a freer unfolding of popular energy. The fact that our earliest evidence of political unrest among the people belongs to the period just subsequent to the coming of the potestà may be taken as a sign that the monopoly of the oligarchs was looked upon as weakened.

For several decades after our first proof of the existence of a popular party we lose sight of it again. Very likely it did not succeed immediately in making itself felt in the public life of the town. It had powerful opponents; it lacked experience; and it had still to perfect its organization. If practical advantages were to be obtained this last point was particularly important, and, as a matter of fact, it received unremitting attention until, toward the middle of the thirteenth century, the organizing work was crowned by the people giving themselves a single head under the title of captain.* As with the captain of the people was associated a council of the people, it became plain that the societas populi senensis was shaping its institutions according to the model furnished by the commune with its potestà and Council of the Bell. However, even before the society reached its final and effective form, it won an immensely significant victory, for in the year 1240 the potestà, though retained as a sort of honorary sovereign with important representative functions, was deprived of the political direction of the city; this responsibility was put into the hands of twenty-four citizens (*I Ventiquattro*), and, what is particularly worthy of remark, one-half of the Twenty-four were required to

* We get our first news of a captain of the people in 1253. Muratori, XV, "Cronica Sanese," ad annum.

General view of the Cathedral

be of the party of the people.* The revolution of the
year 1240, therefore, established a political partnership
between nobility and commoners. Indications are not
wanting which point to the conclusion that the con-
servatives in power did not yield gracefully to the new
order of things, and that it required long and loud
clamor at the gates before the people's party was admitted into the citadel. But, the first success won, that
party proceeded with the remorseless tenacity which
has always characterized a pushing democracy, to follow up its initial victory. Wedging its way into one
communal dignity after another, it had by the year 1262
succeeded in carrying a measure to the effect that one-
half of the holders of all offices must be *popolani*.†
When we observe by a perusal of the great constitution
of this same year that the captain of the people, symbol
and gauge of popular influence, ranked with the potestà
as a political factor, remaining inferior to him only in the
subtle matter of prestige, we can form some idea of the
extent of the popular triumph. The people had built
up a party of commoners to effect the capture of the commune, and, after a struggle of half a century, the movement had advanced so far that the ruling class had been
everywhere obliged to let the upstart representatives
of the people make themselves comfortable at its side.

The rule of the Twenty-four, representing a compromise between the nobility and the people, lasted for a
period of just thirty years, from 1240 to 1270. This
period is not only coincident with what is perhaps the

---

* Salvemini ("Archivio Stor. It.," Serie V, Vol. XXI, 571 *ff.*) defends an
interesting, but not conclusive, proposition to the effect that the Twenty-four
were wholly of the party of the people.

† "Il Constituto," etc., I, 518.

climax of the whole Italian Middle Age, but it also conducted Siena to the summit of her political destiny,
disclosing to her for a moment an outlook as wide and
intoxicating as was ever scanned by Venice or Florence.
The life of the Twenty-four covers the last act in the
tragedy of the Hohenstaufen. By taking the Ghibelline
side with conviction and enthusiasm, the Twenty-four
shared the victories won by Frederick II and his descendants, Manfred and Conradin, and inevitably,
when fate finally declared against the imperial champions, went down with them in a common defeat. The
fact that the Twenty-four, who mark a temporary union
of oligarchs and commoners, followed this policy, proves
that the unanimous sentiment of the citizens supported
the Ghibelline cause. This momentary domestic harmony makes the rule of this particular government one
of the happy incidents of Sienese history, and accounts
in part for the great victory won at Montaperti (1260)
against Florence and the Guelphs. For a tremulous
moment after her sweeping triumph Siena held Tuscany
in her hand. If, as sages and poets have told us, it
behooves men to fill the cup of life to the brim and empty
it to the lees, the fever and triumph, associated with
Frederick and Manfred and Montaperti, were worth
while even at the price of the awful fall which followed.
Disaster, after several vain threats, closed definitely
about the city, when the boy Conradin, last of his line,
was defeated in the year 1268, and on the great market-
place of Naples, in the sight of the court of the French
usurper and the massed multitude of commoners, had
his head severed from his body by the executioner's axe.
From that moment the Ghibelline doom was sealed and

Siena's brief dream of empire vanished in air. The Twenty-four, sponsors of a Ghibelline policy, did not quail before the storm which now broke over them. They met the Guelph onslaught at Colle (1269), where the sentence of Montaperti was reversed. Siena had to become Guelph or be obliterated. The first step in the city's recantation was the snuffing out of the Twenty-four.

To Manfred and Montaperti, as well as to Colle and the Guelph triumph, I shall return in the next chapter. I have introduced them here to explain the greatness and fall of the Twenty-four and to render intelligible the inner changes that signalized the passage of Siena from the Ghibelline to the Guelph side. This was a gradual process, much delayed by plots and disturbances, until the trading elements of Siena made up their mind firmly that there was no salvation for the material interests outside the alliance with the victorious church. Then the merchants resolutely took control. In carrying through their Guelph programme they discovered no need for greatly altering the institutions; their principal measure was to give the political direction into the hands of a group of partisans, business men and Guelphs. The number of members constituting this committee fluctuated for a time—we hear on one occasion of Thirty-six, on another of Fifteen—until it was finally fixed at Nine. The new governing committee— *Li Signori Nove Governatori e Difenditori del Comune e del Popolo di Siena*—exercised much the same sort of power as the defunct Twenty-four, and, becoming a fixture in the year 1292, ruled the city for more than sixty years.

The Nine sound a perfectly definite note in the history

of Siena. They mark the adoption by the city of a
Guelph foreign policy, in sober recognition of the fact
that henceforth there was security only in the camp of
the church. But that is not all: they signify also the
final stage in the conquest of the commune by the
people. During the recent passionate struggle the nobility and commoners had been united by a general
Ghibelline sentiment. The domestic harmony was
consecrated by the Twenty-four, made up in equal proportion of representatives of the two groups. But class
rivalry continued under the surface, and the catastrophe
of Conradin had no sooner drawn the ground from
under the Twenty-four than the local disturbances
flared up more intolerably than ever. Thereupon the
merchants, resolved on peace at all costs, seized the
power, their victory finally crystallizing in the government of the Nine. As the merchants represented the
old societas populi senensis, not content with declaring
prudently for the church, they now resolved to crown the
ambition of their party and complete the capture of the
commune. Accordingly they declared the nobility
ineligible to office, reserving all positions of influence to
themselves. It was a violent measure, which, though of
doubtful wisdom, was yet not without a grim sort of
political logic. Since the beginning of the thirteenth
century the people had demanded participation in the
government only to be thwarted at every point by the
selfish oligarchs. None the less by the middle of the
century they had made important progress, and, under
the Twenty-four, weighed as much in the scales as the
old rulers. But as commerce and industry were giving
an increasing significance to the productive workers with

each new year, it was likely that they would demand increasing recognition, nay, press their claims to the point of an absolute triumph. This uncompromising policy the merchants carried through, thus coupling with the Guelph alliance in the foreign field a local democratic victory.*

It was in the year 1277 that Siena adopted the measure which turned the tables upon the nobility. On the 28th of May a motion was passed in the General Council to the effect that the *grandi* should be henceforth and forever excluded from the supreme magistracy of the republic.† Agreed that the measure was intelligible enough in view of the passions developed by the long domestic struggle, it was none the less in the highest degree regrettable by reason of its breeding in the nobility a justifiable and rancorous aversion against the democratic régime. The magnates of Siena were indeed a difficult urban element, but they were not entirely feudal, for they had gone into trade, and the great commercial companies, named for such families as the Salimbeni, the Tolomei, the Malavolti, and the Piccolomini, were one of the main sources of the city's

* Lack of space makes it necessary to treat the struggle which preceded the overthrow of the magnates in the above summary fashion. I must, however, not fail to observe that the victory of the popolo was much helped in Siena as elsewhere by the division of the nobility into the two groups of Guelphs and Ghibellines. As early as 1262 the Guelph nobles, though a minority, engaged in street riots, which ended in the first great exodus from the city. The exodus was a common weapon of party warfare.. On the Guelph-Ghibelline conflict of 1262 see Muratori, "Cronica Sanese," XV, 33, and Davidsohn's comment, "Geschichte von Florenz," II¹, p. 538. The incident serves admirably to explain the various reasons why the nobility could not be trusted with the government of a democratic community.

† Archivio di Stato. "Consiglio Generale della Campana." Deliberazoni ad annum.

prosperity. It is perhaps an erroneous opinion that, by the adoption of a more generous policy, this class would, in the course of time, have been fused with the people into a truly democratic society; it admits of no dispute that the policy of exclusion was the worst that could possibly have been adopted, since by feeding the audacious self-will of the nobles with a genuine grievance, it created a condition of latent revolt and threw Siena upon an interminable sick-bed.

(B)   THE INSTITUTIONS

I have already said that the victory of the people, won toward the end of the thirteenth century, did not greatly alter the city's institutions. Originally the offices had been filled by the nobles; then they were shared between nobles and people; and, after the exclusion act of 1277, they were appropriated, if not by the people, at least by the upper stratum of the people, the trading bourgeoisie. But, whoever possessed the offices, their form remained essentially unchanged. The fact was that the institutions of Siena were to all intents complete before the people carried their victory to its uncompromising conclusion. Exactly what these institutions were is disclosed by the Sienese constitution, the genesis of which I have attempted to explain. With the copy of the year 1262, the earliest version preserved by the chances of time, before us, we are enabled to reconstruct the whole machinery of Sienese public life. Eschewing so ambitious a project, I shall content myself with isolating for observation and remark some of the more important features of the local political system.

As already stated, some students hold the view that
no sooner did the young republic of Siena usurp the
functions of government than the theoretical sovereignty
passed from the empire and emperor to the body of
citizens assembled in parlamentum. The parliament,
however, in no sense governed, wherefore the practical
sovereignty soon centred in the Council of the Bell.
There are traces in the constitution that the parliament,
though obsolescent by the year 1262, was still looked
upon as a potential factor in the life of the city, but, as
the Council of the Bell did not wish to imperil its own
supremacy, it took care to bury the general assembly in
oblivion by never calling it together. Whoever peruses
the constitution will readily convince himself that the
Council of the Bell is the real core of the Sienese state.
He will learn that it was composed usually of about
three hundred members, distributed equally among the
three *terzi* or sections of the city, that the potestà was its
presiding official, and that its session was legal only if a
general summons had been made by the ringing of a
bell. When the *campana del consiglio* raised its metallic
voice, audible far beyond the circumference of the walls,
three hundred men abandoned ledger, shop, and fire-
side to wend their way to the church of San Cristofano,
which in 1262, and for some years after, still did service
as a city hall. Not only such matters as the voting of
moneys, the making of laws, and the decision over peace
and war, but also the election of the potestà and all
officials whatsoever lay in the hands of the Council.
Such powers indicate unquestioned sovereignty.

Of the many committees of the Council of the Bell
I shall speak only of one, very characteristic of this

formative period, the so-called Thirteen Guardians of the Constitution (*I Tredici Emendatori*). They had special charge of the body of statutes, with the duty not only of incorporating with them the new laws passed by the Council, but also of proposing such changes in the machinery of the state as appeared to them desirable. For the purpose of giving their undivided attention to the subject, they went every year, for a period of not more than eight days, into a kind of religious retreat. The ripe fruit of their deliberations was presented to the Council in the form of constitutional amendments to accept or reject as that body saw fit.*

In the year 1262 the chief official of the state, clothed by the Council of the Bell with full executive authority, was still the potestà, though his authority was by no means what it had been when the office was first instituted half a century earlier. In his first period the potestà not only influenced legislation by sitting with the Thirteen Guardians of the Constitution, but was permitted of his own authority to fix the height of the fines by which the citizens compounded certain transgressions of the law. By the middle of the century (1250) he had been deprived of all such powers of personal initiative and been reduced strictly to the terms of an executive official. Other circumstances, already touched upon, contributed to the diminution of his importance. The steady rise of the people's party had brought their leader, called the captain of the people, forward, with the result that the constitution of 1262 names him as the potestà's alternate in leading the armed host, and puts him on a level with the potestà in many other respects. Further,

* See what amounts to their *breve* in "Il Constituto," etc., I, 137–148.

The Palazzo Pubblico

the fact that the political direction of the government had passed, by the revolution of the year 1240, to a committee of citizens called the Twenty-four, effectively reduced the stature of the chief official. The constitution of 1262 still does full honor to him as head of the commune and successor of the consuls: he is endowed with the insignia of sovereignty; he moves with elaborate state through the city; he presides over the highest municipal court; he may, provided the Council does not prefer the captain of the people, lead the local army in war; nevertheless he is a waning and not a growing power in the commune.

Though the constitution of 1262 undeniably declares that the potestà's decline has begun, this process was greatly accelerated in the generation immediately following. Before the end of the century, not only was he entirely relieved of any connection and responsibility toward the army, but the Nine, heirs and successors of the Twenty-four, dropped all concealment and stepped forth openly into the light of day as the real governors of the city. Therewith the potestà vanished from the purely political story of Siena, though in the chapters dealing with justice and administration he still loomed large for some generations by reason of the fact that he continued to be appointed to preside over the leading communal court and, at the same time, acted as the court's executive official.

Having touched upon the evolution of the potestà we are prepared to attend to the characteristic features of his office, as it was exercised through the greater part of the thirteenth century. The first section of the constitution of 1262 (Distinctio I) is devoted largely to him

and his duties. We there learn that he was elected by a
very complicated process in the Council of the Bell;
that he was to be preferably, though not necessarily, a
foreigner; that his term of office lasted for one year;
that he had to be in Siena on the first of November, in
order to familiarize himself with his duties, which began
on January first. As the commune had only just made
a beginning toward providing itself with buildings for
its functionaries, the potestà was obliged to occupy a
private house, being authorized to pay a rental for it of
XL. libræ et non plus.* Among many additional details none are so curious as those which minutely regu-
late his private conduct. He was indeed surrounded
with ceremony and rewarded with an ample stipend, but,
in return, he could bring only a certain number of carefully specified persons with him in his suite and had to
submit to petty, not to say ludicrous, rules, prescribing
his guests at table and the very hour of his retirement
at night. The fact was the stout burghers, who gave
themselves the foreign potestà as ruler, were devoured
with the suspicion that he might transform his elective
dignity into a tyranny, and controlled his every movement as a guarantee against conspiracies and as a
necessary safeguard of their newly won and precious
liberties.

No less important than the executive provisions are
the administrative arrangements of Siena as revealed
by the constitution of 1262. The document informs us
that the business of the city was largely concentrated in
the hands of four men, called *Provveditori*. Like the
potestà, they were elected by the Council of the Bell, to

---

* "Il Constituto," etc., I, 158.

which, too, they were responsible for the conduct of
their office. They comprised essentially a department
of the treasury in charge of the revenues and expendi-
tures of the state, exercising, in addition, a general control over many minor administrative services.* Their
account books, beginning with the year 1226, are extant,
constituting a source of invaluable information touching
dress, customs, commerce, and an endless variety of facts
illustrating the state of Sienese civilization.† A house
attached to the church of San Pellegrino and used for
their official residence bore, for an unexplained reason,
the name Biccherna, and *la Biccherna* became in popular usage the term of reference to the office of the Four.
Their secretary was called *camarlingo*, and in the early
period of the republic was frequently, because of the
reputation of honesty attaching to his cloth, a Cistercian
monk from the great abbey of San Galgano in the Merse
valley. A charming memorial of this secretary and his
four superiors is preserved in the Piccolomini palace,
the splendid structure of Pope Pius II, which serves at
present as the home of the Sienese archives. To appreciate this memorial we must acquaint ourselves with the
custom of the Biccherna to file away its accounts within
a pair of stout wooden covers, which, moved by the love
of art characteristic of the time, it commissioned some
local painter to grace with a design in color. Many of
these covers have been preserved, all more or less significant, and affording in their sum a rarely intimate and

* The duties of the Provveditori are described in "Il Constituto," etc., I,
381. On their origin see Introduction, p. xxi *ff*.

† The Commissione Senese di Storia Patria has begun the publication of
these account books under the name Libri dell' Entrata e dell' Uscita della
Repubblica di Siena. Thus far (1908) two volumes have appeared.

immediate view of a vanished world. A visit to them, where they hang in a rarely trodden corridor of the great papal palace, builds the road to yesterday with audible whispers of the by-gone years. We see the coats of arms of former Provveditori, which are often splendid designs in mediæval heraldry, the Virgin in the very act of protecting her city in some grave crisis of war or pestilence, and, often, the figure of a white-clad, shrewd-faced monk, bending over a book of figures—our camarlingo.*

Many special studies, based on the constitution of 1262 and utilizing a large amount of other material, have reconstructed the Sienese system of justice as it existed in the thirteenth century. This large subject, which, in order to reach broad and satisfactory conclusions, ought to be considered in connection with the whole question of justice in the mediæval communes, I can no more than hurriedly touch in passing. When the feudal courts broke down, or when they failed to meet the wants of the population, new courts took shape, instituted by the great corporations which came to dominate society. In Siena, as everywhere, there was in consequence a variety of justice: justice of the church, justice of the guilds, justice of the commune. In this situation it was not always easy to say which court had competence in a particular case. The movement toward the unification of these various systems was, in the year

* For an attractive account of these covers see Heywood, "A Pictorial Chronicle of Siena." The whole series of covers has been issued in photographic fac-simile, accompanied by a scholarly Introduction, by Lisini, "Le Tavolette Dipinte di Biccherna e di Gabella." In this connection it should be explained that the Gabella was a minor section of the general financial administration, and that its officials, like those of the Biccherna, had the habit of filing away their records between painted wooden covers.

1262, still so backward, that an able critic has declared the judicial department the weakest point in the organization of the state.* Each of the diverse courts within the walls being independent of the other developed its own procedure, and each rested upon a body of law, containing customary, statutory, Germanic, and Roman elements in varying proportion. Here was abundant occasion fo confusion, which, however, a movement already noted tended to reduce. I refer to the revival in the twelfth century of the study of Roman law in the university of Bologna, which influenced tremendously the legal systems of all the communes of Italy, and led to their absorption of Roman principles in constantly increasing measure.

On every department of public life, on which a student may desire information, the constitution offers full particulars. Of the army I shall speak in another place.† That Siena minted her own money, one of the usual attributes of sovereignty, we know from the charter of Henry VI,‡ but only through the constitution of 1262 are we aware that she took deep pride in her coinage, declaring that none but the best workmen shall be employed in order that the money of the city be both reliable and beautiful.§ However, of all the varieties of information vouchsafed by this document, none would prove more fruitful, especially on the social side, than a study of the municipal taxes. Owing to its great

---

* Zdekauer, "Il Constituto," etc. Introduction, p. lix. For an important contribution to our knowledge of early communal justice, see the same editor's "Il Constituto dei Consoli del Placito del Comune di Siena"; also, Caggese, "Un Comune Libero alle Porte di Firenze," p. 34 *ff.*

† Chapter VI, p. 164 *ff.*   ‡ See chapter II, p. 57.

§ For the *breve* of the lords of the mint—the mint itself was called Il Bulgano—see "Il Constituto," etc., I, 418, 444.

necessities, the commune early in its career put on the tax screws, levying all the direct and indirect taxes known to a modern secretary of the treasury, but perhaps the most significant observation in connection with the revenues is that they show a growing tendency on the part of the authorities to proportion the burden to the wealth of the individual citizen—plainly an affirmation of democratic ideals.*

This rapid sketch of the institutions of Siena covers the period of the Twenty-four, reaching down to the exclusion of the nobility (1277) and to the assumption of political power by the people. Before I carry the domestic evolution further, I must follow the genesis and culmination of the greatest national issue which Siena in all her career was obliged to face, the struggle with Florence for the supremacy in Tuscany. By an interesting coincidence the conflict was at its height at the very period when the constitution of 1262 came into being. At that time, however, the rivalry was already a century and a half old, and by having eaten into the blood and fibre of every Sienese man, woman, and child, ignited, at the slightest provocation, a flame of passion that was fed from every enthusiasm and every rancor of the human breast.

* The direct tax, affirming itself more and more in the Sienese system, was a tax on total wealth and was called *lira*. It was levied for the first time in an experimental way in 1202, but from that time was gradually broadened and regulated in its application by being based on careful registers. On the *lira* see "Il Constituto," etc., Introduction, p. lxviii; also "Conferenze" (1897), p. 132 *ff.*

CHAPTER VI

THE RIVALRY WITH FLORENCE

NO one can follow the story of the long and bloody wars between Siena and Florence without keen distress. Such savage hatred, such din and onset of armed hosts, such wanton butchery of wounded men, such cold torture of prisoners, such harrying of fields at the very moment when the bending corn was ripening to the sickle—*se non piangi di che pianger suoli?* That they, Tuscan cities of the same blood, should have warred upon one another at all, has, at first blush, something unreasonable to the modern mind, though when we recall that the society of which they were a part systematically cultivated a martial frame of mind, that their territories were contiguous and their boundaries uncertain, and that mutual animosity was constantly stimulated by commercial rivalry, we cannot fail to recognize that here were conditions and motives which still operate in our own day to produce armed conflicts. But if the underlying causes of the wars between Siena and Florence are unhappily familiar to our thought and experience, there remains, separated from our modern practice by a gulf of seven centuries, the manner in which these wars were carried on. In this respect Time has wrought an immense improvement, of which we must take exact account if we would seize the peculiar atmosphere enveloping a mediæval campaign. Apart from our medical service, which as a very recent achievement of science affords no basis for comparisons, we have an elaborate international war-code, under which non-combatants are safeguarded, prisoners treated with humanity, and every care taken to eliminate merely wanton cruelty. Many of the baser passions had to be tamed, a process involving a radical reform of conduct, before mankind could make this general advance. In the campaigns, not only of Siena and Florence, but of all the Italian cities, the absence sometimes of even the most rudimentary humanitarian impulses forces itself on our attention, and the brutality, the uncontrolled fury, the total surrender to the pulses of hate, burn us as with fire. Hear, for example, the words of a poor Franciscan, Brother Salimbene of Parma. Listening from his quiet retreat in the Emilia to the noisy march of the world, he entered in his chronicle with the pardonable garrulity of old age all that he could learn about the great sea-fight of the year 1284 between the Genoese and the Pisans. The slaughter was terrible, and when the victorious Genoese had sailed away with those whom they had spared as prisoners in their hands, the women of Pisa went on foot to seek out their husbands, sons, and brothers.

"And when the aforesaid women sought out their captives, the jailers would answer them: 'Yesterday thirty died and to-day forty. We cast them into the sea, and thus we do daily with the Pisans.' So when those ladies heard such news of their dear ones and could not find them, they fell down amazed with excess of grief, and could scarce breathe for utter anguish and pain of heart. . . . For the Pisans died in prison of hunger and famine and misery and anguish and sadness." And he closes a heart-rending

passage with this significant statement: "Note, moreover, that
as there is a natural loathing between men and serpents, dogs and
wolves, horses and gryphons, so is there between the Pisans and
Genoese, Pisans and men of Lucca, Pisans and Florentines."*

Horses and gryphons! An amusing mythological
intrusion, but incapable of weakening the vibrant force
of the old man's statement. Like his spiritual father,
St. Francis, like the best men of the church for ages past,
he bewailed this unmitigated manner of carrying on
war; but many generations were to come and go before
the voice of humanity made itself heard above the
tumult of violence.

Let us give ear to one more and the weightiest witness
touching the moral background of the age before we
take up the detailed struggle of Florence and Siena.
Dante Alighieri was a younger contemporary of
Brother Salimbene. What was to him the *summum
bonum*, the supreme hope and desire of mankind?
Listen to this solemn sentence from the De Monarchia
(Book I, chap. 4): "And hence to the shepherds
sounded from on high the message not of riches, nor
pleasures, nor honors, nor length of life, nor health, nor
beauty, but the message of peace." The greatest thing
is the thing we miss most, and Dante neither had peace
in his own life nor did he see it anywhere about him in
the world. Even more moving than his own words is
the glimpse of the great exile which we get in a contemporary letter.† The writer was an inmate in a

* Coulton, "From St. Francis to Dante: A translation of all that is of
Primary Interest in the Chronicle of Salimbene," p. 218.
† The letter of Fra Ilario retains a certain biographical value even if it is,
as some contend, apocryphal. On its authenticity see Bartoli, "Della Vita
di Dante," chapter 12.

monastery high in the mountains above Luni. One
day a wanderer with the sad eyes of Ahasuerus entered
the gate. "Hither he came moved either by the religion
of the place or by some other feeling. And seeing him
. . . I asked him what he wished and sought. He
moved not, but stood silently contemplating the columns
and arches of the cloister. Again I asked him what he
wished. . . . Then slowly turning his head, and looking
at the friars and me, he answered 'Peace.'" The
stranger was the great Florentine.

Peace, the peace which in his poem he said he sought
from world to world,* was the aspiration of his deepest
mood. But here we come upon an anomaly, painful
in such a man, but intensely human. Though he
craved a better day, and dreamt of peace and love, he
was buffeted by all the passions of his age. That was
the price he paid, and probably paid gladly, for being
alive. Does he not share every hatred by which his
fellow-citizens, ranging from the humble wool-carder to
the proud merchant of the Calimala, were fused into a
nation animated by a common patriotism? In his
verse rival Pisa becomes the *vitupero delle genti*, neighboring Pistoia is urged to make an ash-heap of itself for
its sins, and the upland Sienese are sneered at as fickle-
hearted children, a *gente vana*. His attitude is equally
uncompromising toward his fellow-citizens, or rather
toward that presumptuous section of his fellow-citizens
who conducted his beloved Florence along a different
political path from that which he would have wished
her to travel; he has nailed their reputations, while
the world lasts and poetry is power, to the gallows.

* "Purg.," V, 61.

View of the Campo from the Tower of the Cathedral

No, Dante might cry peace, peace, but, while he himself travailed with hate, showing us in the vast panorama of his poem his whole generation stirred in every fibre with the like passion, there could be no peace.

Returning to the rivalry of Florence and Siena, I repeat that it had its origin in a territorial issue, reënforced and embittered by unrestrained commercial competition. The reader will recall that, as soon as the two towns became independent commonwealths, they entered upon a struggle to control each one its own comitatus or county. In the early Middle Age, during the Germanic domination, the comitatus or count's territory was the civil counterpart of the diocese or bishop's territory, and, in a general way, the boundaries of the two administrative units of church and state coincided. But there were regions of divergence. The failure of the Sienese diocesan boundary to include eighteen baptisteries, lying to the east and included within the political boundary of Siena, was at the bottom of the long lawsuit, of which we have heard, between the bishops of Arezzo and Siena. Northward, in the direction toward Florence, there was even graver trouble, to understand which we must familiarize ourselves with certain important facts in the Florentine political development. Owing to some confusion of the ninth century which escapes our knowledge, the county of Fiesole had been united with that of Florence, giving Florence a civil territory larger than that of any other Tuscan town. How far the boundary of the combined county of Florence-Fiesole extended southward was uncertain, but the Florentines raised the claim that it reached beyond the Chianti hills, nay, even to a succes-

sion of points, the nearest of which was not above seven
or eight miles from the Sienese walls.

Apart from the doubt which, in view of the prevailing mediæval confusion in the matter of boundaries, the
Sienese might reasonably entertain concerning the justice of the Florentine claim, they were urged by the most
elementary considerations of safety to keep a neighbor
of the metal of Florence at a more comfortable distance
from the gates.　At this point the reader is requested to
examine the accompanying map* and to take note how
close to Siena the probable southern boundary line
of the combined county of Florence-Fiesole extended.
Even so the Florentines raised objections and claimed
a still further extension southward.　Agreement proving impossible in the face of such insolence, the decision had to be referred to the field, and since, as we
shall presently see, Florence was victorious, her view
naturally triumphed.　As early as 1203 an arbiter, the
potestà of Poggibonsi, rendered a decision favorable in
all respects to Florence, with the result that down to
the last days of the independent existence of the two
republics, the boundary between them practically remained as traced by Florence and confirmed by the
so-called "lodo" of 1203.

During the early mediæval centuries this boundary
dispute between Siena and Florence slumbered, assuming importance only with the twelfth century, for not
till then did the two cities begin to extend their dominions beyond their walls.　In this movement of expansion they had no sooner clashed with the great nobles
of their respective contados than they began to quarrel

* See p. 177.

with one another.   If Siena was hemmed in by the Soarzi, the Cacciaconti, the Aldobrandeschi and other
clans, Florence was hardly less hampered by the two
great houses of the Guidi and the Alberti, who held
scores of castles all around the city.   Under the stimulus of an unscrupulous rivalry, Florence secretly encouraged and often lent open aid to the Sienese nobles,
while Siena followed the same policy toward the Florentine magnates.   When we recollect that each of the
two towns was territorially and commercially in contact
with other towns, Florence especially with Arezzo,
Pistoia, and Pisa, Siena more particularly with Arezzo
and Orvieto, we are prepared to understand that they
never faced each other like two duellists, each of whom
relies upon himself alone, but that their city neighbors
were inevitably drawn into the conflict.   Nor does that
exhaust the political and military factors of which we
must take account in this keen rivalry.   As pope and
emperor enjoyed considerable, if varying, power, towns
so savagely hostile as Siena and Florence would not
hesitate to enlist the support of one or the other for
their side.   When Florence became Guelph, holding
with remarkable steadiness to the alliance with Rome,
Siena had really no choice left but to become Ghibelline
and seek her salvation in a union with the emperor.
Thus the nobles of the respective contados, the neighboring free communes of Tuscany, the emperor and
pope all play parts in the long feud between Florence
and Siena, but while the presence of these numerous
agents often obscures the issue and complicates the
situation, we are certainly not wrong in affirming that
no matter with what helpers and under what battle-

cries the two towns clashed in field and council-
chamber, in the mind and heart of each was ever
uppermost its own security and greatness.

The first armed conflict of Florence and Siena
bringing the territorial issue between them into sharp
relief occurred in the year 1129 at Vignale, a castle
situated in the disputed Chianti territory.* The Sienese
had seized an opportunity to enter and fortify it, when
the Florentines hurried up and drove them out again.
In 1141, we are informed, the Florentines pushed an
incursion into Sienese territory as far as the Porta
Camollia, the north gate of the town, and in the year
1145 we hear of a great Florentine victory on the slopes
of Monte Maggio, that wooded mountain intercepting
the gaze of whosoever standing on the Sienese ramparts
looks toward the setting sun. In the battle of Monte
Maggio the Guidi, the leading feudal family of the Arno
valley, fought on the side of Siena, and though defeated,
or rather because defeated, continued to nurse a rancorous hatred for the Florentine commonwealth. In
company with their ally, Siena, they now planned a
stroke which was to check the further progress southward of the Arno city.

The *via francigena*, of such importance to Siena, followed, as we know, the Elsa valley until it reached the
Arno, crossed the river by the bridge at Fucecchio, and

* The Annales Senenses ("Monumenta Germ.," XIX) report, without
explaining, an earlier clash than the above, a clash of 1114. The wars of
Florence and Siena in the twelfth century are a difficult subject, upon which
many scholars have exercised their ingenuity. In addition to Davidsohn
("Geschichte von Florenz") and Santini ("Contado e Politica Esteriore del
Sec., XII"), much valuable material has been contributed by Villari ("I
Primi Due Secoli della Storia di Firenze") and Hartwig ("Quellen und
Forschungen zur Geschichte von Florenz").

then turned sharply west to Lucca. Half-way down
the Elsa valley lay the hamlet of Poggibonsi, so favorably situated on a hill that whoever controlled it might
hope to hold the key to the whole region. Poggibonsi
was a possession of the Guidi, but lay, so the Arno
burghers clamorously affirmed, in Florentine territory.
Toward the middle of the twelfth century little Poggibonsi on the Elsa became the center of a web of intrigues which almost defies unravelling. Suffice it that
the Guidi, filled with wrath at the presumptuous
Florentines, deftly spun their threads to play Poggibonsi
into the hands of Siena. In the year 1155 the cabal, in
which even the pope was induced to take a hand, scored
a complete success. The Florentines, hurrying up with
an army to protest with force against the diminution of
their authority, were defeated, and Poggibonsi for the
present remained in the hands of Siena, a welcome
guarantee to that town against further Florentine encroachment on the Elsa side.†

If one thing more than another distinguished the Arno
burghers it was that they could bide their time with the
patience of a hunter in the woods. Desirous of trapping
Poggibonsi, they waited for their opportunity nineteen
years. Then they intrigued with the Cacciaconti, lords
of Asciano and neighboring points and ancient enemies
of Siena, and acquired a foothold in the important
Asciano itself. When the Sienese arrived on the scene,
prepared to undertake the siege of the little town, the
Florentines advanced upon them to the cry of San

† Poggibonsi in the twelfth century is a story by itself and a fascinating
one for the student of Tuscany. For a coherent account see Davidsohn, p.
457 ff., and passim; also, Santini, "Contado e Politica Esteriore", pp. 57,
81–83, 100–106.

Giovanni, their patron saint, and defeated them roundly
(1174). In spite of spirited efforts the sons of the
Virgin could not recover from this calamity, and in the
year 1176 were obliged to accept peace at the dictation
of their enemies. The conditions of the victors were
hard: they acquired one-half of the Sienese interest in
Poggibonsi and forced from Siena a recognition of the
Chianti boundary line as drawn by themselves.

The next crisis in the affairs of the two rivals occurred
in the year 1197, when the sudden death of the Emperor
Henry VI broke the tyrannical yoke which his masterful
will had imposed on the Tuscan cities. We have observed how, by the charter of the year 1186, Henry had
in effect limited the authority of the Sienese consuls to
the city itself. The like or a similar policy he had pursued with reference to the other towns, with the result
that they had lost their hold on their respective contados,
ambition and prize of many decades of combat. In
1197, therefore, the towns, relieved of the imperial
incubus, made a general Tuscan alliance with the main
object of permitting each one to repossess itself of its dependent territory. We have taken note of the "submissions," which Siena now successfully enforced from
Cacciaconti, Ardengeschi, and others of her feudal foes.
But the contado issue, revived by the Tuscan league,
naturally brought the old Chianti boundary dispute
once more to the front. Siena was very desirous to
improve her position against her grasping neighbor, but
as Florence would not yield one inch of her historical
claim, the upland city, in order to avoid war, agreed
to have the Chianti matter settled once for all by the
decision of an umpire. The potestà of Poggibonsi was

accepted for this office, and in the year 1203 pronounced the "lodo" already mentioned, favorable in every respect to the Florentine claims.   A little later, in the year 1208, Siena resigned all her remaining rights to Poggibonsi. Thus, after a struggle of almost one hundred years, the defeat of Siena, with regard to the various questions touching her northern boundary, was indisputable and complete.   With the new century the conflict between the now thoroughly embittered towns continued, but Siena, persuaded of her inability to break through the Florentine line to the north, with shifty resolution turned her chief attention in another direction.*

To understand fully the change which now occurred in the Sienese policy of conquest we must return to the Tuscan league of 1197.   From that union of cities Siena received authority to possess herself of her contado. Accordingly, as soon as the nobles had been reduced to obedience, she laid siege to the hill-town of Montalcino, and in the year 1201 raised her banner over its walls. Then, moving step by step, she undertook to subjugate Montepulciano, even more important than Montalcino, for Montepulciano reared its threatening towers not only near the via francigena, but also directly over the road which penetrated eastward to the Chiana valley and to central Italy.   On the basis of an express agreement

---

* Of course Poggibonsi and the northern boundary were not eliminated from the subsequent struggles, for Florence did not enter into permanent possession of the little town in 1208.   The interference of the emperor presently effected the liberation of Poggibonsi, without, however, in the least discouraging the ambition of the Arno burghers.   Throughout the thirteenth century Poggibonsi, when free as well as when unfree, remained a centre of dark intrigue directed against Florence.   For the astonishing vicissitudes of the little town in the thirteenth century see Davidsohn, "Geschichte von F.," especially II^I, pp. 219, 428, 513; and II^{II}, p. 64.

the Florentines had supported the Sienese in their campaign against Montalcino, but now when the latter moved on Montepulciano the Arno burghers took alarm. A strong Siena was not to their taste, and although Montepulciano was proved before commissioners of the Tuscan league to lie, beyond the peradventure of a doubt, in Sienese territory,* and, therefore, to be lawful Sienese prey, the Florentines were ready to resort to any and every device before they sanctioned Sienese rule at that commanding point. The result was war, in fact a whole succession of wars, spun out through the greater part of the thirteenth century, with Montepulciano as the storm-centre, and a number of other Sienese towns, such as Montalcino and Grosseto, involved whenever Florence could induce them to rise in revolt. Between the new wars and those of the previous century over Poggibonsi and the Chianti boundary existed as a bond the inalterable resolution of Florence to thwart the expansion of Siena.

In order to bring the new phase of the struggle before us as succinctly as possible, I shall set down the wars in their chronological order. There was war between Florence and Siena from 1207 to 1208, again from 1229 to 1235, another war from 1251 to 1254, and a final struggle—with interruptions—from 1258 to 1270. Even the intervals of peace witnessed some disturbances, because Tuscany, with its many other cities, provided each with its own set of quarrels, was almost always in a state of confusion, which inevitably reacted upon the delicate relations of our two rivals. I do not purpose

---

* The evidence, taken down by the commissioners and entirely conclusive on the point at issue, may be found in Muratori, "Antiq. It.," IV, 576 ff.

to follow these wars with any detail until we get to
Montaperti and the dazzling prospect, brief as summer
lightning, which it opened to the Sienese.   The military
art of that century was a pitiable thing, and the capricious course of assaults, sieges, and retreats must exas-
perate every modern reader.   To Mr. Maurice Hewlett,
considering the ways of the Tuscan cities,* their campaigns reach unimagined heights of futility.   Siena,
Pisa, Arezzo, Florence and the rest are to his amused
view very like a pack of ill-tempered village curs, who
bark and snarl at one another until with a sudden rush
they roll over in the dust, biting right and left, and then,
yapping rage and victory, make for home.   With due
allowance for the exaggerations of the romantic temperament, it remains none the less true that there is little
profit to be had of the ordinary Tuscan war.   Its background of mediæval manners alone is perenially interesting, and as that can be recovered best out of the mouth
of contemporaries, or from writers who were sufficiently
close to contemporaries to share their sentiments, I shall
content myself with following the events at the hand of
expressive selections from the chroniclers.†

The war of 1207 began with a siege by the Sienese of
Montepulciano.   To make a diversion the Florentines
with their allies—the Aretines and Count Guido, who,
following the wavering practice of his kind, was now on
the Florentine side—attacked the castle of Montalto,
not far from Asciano.   On the 29th of June the Sienese

* In his "Road in Tuscany."
† Readers interested in the political combinations and military incidents of
these wars are referred to the second volume of Davidsohn's "Geschichte
von Florenz."   They will find there a brilliant, detailed reconstruction of
the complicated affairs of Tuscany in the thirteenth century.

came up to the relief of Montalto, and a great battle
ensued, of which a Florentine eye-witness has left a
curious account.

"The Florentines, investing the aforesaid castle, assaulted
it with many mangonels, and in order that the garrison might not
effect a retreat . . . guards were set round about.   On a certain
day, however, when the sun shot down hot rays, and the guards
wearied by work were resting in the shade . . . behold the
Sienese, come to snatch the castle garrison from danger by a sudden
stroke. . . . But the Florentines, seizing their arms, rushed upon
them and drove them into flight, pursuing them for four miles, not
over ways suited for war, but through woods and thickets difficult
even for wild beasts. . . . And the tents and the whole equipment
of the army was seized, and of knights and foot-soldiers twelve
hundred or thereabouts were captured, and very many on both
sides were killed. . . . However, I desire not to omit what,
though I did not see, by virtue of my being of that expedition I
heard, to wit, that the women, coming from afar, with tears,
sought the bodies of their husbands, and each in order to find one
had to turn many corpses over seeking for her own.   They cried
aloud, weeping together, and owing to the altered features scarce
one recognized her husband. . . ." *

That signal defeat obliged the Sienese to desist from
attacking Montepulciano and to make peace.   They
would have to await their opportunity, and the opportunity in the changing circumstances of Tuscany always
came.   Hear the version of the next encounter as given
by the great Florentine chronicler, Villani:

"In the year 1229 the Sienese broke the peace with the Florentines, because against the articles of peace they laid siege to Montepulciano in the month of June of the said year.   On which ac-

* "Sanzanomis Gesta Florentinorum." Hartwig, "Quellen und Forschungen," I, p. 15.

count in the following September, Messer Giovanni Bottacci being
potestà of Florence, the Florentines led an army against the
Sienese and harried the countryside to Pieve Asciata and dismantled Montelisciai, one of their castles not three miles from
Siena. And the next year, Otto da Mandello of Milan being
potestà of Florence, the Florentines led an army against the
Sienese on the 31st of May, and they brought the carroccio with them
and, passing by the city of Siena, went to San Quirico a Rosenna
and dismantled the baths of Vignone. . . . And returning they
laid siege to Siena." *

In the matter of the siege itself—it occurred in the
year 1230—we will give ear to another Florentine, who
offers us a fuller account than the grave Villani. The
Florentine army lay encamped before the north gate,
called Porta Camollia.

"And the Sienese making a sally to defend themselves a great
battle followed; when the Florentines drove them back, even the
women came out to fight, but to no avail, for Count Alberto di
Mangona succeeded in hanging up his shield on the gate"—in
token of victory! "The slaughter was great and the city was
almost completely captured; and if the Florentines had not been
moved by compassion they might have destroyed the whole of it
with fire and sword. They brought one thousand three hundred
and thirty-five prisoners to Florence and, in addition, many
beautiful women of Siena, and them they obliged to become the
concubines of those who had captured them." †

The "compassion" of the Florentines is good, especially in the light of the succeeding item about the
captured Sienese women. But to proceed with the war.
In 1232 the Sienese at last had their heart's wish; they
took Montepulciano and levelled its walls with the

---

* Villani, "Cronica," Libro VI, chap. 6.
† "Die sogenannte Chronik des Brunetto Latini," Hartwig, II, p. 227.

ground. This success was mitigated by a new harrying
of the poor countryside by the Florentines, and in the
next year (1233) came another siege, which was unsuc-
cessful but must have been a sore trial to the Sienese in
more ways than one, for the besiegers "threw many
stones into the city from many engines of war, and to do
despite and bring shame to the besieged hurled asses
over the walls *e altra bruttura*"*—amidst the Homeric
laughter of the embattled warriors from Arno, sadly
addicted, as we may still learn by a perusal of the gay
tales of their countryman, Boccaccio, to *beffe* and practical jokes. When the Florentines came yet another
year in the season of the crops and laid waste the fields
and destroyed more than forty castles and settlements,
the Sienese at last cried enough. One of their own
chroniclers reports the terms of the peace. Of course
Montepulciano had to be set free. "And the Sienese
rebuilt the walls of Montepulciano which cost them
8,000 florins:"† the walls which they themselves had
cast down—a bitter morsel for the stiff-necked burghers
of the upland town! Montalcino, too, the other apple
of discord in the southern district of Siena, had to be
given its independence at the bidding of the victorious
Florentines.

At this juncture we may pause a moment to look into
the composition of the forces which engaged in these
furious expeditions. We have already heard that the
popular army, according to the old Germanic concept of
das Volk in Waffen, was an expressive feature of all the
free communes of Tuscany, but we have not attempted

---

* Villani, "Cronica," Libro VI, chap. 10.
† Muratori, "Cronica Sanese," ad annum 1235.

to develop a detailed picture of such a communal host.
On the safe assumption that the army of one city was
much like that of another, we are justified in drawing
upon a remarkable, I may say a unique, military document, preserved in the Florentine archives.   This is the
so-called Libro di Montaperti, being nothing less than
the administrative records of the Florentine host of 1260,
which, on their capture by the Sienese in the terrible
rout of that year, were jealously guarded as an invaluable
prize through many generations, only to be returned to
the Arno city in the sixteenth century, in visible sign of
the definite supremacy of the Medicean commonwealth.*
With the help of this source, supplemented by the Sienese constitution of 1262,† we can get a very graphic conception of a Florentine, as well as of a Sienese, army
of the thirteenth century.

To begin with, the communal army was indeed democratic in the fullest sense of the word, for, when war was
declared, all the male inhabitants, from the age of fifteen
to the age of seventy, in the city as well as in the county,
were obliged to report for service under threat of heavy
penalties.   Apart from certain inconsiderable bands,
detailed for garrison duty, the conscripts formed one
large field army, composed, in the case of Siena, of
three main divisions corresponding to the three regions
or terzi of the town—Città on the south hill, San Martino
on the east hill, and Camollia on the north hill.   The
Florentine host, according to the division of the Arno
town into six regions, and not into three as at Siena,
was made up of six distinct bodies.   Thus every inhab-

---

* "Il Libro di Montaperti," Pubblicato per cura di Cesare Paoli, Florence,
1889.   † See, for guidance, Introduction, xxxxiv and lxxxviii.

itant within the walls of our City of the Virgin marched
with the men of the terzo in which he dwelt, but as the
terzo system was, for the sake of convenience, extended
also to the county, which we may conceive as composed
of three sectors adjoining the three hills of the town,
every county dweller was carried on the army lists
either of Città, of San Martino, or of Camollia.

When we have understood that the military forces
of San Martino would be normally made up of the city
dwellers of the terzo, increased by the inhabitants of
that section of the county contiguous to San Martino,
and so with Città and Camollia, we may pass on to the
composition of each of the three great fighting corps.
Each was divided into *milites* and *pedites*, that is, into
cavalry and infantry, the enrolment in one or the other
of the two services being determined exclusively by
wealth. The individual whose *lira* or property tax
reached a certain sum had to keep a horse for the commune, and present himself for service with lance, shield,
and other accoutrements exactly prescribed, while he
whose lira fell below a certain sum served on foot and
armed himself according to a humbler requirement.
The arms, it will be observed, were in each case furnished by the citizen and not by the commune. However, milites and pedites did not exhaust the military
categories, for the development of war had favored the
formation of certain special troops, composed of picked
men drafted from the terzi. Thus we hear of a body of
pavesai or shield-bearers, carrying immense bucklers
which were tied together for attack and afforded the
appearance of a moving wall, of a body of *arcadori* or
long bowmen, and of a company of *balestrieri*, armed

The Palazzo Buonsignori

with *balestre* or cross-bows. Among the special arms the cross-bows held the most prominent place, for, when built on a large scale, according to a great variety of patterns, they formed a primitive artillery for hurling stones and arrows, and proved themselves particularly effective in the conduct of a siege. If we add a baggage service of pack-asses, destined to carry the tents and the provisions, we can see that the army, on passing out of the gates, each division under a leader and following a gonfalon or pennon gayly fluttering in the wind, was already far beyond the stage of primitive organization.*

But of all the curious and attractive features of a mediæval host upon the march none would have exercised such fascination upon a spectator of our time as the *carroccio*. We heard from Villani, the Florentine chronicler, that his countrymen carried the carroccio with them in the campaign of 1230, and it is a fact that no city of mediæval Italy undertook any action on a large scale without this strange instrument of war. The Florentine historian, although writing in the fourteenth century, when the carroccio had already fallen into disuse, was sufficiently stirred by antiquarian interest to devote a page of loving description to it. He writes of Florence, but we may safely assume that the Sienese and Pisan and Milanese and every other war-chariot had much the same appearance.

"And observe that the carroccio, which the commune and people of Florence took along with them, was a platform on four wheels, painted crimson all over, and it carried two great crimson

* For an excellent article on the mobilization of a mediæval army see Hartwig, "Quellen und Forschungen," II, p. 297 *ff*. This may be supplemented by comparison with Davidsohn, "Geschichte v. F.," II [1], p. 413 *ff*.

masts from which waved the great standard of the commune, consisting of one white and one crimson bar and yet to be seen in San Giovanni.   And the carroccio was drawn by a magnificent pair of oxen, covered with crimson hangings and reserved expressly for this service . . . and their driver enjoyed freedom of taxation in the city.   And when an expedition was proclaimed the nobles and knights of the neighborhood drew forth the car of state from the Opera of San Giovanni and brought it to the New Market. . . . And the best and strongest and worthiest foot-soldiers were appointed as its special guard and the whole people were wont to collect about it." *

As far as the carroccio had a practical purpose, it served, as Villani's statement indicates, as a rallying-point for the infantry, but rather than a factor of military usefulness it was an agent of pomp and patriotism, and as such became the object of an almost religious veneration on the part of the citizens.   For this reason to lose the carroccio was an intolerable disgrace, and for this reason the Florentines at Montaperti, as we shall presently see, died around it in the same devoted spirit in which crusaders perished fighting for the Holy Sepulchre.

As we approach the middle of the thirteenth century we observe that the local issue between Florence and Siena becomes bound up more inextricably than ever with the ancient quarrel between papacy and empire. Toward the end of the reign of Frederick II, that extraordinary man of genius whose life was a prophecy of the modern world, the relations of this sovereign with the

---

* Villani, "Cronica," Libro VI, chap. 76.   Interesting additions and corrections of Villani's description in Davidsohn, pp. 691–92.   Siena preserves an interesting relic of its carroccio in the two tall, age-browned poles to be seen in the cathedral, clamped against the piers of the cupola.   These poles once served as the masts which crowned the Sienese carroccio, and from them waved proudly the standards of the city.

pope became embittered to the point of irreconcilability, with the consequence that the quarrel of the two heads of society was reflected in every Italian town in fresh and ever more ferocious broils between Guelphs and Ghibellines.   In Florence, in the year 1248, the Ghibellines, encouraged by Frederick himself, drove out the Guelphs, but in 1251, after the death of Frederick, the Guelphs acquired the ascendency and drove out the Ghibellines.   As soon as these Ghibelline exiles allied themselves with Ghibelline Siena, which they straightway proceeded to do, the occasion was supplied for another war.   It broke out in 1251, led to fresh Florentine victories, and ended (1254) ignominiously for Siena by a renewed recognition of the independence of the coveted Montepulciano and Montalcino.   Owing to the temporary elimination of the empire from the affairs of Italy, Siena felt so completely crushed that she presently (1255) joined with Florence in what in the grotesque jargon of the jurists was called "an eternal league of love."   In addition to the pledge to support one another in the case of war, each city agreed neither to receive within its walls nor to shelter in its district the *fuorusciti*, that is, the rebels of the other.

Here was what, on the surface at least, looked like unexampled harmony between the ancient rivals, but it was rendered vain by the fact that it was not the result of free choice but of victory and defeat.   The test of the genuineness of the new friendship came soon enough. In the year 1258 the Florentine Ghibellines who, as happened often enough, had been temporarily reconciled to their Guelph opponents, grew restive.   They entertained hopes associated with a Hohenstaufen

revival, of which we shall presently hear, plotted unsuc-
cessfully against their city, and, finally, in order to save
their lives, decided on a general exodus. At the head of
the Florentine Ghibellines was the Uberti family, of
which the leading member was Manente, known as
Farinata. He, together with many relatives and
friends, made his way to Siena, and, contrary to solemn
treaty obligations, was eagerly made welcome. Therewith another *casus belli* was at hand. The Farinata
degli Uberti, who in clanking armor rode into Siena
with indignation against his native city smouldering
like a live coal in his heart, was the same person whom
Dante, meeting in Hell, has limned for us with his unerring stroke: he rose from his pit of flame, says the
admiring poet, with an action *"come avesse lo inferno
in gran dispetto."* What a man to know more of, if
only the documents were not silent or almost silent concerning him! The new war led to Montaperti and its
glories. Hitherto for a period of one hundred and
fifty years the Sienese had been almost uninterruptedly
beaten. It was with them as with the Celts of whom
a countryman once tragically said: "they went forth
to war, but they always fell." And now Time brought
its revenge.

Before taking up the story of Montaperti * we must
cast a glance at the general politics of Italy as they had
developed after the death, in the year 1250, of Emperor
Frederick II. With the withdrawal of his hand from
the helm, the fortunes of the empire had sunk very low,

---

* On the campaign culminating in Montaperti consult Paoli, "La Battaglia di Montaperti"; Langton Douglas, "A History of Siena," chap. VII;
and Davidsohn, "Geschichte von F.," II [1], p. 460 *ff.*

and the church party might reasonably flatter itself that
its cause had triumphed. However, the dynasty of
the Hohenstaufen still survived, its main representative
being Frederick's acknowledged heir, Conrad, whom
the sovereign, even in his lifetime, had established in
Germany to rule that country in his name. Shortly
after the death of his father Conrad came across the Alps
to assume his Italian heritage of Sicily, but had hardly
received the crown when he died (1254). Even this
premature death did not dispose of the family, for
Conrad, on leaving Germany, had left behind a son and
heir, known to fame as Conradin. For the present
certainly, this lad, being still confined to the nursery,
was eliminated from the situation, and victorous Rome
was the undisputed mistress of the peninsula. So at
least thought the pope, making his reckoning without
another son of the great Frederick, Manfred, who was
treated as a negligible branch of the imperial tree,
because he had been born to the emperor out of wedlock.
On the death of Conrad, Manfred, his younger half-
brother, full of the pride of race, seized the Sicilian
crown for himself, drove the papal agents, who had come
to claim the prize, from his dominion, and by his brilliant successes against the forces of the pope, stimulated
the depressed Ghibellines throughout Italy to new life.
Without Manfred's unexpected triumphs it is not likely
that the Florentine Ghibellines would have plotted
against their city, or that Siena would have affronted
Florence by receiving, contrary to treaty, Farinata and
the other exiles within her walls. That act declared as
plain as words that the City of the Virgin, rising from
its disgrace, again assumed the championship of

Ghibellinism in Tuscany, and, putting its reliance in Manfred and his mounting fortunes, was ready once more to try conclusions with its Arno rival. To so bold a provocation Florence could respond only with war.

The year 1259 was largely spent in preparations. The earlier wars, as we have seen, had rarely been restricted to Siena and Florence, and many neighbors, with or without their consent, had been sucked into the mælstrom. The present war, more than any of its predecessors, affected all Tuscany, for the papacy and the empire were involved, and with them every petty Guelph and Ghibelline partisan. Florence could declare that she was fighting not only for herself, but for the great cause of the church. By such an appeal she succeeded in cementing a league of Tuscan Guelphs, which included the chief cities of the province, for Tuscany at this time, owing to the continued success of the church, had almost entirely gone over to the victorious side. Even Pisa, traditionally attached to the empire, seems to have remained neutral on this occasion, owing to a cloud of distrust which had arisen between it and Manfred. Thus Siena stood, to all intents, alone. Triumphant Florence, not satisfied with the preponderance secured by her many Guelph alliances, did not fail to make her usual appeal to the insidious agent, treason. She incited Montalcino and Montepulciano to make common cause with her, and successfully encouraged Grosseto and the whole Maremma region to rise in rebellion. Caught between the army of the Guelphs and the disturbances in her own house, Siena's doom seemed at hand.

In these straits she turned eagerly to King Manfred.

The Palazzo Tolomei

Was she not fighting his battle and that of the Ghibelline cause? Would he permit the one strong pillar of his throne in central Italy to be broken? In May, 1259, King Manfred and Siena entered into a league, by which the young sovereign, in return for the oath of fealty and obedience, took Siena under his protection. In sign of good faith he sent northward, with a small troop of German men-at-arms, his near relative, an experienced warrior and a man of parts, Giordano, Count of San Severino. In December Giordano rode through the gate of Siena amidst the cheers of the citizens. Elated by this evidence of the king's good will, the Sienese immediately ordered an expedition against rebellious Grosseto, and in February, 1260, after a short siege, once more took the troublesome coast town in possession. They had followed up this success by laying siege to Montemassi, another rebel town of the Maremma, when they received the news that the Guelph army had set out from Florence. The campaign had opened in earnest.

On April 19, the Florentines with the carroccio in their midst, and attended by allies who swelled the total number of the army to thirty thousand men, marched by the Elsa valley to meet the enemy. Two courses were open to them: either to proceed to the Maremma to support the rebellion there, or to strike straight at Siena herself. Unable to make up their minds swiftly, they let the favorable moment pass and turned against Siena when it was too late to take the city by surprise. On May 17, they appeared before the Porta Camollia only to find the gate barred and the Sienese ready to receive them. The very next day a small company of

Giordano's Germans made a sudden sortie, carrying all before them until they came upon the bulk of the Florentine army, which succeeded in repulsing them and in capturing one of their banners. The jubilant Florentines gave vent to their animosity by dragging the royal standard through the mud of the highway. Still the valor of the enemy must have made a deep impression on them, for they immediately withdrew to a safe distance, raised the siege, if siege it may be called, and before the end of May were once more safe at home. Their triumphal entrance into Florence with Manfred's captured banner flattered the love of "pompa e grandigia" characteristic of the age, but hardly concealed the fact of the substantial failure of the expedition. The first engagement of the year was over.

If the Sienese had won no decisive success in the recent campaign they had at least gained time. And time, in view of the double task upon their hands of foreign war and local insurrections, was everything. At this auspicious moment, spreading encouragement and arousing an immense enthusiasm, additional German men-at-arms arrived in the city, sent by Manfred and conducted to Tuscany by that valiant Sienese, Provenzano Salvani, whose energy and courage made him the natural leader of his countrymen in the hour of peril. Accordingly the people resolved to improve the lull in the war with Florence by renewed measures against the rebels of the contado. Great in those summer months was the Sienese activity, and great, too, the Sienese success. Not only did the citizens once more reduce the Maremma to obedience, but they subjected the fields about Montepulciano to an awful harrying by means of an expedition, equipped, we hear, with one thousand new sickles to be tried upon the standing corn, and their energy spread such terror that they actually broke, in the month of July, the resistance of the town. To this long chain of triumphs it remained only to add the capture of the passionately desired and passionately hated Montalcino. In the course of the summer the hill-town was subjected to a vigorous siege.

It was the news that this stronghold was about to fall* that stirred the Florentines to take the field once more. Toward the end of August they left their city, resolved to relieve and reprovision threatened Montalcino. As their way would take them past Siena, some of the more sanguine leaders doubtless hoped to frighten the enemy into submission by a show of numbers, for well-equipped contingents from Prato, Lucca, Volterra, Arezzo, Colle, San Gimignano, and even distant Bologna, swelled the army of the Florentines, as it poured out of the gates, while troops from Orvieto and Perugia joined it on the march. A second time within five months all Tuscany, ranked and invincible, a host composed of probably no less than seventy thousand fighting men, came sweeping down upon Siena.

This time the Florentines took the shorter route, not marching by the Elsa valley as in the spring, but following the Val di Pesa across the Chianti range, and on September 2 were at Pieve Asciata with many-towered Siena full in sight on its high ridge, covered with green vineyards interspersed with rows of silvery

---

* Hartwig, "Quellen und Forschungen," II, p. 309, is very convincing on this point.

olives. Their exultation was immense, the victory in their eyes as good as won. Only this profound assurance can explain the course which they now followed, for they dispatched two ambassadors to Siena to demand in insolent terms the immediate surrender of the town, and then moving leisurely across the Arbia, they pitched camp on a plain called *le Cortine*, and awaited the return of their messengers. The plain was at the foot of a barren range of chalk hills, which bore the name of Monteselvoli and looked across the valley of the Arbia to Siena. There we will leave them while we follow their ambassadors into the city.

On arriving in the town the Florentine spokesmen were led before the Twenty-four, the governors of the city, and haughtily presented their message. In the name of their countrymen they commanded that the walls be torn down in several places, in order that the Florentines might enter the city wherever they pleased, and, further, they continued, "we desire to put a commission in every terzo of Siena and to erect a fortress in Camporeggi . . . ; and with regard to these matters we desire an answer, which not being satisfactory, our army shall fall upon you with the greatest cruelty."* Having dismissed the insolent envoys with a dignified response, the Sienese governors began feverish preparations of defense, encouraged at every step by the splendid spirit shown by Giordano, King Manfred's

---

* My quotations on Montaperti are from two Sienese chronicles published by Porri in his "Miscellanea Storica Sanese," in 1844. The first goes under the name of Domenico Aldobrandini; the second under that of Niccolò Ventura. They are both of the fifteenth century and are patently elaborations of an earlier lost original, probably contemporary or almost contemporary with Montaperti.

vicar, and his tried corps of eight hundred German men-at-arms. A pressing need was money. But the call for a loan had hardly gone forth when up rose in the Council Salimbene Salimbeni and made offer of the whole sum wanted—118,000 gold florins. Salimbene was at the head of one of the greatest of the Sienese merchant companies, which thus demonstrated in his person that money had not destroyed their patriotism nor undermined their courage. "And immediately the said Salimbene went to his palace for the money and put it in a cart covered with crimson cloth and decked with branches of olive, and so brought the money to San Cristofano,"* where the Twenty-four were in session. Financial provision thus made and the Germans heartened with double pay, the rulers appointed Buonaguida Lucari as syndic with full powers. And he, seized with a sudden inspiration, addressed himself to the vast concourse which had gathered in the piazza before the church, inviting his fellow-citizens to attend him in a procession to the duomo, in order to deliver the city, in its hour of need, into the keeping of the Virgin Mary. How Buonaguida stripped himself to his shirt and with his girdle round his neck, like a halter, and, followed by the whole town crying *misericordia, misericordia*, made his way to the cathedral, and how the bishop and clergy received him at the high altar, and how the act of dedication was effected, we have followed in another connection. "And they made peace with one another, and he who had been most offended sought out his enemy to make peace with him."† And thus passed Thursday the second of September.

* "Ventura," p. 39.   † "Ventura," p. 45.

Early the next morning the Twenty-four sent three
heralds, one to each terzo, who ordered the army of
citizens straight to make ready. Then every man
joined his company, and the companies gathered according to terzi, as was the custom, and presently the
host marched out of the gate of Santo Viene, first the
terzo of San Martino under its banner, then the terzo
of Città under its banner, and finally, the terzo of
Camollia under its ancient standard of pure white;
and this, says the chronicler, "gave much comfort, for it
seemed like the mantle of the Virgin Mary." Thus
passed the general muster of the Sienese strengthened
by a few allies, such as King Manfred's Germans, Count
Aldobrandino of the powerful Maremma family, who at
Giordano's solicitation had joined the ranks of the
Ghibellines, and Farinata with the Florentine exiles.
As no city of any importance had sided with Siena, the
Ghibelline host could hardly have exceeded twenty
thousand horse and foot, leaving it numerically in considerable inferiority to the army of the Guelphs. The
leader of the citizen forces was probably, according to
the terms of the constitution, the potestà, one Francesco
Troghisio, who owed his appointment to King Manfred,
although, curiously enough, the chronicles agree in
committing the chief command of the Sienese to Count
Aldobrandino, hardly to be styled a consistent friend of
the commune.* As commander-in-chief of the whole
host of Ghibellines figured, of course, King Manfred's
vicar in Tuscany, the valiant Count Giordano.

* According to a theory, defended by Hartwig, II, p. 310, the potestà was
not in command at Montaperti, because with another section of the Sienese
army he was conducting the siege of Montalcino.

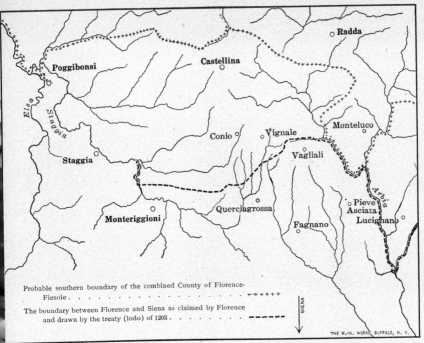

Probable southern boundary of the combined County of Florence-
Fiesole . . . . ⊢+++++

The boundary between Florence and Siena as claimed by Florence
and drawn by the treaty (lodo) of 1203 . . . . – – – –

THE M.-N. WORKS, BUFFALO, N. Y.

The CHIANTI BOUNDARY between FLORENCE and SIENA

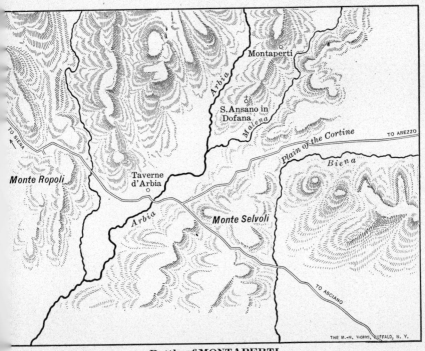

THE M.-N. WORKS, BUFFALO, N. Y.

Battle of MONTAPERTI

As the day was already far advanced the army proceeded only a short distance beyond Siena to the low
range of Monteropoli.   There it pitched camp, with
the enemy at the foot of Monteselvoli in full sight and
separated from him only by the shallow stream of the
Arbia and its valley.   The next morning the Ghibelline
leaders were resolved to launch their attack.   That night
while the Florentine camp was kept in constant alarm
by the sudden swoop of small bands of horsemen, the
Sienese rested quietly.   Then it was that a white mist
was seen to float over the host.   Many anxious people,
sisters and wives, peering into the darkness from the
ramparts of Siena wondered at this phenomenon, "and
some said that it is the smoke of the great fires lit by the
Sienese folk.   Others said: 'Not so, for smoke would
drift, and this rests fast as you see; surely it is other
than smoke.'   Still others said: 'It is the mantle of our
mother, the Virgin Mary.'" *   So passed the night of
the third of September.

When the next day dawned the Sienese commanders
made ready for battle.   Behind the camp of the Florentines the sun had not yet risen and the barren chalk
hills beyond the Arbia, at the foot of which the tents of
the enemy were spread, looked bleak as a desert in the
cold light of morning.   Three corps, with a fourth to
act as reserve, were rapidly formed.   The first, led by
Count Arras, Giordano's seneschal, was ordered to
make a wide detour and lie quietly in ambush behind
the hills under the Florentine left until the favorable
moment came.   This was an unusual piece of tactics
for those simple, forthright days of the military art, and

* "Aldobrandini," p. 10.

probably decided the issue. The second troop was led
by Count Giordano, the third by Count Aldobrandino,
and the reserve by Messer Niccolò da Bigozzi, a worthy
Sienese. Then before the order to attack was given, the
wise quartermasters provided a copious breakfast of
various kinds of roast meat and "perfectly matured"
wines and the finest bread. "And the Germans danced a
beautiful dance to the accompaniment of a song which
in our language began: soon shall we see what hap may
fall."* Thus encouraged with feast and music the
Ghibellines were no longer to be restrained, but presently poured across the Arbia, and in passionate haste
but excellent order began to mount the slopes of Monteselvoli, rushing straight upon the Florentines. These,
ranged by their leaders along the crest, awaited the
attack from their point of vantage.

Just as Giordano's cavalry, which held the van, was
about to open battle, behold my lord Harry of Astenberg make his way to the side of his captain and "with
deep bow pronounce these words: 'All our house of
Astenberg is privileged by the Holy Empire to strike
the first blow in every battle, and this favor, I pray, you
grant unto me.' And it was granted. Whereupon my
lord Walter, nephew of the aforesaid lord Harry, dropped
from his horse to earth, and on his knees spoke thus to
his uncle: 'Whoever receives favors should be disposed
to grant them. Be pleased that I, in your stead, be the
first to lower lance.' Which my lord Harry conceded,
and kissed and blessed him. And my lord Walter
leaped on his horse, and thanked his uncle for the honor,
and put his helmet on his head, and was off at the in-

* "Ventura," p. 61.

stant";* and after him rushed lord Harry with Count
Giordano and his Germans, and after them came
Count Aldobrandino with his troop, and finally all the
people of Siena on foot shouting amain *alla morte*,
alla morte. Thus, the sun looking on from the east,
the battle was engaged on Saturday, September the
fourth.

Battles in those days were usually decided by sheer
push of men on horse and foot. What happened on the
slopes of Monteselvoli during the long hours while the
sun rose to the zenith and sank westward toward Siena
may be left to the imagination. Deeds of blood were
done, deeds of savage courage which fill many pages of
glowing description in the old chroniclers. Suffice it for
us that the day was probably decided by the turning
movement of Count Arras. After an interval, when the
two swaying lines of battle had had time to grow exhausted, he rose from his ambush and suddenly fell
upon the rear of the Florentines. An immediate confusion ensued. The Guelph horse was overwhelmed,
and presently the great standard, carried by Messer
Jacopo de'Pazzi, fell to earth; down it went by act of
foulest treason, says the Florentine, Villani, unwilling
to believe that his people could ever be beaten in fair
fight by mere provincial Sienese, and convinced and
ready to convince others with copious detail that Pazzi
had his hand hewn off by a false friend at his back.
And Dante, another patriotic Florentine, holding the
same belief, met the traitor, one Bocca degli Abbati,
frozen in the ice of deepest hell, and struck his foot into
his face.† Treason or no treason, the attack of the

* "Aldobrandini," p. 19.   † "Inferno," XXXII, 76 *ff*.

Ghibelline cavalry drove the Florentine men-at-arms from the field. Discouraged, seized with panic, they dug their spurs into their horses, leaving the Florentine foot to save themselves as best they could. With splendid courage the Arno commoners gathered around their carroccio, blindly resolved to save the honor of the day. But the Sienese, rejuvenated by the consciousness of victory, swarmed about them from all sides. In the gulches of the Malena, a small stream which empties into the Arbia, a slaughter ensued which colored the water red and piled the corpses in pyramids. "And how many died God knows, for they were not heard when they shouted: I surrender. . . . Nor did it avail to call for aid upon San Zenobio and Santa Reparata"—home saints of the Florentines, plainly poor stuff compared with Siena's Virgin—"for the Sienese slaughtered them as butchers slaughter their cattle on Holy Friday."* At last the Ghibelline leaders took compassion, and gave orders that the butchery cease, and that who would, be taken captive. Whereupon the Florentines in their joy bound one another in order to save their lives. And to supply the touch of comedy which is certain to intrude upon the gravest moments of the human drama, Usiglia, the ancient vivandière, took and bound with her head-band (*benda*) thirty-six prisoners and led them off to camp like a string of geese. Ten thousand enemies or thereabouts lay stretched upon the field, while twenty thousand prisoners and untold quantities of arms, tents, and provisions fell into the hands of the victors.

* "Ventura," p. 68.

On the other side of the Malena, across which a handful of Guelphs had made their escape, took place the closing episode. There on a hill, crowned with a castle known as Montaperti, the weary fugitives made a last stand, but before night fell they accepted the offer of the victors and surrendered at discretion. The inconspicuous mound, at the foot of which the battle expired, has given its name to the historic conflict.

All that day an immense suspense hung over Siena deserted by the male half of its inhabitants. The bishop, surrounded by the clergy and the women, prayed or moved in solemn procession from church to church. The less contemplative—chiefly old men and children— gathered at the foot of the tower of the Marescotti, from the top of which Cerreto Ceccolini, the drummer, spying eastward, gave out the news. The battle was waged only three miles away as the crow flies, and Cerreto's expert vision detected every capital movement among the barren, sun-lit hills. Beating the drum at each announcement he shouted: "They mount the slopes of Monteselvoli; our line gives way, no, it is theirs"; and, finally, "their banners fall, they are broken, they are broken!" A day, we can fancy, far more terrible to those left behind than to them who stood in the heat of the fray.

That night the victorious host rested in its old camp on Monteropoli, but the next day, Sunday, the fifth, rising early, it wound back to Siena to make a triumphal entry by the ancient gate of Santo Viene. By this gate, one hundred and fifty years before, the bones of Sant' Ansano had been brought from their resting-place, hardly a bow's shot from the bloody battle-field, back to the city he had loved. Pious songs of gladness had greeted his home-coming; the victors, returning from Montaperti, where they had staked their wives and children on a throw of the dice, brought and loosed an ecstasy of joy. At the head of the line came one of the Florentine ambassadors who had made the haughty demand for immediate submission. He sat bound, face about, on an ass, from the tail of which dangled, bespattered with the mud of the highway, the great standard of the commune of Florence. Then came Giordano and his Germans, crowned with olive and singing clear songs in their own tongue; close behind followed the victorious carroccio, after which trailed in huddled groups thousands of anguished prisoners; and, finally, amidst wild jubilation, marched past the citizen-soldiers of Siena, the fathers, sons, and brothers of the intoxicated multitude. The host went first to the cathedral to return thanks to the Virgin for the protection she had afforded her people, and then for three days the victory was celebrated with prayers and games and every form of joy and gratitude.

It remained to reap the harvest of the unparalleled success. On September 8 Montalcino surrendered. A deputation of citizens to the number of four hundred presented themselves in the Campo of Siena and with abject mien asked for mercy. Montepulciano had already yielded in July, some months before Montaperti, but, exasperated by the hardness of the victors, it rose once more in revolt. The action, hopeless under the circumstances, led to a new siege and a new surrender. On July 5, 1261, an instrument was signed, by which the town agreed to offer annually, on the occasion of

Fonte Ovile

the August festival, a candle of fifty pounds, and to permit the Sienese to build a fortress within the walls.

Long before the final collapse of Montepulciano a cruel fate had overtaken Florence. Twelve days after Montaperti Count Giordano entered the Arno city and turned its government over to the Ghibelline exiles who rode in his train—Count Guido Novello, Farinata degli Uberti, and their associates. There was no resistance; the remaining Guelph leaders, who by flight had saved themselves from the ruin of Montaperti, had, on Giordano's approach, abandoned the city without a struggle. The Florentine Ghibellines, raised once more to power, had, of course, to show themselves thankful to their protectors, the commune of Siena. On November 25 they signed a treaty renouncing almost all the advanced positions which Florence had gained during the last hundred years, and by which she threatened to strangle her south-Tuscan rival. The treaty not only cancelled all Florentine claims in Montalcino and Montepulciano, which thus at last were delivered over to Siena, but it gave Siena new guarantees along her northern border by obliging Florence to withdraw her hand from Mensano, Casole, Staggia, and Poggibonsi—a line of points which controlled the upper valley of the Elsa. The document, to put its results in a word, realized the long standing ambition of Siena to govern its own county without challenge from a rival. When we consider that it marks no effort to partition the territory of Florence in order permanently to reduce the Arno city from its high rank, we may even find the terms of the peace decidedly moderate. A group of uncompromising Ghibellines indeed, led by Count Giordano, were for levelling

Florence, the secular enemy of the empire, with the earth, but Farinata degli Uberti rose in the council of the Ghibellines at this suggestion and, with his hand laid ominously on his sword, declared that he,would defend his native city from such a fate with his last breath. Thus Florence survived, without being even notably diminished in its territory, but for the time being the proud town was unquestionably subordinated to Siena, since Siena enjoyed an undisputed primacy in Tuscany.

The sweeping victory of Montaperti soon put an end to Guelph resistance throughout central Italy. Town after town, following the Florentine example, purged itself of its Guelph faction, declared for Manfred and Ghibellinism, and joined the league headed by King Manfred's vicar and the Sienese. Lucca was the last to yield, but when in the year 1264 the Lucchese Guelphs, despairing of further resistance, rode sadly across the Apennines to seek shelter in friendly Bologna, all Tuscany was gathered under the twin banner of Manfred and Siena.

As the rise was sudden, so was the overthrow. Three blows, falling in swift succession, shattered the young paramountcy of the city of the Virgin, and shattered it forever. The first was the fall of Manfred. The implacable pope, unable to support the rule of a member of the hated race of the Hohenstaufen almost under the walls of Rome, presently invited Charles of Anjou, brother of the French king, to cross the Alps and seize the Sicilian crown for himself. In 1265 Charles followed the summons, was invested by Pope Clement IV with the southern kingdom, and as a soldier of the church, with the cross upon his shoulder, set out to

destroy "the viper's brood." In the battle of Beneventum, fought on February 26, 1266, fortune declared
for Anjou, and Manfred himself died a death not unworthy of his race. For two days the victor searched
the battlefield for the body of his enemy. At last it
was discovered under a heap of the dead, naked and
hacked almost past recognition. To effect its identification it was laid out before the victorious Charles
seated among his courtiers, while a number of captive
barons were dragged from prison into the usurper's
presence. Among them was the great-hearted Giordano,
Manfred's cousin and his some-time vicar in Tuscany.
Six years had passed since his star stood over Montaperti; six years of good and evil fortune had brought him
here to the bier of his liege. The other barons on being
interrogated maintained a timorous attitude, but when,
says Villani, the turn of Giordano came, his face dropped
into his hands and he sobbed aloud, *omè, omè, signor
mio* *—a cry of the wounded heart that almost strips
that scene of horror of all unloveliness!

Beneventum ended the predominance of the Ghibelline league of Tuscany. The Guelphs returned to
Florence, the Ghibellines were driven out, and Siena,
head of the Ghibellines, found her path beset with
enemies. Nevertheless she maintained her faith in the
imperial cause. When the last offspring of the Suabian
house, Conradin, a lad of fifteen, appeared in the year
1267 in Italy, she received him with loyal rejoicing and
sped him with many a prayer upon his southward
enterprise. With Ghibelline supporters collected from
all parts of the peninsula, he tried the hard feat of dis-

* Villani, "Cronica," Libro VII, chap. 9.

lodging the stout Charles of Anjou from the Sicilian kingdom, and met a fate worse than the worst fears which haunted his despairing mother on his setting out. On August 23, 1268, he was defeated by Anjou near Tagliacozzo, escaped from that bloody field only to be sold to the victor by a traitor, and a few months later, on the present market square of Naples, paid for his daring with his head.

Tagliacozzo was the second blow which staggered Siena and the Ghibellines. The third and last fell in less than a year's time: its name is Colle.

Even the disaster of Tagliacozzo did not turn Siena from her Ghibelline convictions. The leader of the Twenty-four, the guiding spirit of Siena ever since the rise of Manfred, had been Provenzano of the noble house of the Salvani. In the summer of 1260 we saw him lead, amidst rejoicing, a troop of Manfred's horse into the city. He had succeeded in popularizing Ghibellinism in Siena and, with Ghibellinism, himself. His name looms large in the public records of the day, but, as usual, Dante with a line comes nearer to making him live before our eyes, than repeated entries in official documents. He tells us * *colui* . . . *Toscana sonò tutta*, all Tuscany rang with his name, and after this introduction to the blare of trumpets, sketches that imperishable picture of the proud nobleman stooping to collect alms upon the Campo from every passer-by, in order to achieve the ransom of a friend languishing in the prisons of Anjou. While Provenzano dominated the government of Siena, the town was not likely to surrender its convictions, in spite of the fact that the Guelph

* "Purg.," XI, p. 109 *ff.*

tide was steadily mounting. Tuscany had already for the most part subjected itself to the pope and to his representative, King Charles of Anjou, but Pisa and Siena, with the courage of despair, continued to pin their faith to the lost imperial cause. Naturally the exultant Guelph faction believed that the time had come to bring every Ghibelline stronghold to the ground. From Colle on the Elsa, which was held by the Guelphs for King Charles, and where some of the Guelph fuorusciti of Siena had taken residence, they harried the country around Siena and undertook incursions which brought them to the very walls of the town. It goes, of course, without saying that Ghibelline Siena had a Guelph faction among her nobility, just as Guelph Florence had a Ghibelline one. In June, 1269, the government, bent on punishing the repeated Guelph impertinences, dispatched Provenzano with an army against Colle. At the news the Florentines, supported by some French men-at-arms, hurried up, and in the ensuing encounter (June 17, 1269) the Guelphs wiped out the disgrace of Montaperti. Provenzano himself was slain, and his head, set on a pike, was carried in triumph through the streets of Colle.*

Colle destroyed the Sienese fighting force almost as effectively as Montaperti had destroyed that of Florence.

---

*It is difficult to refrain from repeating in this connection a story of Provenzano told by the incomparable Villani. The chronicler believed, as a good Florentine, that Provenzano was in league with the devil and tells (Libro VII, chap. 31) how Satan enticed him into the Colle expedition with an ambiguous prophecy. Of course Provenzano insisted exclusively on the favorable reading, and was promptly caught on the other horn of the Delphic prognostication. Having recounted all which the historian adds gravely by way of warning to his readers: "Wherefore it is folly to put your faith in the words of the devil."

For some months Siena continued to offer a despairing
resistance, until in the summer of 1270 the French
vicar who represented King Charles in Tuscany compelled the city to take back its Guelph exiles. Presently
the Ghibelline nobles were driven from the town, the
government of the Twenty-four, identified with Ghibellinism, dissolved itself, and Siena, without great violence,
under the steady pressure of ineluctable fate, joined the
Guelph league. It remained for a Florentine to raise
the epitaph over the fallen foe. With calm impudence
Villani rendered the significance of Colle in the following
words: "The Florentines drove the Ghibellines from
Siena and pacified the two communes. They have
remained friends and companions in arms ever since.
And thus ended the war between Florence and Siena
which had lasted so long a time."

In this manner Siena turned Guelph, and as long as
she remained Guelph was doomed to rest in dependence
on Florence, as Florence during the brief ascendency
of Ghibellinism had been dependent on Siena. Historians have been inclined to lament the conversion of
Siena to a political programme which put her in an
inferior position. As if it could have been avoided!
Siena yielded to ἡ ἀνάγκη, the great god Necessity. It
takes no profound insight to recognize that the success
of Florence was due to something more than to a victory
in the field, to something more even than to the triumph
of the church, the ally of Florence, over the empire,
Siena's ally. The success of Florence was secured
primarily by her economic advantages, buttressed and
affirmed by the hard, inflexible, and yet adventurous
temper of her citizens. Siena went down under a decree

of fate, but she went down heroically in company with the empire and the Hohenstaufen, in whose compelling tragedy her name shines out with the immortal candor attaching to fidelity and sacrifice.

CHAPTER VII

THE CIVIL STRUGGLE OF THE FOURTEENTH CENTURY: THE NINE, THE TWELVE, AND THE REFORMERS

WE have seen that the fall of the great Ghibelline family, the Hohenstaufen, brought with it the overthrow of Ghibellinism itself. Colle, the special blow levelled at Tuscan Ghibellinism, was the inevitable consequence of Beneventum and Tagliacozzo. After the defeat of 1269 Siena was obliged to become Guelph if she would continue to exist, but the transition was an uneasy and bitter experience. The most numerous faction of her nobility, by virtue of long association and feudal prejudices, held Ghibelline convictions, and the common people, too, inclined to the imperial side, from sentiments deriving from such warlike memories as Montaperti, but chiefly from the ancient and ineradicable hatred of Guelph Florence. For these reasons Siena was a long time settling down to a steady Guelph policy. The Ghibelline and Guelph factions among the nobility vented their spite on one another in murders attended by the usual confiscations and banishments until the city and contado were reduced to a state of chronic disorder. This confused situation at last obliged the *mezza gente*, the trading middle class, to assert itself. Having reached the conclusion that the

192

conditions necessary for the successful prosecution of business could be secured only by a sincere adhesion to the Guelph party, these people had adopted Guelph views. They waited with some patience for the nobility to adjust itself to the new situation, but when the feuds of the great families imperilled the whole social structure they undertook to act without further delay. In the year 1277, as we noted in a previous chapter, they declared the grandi ineligible to office, reserving all the state dignities to themselves. By concentrating the power in their own hands they hoped to be able to overawe the nobility and secure peace. For a time there was a fluctuation in the number of men on the committee entrusted by the victors with the executive power, but the choice settled at last upon nine. Although the mezza gente was really in control from the time when the exclusion bill against the nobility went into force, the regular and continuous rule of *I Nove Governatori e Difenditori del Comune e del Popolo di Siena* dates from the year 1292. Before following the incidents connected with their long reign we must scrutinize more closely the foundation of their power.

We know that the main political struggle of the thirteenth century, the century which closed with the triumph of the Nine, had lain between the nobility, originally in possession of the power, and a party of the people, organized expressly for the conquest of the commune; and we know further that with each decade the nobility had been shut within more and more narrow limits, while the influence of the people had grown in proportion as their enemies had declined. The exclusion of the nobility, therefore, in 1277 from political honors, bore to a certain extent the character of a logical evolution, and logical, too, we are ready to declare, would have been a democratic régime conducted by the whole people. However, the facts do not accord with this last deduction, for with the fall of the grandi not the people, but only a section of the people, harvested the fruits of victory. The reason is not far to seek. The people's party—*societas populi*—which challenged the nobility, beginning approximately with the year 1213, was a union of the local military companies, each of which corresponded in the main to a ward or contrada of the city. Thus the people's party was in effect the Sienese army of pedites or foot-soldiers, but though in many respects a vigorous body, it was, in those days of great material poverty and small political experience, inevitably manipulated by its leading citizens, the well-to-do members of the guilds. In the turbulent times following the Ghibelline disaster at Colle the rich popolani stepped forward, and favored by the party which had been behind them for half a century, seized the reins of power. Then, enthroned on high, they forgot the ladder by which they had mounted. An act of revolting ingratitude if you will, but not without a parallel in the history of other nations, ancient and modern, and particularly characteristic of the young Italian republics. The mediæval city was, as we have seen, an agglomeration of diverse groups, which had formed a commune or state in the correct recognition of growing common interests. They had formed this commune hesitatingly, moving cautiously among a host of long-standing rivalries and new-born jealousies, but, the commune

once formed, each constituent group strove to acquire
as large a share in the new creation as possible. The
nobles, a social group determined by wealth and birth,
appropriated the commune first, until dispossessed by
the gradual encroachment of the people. But the people themselves, far from being homogeneous in the sense
of a modern citizen body, were composed of diverse
groups and factions, each older than the commune and
commanding a ready and profound allegiance: such
groups were, with respect to the church, the parishes;
with respect to the army, the military companies; and
with respect to industry and commerce, the arti or
guilds. These last, the guilds, were of all the various
groups among the people the most powerful and most
enterprising, and of their number the great merchant
guild, together with the one industrial union of any
consequence, the wool guild, held an easy preëminence. These men, merchants and manufacturers,
the mezza gente as they called themselves, deliber-
ately seized the government under the circumstances
which we have traced, and with the exclusive spirit
of the age, converted the offices into a private monopoly. Not only the nobles but the professional classes
of lawyers and doctors, as well as such petty guildsmen as butchers, bakers, barbers, and carpenters,
and, of course, the proletariat of the day-laborers,
were declared ineligible to rule Siena. The men
with money to lend and notes to discount, constituting
the capitalist class, calmly affirmed that the commune, the eternal object of contending ambitions, was
theirs.

Listen to what the victors have to say on this matter

of eligibility in the new constitution* which they imposed on the state. Under the heading, Of Them Who May Be Of The Nine, we read: "Also, that the Signori Nove . . . should and must belong to the merchants of the city of Siena, that is, to the middle class."† And to define this middle class we read in the next article: "Also, it is decreed and ordered that no nobleman of the city of Siena, nor any knight, nor any judge, nor any notary, nor any physician of the city or district may be of the number of the Signori Nove."‡ And still another article declared that all Ghibellines shall be excluded from the supreme magistracy.§ In view of which statutory provisions a profound student arrives at the following summary conclusion: "The leaders of the wool-guild, a few rich members of the other guilds: such in all probability were the collaborators of the powerful merchants, who suffered no other guild to be represented in the government."¶

In their uncontrolled greed of power the merchants did not hesitate to discard the whole theoretical basis of the early commune. We have seen that the sovereignty, which originally rested, at least in theory, with the people

---

* The Constitution of 1309–10, a document which rivals in importance the Constitution of 1262, has been published by the Archivio di Stato in Siena ("Il Costituto del Comune di Siena." Volgarizzato nel MCCCIX–MCCCX, Siena, 1903). Just as the Constitution of 1262 unfolds the picture of the state under the Twenty-four, that of 1309–10 conveys a full knowledge of the political, social, and judicial conditions under the Nine. A part of this constitution, accompanied with sound observations, has also been published by Luchaire under the name, "Le statut des neuf gouverneurs et défenseurs de la commune de Sienne; Extrait des Mélanges d'Archéologie et d'Histoire publiés par l'Ecole française de Rome," T. xxi. Consult also the same author's "Documenti per la Storia dei Rivolgimenti Politici del Comune di Siena dal 1354 al 1369."

† "Distinctio," VI, 5.   ‡ "Dist.," VI, 6.   § "Dist.," VI, 7.
¶ Luchaire, "Documenti," etc., p. XXI.

assembled in parliament, was with the advance of the
consular régime centred in the General Council, called
the Council of the Bell.   The Council of the Bell not
only made the laws, but elected the officials of the state,
and subjected them to its control.   Such powers in a
numerous body and, because of its numbers, difficult to
control, were far from suiting the merchants: they
vested the sovereignty in the Nine, another way, of
course, of vesting it in themselves.   To preserve equality among their number and keep the authority in circulation they limited the term of service of the Nine to two
months.   Examine carefully these prerogatives which
appear from a perusal of the constitution: the Nine
named their own successors; they appointed all the
leading officials of the state; their resolutions were law;
the potestà and captain were obliged to carry out their
orders; they elected the members of the General
Council, suffering naturally only partisans; and, finally,
they appointed the officers (sworn Guelphs and clients!)
of the military companies.   Was it possible to carry the
principle of political exclusiveness further?   And do not
the enumerated privileges create a magistracy of practically absolute power?   The only possible conclusion,
in the face of such functions as the above, is that
the Nine constituted what we may call a distributed
tyranny.   In spite of the delusive drapery of certain
persisting popular forms, as, for example, the Council
of the Bell, we recognize in this constitution that principle of government which, in the more concise and
evolved form of the power of a single man, undermined the democracy of all the free communes of
Italy and established its throne on their ruin:—a

deeply regrettable development, as Sismondi and
other generous hearts have declared in moving
tones; but, what is more to the point, in an objective
analysis of Italian society, an inevitable development
under the group system of the Middle Age. As long as
an association or a league of associations aimed at a
monopoly of the state to the exclusion of all others,
there was bound to be war to the knife, and of this
social war with its tyranny of fluctuating groups the only
possible solution was the military tyranny of One.

The merchants reaped as they had sown. They were
strongly intrenched in power, they were watchful as
Argus, but they could not escape the common lot of
oligarchs. Conspiracy followed conspiracy, chiefly
among the nobles and the more enterprising of the excluded guilds. However, though repression became one
of the constant preoccupations of the merchants, they
did not fail to engage in constructive activities also.
They constituted, when all is said, the wealthiest and
most progressive element in the city, and tirelessly
busied themselves, and with notable success, in problems of public improvement. To these and other
factors, which piece together the historical picture of
the period of the Nine, I shall now give attention, drawing as far as possible, for purposes of illustration, upon
the pages of the Sienese chronicles and, especially, upon
that fascinating narrative, ascribed to Andrea Dei and
Agnolo di Tura.*

First of all, I shall take up the relations entertained
by the Nine with the empire, and, more particularly,
with their neighbors of Tuscany and with Florence.

* Muratori, "Scriptores," XV. "Cronica Sanese."

Almost everything in this connection is said when I
repeat that the Nine were Guelphs, and that the
Guelph faith was a fundamental feature of their policy.
Therefore, under their rule Siena was officially a link
which, with other links like Florence, Lucca, Colle and
the rest, made a chain binding Tuscany to the church.
This polite view of the character of the Guelph League
as an organization founded to support religion and the
pope, while saving the susceptibilities of the members,
did not alter the fact that the alliance was really a creation of Florence, and as such served specific Florentine
ends.   About the same time that the Nine assumed the
power of Siena, the mezza gente or great merchants had
taken possession of the offices in Florence, thus proving
a certain general resemblance in the social conditions
of the two towns.   But this partial identity did not keep
differences from announcing themselves which sprang
largely from opportunity and national temper.   As if it
were not enough that the conditions of mediæval trade
gave the Arno valley a natural and assured preëminence
in central Italy, the Sienese grew timid at the very
moment when the Florentines unfolded a splendid
audacity.   Above all, the sons of the Red Lily followed
tenaciously the immemorial policy of commercial captains: their sleeping and their waking thoughts were
concerned with the conquest of new markets.   Possessed of this spirit it is small wonder that they manipulated the Guelph League for their own purposes,
practically dictating the Sienese foreign policy and dis-
posing of the Sienese military forces as if they were their
own.   If this was a trifle humiliating, the Nine might
consider that they received compensation in the form

of political security, for, while Siena was united with
Florence, the merchants of the Arno city would not only
cease annoying Siena in her contado, but would lend a
helping hand to keep such invaluable allies as the Nine
in the seat of power against the attack of nobles and
every other kind of domestic conspirator.

The rule of the Nine gives at every point the impression
of a government satisfied with a strictly circumscribed
and local independence, purchased at the price of the
surrender of its foreign policy into the hands of a
powerful protector.   Let us follow, to bring this attitude home, the conduct of the Nine when, after more
than fifty years, an emperor once more appeared in Italy.
In 1310 Henry VII descended the Alps, hailed as a
Messiah by the poor remnant of the Ghibellines, dis-
persed, like the race of the Jews, by defeat and misfortune.   His John the Baptist, who went before him, was,
as everybody knows, the great Dante Alighieri.   Here
was an opportunity, a perilous one, of course, but such as
individuals and nations of mettle have run to meet.
The Twenty-four who ruled Siena back in the days of
Monaperti took a much graver risk when they made
alliance with King Manfred.   The Nine by seizing
Henry's proffered hand would have immediately become
the pivot of Tuscany, and Siena the head of a league,
the main object of which must inevitably have been the
overthrow of Florence.   Instead, the rulers chose the
safe course.   When Henry, in the year 1312, laid siege
to Florence, they dispatched military aid to their Guelph
friend, and, if we are to believe the chronicler, saved
Florence from the emperor's clutches.*   The next year

* Muratori, XV, 48, A.

Jacopo della Quercia's Fountain before its removal from the Campo

(1313) Henry passed by Siena on the way south, but the Sienese locked their gates and manned their walls. Matters standing thus, death took a hand in the game. At Buonconvento, sixteen miles from Siena, the emperor, after a short illness, departed this life to enter, as all good Ghibellines believed, straightway and without the need of purgatorial penance, into the joys of paradise. The simple-minded chronicler, exhibiting as usual no sign of emotion, gives a succinct account of the emperor's coming. If the government was Guelph, none the less, in this old Ghibelline stronghold, throbbing with Ghibelline memories, there must have been a great deal of imperial sentiment abroad. Why else did the Nine, just as Henry was expected, "begin to get the chains ready," as the chronicler dryly notes? This military device, aimed at the domestic enemy, consisted of iron chains, which could on short notice be swung across the main thoroughfares, thus hindering the concentration of forces and, above all, the charge of horsemen. The rivets to which the chains were attached can still be seen at many places through the city.* As Henry swept by, the agitated inhabitants crowded towers, walls, and points of vantage, and surely in that throng many hearts shaped silent prayers for his success.

"He left Pisa on the eighth of August with a large and excellent cavalry . . . and on the fourteenth approached Siena on the side of Porta Santo Viene. And his people burnt many houses and did much damage. . . . On the twenty-second of August, being Wednesday, the emperor fell ill. He left Stigliano while he was still ill and moved to Buonconvento; and on Friday, August

* For some interesting notices about these chains, see "Miscellanea Stor. San.," IV, p. 198.

twenty-fourth, on St. Bartholomew's day, in the church of Buon-convento, the emperor died; and on Saturday his army broke camp and returned to Pisa with the body of the emperor, and there he was buried with great honor." *

Following Henry's failure and tragic end the empire counted for less than ever in the affairs of Tuscany, but the troubles of the harassed province did not on that account cease. New conflicts constantly made their appearance, caused largely by the Florentine ambition to rule and the inevitable resistances which that ambi-tion aroused. Daring leaders, Uguccione della Faggi-uola, lord of Pisa, Castruccio Castracane, tyrant of Lucca, administered stinging defeats to the purse-proud burghers of the city of the Lily, but no amount of encouragement could induce the government of the Nine to abandon their political reserve or to be drawn from their allegiance to their city's dearest foe. In every expedition which Florence organized, naturally after loud beating of the Guelph drums, a Sienese troop took part and was duly butchered *pour les beaux yeux* of her Arno neighbor. Of course some small returns the Nine could reasonably ask for such exemplary devo-tion, and some, too, they received not only in the form of the support of the Guelph League against internal foes, but also in the privilege, certainly not inconsider-able, of consolidating and even extending their power in the Sienese contado.

The rule of the Nine in the contado has many points of interest. However, as I shall unfold the fortunes of the contado in the following chapter, it must suffice me here to point out some of the more obvious difficulties

* Muratori, XV, 48.

which the government encountered in the country-side. Although Florence, allied with the Nine, no longer intrigued with the subject towns to persuade them to rise in rebellion, the situation around Siena was anything but tranquil. The spirit of independence died hard, and Grosseto, Montepulciano, and Montemassi— to name only some of the more important points—revolted many times and had as often to be put down. Besides, with Tuscany in disturbance from such wars as those associated with the names of Uguccione and Castruccio, Siena could not hope to be entirely spared from provincial broils, and was frequently alarmed and harried by incursions into her territory. Then there were the city-nobles, sworn enemies of the merchants who had reduced them to political nullity; on slight provocation, and, often on no provocation at all, they raised the flag of insurrection on one or another of their moated castles, and before they could be brought to terms many troops had been mobilized and much money spent. On the other hand, the original feudal nobility made, with one exception, little trouble, for the progress of time had practically wiped this class out of existence. In the southern districts, in the region of Monte Amiata, the Aldobrandeschi still held their own, but in a number of wars waged against them by the Nine, they were signally defeated and obliged to renew all the old treaties of dependence while offering, in addition, the outright cession of numerous lands and castles.* Plainly the proud house was in unarrested decay. It would seem

---

* Not counting the minor conflicts, in the nature of border raids, there were two real wars waged between Siena and the Aldobrandeschi in the time of the Nine, the first in 1299–1300, the second in 1331. See Muratori, XV, ad annum.

that this truth was not hidden from some of the members
of the family itself, for of Count Jacomo of Santa Fiora,
who died in 1346, we hear that he left the commune of
Siena heir of all his goods. Is not such a testament the
sign of a complete discouragement? And is not this
view confirmed by what the chronicler adds in explanation of Jacomo's unusual act? "And this he did," we
read, "because he said that what he had, or the greater
part thereof, he had seized and stolen in the contado of
Siena." * A baron of ancient lineage regretting a little
violence and eager to restore ill-gotten goods! Beyond
the peradventure of a doubt, the feudal character was
passing with the feudal system.

Overshadowing every other question and interest
attaching to the rule of the Nine, is the story of their
relations to their political enemies within the city.
When we recall that the merchants established an
oligarchy which ruled at the expense of the nobility
and the common people, we can form an immediate
conception of their difficulties. The elements with a
grievance would tend to coalesce, and in those violent
days would balk at nothing in order to discrown their
tyrants. It was well for the Nine that they kept their
hand on the local militia by reserving to themselves the
appointment of the officers. Their continued uneasiness, in spite of this prudent measure, is proved by their
employment of a special palace guard which, from 1320
on, was under a foreign commander, the *capitano di
guerra*,† provided with extraordinary powers for the

---

* Muratori, XV, 114, C.

† On this official, who betrays the system of force built up by the Nine, see
Luchaire, "Documenti," p. L.

detection and punishment of political crimes. A
special palace guard! This touch was needed to establish an unmistakable analogy between this republican magistracy and such avowed tyrants as the
Visconti and the Scala, who at this very time had
succeeded in enthroning themselves, with the aid of
hireling soldiers, on the buried liberties of Milan and
Verona.

In addition to minor tumults, more or less dangerous
to the government, the chronicles report three serious
conspiracies aimed against the Nine, each one of which
composes an admirably clear picture of the local situation. We have seen that things could not have been
entirely satisfactory in the year 1313, when the nearness
of Henry VII moved the Nine to serve warning to prospective rioters by closing the streets with chains. The
open outbreak of 1318 could not have been, therefore, wholly unexpected. The chronicle of Andrea Dei
gives the following account of it:

"At this time some of the Tolomei and other grandi of Siena
. . . made a league and conspiracy with the notaries and butchers
and other guildsmen to break and overthrow the office of the Signori Nove and to seize the signiory themselves.

"And on the night of Thursday, October 25th, being the eve of
Saints Simon and Jude, they gathered on the Campo at the mouth
of the Casato" (the aristocratic street, where many nobles dwelt),
"accompanied by a small number of foot-soldiers, and raised the
cry: Death to the Nine. And among them were certain notaries
and butchers and other common people (*popolari minuti*) of
Siena, and they engaged in battle with the forces of the Nine,
drawn up before their palace to the number of one hundred foot-
soldiers. . . . And the notaries and butchers and other conspirators expected that the Tolomei and the other nobles, who were

parties to the said conspiracy, would come to the Campo with their retainers, but they came not. . . . On account of which those who had engaged in this enterprise were broken by the guard of the commune and driven from the Campo." *

The failure was followed by numerous confiscations, executions, and that most puerile measure of political revenge, unhappily practised by all of the Italian cities, the destruction of the houses of the defeated opponents. All which severity did not put an end to resistance. In 1324 there was an attempt which, in its leading features, presents a close parallel to the conspiracy just described. The Nine were too strong and too watchful; they killed the movement in the bud, with the result that they did not have to face another grave local peril till the year 1346. Of this outbreak we read as follows in the chronicle: †

"On Sunday, August 13th, a rumor went through Siena of a league made by certain common people (*popolari minuti*) who elected as their captain Spinelloccio, son of Misser Jacomo di Misser Meo Tavena de' Tolomei" (always a Tolomei in these enterprises!). . . .

"And certain of the said conspirators raised a clamor and proceded to the house of Berto di Lotto, who was giving a feast for some strangers and citizens, among the latter, Giovanni di Ghezzo Foscherani. And while Giovanni was washing his hands, some of the conspirators, among whom was a certain Simone of Volterra, attacked him with knives, and Simone struck Giovanni several blows and ran away, raising the cry through the quarter of Ovile" (the poorest quarter of the town and the most crowded): "'Long live the people and death to those who are starving us (*e muoia chi ci affama*)'; for in that year there was a great famine of grain.

* Muratori, XV, 60, D.   † Muratori, XV, 115.

"At this juncture a son of the above Giovanni, whose name was Meo, seeing his father wounded, hurried home, and, seizing his sword, ran like a madman after Simone with intent to avenge the outrage. On him, too, Simone threw himself with his knife and wounded him in several places; and finally he killed Meo, son of Giovanni de' Foscherani. Whereupon the said Simone escaped without let or hindrance . . . and fleeing and shouting ever: 'Long live the people and the guilds, and death to them who are starving us,' without the least interference, passed through the gate and vanished into safety.

"For which reason the city was filled with suspicion. And the Nine sent into many directions for aid, and from Florence, Pistoia, San Gimignano, Colle, Montepulciano, Montalcino, and our contado a great quantity of horse and foot poured into Siena and guarded the city many days. . . ."

Observe how the brothers of the Guelph League stood shoulder to shoulder, and how Florence was prepared to be at some trouble to keep so useful an ally as the Nine in power. Simone murdering oligarchs in the streets, with everybody apparently standing by with folded arms, was a phenomenon calculated to arouse reflection. The fact was, the position of the Nine, after two generations of ascendency, was no longer what it had been. But of this anon. Before considering their inevitable downfall I wish to refer to a few events, which pieced together with such scenes as the above, perform the service of making the life in the winding streets among the palaces and warehouses, as actual as if we beheld it with our living eyes.

The laconic chronicler upon whom I am drawing never indulges in lavish description. Facts are what he is after with his simple grasp of life, facts that are as

tangible and solid as a floor beam or a paving block.
He takes note of a tower blown down by the wind,
crushing a hundred persons, of an earthquake, a drouth,
a fire, letting no crude, nerve-shaking disaster escape
his attention, but his mind is not yet alive to the subtle
occurrences in the realm of the spirit, and the particular
traits of even those broad events which he describes are
a blank to him.　However, the Renaissance was in the
wind and the Renaissance, among other things, meant
awakened senses, quickened mental processes, and a
more personal relation to society.　Here and there in the
dispassionate record we have quite modern touches in
the shape of descriptive detail, for instance, in connection with the family feuds among the nobles, and particularly in the story of the *grande mortalità* of 1348, the
Black Death of European fame.

In the daily budget of news exchanged by the gossips
congregated in church or on the Campo, the latest incident in one of the many family feuds must have held a
prominent place.　The reader's attention need only be
directed to Shakespeare's Montagues and Capulets in
order to lead him to recall that every Italian city was
stirred with these savage vendettas, survivals of the
feudal preference for the decision of the sword over the
sentence of the law.　In Siena the two most powerful
families were the Tolomei and the Salimbeni.　They
pursued one another in the spirit of the Old Testament
demand of a tooth for a tooth, an eye for an eye.　Over
and over again their murders and riots filled the whole
city with alarm.　To stir further the troubled waters of
civic life, similar feuds sprang up between the families
of the Malavolti and the Piccolomini, the Scotti and the

Saraceni. An event like the following is possible only within the frame of the Italian Middle Age:

"On April 16th (1315) a great conflict and battle occurred between the Tolomei and the Salimbeni, and the whole city armed itself. And the next day the rumor spread that the Aretines, at the bidding of the Tolomei, were coming in their aid, and the whole city armed itself and rushed to the gates and the Campo, but found nothing." *

Not only do the citizens of high birth pursue their ancient and honorable pastimes on the public streets, but they are suspected, and probably not without some ground, of treason! The Florentines, always solicitous for the good of Siena under the pliable Nine, interfered on this and other occasions to compose the feud between the Tolomei and the Salimbeni; neighboring bishops and even the pope may be found at one time or another engaged in the same service; but the peace was hardly sworn when some new excess put everything in jeopardy again. The combat described above still retains something of the air of a knightly tournament, but some of the incidents associated with these vendettas are, viewed in the light of our modern standards, nothing but naked assassinations. Consider this act in the Malavolti-Piccolomini blood-feud:

"On February 19th (1334), just after sunset, four youths of the Piccolomini, to wit, Giovachino d'Andrea di Misser Salamone, Amerigo di Turino, Neroccio di Misser Naddo, and Riccio di Benuccio" (what a sonorous roll-call of brigands! almost capable of reconciling one to being murdered) "with some retainers left their house, and coming to the house of the Malavolti entered the court-yard. There they came upon Niccolò di Misser Cione

* Muratori, XV, 54, C.

Malavolti playing chess; and Giovachino drove a knife into his throat killing him instantly. And then they returned to their house without further incident." *

Another characteristic feature of life in Siena and other mediæval towns were the recurrent famines, usually accompanied with disease and pestilence. The failure from one cause or another of the crops of a particular district always produced a crisis in the Middle Age, owing to the poor facilities for moving grain beyond a certain distance, as well as to the absurd protective views generally current, which caused every state to put the exportation of food-stuffs under a severe embargo. The result may be seen in such a record as this for Siena: 1302 famine; 1328 famine followed by a terrible mortality; 1339 famine and disease; 1346 partial famine. Though the above record establishes an indubitable concatenation between the phenomena of hunger and disease, the Black Death of 1347–48, that scourge unparalleled in the history of Europe, had nothing to do with the Sienese famine of the preceding year. The Black Death—related, it would seem, to the Bubonic Plague, which still decimates the populations of the crowded East—was carried into Europe by Italian merchants. From such seaports as Genoa and Pisa it spread inland with incredible rapidity, leaped the Alps, and presently devastated the whole West. . . . In the spring of 1348 it appeared at Siena:

"In this time began the Great Mortality, the greatest, and most obscure, and most horrible imaginable; and it lasted till October, 1348. It was of such a secret character that men and

* Muratori, XV, 93, D.

women died almost without warning. A swelling appeared in the groin or the arm-pit, and while they were talking they fell dead. The father would not attend to his son; one brother fled from the other; the wife abandoned her husband; for it was said that to catch the disease it sufficed to look upon a victim or to feel his breath. And it must have been so indeed, since so many perished in the months of May, June, July, and August, that it was impossible to find any one to bury the dead. Neither relatives nor friends nor priests nor friars accompanied them to the grave, nor was the office of the dead recited. He who lost a relative or house-mate, as soon as the breath had left the body, took him by night or day, and with two or three to lend a hand, carried him to the church, and with his helpers buried the corpse as best he could, covering it with just enough earth to save it from the dogs. And in many places of the city trenches were dug, very broad and deep, and into them the bodies were thrown and covered with a little earth; and thus layer after layer until the trench was full; and then another trench was commenced. And I, Agniolo di Tura, called Grasso, with my own hands buried five of my children in a single trench; and many others did the like. And many dead there were so ill-covered that the dogs dug them up and ate them, dispersing their limbs through the city. And no bells rang, and nobody wept no matter what his loss, because almost every one expected death. . . . And people believed and said: This is the end of the world."*

But the Black Angel thus reaping up and down the city spared the good Agniolo, called Grasso, and before he died of some other disease, less terrible but just as effective, he wrote the above description, which by reason of a certain rusticity and homeliness has a far greater poignancy than the more literary treatment of the same theme by the famous novellist Boccaccio.†

* Muratori, XV, 123. Agniolo puts the dead at Siena at 80,000; Boccaccio in his Introduction to the Decameron gives the figures for Florence at 100,000 "dentro alle mura."
† Introduction to "Il Decamerone."

With this quotation I shall have to close my illustrations of the life in Siena under the Nine, as depicted in
the pages of the chroniclers. Fairness, however, demands that before relating the fall of this government I
again insist that against its many faults and deficiencies
are set some notable achievements. If it is not easy to
sympathize with the foreign programme of the merchants, which imposed a close dependence on Florence,
if their home policy was dictated by the selfishness of
class interest, they were, nevertheless, in their way,
patriotic and enlightened citizens, and beautified their
town with that keen pleasure with which a lover adorns
his mistress. Since peace was their lode-star, a commercial peace which would enable every man to go
about his daily business, it was at least consistent that the
merchants should give their attention to civic improvements by constructing aqueducts and fountains, by paving
the streets, by erecting public buildings, and generally by
patronizing the arts. The noble outward show, as
noble as may be found anywhere up and down the fair
peninsula, which Siena in this twentieth century still
presents to the eye, is due primarily to the creative
activity of the Nine. The Campo, where they built their
palace, was the particular object of their munificence,
and whoever has seen this unique piazza will agree that
the chronicler was not misled by local pride when, in
1346, in a burst of feeling extraordinary for him, he
wrote. "On December 30th the paving of the Campo
was completed. And with the beauty of the fountains
and of the buildings round about, it is held to be one of
the fairest squares in Italy, and even in Christendom."[*]

* Muratori, XV, 117, D.

Porta Romana

The rule of the merchants for good and for ill was drawing to a close. In the year 1354 an emperor once again descended into Italy. Charles IV was an unimaginative, matter-of-fact politician, who accepted the verdict of history, recognized that Ghibellinism was a dead issue and Italy a lost province, and was content, like a good peddler, to get the best prices he could for his damaged imperial wares. These consisted of privileges and confirmations, to which there still attached a certain value in the eyes of the local governments, for the emperor was, in spite of all that had happened, the theoretical source of all political power; and in any case the imperial diploma with its pendent seal of gold would be a handsome archivial decoration. Naturally at the prospect of so attractive a possession the communes presented themselves before Charles in great number. In view of his conciliatory bearing the Nine, though Guelph, opined that they had nothing to fear from him, and after some hesitation, dispatched an embassy to him at Pisa to offer their homage. To return the courtesy, on his way to Rome, whither he went to be crowned, he came to Siena, entering the city amidst loud acclaim on the evening of March 23, 1355. Considering the strictly commercial interpretation which he put upon his Italian mission, it is not likely that he entertained any plan of overthrowing the Sienese government. From this charge he may be exonerated; nevertheless, he could not hinder his presence in Siena being utilized by the opposition for its own ends. Again and again the nobles and the common people had conspired to overthrow their tyrants, and now no sooner had Charles entered the gate than a new conspiracy sprang into existence. The nobles circulated among the crowd, whispering sedition, and with the first vivas for the emperor mingled also the ominous cry: *Muoia li Nove!* We may fairly believe that Charles was helpless in the midst of the following explosion, the causes of which, as a foreigner, he could not possibly have fathomed. The more closely we examine the course of events, the more certain it becomes that on this, as well as on later occasions, he was hardly more than a cloak for the ambitions of others, constituting, in spite of whatever good-will with which we may credit him, merely an additional element of confusion in an already complicated situation.

The frightened Nine offered no resistance to the new conspiracy. All through the next day (March 24th) the excitement grew, until, on the 25th, the people poured in a surging mass into the Campo and prepared to storm the palace. The emperor was within, consulting with the agitated governors. In order to end the confusion he announced to the populace that the rule of the Nine was over and that a committee would consider the bases of a new constitution. The victors relieved their patriotic enthusiasm in the usual form by the pillage of the houses of the merchants and of all those public buildings which the forces of the emperor did not protect. Abused, cuffed, hunted like wild beasts, the deposed oligarchs fled from the city.

The work of the committee, which was composed of twelve popolani and eight nobles, that is, of representatives of the two groups which had triumphed in the revolution, ended with the establishment of the government of the *Dodici*, twelve rulers in place of nine, all of the victorious people. The merchants paid the price of defeat by being excluded from the offices. The nobles, represented, as we have seen, on the constituent committee, were at first treated with distinction and a council of twelve of their number was appointed to act as a consultative body with the governing Twelve. However, this council was presently discontinued as conferring too much influence, and the grandi were asked to content themselves with some purely administrative posts. In consequence, cheated of their hopes, they took to lawlessness, while the old Salimbeni-Tolomei feud, which had rested for a time, flared up again, carefully nourished by the new rulers in the hope of weakening their enemies. The next few years once more proved the inability of the people to assimilate the noble element, and amply illustrated the countless woes inflicted on the commonwealth by the persistent social schism.

Immediately after the March revolution the emperor had left the city for Rome and did not return till some weeks after, when the work of the commission, appointed by himself, was done. In his presence and with his sanction the new constitution was, on May 1st, put in force, and the first Twelve took up their residence in the Palazzo Pubblico. Their term of office was to last, as with the Nine, two months, and all the citizens, except the nobles and the merchants, that is, the earlier governing classes, were to be eligible to the palace. Again at this point we touch the radical flaw in the political edifice of Siena and of every other commune in Italy: the commune having its origin in a union of groups, never succeeded in fusing them into a whole, composed of elements equal among themselves and equally subordinated to

the government. Out of the conflict of social classes,
military companies, guilds, interests of all kinds, that
longed-for product, the modern state did not emerge.
The inevitable result was the perpetuation of the group.
The nobles, divorced from power by a renewed exclusion, hardened more and more into a political party,
called in the political jargon of the period, *il monte dei
Gentiluomini*. The merchants, branded and disgraced,
formed another party, *il monte dei Noveschi* or of the
Nine, while the victorious people, identified with the
Twelve, were called *il monte dei Dodicini*. A *monte*
was a thing like an oriental caste, into which a man
found himself born and from which there was no
escape except by death. With attachment to the monte
superseding every other loyalty, the party in power felt
no scruples about securing by open violence or by the
most disingenuous sleight of hand the possession of the
honors and emoluments.*

The new government, though a party affair, had at
least the advantage of resting apparently on a broader
foundation than its predecessors. The common people
had won the victory, and the earliest enactments of the
new government not only employed a very democratic
language, but apparently pursued the plan of organizing
the state according to a truly democratic ideal. Twelve
reorganized guilds—the shattered merchant guild was,
of course, not among them—received official recognition,
and every citizen was invited to register in one of them.
The total guild membership constituted the body of
eligible or governing citizens. So far the new theory;

* On this matter of parties see Paoli, "I Monti nella Repubblica di Siena."
Nuova Antologia, Serie terza, 1891.

the practice was entirely different. The social layer just below the great merchants, shop-keepers and notaries for the most part, found itself in power on the morrow of the March revolution, and was resolved to hold fast to what it had secured. No man stands socially so low that he cannot find somebody still lower whom he may freely despise. If the social group just defined was envious of its superiors, it had no love for the common people beneath it, and apart from a liberal alms of democratic phrases, had no mind to rub elbows with workingmen. Through various kinds of manipulation, which are common to the professional politicians of all ages, the Twelve were presently chosen from as limited a circle as ever the Nine had been, and Siena awakened from its revolutionary dream to discover that it was the victim of a shrewd band, which in dignity, prestige, and experience of life stood far below the former rulers.

Such a government as this, guilty of monstrous deceit, issuing democratic promises while concerned only with distributing political favors among a small circle of initiates, did not deserve to live. In truth, its difficulties were, from the first day, enormous. On the news of the revolution in Siena many places in the contado, such as Grosseto, Montalcino, and Montepulciano,* revolted on the convenient pretext that they had sworn loyalty to the Nine; the discontented nobles spread a constant feeling of uneasiness; that dreadful scourge of mediæval Italy, the companies of adventure, put in an appearance and had to be bought off by a timorous government with

---

* Montepulciano submitted to Perugia and caused the Perugian war of 1357–58. On this conflict see Heywood in "Bull. Sen.," XIV, p. 425 ff.

huge sums of florins—admitting that here were troubles
inseparable from rule in those days, the fact remains
that never did a government prove more weak, irresolute,
and incompetent.   The wonder is that it lived for thirteen years, especially as divisions soon appeared in its
own ranks.   The one creditable act of that whole period
was performed in its despite by the general of the
Republic, a Roman noble of the Orsini family, who diso-
beying, in an access of manly indignation, the orders of
his pusillanimous masters, attacked the plundering
mercenaries, known as the Company of the Hat, and put
them to rout (1363).   For which uncommanded victory
he had reason to be thankful not to have been made to
pay with his head!   What the state of public opinion
was within the walls, with Gentiluomini, Noveschi, and
the cheated people muttering wrath, is well brought out
by the chronicler in a strikingly picturesque passage:
"And the Signori Dodici entered into great fear of the
air (*grande paura dell'aria!*) and appointed police
captains in every terzo of the city with many soldiers
under them;   and to these officials they gave ample
authority to behead whosoever should cough against
them (*chiunque tossisse contra loro*), and they issued
many and strict orders against whosoever should bring
to remembrance the emperor,"* ever the extreme hope
of the lovers of change.   Is another touch needed
to complete the picture of a tyranny, which, shut up
in its palace, trembles at every chance noise in the
streets ?

The mere news that Charles IV had come a second
time to Italy—evidently his exchequer needed to be

*Muratori, XV, 192, E.

replenished—sufficed to overthrow the Twelve. Again a critical examination of events will establish that if the emperor's power was small, his prestige was still considerable. Men of influence and ambition—and there was no dearth of them in Italy—could always create serious trouble in alliance with the sovereign. Pushed to the front by skilful politicians, this high personage might deceive himself into thinking that he was playing an imperial rôle, while he was really no more than a puppet in the hands of clever manipulators. Charles came to Italy a second time, and in the year 1368 appeared again in Siena, but except as a centre of intrigue and confusion we can eliminate him from the extraordinary succession of disturbances which accompanied his arrival. The autumn of 1368 established a record, which it would be hard to match even among the turbulent Italian cities —four revolutions in less than four months!

Revolution 1.—On September 2d, the nobles, temporarily composing all their difficulties, above all, patching up the ancient Salimbeni-Tolomei feud, proceeded to the Palazzo Pubblico, and "senza colpo di spada" put the Twelve out. A fall, worthy of this ignominious company. Then the nobles set up a government of their own, a strictly nobiliary government such as Siena had not seen since the days of the consuls, more than a century and a half ago. Of course this anachronism had no chance to live. As soon as the emperor's vicar, Malatesta, commanding an armed force, arrived within bow-shot of the city, new plots took shape. Joined with the Salimbeni, who at this juncture deserted their noble brethren, Malatesta encouraged a rising of the people.

Revolution 2.—On September 23d Malatesta, the
Salimbeni, and the people engaged the nobles, and after
a bloody fight drove them from the palace and the city.
Accordingly, the victory being in the main a popular one,
a government of twelve popolani was set up, wherein all
the various parties of the people were represented.   The
Noveschi secured three members, the Dodicini four, and
il popolo minuto, the hitherto excluded lowest ranks of
the people, five.   The Salimbeni, in reward of their
powerful aid, received a number of special concessions,
among others, six castles in the contado.   Of course
these fine folk had not played the traitor to their class
for nothing.   The upshot of the successful revolution
was that the people were again in control, three groups
thereof, but naturally no one group felt contented with
the share secured by itself.

Revolution 3.—On December 11th the popolo minuto
stormed the palace and put the Noveschi and the Dodicini out.   That left five of their own kind in office, to
which number they added ten, making a chief executive
of fifteen, all of a single political affiliation.   As the council, in coöperation with which the new executive carried
on the government, was called the Council of the
Riformatori (Reformers), the new party took the name
of *il monte dei Riformatori.*   That meant the creation
of a fourth monte, the earlier three being the Gentiluomini, the Noveschi, and the Dodicini.   Each one of
them, let us remember, had no political programme
other than is expressed by the simple predatory formula:
to the victors belong the spoils.

Revolution 4.—On December 16th (*apparently* on
the 16th, for the records of these days are inextricably

jumbled) the Council of the Riformatori resolved,
probably on account of risings of the Noveschi and the
Dodicini, to readmit these parties to office, but not in the
original proportion. The governing committee was
still to be fifteen, of whom eight must be Riformatori,
while four seats were conceded to the Dodicini, and
three to the Noveschi. Though it must strike us as
something of an innovation for a victorious party not
only to agree that rival parties had a right to live, but to
make a place for them at its side, let us not fail to note
that the Riformatori were careful to secure a clear preponderance to themselves. The exclusion of the nobility was of course maintained.

When after three months of perpetual disturbances
the new government, called the Fifteen, or, more usually,
the Riformatori, was installed in the palace, Charles IV
arrived in Siena. He entered the city on December 22,
1368. He had always kept up a special intimacy with
the Salimbeni, and the Salimbeni, at outs with their
own class, and in need, in the dangerous local game, of
allies, usually coöperated with the Dodicini. Charles's
friendly relation with the Salimbeni, at whose palace
he took up his residence, led to his undoing. He agreed
to help in an attempt to overthrow the Riformatori, and
on January 18, 1369, the plot came to a head. Then
the people showed some of their ancient quality. In a
fierce battle for the possession of the Campo, Charles's
knights were beaten back and broken by the almost
unanimous forces of the citizens, who hurriedly patched
up their local differences in the face of an attack on their
independence by a foreign usurper. At nightfall the
emperor found himself shut up as a prisoner in the

houses of the Salimbeni. On being visited by the victorious rulers he showed the stuff he was made of. He
sobbed, wept, threw his arms about every one who came
within reach, protesting—as was probably true—that he
was the victim of the misrepresentations of the Salimbeni
and the Dodicini. He was ready for any concession.
The Riformatori had his notary draw up an imperial
privilege, nominating them vicars of the empire, and not
without scorn, we may believe, permitted him to withdraw from the city. Charles's terror, great as it was,
did not so get the better of his greed as to induce him to
forget to ask for the usual compensation accompanying
a diploma which emanated from his chancellery.

This event, particularly interesting in showing that
the civic spirit had not yet been entirely killed by the
frenzy of party, made only a passing impression on the
life of the city. The Riformatori hopefully tried to take
advantage of the momentary outburst of patriotism in
order to heal the local schisms. They commanded
(January 31, 1369) a solemn mass of peace (*messa della
pace*) in the cathedral to be attended by Noveschi,
Dodicini, and Riformatori, that is, all the popular parties,
on the conclusion of which they should make peace with
one another and promise to be loyal to the existing
government. The Fifteen had already attempted to
replace the odious party designations with new and more
honorable terms, which recognized the tie of civic
brotherhood: the Noveschi were to be called *popolo del
piccolo numero* (People of the small following), the
Dodicini, *popolo del numero medio* (People of the moderate following), and the Riformatori, *popolo del maggior
numero* (People of the largest following)—all to no

effect. True, the Riformatori showed a greater liberality than their predecessors by admitting Noveschi and
Dodicini to office along with themselves, but by setting
up a machinery which planned to secure their permanent control of power, they showed that they were devoted to an undemocratic principle which could not
possibly serve as the seed of the modern state.

The Riformatori held the helm for seventeen years
(from 1368 to 1385) in the midst of a situation which
grew not better, but seemed daily to grow worse. The
companies of adventure continued to molest the countryside. Famine and famine prices were added to the now
permanent industrial depression. In 1371 the starving
woolen workers of the quarter of Ovile rose and partially overthrew the government; thereupon the Salimbeni and the Dodicini, falling on them at an unexpected
moment, took revenge by a terrible massacre of these
poor wretches. Crimes were of daily occurrence, and
men grew brutalized by the chronic disorder to the point
of taking delight in intolerable cruelties. What are we
to think of a civilization which suffered its criminals to
be torn to pieces with red-hot pincers while bound upon
a cart moving along the street at a walking pace?*
Small wonder that the good chronicler waxes despond-
ent. He can account for the wickedness of the time
only by the operation of occult influences:†

"At this time there reigned in the world a planet which had
these effects: The brothers of S. Augustine fell upon their provin-

---

* Muratori, XV, 250 B (1377). However, this punishment was not
peculiar to Siena, but common to the criminal justice of the Middle Age.
See Molmenti, "Venice," Part II, Vol. I, 39.
† Muratori, XV, 238 B (1373).

cial with knives and killed him. . . . At Assisi the Brothers Minor
fell to quarreling and butchered some fourteen of their number.
Everywhere in the world apparently there were dissensions and
bloody encounters innumerable, which I mention not for very
shame. In Siena no man understood or kept faith: the Gentiluomini kept it neither among themselves nor with others; the Noveschi neither among themselves nor with others; the Dodicini
neither among themselves nor with others; and the Riformatori,
to wit, those that ruled, neither with one another nor with others
in any perfect wise. And so the world is all one darkness."

And so the world is all one darkness! The cry, we
may note in passing, of some chronicler at almost every
period of the Middle Age.

In the year 1385 the Riformatori were overthrown
and another government formed which, excluding them,
was composed of Noveschi, Dodicini, and another party
organized from a social stratum still lower than the
Riformatori, and called for short *Il Popolo*. Naturally
this group formed a new monte, *il monte del Popolo*,
the fifth, and we are relieved to find, the last in the
distraught political history of Siena. There is no profit
in following the tale further. Henceforth no one
monte dreamt of being able to exclude all the others,
but each plotted to get improved terms for itself, entering
into alliances which shifted as the interest of the moment
dictated. Never in old Hellas was there a more self-
ensnarled city than Siena, and as in Hellas, the only
remedy for a state which could not compose its quarrels
became the tyrant. Men being men, which is to say,
when their passions are aroused, not far above beasts of
the forest, the tyrant was the only conceivable door
through which mediæval society could pass to the realiz-

The Palazzo Piccolomini

ation of democratic justice and equality. With matters
at this pass the chief regret must be that the tyrant so
long delayed his arrival.

This hurried review of the political movements of
the fourteenth century has omitted or blurred the
numberless details which enter into each particular situation. To some factors I have not given sufficient prominence, others I have passed over with silence. I venture to hope that I have at least made clear why the
Sienese people, though haunted by democratic longings,
never succeeded in establishing an effective democracy.
But the disheartening evolution, which we have followed
to a kind of political stale-mate, cannot be explained
entirely by the furious party spirit, or by the fickleness,
the excitability, and the other defects of the Sienese
temper. There is another cause which must at least
be mentioned in this connection. I have already pointed
out the intimate relations which necessarily existed
from the first between the political movements in the
city and its economic development. Now, economically,
Siena fell into a sad decline in the fourteenth century.
If, during the first decades of that century, at the height
of the power of the merchants, industry and commerce
continued, in the main, to grow, they certainly did not
advance at anything like the pace maintained by
neighboring Florence. As a money centre, in which
capacity we found Siena enjoying preëminence and
harvesting wealth about the year 1250, the town had
fallen into the background. The popes from the period
of Montaperti gave preference to the Florentine bankers,
until in 1309 they dropped suddenly and entirely out of
the Italian financial world by deserting Rome and es-

tablishing their residence across the Alps in far-away Avignon. However, this withdrawal of the papal moneys from Sienese hands was not in itself an irreparable blow, for truth to tell the pontiffs were already completely superseded as a factor in the financial world by the great merchants. These had captained the vast movement of commercial expansion, which showed a splendid energy especially early in the fourteenth century, and which more than the revival of learning, the religious unrest, and all other causes whatsoever, impressed the modern stamp upon the European world. Of the new system of capitalistic production, created by the quickened pace of industry and commerce, Florence became the undisputed head. Absolutely, the resources of Siena continued to grow, but, relatively, the increase was insignificant, compared with that of Florence, Genoa, Venice, and a dozen other centres, more favorably planted along the great international highways. The town, regarded from the economic point of view, did not perish, but it was left behind in the race.

Hand in hand with the decline in banking and commerce went the decline in industry. In spite of the difficulties experienced by the wool-guild, difficulties, it may be remembered, springing largely from the lack of water, the manufacture of woolens continued in the fourteenth century to be a considerable source of wealth and to give employment to many workers. The proletariat of this industry, concentrated largely in the quarter of Ovile, numbered several thousands. In the recurrent periods of industrial depression or in time of high bread prices, their condition must have been terrible. That they organized in 1371 and sought redress by violence proves that they were growing desperate; decimated for their pains by a cowardly massacre conducted by the Salimbeni and the Dodicini, they and other workingmen of a too independent leaning were, on the fall of the Riformatori (1385), expelled, to the number of four thousand, from the city.* This almost ludicrous act of party fury may be taken to mark the end in Siena of capitalistic production on a large scale. To be sure, almost every known craft continued to be represented on the roster of the city's activities, but they were all conducted, in prevailing degree at least, under the system of private or individual production, characteristic of a backward industrial community.

In the decline of Siena the fortunes of the contado had a considerable share, for an uninterrupted chain of wars, risings, and deeds of petty lawlessness gravely affected agricultural production. A leading source of trouble in the countryside was ever the nobility. Siena had to pay a terrible price for being able neither to destroy nor to assimilate this class. From the hills, where their castles were situated, they could always harry the burghers at will, and though beaten again and again, were not, till considerably after the period which we are glancing at, definitely reduced to order. If Siena had become really industrialized, the organized power of the citizens would have irresistibly swept the nobles from their points of vantage; that is what came to pass in happier Florence. Add to the difficulties associated

---

* Even the chronicler cannot refrain from crying out upon this folly: "E io scrittore, che non so' di' Riformatori, giudicai essere mal fatto, perche si guastò e disfece la città di Siena, che in più volte furno cacciate più di quattro mila buoni artigiani Cittadini della città, che non ne torno mai el sesto." Muratori, XV, 294.

with the nobles the raids of the companies of adventure
which, throughout the second half of the fourteenth
century, killed peasants, burned farmsteads, drove off
the herds of sheep, goats, and cattle, and we shall understand that the troubles of agriculture were no less grave
than those of manufacture, and that their interaction
must have affected disastrously the material welfare
of every man, woman, and child of the town's jurisdiction. So much for the affairs of the contado at this
point; in the following chapter I shall attempt to develop
a connected picture of them.

In view of facts such as these, the opinion is untenable
that Siena owed her decline to her political ills. She
owed it to these ills in association with a score of economic
factors, glanced at in the above analysis.* In any
case she declined, not absolutely, let me remark again,
but relatively, and steered her course to that haven of
provincialism, where happily or regrettably, according
to the reader's point of view, she has ridden at anchor
to this day.

* A programme of reforms, drawn up in 1382 by a special commission,
unfolds a most cheerless picture of the city's finances. A government's
finances are, let us remember, an excellent indication of its general state of
health. The monthly expenses surpassed by 4,000 florins the monthly
revenues and the city was heavily in debt. The report is a cry of despair.
It has been published by Lisini, "Provvedimenti Economici della Repubblica
di Siena nel 1382."

CHAPTER VIII

THE SIENESE CONTADO

THE intimate relation subsisting between Siena and its contado makes it desirable to give special attention to some of the problems and conditions of the wide region around the walls. We have seen how the rising commune reached out to control the great highways, and how its action not only led to a clash with the feudal lords established along their course, but was also at the bottom of the rivalry with Florence and other city neighbors, moved by a similar ambition. While I have traced the general march of affairs, showing the gradual subjugation of the Soarzi, Cacciaconti, Ardengheschi, and other noble houses to the young commune, and while I have followed the wars with Florence over Poggibonsi, Montepulciano and other provincial points of vantage, I have not examined the country for its own sake. I purpose to do that now, starting with the period of the potestà, when the feudal lords, although still powerful, were beginning to show the effects of the long battering to which they had been exposed in the era of the consuls.

In the course of the thirteenth century the great families of the contado were broken up, and, with few exceptions, vanished from the scene. A handful had the good fortune or rather the intellectual elasticity to adjust themselves to the new conditions. Thus one line

of the many-branched Cacciaconti moved to Siena, took
up a mercantile career, and conducted successful
financial operations on the fairs of Champagne.   After
a generation it was probably indistinguishable from the
city nobility, which, of course, readily admitted wealthy
newcomers of approved station into its ranks.   However, in general, the feudal lords, perplexed by the urban
movement and hindered by it in the exercise of their
accustomed liberties, hated it with all the vigor of a
whole-hearted prejudice.   Over such obdurate noblemen time passed pitilessly with its iron car.   When
they were not sought out on their hill-tops by the
burgher host, which piled their ruined castles over them
for a monument, they fell victims to the new civilization
in a more insidious manner.   In some cases they would
enter into an engagement with the city with regard to
one or another of their castles, and when they failed to
observe the terms of the treaty, the municipal authorities
would seize the forfeited property.   Or, fond of display,
and persuaded that their station obliged them to parade
a new war horse or a suit of sables, they would make a
light-hearted loan of a prosperous banker, who presently
placed a bailiff in the court-yard.   One authentic
example, showing how poverty waited upon grandeur,
may serve in place of further explanation.   In the year
1296 we find a curious entry in the city account books:
"item, three lire for a cloak given to Nicholas, count of
Rocca di Tintinnano, *causa paupertatis*"—by reason of
his poverty! *   And two years later the gift is repeated,
and with a fine regard for a gentleman's necessities, a
pair of boots thrown in.   The Rocca di Tintinnano,

* Archivio di Stato.   I Libri della Biccherna, 1296.   Uscite c. 233.

rising high over the via francigena at the point where
the great road crossed the river Orcia, was a position of
inestimable advantage.   Toward the middle of the
thirteenth century the counts, harassed by debts, sold
it to Siena,* and before the century had drawn to a close,
a decayed but authentic descendant, the above Nicholas,
scraped his thanks to the Signori Nove for the gift of a
cloak.   A pathetic evolution this, probably not untypical
of the fortunes of the landed gentry after the grinding
process, to which the old order was subjected by the rise
of new classes, had continued for a few generations.

If, in the course of the thirteenth century, the original
feudal masters of the contado almost disappeared, a
partial exception to this general decline is to be noted
in the case of the most powerful of all the great families,
the Aldobrandeschi.   Their distance from Siena and the
vastness of their territory, as well as its wild, inaccessible
character, explain why they were able to maintain
themselves somewhat longer than others of their kind.
When, as has been recounted, Siena in the year 1224
seized the town of Grosseto, she got a foothold at a
point of vantage, from which she could gradually work
her way toward the baronial strongholds in the scarped
and wooded Monte Amiata region.   As late, however, as
the time of the Nine, the great Maremma counts, who
had meanwhile split into the two branches of Santa
Fiora and Pitigliano, continued to make occasional
trouble for Siena,† but treaties of alliance, shrewdly
transformed by the grasping burghers into treaties of
subjection, ended by absorbing the Aldobrandeschi
estates into the dominion of the Republic.   When, in

* Bull. Sen, III, p. 327.   † See chap. 7, p. 203.

the early fifteenth century, the last male of the family died, the fortunes of the house had sunk so low that the event hardly attracted the notice of contemporaries. For the student of Italian feudalism, above all on its social side, it would be difficult to find a more engaging field of inquiry than the rise and decline of the great clan of the Aldobrandeschi.*

While the burghers inhabiting such great commonwealths as Florence and Siena are chiefly responsible for the overthrow of the feudal nobility in Tuscany, another social element, to which I desire now to call attention, contributed in no mean manner to the passing of the order. I am referring to the peasantry, who, though poor and down-trodden, were none the less deeply affected by the passion for civil liberty marking the twelfth century and culminating in the establishment of self-governing consuls in all the Italian towns. The simple fact is that the breath of freedom wafted abroad waked even the most remote agricultural districts to new life. It may prove interesting to inquire a little more particularly just what changes this liberating movement brought about, first, in the relation of the lords to their peasants, and, second, in the general level of comfort and dignity maintained by the humble tillers of the soil.

Originally, wherever feudalism held sway, the country folk were largely serfs who cultivated their lands under a system of tenure, obliging them to pay

* Such a social-political study as I have in mind has never been undertaken, though much material dealing with the Aldobrandeschi fortunes has been diligently collected. See Berlinghieri, "Notizie degli Aldobrandeschi"; Milanesi, "Periodico di Numismatica," Vol. I (1868), p. 110 ff.; Repetti, "Dizionario geografico," Appendice, chap. 12; Davidsohn, "Forschungen zur Geschichte von Florenz," Vol. I, p. 94; and numerous notices (*passim*) in "Bull. Sen." and "Mis. Stor. Sen."

The Ancona

By Duccio (in the Opera del Duomo)

certain customary dues, in the form of personal services, farm products, or money to their lords. It lay in the haphazard nature of the feudal bond—to dignify it with the name of the feudal system is an act of excessive courtesy—that these dues varied greatly from province to province, often from neighbor to neighbor. The lord dwelt in a fortified castle, wherein, however, his dependents were not without rights, for they stored their grain and wine within its walls. Davidsohn, writing of the Arno valley,* has shown how this common interest in a central stronghold gradually led to definite agreements between the lords and the agricultural population, and how these agreements exhibit a steady improvement in the social and economic status of the peasantry. It is with distinct surprise that the student, accustomed to think of the feudal age as one of unlimited petty tyrany, will learn that by the twelfth century the peasants, usually grouped together in a village at the foot of a castle, had generally acquired an appreciable measure of self-government. For the Sienese contado the proofs of this advance are numerous. We have heard of the Rocca di Tintinnano whose impoverished count, shortly before the year 1300, had become a pensioner of Siena. In 1207, when the needy Nicholas's ancestors still breathed the free air of the Orcia valley, they conceded—hardly of their own will, we may opine —a *carta libertatis* † to the villagers. This instrument recognized a consul of the community of peasants, who exercised certain functions of government and received

* Geschichte von Florenz, chap. 8.
† Published, with valuable comment, by Zdekauer, "Bull, Sen.," III, p. 327 ff.

a certain share of the dues, while a second consul, representing the lords, received the remaining and more considerable part of the imposts. Although the continued exploitation of the peasants appears unquestionably from this document, the weighty fact remains that the counts came to terms with their dependents, and that the conceded charter was, if not a guarantee of absolute justice, at least a check upon unlimited abuse. And what happened at Rocca was duplicated at about the same time in the hundreds of *castelli* and *borghi* which, like giants in ambush, lay hidden among the woods and hills of the Sienese contado.* Must we infer that humanitarian principles were beginning to make their way among the landholders, possibly through the teaching of the church? Certainly not. The growth of the cities in the twelfth century reacted favorably on the country, higher food prices prevailed, and the peasants necessarily benefited from the general prosperity. When to the economic advance was joined the spirit of liberty emanating from the great communes, the peasants irresistibly forced a reduction of the feudal services and their admission to a part-control of whatever was common to themselves and their masters. By the middle of the thirteenth century the grip of feudalism upon the lives of its agricultural dependents was visibly relaxing.

At the very time when the lords were confronted with

---

* See on this point Zdekauer "Sugli Statuti del Monte Amiata (1212–1451)," published in Studi Guiridici Dedicati a F. Schupfer, Torino, 1898. In this article Zdekauer, examining a half dozen little communities subject to the abbot of S. Salvatore of Monte Amiata shows (1) their political restlessness, and (2) their steady wrenching of self-governing rights from an unwilling master.

the danger of a peasant agitation, they were obliged to
meet, as we know, an attack from another side—from the
side of the commune of Siena determined to extend its
political territory. In this struggle the burghers were
successful, adopting in general toward the defeated
barons the following procedure: At first they were
content with a rather vague "submission" of the feudal
owners of the soil, taking the form of a tribute to the
Virgin on the occasion of her Mid-August festival; but,
presently, discovering that such a relation did not sufficiently bind the unruly lords to the city, they tried, either
by purchase or conquest, to detach the ancient masters
entirely from their possessions. To refer again, for
purposes of illustration, to the now familiar Rocca di
Tintinnano, we find that Siena, after experimenting
with the loyalty of the owners, bought them out fully
and completely in the year 1250, and obliged them to
remove from their hereditary seat. The step involved
the extension of the municipal administration to the
appropriated district. Accordingly, the city placed a
paid official, called *castellano*, in the Rocca, and of
course followed the same plan with regard to other
strongholds seized under similar conditions. A castellano, while exercising, in the name of the commune,
all the rights of his feudal predecessor, might be supposed to foster and strengthen the self-governing institutions developed by the peasants who dwelt at the
castle's foot. The evolution thus effected from feudal
to burgher rule promised the villages a fair share in the
golden future of Siena.

Unfortunately, however, this promising development
was choked while it was yet in the bud. Siena was

playing, in the thirteenth century, a big political game of the kind we now designate as world-politics. The prime requirement for world-politics then as now is money. The fiscal needs of the city in the prolonged Tuscan turmoil were very great, and brought with them not only increasing taxes, but also loans at usurious and often ruinous rates. The loan money was supplied by the great merchant houses, the Tolomei, the Salimbeni, the Buonsignori and the rest, who, beginning with the practice of taking in pledge the communal property, and more particularly the conquered feudal castles of the contado, ended by assuming full rights in the mortgaged possessions. What was the result? Toward the year 1300 the original country nobility had been largely replaced in its ancient strongholds by the newer city nobility, who, after the manner of upstarts, insisted jealously on all the rights that went with their titles, and who, in their capacity of absentee landlords, were less cordially united with the peasantry than the vanished masters. Thus the Rocca di Tintinnano, repeatedly referred to, received a charter of liberty from its feudal masters in 1207, and saw them take their definitive departure in 1250, when Siena acquired all their rights for a round sum; a generation later, in 1274, the Rocca was in the hands of the Salimbeni, probably as payment for financial help extended during the recent war with Florence. Innumerable are the examples showing that this devolution from baron to banker denoted a typical process throughout the country. I cite only one more case, that of San Giovanni d'Asso, an important castle to the east, not far from Asciano.* Its feudal masters were the

* "Misc. Stor. Sen.," II, p. 90.

great counts Forteguerri, who as early as 1151 mortgaged it to Siena—the usual financial preliminary to
political disaster. Accordingly, in 1208, we find the
Forteguerri out and Siena in; but not for long, for in
1256 we learn that San Giovanni d'Asso has passed into
the hands of the Buonsignori, there to remain till that
famous banking house went into liquidation; finally, in
1303, the Salimbeni, presumably owing to a forced sale,
took possession. Can we want a better example of
how the state made over its assets to the money-lenders
who financed its political ambitions, thereby thoughtlessly creating a second country nobility on the ruins of
the older baronage destroyed by the sword ?

Thus did the city, after holding out to the peasant
communities for one radiant moment the delusive hope
of liberty, yield to its cruel needs and thrust the villages back into their old dependence. World-politics,
I say, with their inevitable bill for military glory.
To this feature of the hard lot of the struggling
peasantry should be added as a factor of at least equal
importance, the economic selfishness which has always
characterized city-states in their treatment of subject
populations. In distributing the taxes urban rulers
have rarely scrupled to lighten their own burdens at the
expense of their agricultural clients. At Siena the great
preoccupation of the various governments—the Twenty-
four, the Nine, the Twelve and so forth—was cheap
food for the dwellers within the walls, no matter what
violence had to be done to achieve the result. Cheap
food would help keep the urban masses quiet, besides
making it possible for the manufacturing interests, with
which the life of the city was bound up, to pay low

wages. Therefore mediæval Siena always followed a
policy of most arbitrary interference with the laws of
exchange. To send breadstuffs across the boundary to
Florence or other centres was rigorously forbidden.
Producers had to market their harvests in Siena in the
hope that a continued abundance would depress prices;
and if the prices did rise, as they would in years of poor
crops, the city governors made sure that the growers
received no benefit from the circumstance by fixing a
maximum price for all leading articles. To hinder
monopolization—really a very constant peril in an
artificially limited market—an elaborate legislation was
formulated with the object of eliminating the middleman
and transferring the necessities of life directly from the
producer to the consumer. All such manipulation of
the natural processes of exchange must strike us as the
height of folly as well as of injustice, unless we keep
before our minds that in the Middle Age we are dealing
not with the vast national agglomerations of to-day but
with small urban units, and that the victorious burgher,
devoted passionately to his particular commune, made
everything else subservient to its interests as these
defined themselves to his understanding.*

Nor does this complete the tale of the oppression

* The policy of the artificial control of the food market, imposed by the
bourgeoisie, grew more rigorous in measure as the people drove the nobility
from power. At first, therefore, the *divieto* or prohibition to export agricultural products was exceptional. By the time of the Constitution of the
year 1262 the divieto had already become more or less permanent (Dist., I,
24), but full and comprehensive legislation on the subject was reserved to
the Nine (Statuto del Divieto del 1300 in the Arch. di Stato). See on this
question Salvemini, Magnati e Popolari in Firenze, pp. 47–50, and Caggese,
Siena e il suo Contado, Bull. Sen., XIII. See further on the whole economic
issue, Mengozzi, La charta Bannorum etc., Bull. Sen., XIII, 381 *ff.*, and
Lisini, Provvedimenti Economici della R. di Siena nel 1382.

practised by the city against the country population. In addition to the above burdens resting on the free exchange of farm products and constituting a series of indirect imposts, a direct sum was assessed annually on every country community, while a tariff on all manufactures imported into Sienese territory increased the price within the district of shoes, clothing, and agricultural implements. In the face of such a policy, there can be left room in no one's mind for doubt touching the reckless exploitation of the country folk whom fate had delivered into the city's hands. The sad truth is that in the fourteenth century the village communities, which in the previous century had been visibly prospering, were slowly sapped of their vitality and the villagers themselves reduced to desperation. A recent student * is right when he describes the town as a tree fed by roots which radiated over the contado, and as flourishing by relentlessly consuming the soil. The patent inference is that although the tree might thrive apparently by systematically exhausting the ground which nourished it, in the long run it only prepared its own destruction.

As if this economic policy, built on false assumptions and inspired by the sole consideration of urban necessities, were not enough to reduce the country to a condition of profound prostration, a veritable rain of additional afflictions fell upon the poor peasantry. We are familiar with the insecurity of life and property prevailing in the feudal age, but this insecurity was not removed by the victory of the commune. If anything, the fourteenth century makes a more chaotic impression

* Caggese, Bull. Sen., XIII, p. 73.

than its predecessor, for to feudal violence, become a confirmed habit, was added the terrible curse of the companies of adventure.

If we would form an adequate idea of the disturbances to which country life was exposed during the Middle Age, we must not limit our view to the private feuds among the nobility or to the wars between the nobility and the towns. As a matter of fact the feudal habit of putting even the most trifling differences to the decision of the sword possessed all classes of society alike, and would continue to possess them until the state had acquired sufficient strength to enforce respect for the slow processes of law. The familiar form of rural disturbance was indeed associated with the nobility, who carried on vendettas in their own ranks, or plotted against the ambitious commune, or, falling on some defenceless abbot, appropriated his lands; but other social classes or political entities, as, for instance, the village communities, occasionally contributed to the confusion. To present a case in point, the little *borgo* of Castiglione, in that lively storm centre, the Val d'Orcia, looked with unconcealed hatred upon the monastery of Vivo because of a dispute about the use of certain meadows. In 1328 the Castiglionesi to the number of two hundred suddenly fell on the monastery, raised their banner over its campanile, pricked* with their swords and lances, evidently in the spirit of rude horse-play, Frate Ranieri, who was celebrating the Mass, robbed the furniture and cattle, devastated the fields, in short,

* *Ponteggiaverunt* is the excellent word of the original declaration. See Bull. Sen., X, p. 44. Article by Bandi, I Castelli della Val d'Orcia. This article, together with those by the same author in Vol. IX, gives a good idea of the troublous life in the Sienese wilds.

conducted themselves in a manner entirely worthy of their aristocratic exemplars.

Public opinion rather approved than condemned such actions, provided they were carried through with boldness and success. Grown-up men, much like school-boys of our own time romantically excited by tales of frontier heroism, even entertained an open admiration for a courageous highwayman. A civil spirit, like Dante, might condemn these gentry, "che fecero alle strade tanta guerra,"* and might consign them to nameless horrors in hell, but the average man, used to violence, practising it himself, made light of their crimes. One of the worst of this pestiferous tribe, operating, in the period of the Nine, in the Monte Amiata region, was Ghino di Tacco. What Dante with his inflexible standards of right and wrong thought of Ghino and his likes I have stated, but I suspect that not Dante but Benvenuto da Imola, one of the poet's earliest commentators, reflects the true contemporary sentiment about Ghino when, at the mention of his name, he bursts into nothing less than lyric encomium, calling him "vir mirabilis, magnus, membrutus, . . . fortissimus . . . prudens et largus."† Although Ghino, as is amusingly confirmed by a story of Boccacio,‡ may have been a gentlemanly robber, he hardly deserves an epitaph which would honor the shade of a Miltiades or a George Washington.

Nevertheless the exploits of the Castiglionesi and the violences of Ghino di Tacco represent minor troubles of the contado which would not have persisted long, if they

---

* Inf., XII, p. 138. † Bull. Sen., X, p. 37 (note).
‡ Il Decamerone, Giornata Decima, II.

had not flourished under the shelter of the turbulent conditions created by the perennial wars of the nobles among themselves and with Siena. Of these wars I have already said enough to make it unnecessary to add, at this point, more than a few details. We have seen by what degrees, and owing to what policy on the part of the commune, the city nobility came, at least in large part, into possession of the castles of the original feudatories. With the transfer of their interests from the town to the country the Tolomei and their compeers, although they did not immediately drop their mercantile connections, began to assume more and more the habits of the class which they succeeded. The unfortunate fact that, from the year 1277 on, they were the victims of manifest injustice by being excluded from the government of their native city, made them more prone than ever to plots and violence. Their exclusion, it may be remembered, was the consequence of the Guelph-Ghibelline feuds among them, which they insisted on fighting out in the streets, regardless of the security of the common people tranquilly going about their business. But these givers and takers of hard blows clashed not only in the city but also in the country; preferably, indeed, in the country because there they were much less likely to be interfered with. The signal victory of the Guelph party in Siena, as well as in all Tuscany, should logically have put an end to the Guelph-Ghibelline animosities. But such was the bitterness of faction and the devotion to the spirit of vendetta that the local noble feuds continued to shake the city long after the emperor's power was broken. Among the family quarrels of Siena the vicious warfare between the Tolomei and the Salimbeni easily overshadowed all the rest. The quarrel of these great houses continued, interrupted by frequent spectacular reconciliations emphasized with false oaths before the altar, throughout the period of the Nine, to be replaced in its turn by one of the strangest wars recorded in the annals of a free community.

In narrating the overthrow of the Nine (1355) I showed that the Salimbeni once more came to the front politically, owing, in part, to their influence with the emperor, Charles IV, and, in part, to their alliance with the party group or monte, known as the Dodicini. During the disturbed period that followed, they succeeded by clever, unscrupulous tactics, in manœuvring themselves into a position from which they dominated the state almost at will. They had long, in return for money lent to the state, enjoyed the possession of many castles—among them La Ripa, Vignone, and the invaluable Rocca di Tintinnano—and in the year 1368, for services rendered to the cause of the people during that year, received in reward Castiglione d'Orcia, Mont' Orsaio, and other places, which, added to their earlier acquisitions, made them unquestioned masters in the Val d'Orcia and throughout the southern section of the contado. Encouraged to defy their native city which thus thoughtlessly elevated a single family at its own expense, they presently entertained the ambition of raising their possessions into an independent kingdom, in the ulterior hope, it was openly whispered, of acquiring the hereditary lordship of Siena itself. Such a project the republic had, of course, to repulse with vigor. A war ensued between Siena and its leading family, which, punctuated with truces and dishonest agreements, lasted half a century. Although the city was torn with the feuds of the monti, and the military position of the rebellious Salimbeni along the steep banks of the Orcia was almost impregnable, once alive to the issue, Siena had still sufficient resolution left to fight for its life, and, in the end, came out victorious. Its culminating triumph, the capture in 1418 of the Rocca di Tintinnano was accomplished by treason,* but as that was a weapon of warfare familiar to both sides, we have no occasion to feel that the city by the use of such means defiled its honor. With the Salimbeni decimated by the long struggle and their castles once more in the hands of the government, the inordinately extended reign of feudalism in the wooded Val d'Orcia was, after a struggle of three centuries, at last definitely broken.

To the reader, now sufficiently familiar with the excesses of mediæval warfare, there is no need of explaining how the long Salimbeni conflict devastated the Orcia valley. Contemplating this calamity in connection with all the other miseries with which the country was regularly visited, one marvels that the whole region was not depopulated by a unanimous migration. Verily, man is strong to endure, and the love of home passes understanding. For even now I am not at the end of my narrative of the afflictions of the contado. Worse in its sudden fury than any of the ills yet enumerated, though not so steadily recurrent as some of them, was the curse of the predatory companies. Throughout the second half of the fourteenth century this evil befell not only Siena and Tuscany, but all Italy. That a band of assassins, calling themselves soldiers, could, under an

* Malavolti, Historia di Siena, ad annum 1418.

The *Majestas*

By Simone Martini (in the Palazzo Pubblico)

audacious leader, march up and down the peninsula, levying contributions on popes, princes, and republics, is an eloquent comment on the helplessness of the Italian governments. Perpetual rivalries among neighbors added to the eternal domestic strife had so paralyzed the national will that it proved incapable of destroying a thieving pack of wolves, the enemies of everybody.

The origin of the companies of adventure is to be found in the evil custom of the Italian states of the fourteenth century of doing their fighting not with the local militias but with mercenaries, usually from beyond the Alps—Germans, Frenchmen, Hungarians, and English. The national army of Siena, created in the consular era, still existed and was occasionally called out for service, but, as a sort of parliament of the people, it was distrusted by the ruling clique, and, furthermore, in the matter of efficiency could not match itself with a corps of trained, professional soldiers. That these mercenaries, on being dismissed at the termination of a war for which they had been engaged, should have bethought themselves to take advantage of the impotent but wealthy governments of Italy, is not strange.* The initial act of audacity, as far as Siena is concerned, was committed by a German leader, Werner von Urslingen, when, in 1342, the republic of Pisa cancelled his engagement. He avowed with the frankness and emphatic rhetoric characteristic of his craft, his freebooter's point of view by the inscription on his breastplate: *Enemy of God, of Pity, and of Mercy.* Such men can be tamed only with cold steel. Siena—it was the time of the Nine—offered him money, some twenty-

* Professione, Siena e le Compagnie di Ventura.

five hundred florins, with the request to go away and cease from further troubling honest folk.* Equally successful throughout Tuscany, Werner made his way northward and crossed the Alps, trailing behind him an immense booty.

Such success was sure to create imitators. Hardly ten years had passed, when the company of a Provençal, called Fra Moriale, descended on the Sienese and plundered at will, pending the agreement concerning their gratuity (1354). The Nine bought poison—no less, we hear, than one hundred and thirty-five pounds of it!—to mix in the enemy's food, which ingenious substitute for fighting failing in its effect, they weakly paid their tormentors a large sum of gold florins.† Money again, food also—everything except forged iron, the only coin of courage! And now the gates were open, and the floods devastated Tuscany with unchecked fury. We hear of the company of Count Lando, of that of Anichino, of the White Company, the Company of the Hat, the Company of the Star, of a succession of mercenary hosts with each one of which is associated a monotonous tale of murder, rapine, and conflagration. For more than a generation this pest afflicted the Sienese state, sometimes raging once every few years, occasionally several times in one year. And the Sienese, cringing behind their impregnable walls, always paid, always, with one exception, due to the fact that the leader—it was the captain of the Breton Company of the Hat—did not want money but territory. At the end of his patience and against the express orders of the Signori

---

* Muratori, XV, "Cronica Sanese," 105, E.
† Muratori, XV, "Cronica Sanese," 141, D.

Dodici, the Sienese general, one of the Roman Orsini, fell upon the Bretons and signally defeated them (1363). It was an isolated act of manhood without further effect; for, eight months later, behold, in place of the Company of the Hat, the Company of the Star, which made itself at home in the country until persuaded to depart with a bribe of over fifty thousand *fiorini d'oro.** But even that huge sum was small compared with the money paid out to the famous commander, John Hawkwood, an Englishman, reputed to have laid his long fingers during his career on several hundred thousand florins of the Sienese exchequer. What wonder that Siena was reduced to terrible financial straits, made reckless loans, and put the tax screws on the subject population! Selfish as the burghers were, and cowardly as their behavior toward the blackguard scum of Europe looks to our eyes, they were neither without pity for the cruel harrying suffered by the undefended peasants, nor without the desire to save them from excessive taxes. But what could they do, themselves the victims of hard necessity?

Marshalling all these facts concerning the contado we are obliged to agree that Siena did not always deal righteously with her dependent territory nor prove herself the mother of bounty and felicity. It would almost seem that the town set itself a larger task than it could master. That task, historically stated, was to uproot

---

* The impression of pusillanimity made by the Dodici is completed when we read: "And the Sienese sent"—in addition, be it observed, to the money— "to Misser Anechino, Captain of the said Company, beautiful and rich presents, to wit, a magnificent horse with hangings, and much wax and sweets"—of which the Middle Age was very fond—"and well-aged wine, and corn and other things." Chronicle of Neri di Donato, Muratori, XV, 183, E.

feudalism and to extend to the country all the benefits
of the new civilization which the free communes had
evolved. Some towns, like Florence, succeeded in this
mission with comparative ease. Siena, because it commanded fewer resources than Florence, and because its
feudal adversaries were more numerous, more powerful,
and better protected by natural defenses than those of
the Arno city, did not bring the struggle to a close till the
fifteenth century. As an additional circumstance,
retarding the overthrow of the feudal agents, must not
be forgotten the necessity, under which Siena was, of
dividing her forces by defending herself against ambitious and encroaching city neighbors. If Siena had
been an island unthreatened by a foreign foe, we can
hardly doubt that feudalism would not have remained
ensconced for long in the fastnesses of the hills, however
inaccessible they may have been. But in spite of all
difficulties, in spite of the grinding of the peasants under
excessive taxes, in spite of the rise of a second giant
brood of feudalism after the first had been laid low, in
spite of the harrying of the fields by the companies of
adventure, early in the fifteenth century the city's purpose
was, in the main, attained and the country fused with
it under a government which, however imperfectly
democratic, was none the less an immense advance over
the political and social system designated by the name
of feudalism.

For this reason we may call the period from the first
vernal budding of communal freedom to the completed
conquest of the countryside the heroic period of Siena,
and single it out of the long life of the town for special
study. Compared with it, the periods which followed

were, as far as their political history is concerned, unsteady, bewildering, and even meaningless. Certainly they do not sound the clear, high note which we detect wherever life is hopeful and society adorns itself daily with some new work of civilization. The organizing and constructive activity of Siena, taken at least in any large sense, came to an end with the beginning of the fifteenth century. Henceforth we look in vain for any essentially new germs. As soon as the communes of Tuscany had conquered their respective contados, the next step in the political evolution plainly was the fusion of the communes into a provincial unity; Tuscany, Lombardy, Umbria and the rest, once unified, might then have proceeded to constitute the larger unity of the Italian nation. But this indispensable work the communes proved themselves incapable of carrying to a successful issue. We have heard something of their rivalries and hatreds and have received a lively impression of the persistence of the stupid prejudices which divided them. The upshot of fruitless quarrelling was that the communes were driven into a blind alley and like every man or society without a clear purpose, presently began, in varying degree, to stagnate; which process, long resisted by the splendid vigor and elasticity of the Italian mind, engaged just then in culling the fruits of the Renaissance, gradually but ineluctably paralyzed the multifold energies of the peninsula. Italy, cursed with political impotence, was a doomed land. A chapter of that doom, to which I shall return, is entitled the Twilight of Siena.

CHAPTER IX

THE RELIGIOUS SPIRIT AND SAINT CATHERINE

IN an earlier chapter I took occasion to show that the official church, though an intensely popular and a by no means inelastic institution, was not always able to satisfy the extraordinary religious passion of the Middle Age. Whenever this passion inflamed large groups of men and women to devote themselves to the quiet contemplation of the goodness of God or to the active service of the sick and outcast, the church had no great difficulty in retaining the allegiance of her over-zealous subjects by organizing them in monastic societies. As outlets provided to relieve the periodically mounting floods of fervor, the companies of monks, nuns, and friars rendered an incalculable service to established religion. But time and again the waters burst all bounds, and the church, a majestic edifice with far-flung buttresses of stone, suddenly found itself enveloped by a raging stream, while the agitated occupants sustained their spirits with the knowledge that such violent crises had occurred before, without further consequences than the deposit of a heap of unsightly wreckage along the track of the torrent. A common enough spectacle throughout the whole Middle Age it was to see bands of excited seekers of salvation infest the highways of the land, lacerating their flesh with brandished thongs, singing lauds or chanting dirges, according to their mood, and summoning the world to repentance. Let him who has any curiosity on this subject turn to that most direct and communicative of all mediæval documents, the chronicle of Brother Salimbene. What a record of processions, extravagances, miracles, and pious frauds, constituting, in the eyes of the average modern reader, a chapter of unmixed midsummer madness! Salimbene was a boy of twelve, residing in his native Parma, when a revival struck northern Italy with the vehemence of an earthquake. Peasants left their ploughs to listen to song and sermon, burghers folded their ledgers and proclaimed a truce to party fury, nobles, divided by inherited feuds, embraced amidst tears; for, says Salimbene, "no wrath was left among them, no trouble or hatred; they had drunk of the wine of the sweetness of God's spirit, whereof if a man drink, flesh hath no more savor for him."* Men called this revival, conducted apparently on an unprecedented scale, the *Alleluia*, and during the few weeks of the year 1233, while it lasted, it made our sordid earth seem a thing radiant and immaterial in the eyes of hundreds of thousands of human beings.

Such elemental movements can only be explained on the ground that the mediæval period conceded to religion a larger share in life than our time is inclined to do. On account of this unchecked indulgence in religious emotion we frequently designate the departed centuries as the Age of Faith, and a group of romanticists among us never ceases to regret that our scientific pursuits have provided us with a set of inhibitions which lay a crushing burden on enthusiasm. These fond dreamers very

* Coulton, "From Saint Francis to Dante," p. 21.

generally owe their views to a deliberate concentration
of attention upon a single aspect of mediæval Christianity. They see the sublime self-oblivion, induced by a
surrender of the individual to the will of God, but they
do not see, or, having seen, wilfully ignore those many
sinister phenomena which, though by no means an
essential part of Christianity, are none the less associated
with the mediæval practice of religion and with its ready
exaltation of passion over reason. The revolting
cruelty of the time, for instance—where is its ultimate
root to be found but in the habit of yielding to every
impulse, noble or ignoble ? Leaving entirely out of consideration the horrors practised under the name of warfare, we are aware that monstrous excesses, closely
resembling those of the battlefield, were common occurrences in the domestic life of every Italian community.
Let the reader recall such an act as that of the year 1371,
when the Dodicini and their friends, the Salimbeni,
wantonly exterminated the poor wool-carders of the
Compagnia del Bruco.* Or let him weigh the significance of such a cold item as the following in an inventory
of public property taken in the fifteenth century: "a
knife for quartering men *at the window of the Martin-
ella,*" that is, at a window of the Palazzo Pubblico
where all the town could participate in the awful
mutilation perpetrated under the name of justice; and
further, "two pairs of pincers for tearing the flesh from
men *at the said window.*"† It would not be difficult to
collect evidence on this point filling many volumes.
The nameless sufferings of Dante's Inferno, far from

* Chapter 7, p. 223.
† Paoli, "Libro di Montaperti," p. XLIIII, (note).

being a pure invention of the poet, were only too often the truthful transcript of an experienced horror which had seared itself upon his memory. Is there anything even in Dante more blood-curdling than the following trait reported of Ezzelino, lord of Treviso: "On a certain day he caused 11,000 men of Padua to be burnt in the field of St. George in the city of Verona; and when fire was set to the place in which they were confined, he jousted around them with his knights as if in sport."* Dante belonged to the next generation after Ezzelino, but often in his youth must have heard old men recount this and a score of similar tales about the unbridled despot.

But let us guard against too strong an emphasis of this aspect of the time—a proceeding which would be quite as reprehensible as the practice of the romanticists of viewing the past exclusively in the rosy light shed by some unreflecting act of love and sacrifice. Let us rather be content to observe that the sharp contrasts existed everywhere—acts of burning devotion flourishing by the side of senseless deeds of violence—and that these contrasts are not only a memorable characteristic of the age but an inevitable consequence of its peculiar evaluation of the elements of conduct. The mediæval period consistently magnified the emotions at the expense of reason which it belittled and decried. The Nothing Too Much of ancient philosophy, extolling a perfect equilibrium of all the human faculties, was an

* Coulton, "From St. Francis to Dante," p. 115. Many authorities report the eating of human flesh by enraged adversaries. See Villani, "Cronica," XII, 17. "Ed ebbonvi de' si crudeli, e con furia si bestiale . . . che mangiarono delle loro carni crude." The author is speaking of the uprising of 1343.

abomination to a society which set above all else the primal satisfaction of the quickened pulse-beat, whether of love or hate. In this passion for excess, crystallized into a code of conduct, most of the social phenomena which fill our sober minds with amazement at the vanished past have their philosophic explanation.

If such a revival as the Alleluia of the year 1233 attracts our attention by reason of its magnitude and universality, other movements of lesser scope, avoiding the mobilization of great masses and aiming at some definite reform of society and the individual, achieved far more permanent results. Of these local actions, associated usually with the name of some visionary, not a town of Tuscany is so poor as not to boast a long succession; and of all the Tuscan towns none might venture to compare itself, in respect of prophets and religious leaders, with Siena. Doubtless the imaginative temper of the Sienese, coupled with their half-pagan sense of the perpetual nearness of celestial agents, rendered them peculiarly responsive to the influence of Roman Christianity. How else account for the long list of native sons and daughters who, to the admiration of a greater or lesser following, stirred the potent sentiments associated in the mediæval mind with God's wrath and man's depravity? In the days of Dante we hear of a certain Peter who traded in combs (*pettini*) and therefore went by the name of Pier Pettignano. His fame for holiness had gone abroad, for the Florentine poet declares that Peter's intercession saved from worse punishment the blinded Sapia who spoke the awful blasphemy.* The pious comb-seller was deeply

* Dante, "Purgatorio," XIII, 106 *ff*.

venerated by his countrymen, and when, in the year
1289, he died, almost a hundred years old, the republic
declared him holy, and supported its conviction by
voting him a monument at public expense—*unum
sepulcrum nobile*.* Scant as this material is, we know
even less of the Dominican friar, Ambrogio, who seems
to have been a member of the noble house of the
Sansedoni. He was a contemporary of Pier Pettignano,
and, not long after he died in the year 1287, was
canonized by the church. From the circumstance that
he long continued to be worshipped at many Sienese
altars, we must conclude that he made a considerable
impression in his day.†

With the coming of the fourteenth century the veil
lifts, giving us a much clearer view of the holy men and
women of Siena as they went about their chosen work
of salvation. The Blessed Bernardo Tolomei (b. 1272)
—of the noble family of that name—wonderfully combined the two Christian ideals of contemplation and
service. A strain of asceticism drove him into the bare
chalk hills to the east of Siena, where with steady labor
he made a little garden-spot, and called it Monte
Oliveto. He lived to found an order—the Olivetans—
organized under the rule of Saint Benedict; but for
all his joy in his pleasant retirement Bernardo did not
refuse to help his countrymen in a great crisis. When
the plague of 1348 devastated Siena, he left his quiet
hills and met his death heroically while attending the
poor victims of that awful visitation.‡ Another founder

---

* "Misc. Stor. Sen.," IV, p. 42.   † "Misc. Stor. Sen.," IV, p. 164.
  ‡ On the Blessed Bernardo Tolomei see a series of articles by P. Lugano,
"Bull. Sen.," IX–X.

of an order was the Blessed Giovanni Colombini
(1304?–1367) with whom originated the Poveri Gesuati.
Of him it is reported that he was a merchant of great
means, when, as he was verging on old age, illumination
descended on him like a dove from heaven. Straightway he divested himself of his wealth—chiefly, like a
good Sienese, in favor of the hospital of the Scala—
espoused the Lady Poverty, and wandered through the
streets and lanes perpetually praising God. Some of
the lauds which he and his followers sang have come
down to us under the name of *rime spirituali* and are,
if monotonous in matter, still tremulous with the joy
of the convert.* But more celebrated than any of the
aforementioned, second only among Italian saints to
Saint Francis, are Saint Catherine and San Bernardino.
Of the latter, as belonging to a relatively late period,
I shall speak briefly in another place;† before taking
up the life of her, who marks the culmination of Christianity within the bounds of Sienese influence, I may
be permitted to call attention to the reverse of the medal
and to speak of the occasional appearance in the city
of heretical views and sects.

Though Siena was profoundly religious and affirmed
her fidelity to the church by adding numerous names
to the roster of saints, no less than every other city of
Tuscany, she was guilty of certain irregularities of
thought and practice defined as heretical. In this
connection it is well to recall that our precise modern
idea, that heresy consists in formulating and defending
an unorthodox theological opinion, must be revised for

* "Bull. Sen.," II, 1 *ff*, discusses his life, and on p. 47 gives one of his
lauds.   † Chapter 14.

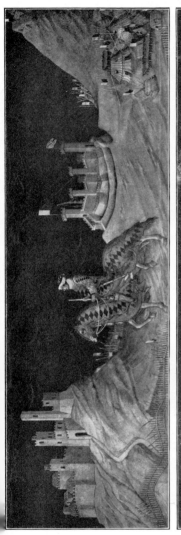

Guidoriccio da Fogliano.   By Simone Martini (in the Palazzo Pubblico)

Allegory of Good Government.   By Ambrogio Lorenzetti (in the Palazzo Pubblico)

mediæval times in view of the custom of throwing alchemists, epicureans, astrologers, and wizards into a common class with the religious innovators. Such summary procedure saved thought on the part of the authorities, and, further, may have recommended itself as an easy way of periodically purging society of its restless and dangerous elements under the pretense of defending the imperilled church. True, belief in love draughts, in the influence of the stars, of the possibility of transmuting baser metals into gold, was general,* for the age was one of extraordinary superstition, but a revulsion, due to religious fear, was certain to follow sooner or later, and then the thaumaturgists, representing a strange mixture of charlatanism and honest zeal for knowledge, paid for their brief popularity with their lives. A typical case is that of Capocchio of Siena, who aroused the suspicion of the authorities in consequence of his devotion to the primitive science of the thirteenth century, and perished at the stake.†

But much more interesting than the misled and misnamed scientists who might from time to time fall under the imputation of heresy are the representatives of movements consciously religious in character and openly or secretly directed against the church. The student of the Middle Age, who knows that great concerted agitations repeatedly threatened the ascendency of Rome, will not be surprised to

---

* On this subject of superstition see "Misc. Stor. Sen.," I, 124. The government *officially* employed wizards, prophets, and exorcisers.   On the opening of a campaign with Florence it was a common practice to hire a magician for the purpose of having him concoct a powder to scatter among the enemy!

† Dante met Capocchio in hell, "Inferno," XXIX, 133 *ff.*

hear that almost all of them could claim a following in Siena. The Manicheans, and after them the
Paterini, who bore a certain inner resemblance to
the Manicheans, had a strong following in southern
Tuscany throughout the early Middle Age,* while in
the thirteenth century we hear of Sienese supporters of
the thrice cursed Albigensian heresy, and in the fourteenth of a group of Franciscan rebels against Rome
called Fraticelli.† These various sects did not by any
means occupy the same theological ground, but they
were all agreed in their opposition to the dominant
church. Therefore the bishop of Siena, supported
from the thirteenth century on by the new and famous
institution of the Inquisition, was obliged to exercise
constant vigilance. The Inquisition differed from the
old episcopal supervision in matters of faith in that it
was centrally operated from Rome, chiefly through
the agency of the Dominican order, and that it proceeded in accordance with much more rigid principles.
Bishop and Inquisition alike enjoyed, though with
varying fervor, the coöperation of the Sienese state,
and from the earliest constitution which has reached us,
the Constitution of 1262, we may learn that the state,
anxious to avoid the censure of the church, legislated
with the utmost severity against *heretici et pactareni*.‡

Catherine Benincasa, the most fragrant and exquisite representative of Sienese Christianity during the

* Davidsohn, "Geschichte von Florenz," I, 721 *ff*., II¹, pp. 302–4,
presents a careful review of the Paterini in Florence and Tuscany.

† For the edict against them see Cappelletti, "Storia delle Chiese d'Italia,"
XVII, p. 484. On the general subject of heresy consult Tocco, "L'Eresia nel
Medio Evo," Florence, 1884.

‡ Zdekauer, "Il Constituto di 1262," I, 118. The legislation on heresy
tended to become more and more rigorous, as may be seen by consult-

whole Middle Age, was born on March 25, 1347. Her
father, Jacopo Benincasa, a dyer by profession, conducted his business on the steep slopes of the street
which led down to one of the famous fountains of the
city, the Fonte Branda.   Jacopo and his wife Lapa
were honest working people, poor in everything except
in offspring, for Catherine—not the smallest marvel in a
marvellous career—was, according to her biographer,
Fra Raimondo, the next to the last in a succession of
twenty-five children, who singly or in pairs came to
make their home under the dyer's roof.   The Benincasa
house still stands, provided in the sixteenth century
with a beautiful loggia both in the front and in the rear,
and otherwise altered to meet the requirements of a
sacred museum, but the essential changes are slight,
and the immediate environment bears to this day much
the same aspect which marked it in the time of the
saint's youth.   Here the working people continue to
make their home; the street, too precipitous for even
the lightest vehicles, swarms with riotous children,
swarthy with the wind and sun; and the air is full of
the pungent, not unpleasant odor rising from the vats,
around which the tanners ply their immemorial trade.
Over the dusty flags the baby Catherine must have
rolled, watched by the busy Lapa out of the corner of her
eye; like the urchins of our day, she must have toddled
down to Fonte Branda, where the press of men and

ing "Il Constituto di 1309-10 with regard to its heretical provisions."   The
ecclesiastical ideal in the matter of persecution was represented by the
hideous laws promulgated in the years 1232 and 1238 by Frederick II, in
order to curry favor with the church.   Monumenta Ger., Leges II, p. 286,
p. 326.   Whenever Siena or another commune wished to stand well with the
pope, it made a show of incorporating these laws in its statutes.

women, come to draw water for the house and shop,
provided a never-failing spectacle; and perhaps her
first adventure was to scramble up the steep hill flanking
the ancient fountain, in order to have a peep into the
cool interior of the great church of San Domenico,
which reared its transept almost vertically above her
father's roof.*

The church of San Domenico, perpetually in view on
its high eminence, was destined to play a directing rôle
in Catherine's career. The good brothers of the
monastery, who came sometimes to visit her parents,
were struck with the self-contained manner of the
child, and gladly undertook her spiritual guidance.
Without believing to the letter all the miraculous things
reported of the youthful Catherine, we may rest assured
that she had a strong religious bent from her birth,
which, being carefully nursed by her Dominican friends,
presently took the form of an overpowering enthusiasm
for the life of a Christian ascetic. In spite of the
remonstrances of her family, in the year 1362, when she
was only fifteen years old, she joined the Order of

---

* The literature on Saint Catherine is rapidly assuming vast proportions.
For a good review of the sources see the Bibliography appended to Gardner,
"Saint Catherine of Siena." The original life, called the Legend, which has
principally supplied later writers with their facts, was written in Latin by
Catherine's confessor, Fra Raimondo of Capua. Far and away the most
important source for an intimate knowledge of the saint are her Letters.
If all the material furnished by the hagiographers were lost and these unique
epistles spared, her historical portrait would not suffer the loss of a single
significant trait. Of the several editions, I have used the edition of Gigli,
reprinted in 1842 at Milan. Her complete works, including the "Dialogo"
and Fra Raimondo's "Life"(in Italian), were published by her devoted admirer, Girolamo Gigli, early in the eighteenth century. Of recent works, the
most important are Drane, "The History of St. Catherine"; Capecelatro,
"Storia di S. Caterina da Siena"; Scudder, "Saint Catherine of Siena as Seen
in Her Letters"; and Gardner, "Saint Catherine of Siena."

Detail—Guidoricc o da Fogliano. By Simone Martini (in the Palazzo Pubblico)

Detail from the Allegory of Good Government.
By Ambrogio Lorenzetti (in the Palazzo Pubblico)

Penance of Saint Dominic, the saint of her particular
devotion, and became what the Sienese called a Mantel-
lata.   The Order of Penance was a lay order, embracing
both sexes and planned to supplement the work of the
Dominican friars, but its members wore religious dress
and dedicated themselves, as far as their secular condition permitted, to the duties of their faith.   On assuming the mantle Catherine continued to dwell at home,
where she converted her room into a cell, and gave herself wholly to the contemplation of the mysteries of
Christianity.   For years she led a life of strictest
confinement, abandoning her solitary retreat only to
attend mass and receive the eucharist in the church of
her order, which had come to stand in her exalted mind
for the promise and glory of the cross.

A pure and simple-minded girl, burning out her
life like a taper before the tabernacle of the Lord—that
is all there might have been to the uneventful history
of the maid Catherine, if, in addition to her love of God
and yearning for heaven, she had not also felt the passion to serve mankind.   This is a fundamental trait
of her character, giving her life a human zest generally
lacking in the pallid ranks of the brotherhood of
mediæval saints.   For a brief period in her zealous
youth she may indeed have sealed her senses to the
sights and sounds of the world, but she was too utterly
human to persist long in so narrow a course.   The fact
is, the world rang like a trumpet in her ears and gave
her no rest.   The miseries of her age invaded her cell,
but, instead of driving her into deeper solitude, they
aroused her will to wrestle with them to the end of
making the earth she lived in a more godly habitation.

And what a desolating picture it was which society spread before her eyes! While the pope was an exile in Avignon, apparently content never to return to his hereditary seat at Rome, the emperor, sunk even to baser depths than his spiritual rival, looked upon his office as a mere device for raising revenue. In 1355 Catherine with her own eyes may have seen an emperor, after an interval of a century, ride through the streets of Siena, and possibly she shared for a brief hour the dream that his coming meant an end of domestic confusion. But instead of peace Charles IV brought new civil wars and the government of the Twelve. At her father's table this event must have given rise to brisk and gleeful comment, for the clan of the Benincasa belonged to the new monte of the Dodicini, and for a short space (1355–68) took rank with the rulers of the city. But the Twelve, as we know, were a wretched magistracy under whom the state enjoyed hardly a moment of peace. The city rang with the lawless deeds of the Tolomei and the Salimbeni, and no sooner was the din raised by these cantankerous noblemen somewhat quieted, than there sounded across the contado the wail of the poor peasants, plundered and put to torture by the prowling bands of Hawkwood and similar adventurers. Violence, blasphemy, greed, and oppression met the young girl at every turn until her heart swelled with all the sorrows of the race. Had thirteen hundred years of Christianity been all in vain? "I die and I cannot die," was the agonized cry she raised again and again.* But in spite of her anguish she sought the burden of the world, courag-

* See, for instance, "Lettera 90," III, 28.

eously resolved to do her part to realize a nobler brotherhood of man.

The work done by Catherine in the service of her fellows is generally regarded as the most memorable chapter of her life. That view, however, is not shared by all her admirers. Fervent Catholics, in particular, love to linger on the many temptations which she victoriously overcame, or to contemplate the glowing trances during which the heavens opened and she gazed upon the serene features of the Virgin and her Beloved Son. The ecstasies of Catherine constitute a chain of fascinating incidents, in which a modern psychologist should find a rich treasure of evidence bearing upon the tenuous character of what in common phrase we call reality. How Saint Catherine in a vision was wedded to Christ, how she exchanged hearts with her heavenly Lover, how, finally, she had seared upon her flesh the Five Wounds—these and similar holy experiences narrated by her particularly impressed her age, as chapel walls and panels, glorified by the great masters of painting, still eloquently testify throughout the length and breadth of Italy. All her communications with the divine powers occurred in the state of trance, during which, according to an eye-witness, "she appeared like a statue which retains nothing but the human form."* She passed into this condition most readily after having partaken of the sacrament, when, being upon her knees, her head would fall forward on the altar rail, and she would lose all consciousness of time and place. Once, as she lay thus abstracted from the world, a shameless woman, we are told, moved by

* Evidence of Caffarini. See Drane, p. 71.

scepticism or curiosity, drove a needle into her foot. She gave no sound of pain, but an hour later, when she awakened from her trance, she complained of suffering and walked with a limp. No student of human nature will be inclined to minimize this side of her career—the side by which she takes rank with Saint Theresa and the great visionaries—but no one, responsive to the *allgemein Menschliche* by which she is related to our common human lot, will protest against devoting particular attention to her public acts and private charities, the moving record not of her dreams but of her earthly destiny.

Catherine had borne the robe of penance for hardly three years when she began to give up her life of close confinement, irresistibly drawn to the world by the passion of service. Love henceforth became the substance of her days, the love which flows from God like a radiance and is the one sure bond uniting His creatures. To rich and poor, to rulers and ruled, to oppressors and oppressed she preached the same doctrine, convinced that there were no ills which would not yield to the divine cure. All the sins of the world, she says somewhere in her passionate and picturesque way, are but a drop of vinegar in the boundless ocean of God's love. This is the enveloping element, not God's wrath, as the doctors of theology, her predecessors and contemporaries, had been sternly telling a credulous and frightened people. With this old-new message she moved like an angel of light along the streets of her native town, recalling a blasphemous youth to the thought of God, giving food to the needy, speaking a word of good cheer to the sick and dying. Among the relics which Siena still possesses of her—and the relics are not all of this acceptable human sort—is the iron lamp she lighted when called out suddenly at night upon an errand of mercy. How often may she have lighted it in the grim years when pestilence swept over the hills like a poisonous mist from the sea, and her word of comfort was wanted at all hours in every quarter of the city! But the healthy, too, had need of her ministrations, the physically healthy, whose souls were eaten with canker. For the fierce party and family feuds which tore the entrails of her native town she never ceased recommending her panacea of regenerating love. The conversion of the young patrician, Stefano Maconi,* from his sworn vendetta, forms one of her noblest conquests, but yields in interest to the well-known incident connected with the name of Niccolò Tuldo, of whose change of heart she herself has left a moving record.†

Niccolò Tuldo was a Perugian youth who, during a visit to neighboring Siena, called attention to himself by offensive criticism of the government.‡ He was seized, and immediately, according to the inhuman justice of the day, condemned to death. The sentence, falling on him like a bolt from the blue, almost drove him out of his mind. He raged, cursed, and refused all religious consolation, until Catherine, prompted by her quick sympathies, came to knock at his prison cell. With sweet compulsion she recalled him to himself, and in a few visits converted the young worldling into a

---

* Gardner, p. 168 *ff*. The episode probably belongs to the year 1376.
† "Lettera 97," III, p. 58 *ff*.
‡ If the party in power was the Riformatori, as is probable, the incident would belong to some year after 1368; Gardner assumes the year 1377.

soldier of the cross, for whom death lost every aspect
of terror.　Having promised to be with him at the hour
of trial, she awaited him at the foot of the scaffold,
around which crowded the usual multitude of eager
spectators.

"He arrived like a gentle lamb, and seeing me,
began to laugh, and desired that I make him the sign
of the cross; and when he had received the sign, I said
'down; down to the espousals, my sweet brother,
which will bring you quickly to everlasting life.'　He
sank down with great humility, and I laid his head upon
the block, and knelt at his side, and recalled to him the
blood of the Lamb.　His lips kept repeating the words
Jesus and Catherine, and he was still speaking when I
received his head in my hands. . . ."

Then Catherine kneeling and pressing the head to
her bosom passed into an ecstasy in which she saw the
soul of Niccolò mount upward to where Christ waited,
clothed in the radiance of the sun.　And a remarkable
feature of this ecstasy was that it took place amidst a
perfect riot of the overwrought senses.　With hands
and dress bathed in the blood of the victim, which
somehow in her mystic joy she associated with the
blood spilt by the Redeemer, she wrote these intoxicated
words: "And the fragrance of the blood brought me
such peace and quiet that I could not bear to wash it
away."

The great reputation won by Catherine among the
people of Siena soon spread to neighboring parts and
created a general demand for her beneficent presence.
Montepulciano sent for her to make peace between two
hostile families; Pisa and Lucca desired her fertile

counsel;* and presently Florence sent a messenger to
invite her visit.   The Florentine business was concerned
with the papacy and produced that incident in her
public career by means of which she assumes a place
in the political story of Italy.

In the year 1375 Florence, the old Guelph centre,
had fallen out with its natural ally, the papacy, over
a number of matters, the most immediately pressing of
which was the economic policy of the States of the
Church across the Apennines.   Owing to a scarcity
of provisions threatening a dire famine, the Arno city
attempted to import food-stuffs from Bologna, but the
papal legate at that post defeated the plan by a general
prohibition.   Perhaps the papal legate, as the Florentines averred, was plotting to overthrow the democratic
government in their city; perhaps the Florentines were
jealous of the consolidation and increase of the papal
states which had lately been effected by the famous Cardinal Albornoz.   At any rate, popular excesses against
ecclesiastics were followed by preparations for war,
which were still going forward, when, in December,
1375, the Florentines achieved the great success of in-
ducing the lords and cities of the papal territory to rise
in revolt against their master.   At the same time all
Tuscany declared its adhesion to the Arno city.   By the
spring of 1376 the pope in distant Avignon faced a situation which must have filled him with consternation, for
not only had he lost most of his Italian patrimony, but
as long as he was involved with all his resources in a war
with Florence, he could hardly hope to take effective

* The Montepulciano incident belongs to 1374; the visits to Pisa and Lucca
to 1375.

steps for the recovery of his territory. He showed his resentment by placing the presumptuous city under the interdict. Nothing daunted, the Florentines, or rather the war party among the Florentines, maintained their policy, though a conservative group, shocked at the rupture of the ancient bonds between Florence and the church, applied itself strenuously to the reëstablishment of peace. It was this party which in the month of May sent for Catherine, in order to request her to act as mediator at Avignon.

Although gladly complying with the wishes of her Florentine friends, Catherine did not fail to see that her journey would enable her to promote an enterprise even nearer to her heart than the cessation of hostilities in central Italy. She was indeed a Christian mystic, but she was also a devoted Catholic, firmly convinced that the salvation of mankind could be wrought only through the agency of the church. Two things, therefore, grieved her spirit above all others: first, that the ministers of the church, especially the highest prelates, were so often corrupt and worldly, and second, that the chief pastor chose wilfully to absent himself from his appointed capital. With her usual candor she wrote of these grievances to the pope in letters which announced her approaching visit, and on June 18, 1376, attended by a group of faithful followers, entered the gates of the transalpine town. The reigning pope was Gregory XI, a slight, pale-visaged Frenchman, who listened to her impassioned communications with wistful longing. He was ready to make peace, and peace would have promptly followed if the Florentines had really desired it; more than that, he was ready to go to

Rome, and in support of his declaration could point to
a circular letter to the princes of Christendom of over
a year ago, wherein he had registered a promise to that
effect. But there were difficulties. The cardinals,
Frenchmen in their vast majority, were unwilling to
exchange the luxurious palaces of Avignon for the
squalid ruins of Rome, and belabored him ceaselessly
in the hope of undermining his resolution. Knowing
his timorous disposition, they even sent him a letter,
purporting to come from some eminent authority across
the Alps and hinting at the perils of Italian poison. At
this ruse Catherine's indignation brimmed over.

"In the name of Christ Crucified," she wrote him,
"I beg you to be not a fearful child but a man; open
your mouth and swallow the little drop of bitter medicine. . . . By the infinite and inestimable goodness of
God I hope that you will prove yourself firm and stable,
and will not be disturbed by reason of any wind or
trick of demons" (messers, the cardinals, to wit!) "but
will follow the will of God, and your own pure desire,
and the counsel of the servants of Christ Crucified."*

Many such words pronounced without fear or favor,
words which scorched as with fire the lordly prelates
anxious for their ease and comfort, the holy maid spoke
at Avignon, where the cooks were more exquisite, the
tailors more expensive, and the minstrels and courtesans
more numerous than anywhere else in Europe. It is to
be regretted that no contemporary writer exhibits her
in the midst of these splendors. Catherine, before the
wealth and color and laughter of the leading court of
Europe, makes one of those striking contrasts in which

* "Lettera 10," I, p. 59.

her age, an age of transition, abounded. Half concealed from view in her black mantle, with her eyes turned inward, she doubtless walked the streets of the fair town, spread beneath the blue sky of southern France, without noting overmuch those signs and trappings which she would call mere phases of corruption, but from her letters we gather that she saw enough and more than enough to confirm her in her worst suspicions of the state of the church.

Fortified by Catherine's indomitable spirit, Gregory at last found the needed courage, and setting out from Avignon, on January 17, 1377, arrived at Rome amidst frenzied popular rejoicings. Thus ended the long Babylonish captivity, not without the important participation of the Sienese virgin. The great benefits, however, which she anticipated from the transfer of the papal capital were slow in appearing. The Florentine war party maintained the upper hand in the Arno city, and throughout the pope's first year in the peninsula the conflict between himself and the stubborn democracy continued unabated. Catherine bled and agonized over the miserable issue. In the early spring of the year 1378 she came to Florence in the pope's name to arrange an honorable peace, and, in spite of difficulties and even riots, in one of which she almost lost her life,* at last brought the troublesome matter to a successful termination. But Gregory was not destined to be cheered by the good news. Long broken in health he had died in the month of March, and with his death the latent Franco-Italian quarrel in the college of cardinals stood revealed before the world.

* Her own account, mystically transmuted, in "Lettera 96," III, 52 ff.

The election which ensued of the Italian prelate, Urban VI, is one of the most thrilling incidents of church history.* But Urban was hardly elected when the French faction, repudiating him, chose one of their own number under the title of Clement VII, and thus precipitated the famous crisis called the Great Schism.

How this new calamity hung with a pall the ardent mind of Catherine, who had freely predicted some such trouble as this unless the poisonous plants were weeded from the garden of the church, may be left to the imagination. The unity of the church, as represented by the person of the pope, was to her a sacred thing, and now she was called upon to be a spectator while the cardinals tore the seamless coat of Christ. She was not a moment in deciding where she stood, for, once assured that her Italian compatriot was canonically elected, she had really no liberty of choice. Her letters to Urban, rising almost to shrillness in their tender solicitude, are assertions of his inalienable right, and mingle ringing encouragements with constantly renewed appeals to effect at last the cure of the church's evils. But beyond instilling her own high courage into the pope, she could in this vast crisis do little but pray. Therefore her political career ceased with this new phase of Italian history. In November, 1378, she went, at the pope's request, to Rome in order to lend him the benefit of her wise counsel, and although her presence was felt by the pontiff as a strengthening draught, and although she wrote letters in his behalf to kings and princes, and pleaded affectionately with the sulky Romans, always on the point of insurrection, she was never again lifted

* Gregorovius, "Geschichte der Stadt Rom im Mittelalter," VI, 481 *ff.*

high into the sight of all by a public mission.   During
these her last months on earth she was racked with
many pangs of the body admirably borne, the result of
her persistent disregard of the laws of nature.   For
years she had starved herself so that her stomach
could no longer support more than the merest mouthful
of food.   It was even currently believed that she sustained life without other nourishment than the bread
received in communion.   This could be disproved, if
one were not satisfied with the verdict of common-
sense, out of the records left by her disciples, but in any
case it is sure that she carried the mortification of the
flesh to such a point that she was frequently heard to
say that the mere thought of a meal was like going to
execution.   Bodily disease, added to her mental agony
over the condition of the church, was more than she
could bear; she failed steadily through long weeks, and
on the 29th of April, 1380, died, lovingly attended to
the last by her sorrowing disciples.   Her mortal remains were interred at Rome in the Dominican church,
called the Minerva.

After her death the fame of Catherine grew rather
than diminished, in consequence of which fact many
worshiped her as a saint without awaiting the formal
authorization of the church.   At last, in June, 1461,
the Sienese pope, Pius II, besides gratifying his own
love for his native city, met a very general demand by
publishing a bull which raised her to the honor of the
altars.

So far has the story of the daughter of Jacopo Benincasa travelled that to many people in the remoter out-
posts of Christianity Siena is merely the town of Saint

Madonna and Child

By Ambrogio Lorenzetti (in S. Eugenio Outside Porta S. Marco)

Catherine. But if the holy maid has carried the fame of the city abroad, Siena has repaid the service by lovingly cherishing her memory. Whoever visits the Tuscan town will find at almost every turning some token which brings her to the mind, but most especially will her memory attend him along the steep street where she was born, and on the hill above it which bears the venerable church of San Domenico. For the house of her father and the temple where she worshiped not only are hallowed by her spirit, but also cherish some authentic relics of her life on earth, preserved in a setting upon which a number of eminent artists have expended their best effort. To San Domenico, in particular, no admirer of the maiden will fail to make a pious pilgrimage. If he is not greatly drawn to the relics of her bodily life, for the church boasts the possession of her head and one of her fingers,* he will at least take curious and vivacious notice of what art has done with the wonderful material of her life. In a chapel built in her honor after her death, the Lombard Sodoma has portrayed her in a series of much-praised frescoes. Sodoma lived in the sixteenth century when painting had already divorced itself from religious feeling. It need cause no surprise, therefore, that, though his work in Saint Catherine's chapel is not without a certain sensuous charm, it should be marred by an almost total lack of sympathetic insight. Much more true to the honest spirit of the saint is the unadorned portrait of her by her contemporary and

* These were sent to Siena shortly after her death by her confessor and biographer, Fra Raimondo, and are exposed on her annual festival, the 30th of April.

disciple, Andrea Vanni. It hangs over the altar in the actual chapel—the *capella delle volte*—where she prayed and was rapt away to some of her most resplendent visions. Standing in this consecrated enclosure before her sweet and solemn countenance, we realize that one of the highest functions of art is to preserve the memory of the noble dead, for, gazing, we are drawn close as never before to her gracious being, and in a revealing flash see her as she was, the maid, who

> . . . "mixed herself with heaven and died;
> And now on the sheer city-side
> Smiles like a bride."

CHAPTER X

THE CIVIC SPIRIT AND THE BUILDING OF THE CITY

ON September 2, 1260, Siena, by unanimous impulse of her citizens, dedicated herself to the Virgin, and two days later touched the zenith of her political fortunes in the great victory of Montaperti. The hundred years following Montaperti constitute the period in the evolution of Siena during which she participated most vitally in the life of Italy, and won such a place as she holds among the communes of the peninsula. Although this statement has already been illustrated to a certain extent in the previous chapters, a very suggestive line of evidence remains yet to be adduced: in the foremost century of her existence Siena raised her cathedral and her Palazzo Pubblico, adorned herself with fountains, girdled herself with walls and gates, in a word, assumed the characteristic garment which she was to wear for all the following ages. Who makes the acquaintance of the Siena of to-day finds spread before him substantially a fourteenth century town. And because the subsequent centuries, effecting innovations and changes almost everywhere else in Italy, hardly turned a stone in this upland town, no other city throughout the length and breadth of the peninsula strikes so resonantly and significantly the mediæval note. Her monuments of brick and stone affirm gracefully and ponderously by turn, but never doubtfully, a distinctive personality, and as we are seeking better acquaintance with this personality, as it constitutes in fact the real object of this book, I must consider myself well employed in following the leading phases by which the town became materially what it is.

The original nucleus of Siena was that highest point in the southern section of the town, still called Castello Vecchio or the Old Castle. The ridge of Castello Vecchio drops gently till it encounters two other ridges from the north and east respectively at a place of meeting known by the name of Croce di Travaglio.* Immediately below the Croce di Travaglio, in the pocket between the ridges from the south and east, lies the great public square or Campo, which antiquarians incline to identify with the forum of Roman times. In the avenues of communication following the three ridges, in the Croce di Travaglio, and in the Campo, we have the main features which determined the physical aspect of Siena.

Owing to the fact that Siena was built upon three ridges, the town appears from remote times as divided into three sections called terzi. The terzo lying to the south and embracing Castello Vecchio and its ridge was called, in deference to its age, Città, that is *the* city; the terzo to the east was named San Martino; and the

---

* This mysterious term may refer to some cross (croce) which once rose here to mark the intersection of the three Sienese spurs, or, quite as possibly, to the cruciform shape of the place itself, with arms running off in different directions. According to the best opinion the word travaglio is an Italian corruption of the Latin trium vallium. See Heywood, "Guide to Siena," p. 81 (note).

northward terzo bore the designation Camollia. The houses, massed at the point of junction and running out along the narrow ridges, give Siena, when seen from one of its high towers, the appearance of the claw of some huge bird of prey. The division into three parts, commanded by nature itself, was of the kind to become deeply imbedded in the consciousness of the Middle Age, which we have come to know as the period of home feeling and neighborly associations. In fact, as soon as we hear of a commune of Siena, we are informed that at its head stood three consuls or some multiple of three: the terzi evidently insisted that in the formation of a common government they should be all equally represented. When the consuls were superseded by a potestà, who came from foreign parts, he was obliged to choose his residence in a different terzo from his two immediate predecessors, in order that each terzo might in turn harbor the chief dignitary. When a party government replaced the potestà in the political direction of the town we may discover in such magistracies as the Twenty-four, the Nine, the Twelve, the Fifteen— all multiples of three—the persistence of the terzo jealousy. No less vigorously than in politics the ancient sentiment expressed itself in common social relations, as may be vividly seen, to mention only a single instance, in the game of *pugna*, really hardly more than a general street-fight by three bands, representative of the three sections; these three hosts met from time to time in the Campo and a curious detail of their battle of fists and stones was that Camollia and San Martino regularly united against Città, thereby clearly betraying a long-standing resentment against the original settlement and against certain airs of superiority by which its inhabitants may have given offence.

But the physical separation of Siena into terzi is only the beginning of the long tale of her local divisions. In the days of the consuls the grandi formed, by reason of their wealth and habits of life, a class sharply marked off from the rest of the people. Their superiority showed itself in their very houses, which, built of stone and brick, occupied the ridges, while the common people, housed wretchedly in wooden huts and in those caves and cellars, specimens of which still abound and which are made possible by the soft clayey character of the soil, spread in careless disorder along the slopes of the hills. The original houses of the grandi were really rude castles, consisting of buildings clustered without any effort at beauty or order around an open court, and inhabited, in addition to the family or clan, by retainers and petty craftsmen, huddled in dark shops on the street level. An excellent example of such a composite dwelling, called *castellare*, may still be seen opposite the church of San Vigilio. It is the most complete monument the remote Middle Age has left in Siena.* But sombre as it is, and impressive in spite of its being a mere formless heap of masonry, time has deprived it of the most conspicuous feature of a feudal residence— the tower. In the early days every castellare had a tower, built to exceed in height, if possible, the tower of the neighboring castellare. For not only was the tower the best possible security against an enemy, but,

* Heywood (The "Ensamples" of Fra Filippo, p. 34 *ff.*) draws a vivid picture of the appearance of the streets and houses of thirteenth century Siena.

by letting it soar high over the roofs, the owner proclaimed, with the ingenuous boastfulness of a primitive
race, his greatness to his fellow-citizens. As late as the
sixteenth century a sufficiently large number of these
towers was left standing to make Siena look at a distance, we are told, like a canebrake,* and even after
the wholesale destruction ordered by the Emperor
Charles V to supply the material for the fortress with
which he planned to tame the turbulent town, so many
towers continued to scale the sky that a northern gentleman on his grand tour might readily imagine that he
had dropped among a strange race of cliff-dwellers.
Only a comparatively recent period has effected their
complete removal, when, in consequence of the appearance of rifts in their walls, they threatened the
safety of the citizens.

Such was Siena in the consular period: a mass of
castellari along the heights and over-soared by towers;
with the congested quarters of the poor, largely of
wood, clustering round and spreading down the steep
declivities. The main thoroughfares along the ridges,
traced in Roman, and possibly Etruscan, times were
reasonably broad and straight, but on the slopes there
was an inextricable maze of dark by-ways, due to
personal caprice unchecked by anything resembling an
effective social control. In sign of this confusion
Siena, although never a town of great extension, possessed in 1301 as many as thirty-six gates,† whereas

---

* Ugurgieri, "Le Pompe Sanesi," II, 307. "Erano tante torri in Siena
che la Città pareva un canneto." See the old print of Siena in chap. 14.

† Bargagli-Petrucci, "Le Fonti di Siena," I, 256, note 1. The author
finds an additional reason for the large number of gates in the successive
circles of walls.

some generations later, when useless walls had been
leveled and the side streets rectified in accordance with
the more rational plan imposed by a central government,
one-third that number was found to be ample.* If,
to complete the picture of feudal independence, we
recall that the nobles in addition to dominating the city
from their castellari were leagued together in *consorterie*
or associations, the members of which were pledged to
help one another and to take justice from the hands
of their officers, we shall have formed a conception of
the difficulty of reducing a class, inoculated with ideas
of might and grandeur, to a system of civil order.

The clergy, which, owing to the dissipation and exhaustion of the authority of the state in the period of
the Germanic conquest, had practically succeeded in
separating itself from lay society, represented another
difficulty of the early commune. Its independence, at
first an affair of custom, had been confirmed by solemn
compacts, the slightest encroachment on which was
sure to excite a fiery fulmination from the Holy Father
at Rome. But the numerous body of citizens of clerical
degree was by no means one and undivided. At their
head stood indeed the bishop, but within the imposing
organization what a profusion of elements, all more or
less self-governing! Immediately under the bishop
were the cathedral canons with their own palace, their
own property, and their own policy, and throughout the
city were convents, male and female, large and small,
some strictly local, and others affiliated with such universal orders as the Benedictines, the Cistercians, the
Dominicans, and the Franciscans. Among the laity,

* Nine is the number of gates Siena has to-day.

hardly less penetrated with the spirit of religious association than the clergy itself, we encounter not only voluntary societies, whose members wore a clerical-looking gown and devoted themselves to deeds of charity, but also more formal corporations called confraternities, not unlike our secret and mutual aid societies, and pledged to render service to their bretheren in misfortune, sickness, and death. Bishop and parish priests, canons, the innumerable convents, confraternities, and lay charitable unions give some idea of the varied and picturesque aspect of mediæval religious life.

So much for the nobility and clergy; below them was the body of the common people who lived by the sweat of their brows and whose numbers grew constantly greater with the development of civil society. One of the first signs they gave of a renewed energy was by the formation of military companies. Apparently one such company sprang up in each parish, while the union of all of them constituted itself as the armed host of the republic. Another assurance of growing vigor was furnished by the industrial organization of the commoners, effected by means of the guilds or arti. The arti, in measure as they accumulated wealth and influence, yielded to the corporative bias and exercised an increasing sway over their members through a mechanism of officers, police, revenues, and justice. Small wonder, in view of this ubiquitous group activity, that a distinguished student of the Italian Middle Age has expressed the opinion that the mediæval town was a very miracle of internal divisions.

And now we are in a position to appreciate the herculean labor undertaken by the new political entity, the commune.   Not only were the clergy, nobles, merchants, and artisans, used to independence and exercising it daily, to be fused into a body of citizens subjected to a common law and recognizing a common duty, but out of the various loyalties, bound up with geographical, military, and professional associations and communicated to the blood and marrow through ancient habit, was to be created a higher loyalty attaching to the new-born commune of Siena.   Only as that loyalty, called patriotism in our day, should grow and flourish, could the town generate the civic spirit, upon the health and vigor of which depended its greatness. And, in spite of difficulties, jealousies, clashes, the civic spirit was born and stood forth in the light. Without it there would have been no history of Siena capable of holding our attention for even a moment. The achievements of that spirit in the constitutional, administrative, and political fields we have already examined; we shall now proceed to examine the remembrance it has left of itself in monuments of public utility and beauty.

It is characteristic of all the Italian communes that their earliest municipal enthusiasm gravitated toward the church.   Not only were mediæval men wrapped up in religious practices much more than it is easy for us to understand, not only was the church the object of a veneration deep as the springs of life, but the cathedral of the bishop, not waiting to be created like the commune, but existent and tangible, though often of small dimensions, was the natural focus of that sentiment, the most ineradicable experienced by the human heart, the love of home.   No sooner had this feeling been roused from passivity to action with the stir of new life in the towns, than the people of each exhibited discontent with the petty proportions of their central house of worship. Its abolition to make room for a more magnificent structure became the universally chosen means of declaring that the town was reborn. Every visitor of Venice grows instinctively aware how all the struggles and triumphs of the young republic are entered in that wonderful volume which bears the name of the basilica of St. Mark. Whoever has stood before the cathedrals of Pisa, Florence, and Lucca has been able to read upon their walls, as if written with illuminated letters, the story of the communes to which they bear perpetual witness. Just so is Siena bound up with her cathedral, which we may rightly name the first labor of her civic spirit.

It was in the second quarter of the thirteenth century when, under the guidance of the Twenty-four, the town was mounting to its meridian, that the citizens of Siena resolved to tear down the old cathedral, named for the Virgin, and to build a new one which, dedicated to the same supreme Lady, should be commensurate with the growing wealth and political importance of their commune.* The historian Malavolti assigns the beginning of the work to the year 1245; not improbably it was initiated a few years earlier. The original architect has not been discovered, and no *operaio* or head of the works is named in the documents till we get down to

---

* The literature on the cathedral is extensive. I refer the reader to: *Milanesi,* "Documenti per la Storia dell' Arte Senese"; *Borghesi* and *Banchi,* "Nuovi Documenti per la Storia dell' Arte Senese"; *Richter,* "Siena"; *Langton Douglas,* "History of Siena," p. 265 *ff.*; *Canestrelli,* "Bull. Sen.," XI, p. 72 *ff.*; *C. E. Norton,* "Church-Building in the Middle Ages."

1257, when we find a Cistercian monk from San Galgano, Fra Vernaccio, in charge. This circumstance has misled some scholars, inclined to give more weight to literary arguments than to the evidence of the senses, into the belief that the style of the cathedral was borrowed from the wonderful abbey of San Galgano, which had just risen on the banks of the Merse, some fifteen miles to the south. Nothing could be more erroneous. San Galgano is, as we shall see hereafter, a remarkably pure production of French Gothic inspiration, while the cathedral is an Italian structure of prevailingly Romanesque character. Fra Vernaccio was succeeded presently by Fra Melano, also a Cistercian from San Galgano, and during his incumbency occurred, on September 2, 1260, the stirring dedication of Siena to the Virgin under the direction of Buonaguida Lucari and the bishop, and with the passionate participation of the whole citizen body. At the time of this event the distinctive feature of the structure, the great cupola over the crossing, was practically finished, together with the towering campanile, a part of the transept, and all the west end as far as it was then planned to be carried, which was, however, two bays short of the present length. Thus it will be seen that the cathedral in which Siena prepared her spirit for the great trial of Montaperti, and to which she carried her thank-offerings after her victory, was hardly more than half the size of the final edifice.

Fra Melano continued in charge for more than a decade, during which time he extended both the right and left transepts by a bay, and called Niccolò Pisano— the summons occurred in 1266—to erect the famous

Madonna, Child, Saints, and Angels
By Matteo di Giovanni (in the Galleria delle Belle Arti)

pulpit, which still constitutes one of the main decorations of the interior. Before the downfall of the Twenty-four, occasioned by the overthrow of Tuscan Ghibellinism at the diastrous battle of Colle (1269), the cathedral was done as originally planned except for the façade. As Giovanni Pisano, the equally famous son of Niccolò, was operaio from 1284 to 1298, it has been surmised that he was employed for the precise purpose of giving the building its missing front; however, as the first façade was torn down at a later time to make room for an extension of the nave, the Pisan artist's authorship of this section is no more than a reasonable conjecture. In no case can he have had anything to do with the existing façade, though a current tradition persistently refers to him as its author. Thus the eager activity of hardly more than a single generation of men had given the Virgin a new home and endowed the Sienese with a treasure of beauty in which rich and poor had an equal share.

However, after some decades, following the common fashion of fickle man, the citizens began to exhibit discontent with the house of their Protectress. Florence and Orvieto, neighbors to the north and south, were engaged upon more spacious cathedrals, and Siena had no desire to be thrown into the shade. The Nine, that capable though partisan government, representative of the merchant class and borne just then on the mounting tide of prosperity, shared fully the popular sentiment, and in the year 1315 undertook an enlargement, inaugurating thereby a second period of construction in the history of the cathedral. The plan adopted was to build a choir eastward behind the cupola, and, as the

ground in this region descended precipitously, it was
resolved to lead out the choir like a viaduct over powerful piers, which would offer the additional advantage of
affording room, among their masonry, for a new baptistery. It may have weighed with the architects that at
Assisi a magnificent effect had been produced by throwing out vast buttresses over the brow of a hill for the
support of the great central church of the order of
Saint Francis. By the new plan the cathedral would
be enlarged at least one-third, while a worthier structure
would be obtained to take the place of the old baptistery,
which lay to the right of the cathedral and had fallen into
contempt as the relic of a barbarous time. The new
work was advancing slowly, owing to the difficulties
of the site, when a commission of experts, called together
in 1322 and having among them the famous Sienese,
Lorenzo di Maitano, architect at Orvieto, declared the
recent construction unsafe, and recommended the building of an entirely new church. As this advice was too
startling and audacious, it was rejected by the government and the old plan adhered to for another seventeen
years. At the end of that time, while the choir and
baptistery were still struggling with apparently unsolv-
able difficulties, the idea of a new church had made so
many proselytes that the sentiment in its favor carried
the day. On August 23, 1339, the momentous decision
was made; Lando di Pietro, a Sienese in the employ
of the king of Naples, was called from the south to take
charge; and in the following February the first stone
of the new structure was set in place. The proposal
was to erect the *duomo nuovo* at right angles to the
existing edifice, thus preserving the latter but reducing

it to serve as transept for a new and magnificent nave with aisles. If the project had been carried out a provincial town of southern Tuscany would have boasted the most splendid temple of Italy. The very thought explains the doom which overtook the structure. Siena had overreached herself; although she was still animated with hope and overflowing with life, such a central church decidedly overstated her importance among the Tuscan communes. The *gente vana*, whom even the stern Dante reproved more in sorrow than in anger, had with the impulsiveness of children undertaken an enterprise beyond their strength, and presently, when difficulties accumulated in their path, impulsively gave it up. The difficulties, however, it must be granted, were enormous. First came the plague of 1348, bringing manifold ruin to the city, and presently, cracks appeared in the new parts, telling an ominous tale of faulty construction. This discouraging circumstance, by the way, had attended the building of the cathedral from the first, and justifies the assertion, supported by copious evidence from other towns of the peninsula, that the Italian architects were as deficient in technical knowledge as they were abundantly possessed of audacity, imagination, and æsthetic perception. While the work came to a standstill and experts insisted on the necessity of taking down the injured vaults to prevent a catastrophe, the Nine, patrons of the new dome, were themselves overtaken with ruin (1355). They were followed by the Twelve, mean folk of reduced vistas, who, after ordering, in the year 1357, that the unsafe portions be removed, let the whole plan quietly lapse into oblivion.

The visitor to Siena never fails to be arrested by the few arches which still stand of the famous dome of Lando di Pietro. The slender piers support a succession of round arches as bold and graceful as any to be found in the peninsula, where boldness and grace are the recurrent expression of the national genius. But even the chance traveller can see that these exquisite piers would be unable to support the vaults of the colossal nave which defied completion, and that the colossal nave itself was the dream of a people, splendidly courageous indeed but lacking in that self-command and just measure which are the spiritual groundwork of every enduring success.

The abandonment of the impossible carried the mind back once more to the possible, with the result that the old project of an extended choir led out over the brow of the hill on massive foundations was again taken up. If Siena would have to be content with the cathedral she possessed, she could at least add to the size and the beauty of the existing structure. This clear resolution must be put at the side of the disastrous inconsequence connected with the new dome, if we would do justice to the moral reserves of a race, which, often as it yielded to its reckless instincts, never failed to disclose, when the need was greatest, a sufficient fund of manly persistence. By the year 1370 the choir end had been completed, and, immediately after, steps were taken to enlarge the opposite or west end. The old façade,* possibly the work of Giovanni Pisano, was removed, and, after the

---

* Some notion of the appearance of this first façade can be gained from an old book-cover of the Biccherna, preserved in the archives and reproduced by Richter, "Siena," p. 46. A modest performance, this, in pleasing contrast with the pretentious front which replaced it.

nave had been lengthened by two bays, a new façade, conceived as the fitting crown of the enterprise, was taken in hand. The work was begun in the year 1377, and advanced so rapidly that by 1382 the Board of Works could again transfer its attention to the east end and to the problem of a suitable frontispiece for the recently completed choir and baptistery. On a sketch furnished by the painter, Jacopo di Mino di Neri del Pellicciaio, and still to be seen in the museum of the Opera, the east façade was carried to the present height and never finished. The difficulties, which even the untrained eye can appreciate, were too great for the science of the Italian architects.*

A thing highly remarkable, in view of the capricious history which I have traced, is that to step within the cathedral of Siena is to receive a perfectly consistent artistic impression. This impression arises from the character stamped upon the structure by the earliest operaii and maintained, in spite of slight deviations of taste, by all the subsequent builders. The cathedral is a thoroughly Italian edifice, employing the constructive forms of the Romanesque style as developed in Lombardy, and fusing them with certain elements, chiefly decorative, which derive from the Tuscan school of Pisa. The Lombard vaulted architecture, containing the germ of Gothic but utterly lacking in Gothic elevation and flight, produced a low, massive, and ill-lighted

* To render complete this long story of construction, I add that a hundred years later the interior was adorned with two features which are the object of much admiration: The small and delicate Baptistery in the northwest angle of the left transept was built in the year 1482, and the Piccolomini Library, containing the celebrated frescoes of Pintoricchio, in 1495. Both of these additions employ the forms of the early Renaissance, but, lost in the vast edifice, do not modify the general mediæval effect.

structure, pervaded by a startling effect of brooding sombreness. Sant' Ambrogio, that ponderous though hardly beautiful church of Milan, is an excellent example of what the unadulterated Lombard principles æsthetically signify. The cathedral of Siena makes a similar appeal, considerably modified, however, by the presence of certain Pisan features. The Pisan school, as may be seen by the unique and overwhelming group of cathedral, baptistery, and campanile in that solitary, grass-grown square of the Arno town, cultivated, by means of beautiful arcades and a subtle use of different colored marbles, a style which associates itself with the free and sunny traditions of classical Italy. The earliest architects at Siena, whoever they were, were imbued with Lombard ideas, but, owing to an acquaintance with Pisan results, wished to graft the charm and elegance of the neighboring school on the Lombard stock. If the thought in itself was good, the execution is subject to some heavy strictures, for the slight arcade around the cupola hardly suffices to produce an effect of elegance, and the alternate bands of black and white marble, representing the Sienese version of the Pisan brilliancy of surface, instead of supplying a note of gaiety, only deepen the natural gloom of the edifice. That the Board of Works was itself not delighted with the misapplied Pisan effect is proved by the circumstance that, when the choir was reached, the amount of black marble used in piers and walls was considerably reduced, to the immense brightening of that section. A similar tendency to excess, the usual fault of youth and inexperience, may also be observed in the extraordinary cornice, which, composed of the heads of the long succession of the popes, circles the whole nave and choir. These and other features, over which experts doubtfully shake their heads, and which tend to puzzle the visiting dilettante, do not, however, succeed in keeping the cathedral from making that triumphant impression, which, however achieved, we know to be a thing rising above details and defying intellectual analysis. Especially when the evening light sifts through the clerestory, softening the harsh dispute between the banded black and white, and spreading a warm gloom among the tall piers, stretching in solemn rows through nave and transept, the spacious beauty of this interior will unfold itself to every one whose approach to the world of art is unvexed by thought, and who rates a genial and naïve simplicity above the correctness of an unerring taste.

When I said that the cathedral strikes unhesitatingly the Romanesque note I did not mean to imply that it is entirely free from minor Gothic traits and adornments. Gothic forms succeeded in obtaining so universal an ascendency in the course of the thirteenth century that they were certain to insinuate themselves even into a building deriving from an earlier inspiration. In the Sienese cathedral they meet the eye at every turn, in the forms of the windows, in the capitals, in the profiles of the ribs, but wherever they occur they are absorbed into a perfect harmony with the prevailing style.

When we step from the nave into the open air to receive the impression which the exterior view makes upon the mind, we are likely to surrender ourselves, first of all, to the happy sense of release attending our passing from a place of solemn gloom into the clear, boundless light of an Italian day. This long edifice,

enveloped in shining marble and crowned by cupola
and soaring campanile, has under the blue sky an air of
frank communication which is in the sharpest possible
contrast with the ghostly suggestion and whispered
messages of the interior. How imposingly and with
what a sense of ease it spreads its huge mass over the
hill! What a crown to shine forever, white and pure
above the clustered houses of the city browned with
age and, at the hour of sunset, glowing dull red as in
memory of the spilt blood of civil feuds! If, in the
lonely piazza of Pisa may be seen greater charm and
grace, elements of charm and grace are here also, in the
smooth garment of marble and in the cupola with its
delicate arcade. If, as close by as San Galgano, we
may see nobler Gothic, these windows of aisle and clerestory have at least an undoubted distinction and finish.
So runs our impression till, slowly swinging round the
square, we stand face to face with the façade. Except
as a curiosity, a tour de force, it is incredible that any
one should have patience with this celebrated feature
of the exterior, and support the shock with which it falls
upon the sensibilities. It was planned as an adaptation
of the façade of the cathedral of Orvieto which, though
it, too, has little organic connection with its interior
and is made to play the part of a mere screen, achieves
a beauty all its own, due to a fusion in admirably chosen
proportions of architecture, sculpture, and mosaic.
Of this merit, a merit of harmony, there is nothing in the
Sienese counterfeit; in its place we meet that barbarous
spirit of excess, of which we have found other traces
in the building, and in which we are obliged to recognize
a national trait. The superabundance of sculpture,

not in subdued relief as at Orvieto, but in the round
and of all sizes, has, quite apart from the wilful blurring
of the great structural lines, practically obliterated the
architecture.   The façade exists for the sculpture only,
which circumstance, in view of the necessarily ancillary
function of sculpture, removes every doubt concerning
the fitness of this terminal production.   It is the Christmas dream of a fanciful but undisciplined child, not
only disorganized and bewildering but, owing to a recent
restoration, deprived of that saving grace of many a
mediocre handiwork of man, the ivory tint of age.   In
sharp contrast to the west front, the baptistery end was
planned in a modest, attractive, and wholly Sienese
adaptation of Gothic principles, and, although un-
finished, may boldly be called the most satisfactory
feature of the whole exterior.   In west and east end
respectively we may see two significant and contrasting
phases of the Sienese temper.

Again I submit, that for all the strictures and problems
cast up by the detailed examination of this cathedral,
there is a simple remedy which blots them out of existence.   We have only to withdraw our attention from
youthful violences and unassimilated experiments pushing themselves into notice here and there, in order to
take in with a creative sweep the marvellous image of the
whole, and we must fall under the spell of the splendor
and majesty of this monument, to which many generations gave their love and labor, and where we may read,
expressed in stone and marble, the passions, the faults,
and the destiny of a nation.

A similar atmosphere lends a romantic charm to that
other great emanation of the civic spirit, the Palazzo

Pubblico.* We have seen that in the early days of the commune the new government followed the practice of putting the churches to public use, and of renting private residences in order to house its officials. The Constitution of 1262 showed us the Council of the Bell in session in the church of San Cristofano, while the potestà held court in San Pellegrino and dwelt with his suite in a mansion rented from a citizen. These arrangements, unexceptionable in the nursery days of the commune when its business was inconsiderable, would be found unsatisfactory in the period of manhood; and, in fact, as early as 1193, we encounter a measure proving that the republic had awakened to the new necessities of its position. In that year the consuls acquired land on the lower edge of the Campo, and after filling in the ground and building a retaining wall—a measure necessitated by the sharp declivity at this point—erected a modest edifice of probably no more than a single story on the higher or Campo side. This was the nucleus of the great palace of later days, and in it were housed the *dogana del sale e dell' olio* and the public mint, called *il bolgano*. Thus matters rested for about one hundred years, when the inconvenience and lack of dignity attaching to the haphazard installation of the potestà and Council of the Bell led to a succession of improvements. In this connection it must again impress the modern mind that there was nothing suggesting dispatch or precipitation in the founding of a mediæval commonwealth. Every step was taken after

* Scattered contributions on the history of this structure, together with abundant archivial material, have been utilized in the valuable study of *Donati*, "Bull. Sen.," XI, p. 311 *ff*. As my story of the construction of the palazzo is based upon Donati, I refer to him, once and for all, at this point.

ripe consideration and under pressure of ineluctable necessity. The necessity, in the case of the Council of the Bell, was that ever since the year 1271 it was without a home, and reduced to a very disconcerting and nomadic existence, because San Cristofano had to be abandoned by reason of injuries received in connection with the spiteful destruction of the houses of the famous Provenzano Salvani which abutted thereon. For more than a decade the Council was obliged to meet in private houses, rented from great nobles, until the humiliating situation was ended (1284) by the construction, within the Dogana, of an appropriate council chamber. In the same year the potestà was permanently assigned to a rented house to the right of the Dogana, and the Nine, whose period of power had just dawned, shortly after leased and moved into a house on the left of the communal structure. The main branches of the public service were now at least concentrated at one point.

With the question of the communal offices clearly put, the movement had inevitably to continue until the republic had provided itself with a specially constructed palace commensurate with its position in the Italian world. In 1288 a resolution was passed conformable to this idea, and was shortly followed by the purchase of the rented houses on either side of the Dogana. Not till ten years later, however, was actual work begun on the famous municipal residence which still stands— work which, from the nature of the case, was not entirely new construction according to a general plan, but which consisted in considerable part of a remodelling of existing buildings. In a comparatively short time the central section or *torrione* had taken the shape we now

see; as early as 1299, we are informed, it was completed
to the very battlements. And now any further delay
which occurred was due solely to the lack of funds.
Early in the fourteenth century we hear that the potestà's
wing to the right of the torrione was under way, and in
1310 the left wing, or wing of the Nine, was ready for
occupation. The palazzo thus completed in a period
of hardly more than ten years is substantially the
palazzo of to-day except that it was a story lower in
each of the wings. Within were two open courts, one,
which may still be admired, in the section of the potestà,
the other, enclosed in modern times and encumbered
with a broad stairway, in the wing called of the Nine or,
as frequently, of the Signoria.*

In the subsequent years followed many additions and
improvements. We learn that the treasury office or
Biccherna, which had found a home in the central
secion, received a stone vault, and that the walls of
various rooms were made beautiful with paintings, but
we perceive that no further important work in construction took place on the Campo till the government
resolved to build itself a tower for its bells. The town
bells, which summoned the members of the Council to
their deliberations; which announced the dawn of
another day of work,† and at night tolled the curfew,

* This suppression of one of the interior courts was effected, in order to
meet some fancied needs, in the year 1680. In the same year another even
more important change was made, for the wings on either side of the torrione
received their second story. Clear evidence of the original height of these
wings is furnished by the rows of arches which are still visible under the
second story windows, and which supported the original battlements. The
wonder is that the seventeenth century should have effected a remodelling
of the front in so chaste a spirit.

† The Constitution of 1262 declared (I, 304) that every dawn the bell
must be rung *per magnam horam*, a full hour!

Charity.   A detail from Jacopo della Quercia's Fountain

In the Loggia of the Palazzo Pubblico

clearing the streets and squares of chatter and business; which, in the absence of clocks, were relied upon to give notice of the passing hours—the town bells, I say, had a share in mediæval life which made them an object of almost superstitious veneration. Following the general custom, they had been hung originally in rented towers, until the resolution was taken to build a worthy struc- ture for them at public expense to the right of the palaz- zo. On October 12, 1325, the corner-stone was laid with the usual religious ceremony, after which, accord- ing to an ancient chronicle, messer Ugo de' Fabbri, who had the work in charge, "put into the foundation of the said tower some pieces of money . . . and set in each corner a stone with bits of writing in Hebrew, Greek, and Latin letters to make it safe against injury from thunder, lightning, and tempest."* Thus did messer Ugo de' Fabbri, convinced, like every good mediæval Christian, of the powers of necromancy, make shrewd double provision for the security and long life of his enterprise. In connection with the tower the whole wing of the palace adjoining it underwent changes both of adjustment and enlargement. This had be- come pressingly necessary because the quarters of the potestà had been found too small for him and his numer- ous suite. For some reason the progress was slow, for we find that the potestà did not take possession of his improved residence till the year 1330, and that in 1338 the tower had not yet risen above the walls of the palace. Only then the work began in earnest on what

* The original is delightful: ". . . e fuvvi messa in ogni canto una pietra co' lettare ebraiche greche e latine, perchè non fosse percossa nè da tuono, nè da sætta, nè da tempesta." Chronicle in Biblioteca Comunale, Cod. A., III, 26, c. 83.

the almost unanimous voice of the lovers of art proclaims
to be the most beautiful tower of Italy. Signor Lisini
has discovered that its architects were two Perugians,
Minuccio di Rinaldo and Francesco, his brother, who
were, however, superseded before the completion of
their work. The noble ornament of gray stone, which
crowns the slender shaft of brick, or rather issues from
it as naturally and gracefully as the lily bursts from its
sheaf, was completed after a plan furnished by the
painter, Lippo Memmi. In the year 1344 the tower
was put into service and the citizens let their work rest
for a moment to listen joyfully as the first bell sent its
clamorous summons from a height of almost three
hundred feet.* During the next years the final touches
were added and some changes introduced, of which I
note only one because it furnished the tower with its
curious name. A mechanism, built in imitation of a
man, was installed aloft to strike the hours, and to this
man of wood, replaced afterward by a more splendid
one of brass, the people humorously gave the name of
the live bell-ringer whom the too inventive spirit of the
age had deprived of his occupation. The supplanted
bell-ringer seems to have been something of a butt
among the loungers that gathered in the wine-shops,
and went among them by the amusing name of *Mangia-
guadagni* or spendthrift. The designation of Man-
giaguadagni, or Mangia for short, was presently
transferred to the automaton, and, in the course of
time, attached itself to the whole tower, known therefore to this day as *la torre del Mangia*.†

* To be exact the tower measures 86⅔ meters.
† This luminous explanation of the name Mangia originated with Lisini,
"Misc. Stor. Sen.," I, 26.

And still the work of supplying the growing public needs with buildings specially constructed for the purpose continued. The prisoners of the town, who had been miserably housed in narrow rented quarters that, apart from the memories clinging to them of nameless horrors, were veritable breeding places of pestilence, were in the year 1330 transferred to the first municipally owned prison, erected behind the palace of the potestà; and, shortly after 1342, a new and vast hall for the General Council was raised over the gloomy rows of cells. Such an association, amounting almost to physical contact between the rulers of society and its broken victims, would be intolerable to our feeling, but seems to have aroused no comment among a generation of men endowed with enviable nerves of iron. The great *sala del consiglio* was in the bureaucratic sixteenth century, which had neither understanding nor reverence for the relics of a free society, reduced to a theatre, and gradually put through such changes as to obliterate every feature of its original style.

To render complete the history of the palazzo, I must add a word touching the outer chapel at the foot of the Mangia tower, the *capella di piazza*. This chapel owes its origin to a vow addressed to the Virgin during the *grande mortalità* of 1348, but its construction was not begun till four years later. Owing to muddling, both official and professional, it long defied completion, and was at length, in an access of despair, covered with a temporary roof at the height of the capitals. Not till a century later, in the period of the Renaissance, was the work again taken in hand, and being entrusted to the capable Federighi, was soon vaulted over and finished with pleasing decorations, chief among them an effective frieze of gryphons (1468–70).

At last I have arrived at the end of this long-spun and complicated story of a municipal structure which took one hundred and fifty and more years to bring to completion. This deliberate procedure, while corresponding to the slow economic expansion of the mediæval commune, also gives the measure of the very gradual manner in which the consciousness of a new society and its needs dawned upon those blindly groping generations. The rich experience of the many subsequent centuries, laid down in an effective science of government and in a knowledge of mechanics which laughs at difficulties, has changed completely our manner of approach to the problem of providing a fit home for our ruling bodies. A modern architect would undertake to erect and finish a building of much greater bulk than the Sienese palazzo in less than a year. But would he, so infinitely superior in the means at his command, venture to promise that it will endure as long, and be an object of beauty and a source of joy six centuries after the laying of its corner-stone?

The palace of Siena, composed of a central mass and wings and flanked by the tower which soars upward like an arrow released from the bow, ranks with the great municipal residences of the Middle Age. The forms which it employs—the pointed arches of the ground floor, the ample three-light windows, the square battlements—speak the common language of the Gothic period, but they are so combined and modified by local sentiment as to result in a highly idiomatic creation.

The union of stone in the lower story with brick in the
superstructure has produced a delightful variation of
surface, which is a subtle source of pleasure to the eye.
The final grace, however, is conferred upon the palace
by its position on the Campo.   This remarkable square,
which, as already observed, may owe its shape to a
preëxisting Roman forum, is neither quite an oval nor
quite a semicircle.   Its capricious refusal to be classi-
fied under any known geometric form is one of its charms,
to which must be added the natural tilt of the ground
toward the Palazzo Pubblico.   As the entrance to the
Campo is from the elevated ridges which meet in the
Croce di Travaglio, the communal palace with its
battlemented sky-line, its gloriously patinated surface,
and its slender tower is placed at just the point where
it presents itself to view with the greatest possible
effectiveness.   Strange to say the houses fronting on the
Campo, though they have for the most part gone
through modernizations, especially as regards the
windows, hardly attenuate, by reason of their wise
subordination to the palace, the consistent mediæval
impression of this square.   In the days of the republic
when, owing to a formal ordinance, Gothic windows *a
colonelli* prevailed around the whole enclosure,* the
effect must have been magnificent.

The ordinance just referred to, enforcing the style
of the municipal residence upon the houses of the
Campo, may account for the fact that this building
served as the model for the private palaces throughout
the city.   In such edifices, raised shortly after the

* The ordinance in question was passed in 1297.   Borghesi and Banchi,
"Nuovi Documenti," etc.

Palazzo Pubblico, in the period of the Nine, Siena is peculiarly rich. To pass them in review—the tall, inscrutable Palazzo Tolomei, the rude and yet distinguished Palazzo Saracini, the Palazzo Sansedoni, set in the high fellowship of the Campo and washed with soft pink as from a perpetual dawn, the Palazzo Grottanelli, splendid with the coats of arms of its former residents, the Captains of War, the Palazzo Salimbeni with its air of feudal insolence, the Palazzo Buonsignori crowned with beautiful battlements—is to receive an overwhelming impression of the fourteenth century greatness of this city. These buildings, one and all, rest architecturally upon the communal palace: they employ the same materials of construction with a frank preference for brick; they exhibit the same Gothic ornaments; but each one is so entirely free in its use of what it borrows that the result never fails to be artistic and original. Concerning the Tolomei palace, and concerning it alone, a doubt may reasonably be entertained touching the asserted derivation from the Palazzo Pubblico. The residence of the Tolomei, perhaps the most wonderful of all by reason of the union of great simplicity with fine proportions, is declared by an ancient chronicler to have been begun in the year 1208, that is, several generations before the palace on the Campo.* The same chronicler speaks, too, of subsequent injuries suffered through fire and political malice. The evidence still supplied to the eye would seem to show that there was an early Romanesque palace from which the present structure derives its general frame of stone,

---

* Muratori, XV, "Cronaca Sanese," ad annum.   "Fecesi el Palagio de' Talomei."

Wrought-iron Gate of the Chapel of the Palazzo Pubblico

especially the tall first story and the fine lions of the
lintels, but that it underwent important changes in the
fourteenth century, when it received its Gothic im-
print, noticeable, above all, in the windows with their
graceful tracery.

A body of courageous citizens, who had built through
generations and with many sacrifices a cathedral and a
municipal residence, were sure to address themselves
with proportionate energy to all minor public works.
Chief among them in a city situated like Siena were the
fountains.   They had received the care of the parishes
and neighborhood associations long before there was
a commune, and, naturally, with the rise of the commune, their improvement became one of the chief
objects of the new government.   In fact, among the
earliest notices we possess of Siena is a reference to
Fonte Branda.   An inscription, still imbedded in the
wall of this fountain, informs us that one Bellaminus
built it in the year 1193, while a second inscription of
1246 makes mention of additional labors of construction, a reference presumably to the heavy stone vault
which encloses the work.*   Fonte Branda was an
exceptionally handsome fountain in its day, with a
copious flow constantly enriched by the extension of the
subterranean aqueducts upon which it depends for its
supply of water.   In modern times it has lost its battlements and has acquired a squat and inelegant appearance through the burying of its piers to over half their
length by the gradual filling in of the soil, but Dante

---

* For the history of Fonte Branda and of every other fountain of Siena,
the reader may turn to the scholarly work of Bargagli–Petrucci, "Le Fonti di
Siena"; for Fonte Branda in particular, see Vol. I, 182 ff.

gives ample evidence that its fame in the days of its splendor had gone over Italy.*

Other fountains, similarly enclosed in walls and heavily vaulted, lend picturesque touches to various quarters of the town. Around the great open basins may be seen at all hours of the day the women of the neighborhood, gay with colored kerchiefs and chattering merrily as they bend over the household washing. Such fountains are Fonte Nuova in Vallerozzi, Fonte d'Ovile outside the gate of that name, and Fonte Follonica, left in a romantic abandonment amidst the kitchen gardens behind Santo Spirito. A fountain of a different kind, not meant so much to serve the needs of the citizens as to give expression to their love of home and their passion for beauty, was the celebrated fountain of the Campo. That it should have occurred to an artistic people to add to a square, which was their pride, the charm of running water is not strange. The difficulty was to find the requisite supply. In the year 1334 work was begun to collect water by means of subterranean channels outside Porta Camollia, and after a heavy expenditure of money and labor, a thin stream at last issued forth upon the Campo (1343). It was enough to loose a bedlam of joy. For fifteen days, we are told, the citizens held carnival, instituting games and dancing in companies amidst music and laughter through the streets.† They were a light-

---

* The man in hell, agonized by thirst, would rather see his enemies at his side suffering his pain than have all the waters of Fonte Branda: per Fonte Branda non darei la vista. "Inf.," XXX, 76–78. Petrucci seems to prove successfully that the reference is to the Sienese fountain and not to one of the same name in the Casentino.

† Muratori, XV, "Cronaca Sanese," 106. ". . . e per la detta cagione si fece tanta allegrezza in Siena e tanti balli . . . che sarabbe incredibile a

hearted folk, the mediæval Sienese, and never let an
occasion for merry-making escape. After this there
could be but one name for the new fountain: it was
called Fonte Gaia. A drop of wormwood in the full
goblet was the meagre flow, which the signoria set
itself to remedy by an ever renewed search for springs
along the northern ridge. Early in the fifteenth century
the government resolved to transform the receptacle in
the central square into a magnificent structure of
marble. By a fortunate coincidence the right man for
the work was close at hand, Jacopo della Quercia,
a Sienese citizen and one of the greatest names of
Italian art. After a labor of ten years, often interrupted
by the need of his restless genius to engage in a variety
of enterprises, Jacopo completed, in the year 1419, such
a monument as was boasted in the Middle Age neither
by imperial Rome, ever echoing with the murmur of
water, nor by Venice, maid of the sea. However, in
the course of the ages Jacopo's fountain suffered such
serious injury that to avoid total destruction it had, in
the nineteenth century, to be removed from the Campo.
Its remnants may now be seen in an environment that
could not have been better chosen, the upper loggia of
the Palazzo Pubblico. The broken pieces, like a Greek
torso recovered after centuries from a temple ruin, are
touched with imperishable beauty.

An appreciable factor in the mediæval impression
still conveyed by Siena are her walls and gates. Naturally they were an early and a constant preoccupation

dire e a credere chi non l' avesse veduto; che quasi ciascuna Arte otto dì
prima e otto dì poi per se fece una brigata . . . ballando e danzando e
cantando per la città insino alla notte."

of a republic surrounded by enemies. This is not the
place to discuss the difficult question of the successive
extensions due to the growth of the city. Malavolti,*
beginning with the Etruscan castle, speaks of six
circles of walls, which, of course, is not to be taken
literally but to be interpretated as referring to six
distinct periods of enlargement.† In any case, when
we reach the days of her power under the Nine, Siena
had substantially the walls and gates of to-day. Minor
portals have been closed, the principal ones have under-
gone repairs and alterations, but the fourteenth century
is still forcefully impressed on the defences behind
which she defied her foes. The Porta Romana, the
Porta de' Pispini, and the Antiporta of Camollia, a
single round arch of magnificent sweep, have that precious quality called character, which, if not identical
with beauty, bears a close kinship to it. To receive the
message which Siena conveys it is necessary to have
looked at her gates with reverence, as it is also necessary
to have walked around her walls, especially the picturesque stretch from Ovile to Pispini. Whoever has
followed in an afternoon's excursion their sudden
plunge and ascent along their broken path, and soothed
his senses with their perfect tone of pink and gray, will
have mastered one of the secrets of the spell exercised
by the ancient city.

In the fifteenth century the vital force of Siena, which
had been visibly failing for some time, still showed itself

---

* Malavolti, Prima parte, 13, 15, 21, etc.

† Bargagli-Petrucci, "Le Fonti di Siena," has a map at the end of Volume I
in which he gives with admirable clearness his version of the six circles. He
also traces a seventh and last circle, resulting from the construction in the
sixteenth century of the fortezza di S. Barbara.

in occasional creative outbursts. Such a one is associated with Jacopo della Quercia's fountain; at the
same time, but with different artistic result, was built
the Loggia della Mercanzia (1416), fronting the Croce
di Travaglio, and hardly to be found other than heavy
and ill-proportioned by the side of the great Florentine
loggia with which it naturally invites comparison. For
some years now conspicuous enterprises ceased till,
shortly after the middle of the fifteenth century had been
passed, there was a brief stir of architectural activity due
to the impulse of a single man, the famous Sienese pope
of the Piccolomini family, Pius II. Then were built
the charming Piccolomini Loggia, the Palazzo Piccolomini, the Palazzo Nerucci, and the Palazzo Spannoc-
chi, all planned either by Florentine architects or by
architects under Florentine influence. These splendid
structures give the Renaissance touch to Siena which
no one would care to miss; nevertheless, they not only
represent an artistic importation, but are impotent to
drown the mediæval note so formidably struck by the
city's ensemble.*

Thus through continued efforts, chiefly of the thirteenth and fourteenth centuries, was Siena endowed
with the various monuments which are the expression
in durable material of her character and history. Add
the humble but never unsightly houses of brick and

* It must strike the reader's attention how little the churches, apart always
from the cathedral, count in this ensemble. That is due to a variety of
reasons. In the first place the two great houses of the begging orders, S.
Francesco and S. Domenico, are architecturally of little or no interest, being
nothing more than huge barns; and, further, the very ancient parish churches,
such as S. Vigilio, S. Cristofano, and S. Martino, which, if small and rude,
must have possessed a definite mediæval character, were in the Renaissance
centuries done over in the prevailing style.

stone along the sharp slopes and winding streets by
which the poorer classes gradually replaced the wooden
dwellings of an earlier time, and we have before us the
picture of the commune at the height of its destiny.
If our hearts are moved by this age-browned city, lying
high upon its hill and lifting up its white cathedral like
a shrine of pearl, it is not merely because our imagination readily makes a romance of the past, but because
we perceive in its strong and ordered masonry the admirable effects of a creative civic spirit.

CHAPTER XI

THE ARTISTIC SPIRIT AND THE ADORNMENT OF THE CITY

OWING to the cosmopolitanism of our time, with its growing tendency to obliterate mental boundaries and create a uniform civilization, the purely national element in a work of art is not as prominent as it once was. While an artistic production is received by us primarily in the light of a personal statement about life, in the Italian Middle Age it represented far more truly the version current among a particular school or group, with the passions and prejudices of which the individual artist was content to be fully identified. The neighbors of shop and street, enclosed by the same wall, constituted the people of his choice and love, distinct not only politically from the rival peoples established in the surrounding towns, but differentiated from them morally and mentally, as well as by innumerable peculiarities of dress, habit, and sentiment. The work of the mediæval artist possesses therefore in the highest degree the flavor of the immediate soil from which it sprang.

This idiomatic result, due to the stubborn self-sufficiency of the early commonwealths, was confirmed and fortified by still another circumstance. As the communes acquired strength and vigor they set them-

selves as one of their chief tasks the upbuilding of a
home, worthy, noble, and beautiful. I have already
spoken of this common mediæval passion, showing how
in Siena it produced the cathedral, the Palazzo Pubblico,
and the whole town as it still stands. But as the
national enthusiasm did not rest here, as the walls
raised by the architects were susceptible to the manifold
adornment which are the special province of sculpture,
painting, and the minor arts, these arts no less than
architecture, and certainly to an extent utterly unknown
in our day, were informed with the civic spirit and
moulded to its uses and ideals. In view of these circumstances, which bring home to us the picture of a
long continued isolation, coupled with a fiery local
passion, it is not strange that all work issuing from the
botteghe of the Sienese artists should have a distinctive
quality, in which we may, without falling into exag-
geration, recognize the special genius of the Sienese
commonwealth.

The identification of the mediæval artist with the
group claiming him by birth is fully illustrated by the
great work which inaugurates the history of the Sienese
school of painting.* I am speaking of Duccio di
Buoninsegna's famous Ancona, painted for the duomo
and enthroned on the High Altar, directly under the

---

* The literature on Sienese painting is immense. For an analysis of the
æsthetic elements of the school nothing exists to compare with the essay of
Berenson, "The Central Italian Painters of the Renaissance." On the
history and the production of the school see Milanesi, "Documenti per la
Storia d'Arte Senese"; Borghesi and Banchi, "Nuovi Documenti," etc.;
Vasari, "Le Vite de' più eccellenti Pittori," etc., edited by Milanesi; Langton
Douglas, "A History of Siena," chap. 18; Heywood and Olcott, "Guide
to Siena," Part II; Burckhardt, "Der Cicerone," 9te Auflage; E. H. and E.
W. Blashfield, "Italian Cities." Vol. I.

cupola, in the year 1311.   There was painting in Siena
before Duccio's day, enough to have led to the formation of a very active guild of the practitioners of the art,
but, judging by its best known work, the madonna by
one Guido da Siena, hanging in the Palazzo Pubblico,
it was without any special significance.   Duccio first
blew Guido's poor embers into flame and is the true
founder of Sienese painting.   Guido, his predecessor,
and the long line of earlier craftsmen in whose tracks
Guido followed, were the degenerate heirs who administered with laughable ineptitude the great patrimony of the Byzantine Greeks.   Ages before, in the
fifth and sixth centuries, this people, spanning the
Bosphorus at the meeting-point of East and West, had
developed out of Asiatic and Hellenic elements a new
decorative system which for richness and solemnity of
effect has rarely been surpassed.   At Ravenna, hailed
as bride of the Adriatic until displaced by mounting
Venice, the eastern artists worked for several generations and to such good effect that we may still, by a visit
to that marsh-encircled town, assure ourselves that a
Greek mosaic of the early Christian era, set together of
little cubes of colored glass, has not only a permanency
—itself no mean merit in a work of art—but a glow
and majesty which takes possession of our delighted
senses like orchestral music.   No artists have ever
achieved more with pure color than these Christian
Greeks; their designs, on the other hand, while fulfilling,
at least in the earlier examples, the minor part reserved
for them in the general effect, tended to become, as the
years rolled on, more and more conventionalized, and
the human figures in them increasingly stiff, lifeless,

and hieratic. In the mosaics of Ravenna, Rome, and many scattered places we may recognize the models as well as the starting-point of Italian painting. However, under the disintegrating influences of the Germanic conquest and settlement, the young art failed to take firm root, and, though imitating the eastern productions, soon lost all sense of the Byzantine graces of form and color, and ended in producing those palsied and revolting Christs-upon-the-cross, examples of which are to be found in the early rooms of every Italian museum. Although Guido da Siena's madonna, which bears an inscription with the date 1221—a date, by the way, which most authorities look upon as impossible, prefering to substitute for it 1284 *—enjoys the distinction of marking a reaction from the prolonged and intolerable degradation of the graphic arts, the painter's improvement is not sufficient to carry him forward into a land of promise. That step was reserved to Duccio.† Did Duccio in his youth have under his eyes by any chance the old mosaics of Ravenna and Rome, or did he go further and travel to distant Constantinople to apprentice himself to some Greek master in whose shop the majestic traditions of his craft were still current? These questions, imposed by the character of the young innovator's work, have been frequently put, but belong to the realm of conjecture. What is certain and beyond conjecture is that Duccio somehow and somewhere quickened his spirit and steadied his hand by contact with the genius of Byzantium. To be sure he did not work in

---

* On this controversy see Langton Douglas, "Siena," 481 ff.

† Duccio was active in Siena as early as 1278, and probably died shortly after 1313. See for a few certain facts, extracted from the public records, the article by Lisini, "Bull. Sen.," V, 20 ff.

mosaic, but in the slighter and more fluid medium of paint, which had succeeded to the favor once enjoyed by the colored cubes. But his painting is for all the world like a mosaic which, in the course of its transfer from an ancient wall or apse, has, not without some paling of its glorious surface, acquired a greater freedom of line and a closer relationship to the actual forms of life.

While Duccio renewed the art of painting and became the father of a school, down in the Arno valley, at Florence, a similar mission was fulfilled by Giotto, son of Bondone. Because Giotto, giver of life to the school of Florence, was somewhat younger than Duccio, it has been urged by occasional partisans that the school of Siena enjoys a clear priority over its Florentine rival and must stand at the head of every history of Italian painting. That was not the view of Messer Giorgio Vasari, the first great historian of the arts, who, though an Aretine by birth, became a passionate partisan of the greatness of Florence, his city by adoption. On the strength of the reputation of a certain Cimabue, named by Dante as the forerunner of Giotto and older by a generation than Sienese Duccio, he imperiously assigned all the credit for reviving what he called "the noble art of design" to his fellow-citizens of Florence. He would have it that painting is specifically a Florentine invention, and the school of Siena no more than the seedling of a famous stock. But unhappily Cimabue, in spite of Vasari's generously inventing a life for him and of supplementing the act by a liberal catalogue of works, has, under the searchlight of modern criticism, shrunk to such an extent that not a single authoritative painting remains to make him credible and

real.*   With Cimabue eliminated from the argument, at
least until new facts come to light, the wordy war between
the champions of Florence and Siena, touching the age of
their respective schools, would appear to settle itself, if
that were anything gained.   For the student, however,
whose mind turns instinctively to essentials, the question
of priority—a question of dates—is of little importance.
He will gladly dismiss every mere *querelle allemande* to
fix his attention upon such simple and indubitable facts
as these, to wit, that Duccio and Giotto are the
acknowledged originators of two splendid schools of
painting, that they are to all intents contemporaries,
and that they are independent and largely self-inspired
workers.   Independent, I say, for Giotto, though
somewhat younger than Duccio, did not fall under the
influence and was not the plagiarist the Sienese master,
but strove to give expression to the forms of his imagination by following the light of his own soul.   In the
course of his long self-education he did not turn back
to the Byzantine world; something imposed itself on
him more imperatively than the work of the Greeks,
and that was nature herself.   He dipped into the
fulness of life and by so doing opened a book
from which his countrymen, hailing him as their
leader, drew their chief joy and profit for many generations to come.   Duccio, thrilling to the wonders of
Byzantium, became a decorator with only a languid
interest in the natural world, and his followers of Siena,
receiving their inspiration from him, remained for the
two hundred years the school flourished, decorators

* For the case against Cimabue see an article by Langton Douglas in the
"Nineteenth Century" of March, 1903.

also, who only now and then, and always with something
akin to distaste, turned to refresh their splendid though
formalized art by contact with the shapes and movements of animate life.

Duccio's altar-piece owes its origin to the commune,
which, ever solicitous for the great cathedral erected by
its efforts, wished to make that structure as beautiful
in all details as lay in the power of the age to accomplish.
As the cathedral was dedicated to the Virgin, it was
highly proper that her image should adorn her temple.
The task was assigned to Duccio by a sort of referendum
of his countrymen who, weary of the tortured and
meaningless figures of the old art, found themselves
carried away by the novelty and charm imparted to his
panels by the new master in their midst.   However,
though enjoying the fame of a bold innovator, not till
he undertook the Ancona of the Virgin did Duccio reach
the full expression of his talent.   It was the national
undertaking, performed with all Siena looking on, that
gave him his inspiration and made him the founder of a
school.   The work, which the solid and thrifty rulers,
with fine disregard of cost in such an enterprise, urged
him to make as splendid as lay in his power, was
assigned to him in 1308 and was completed in less than
three years.   Then, the long labor done, the artist
added, by way of signature, an inscription which has the
faint, delicate fragrance of that loveliest product of
monastic Christianity, the Fioretti of St. Francis.
"Holy Mother of God," it reads, "give Siena peace and
Duccio life because he painted Thee thus."*   On the

* "Mater Sancta Dei Sis Causa Senis Requiei Sis Duccio Vita Te Quia
Pinxit Ita."

appointed day the great altar-piece was carried to the house of the Virgin; and, a contemporary chronicler recounts, "the bishop ordered a great and devout company of priests and friars to attend in solemn procession the Signori Nove and all the officials of the commune and all the people; and all the greatest citizens in turn with lighted candles in their hands escorted the said picture, and behind them followed the women and children with much devotion. And they accompanied the said picture all the way to the duomo,"* amidst the ringing of bells and the blare of silver trumpets. With such general delight did the Sienese receive into their keeping the monumental work of their fellow-citizen, and with favor and reverence they continued to look upon it for many generations. But at last a new taste came to prevail, and in the sixteenth century the picture was removed from its place of honor to suffer various translocations and indignities until in our time it has found a resting-place, incomparably better than the ordinary gallery, in the quiet *opera del duomo*. There it may be visited with that peace of mind which is indispensable to its understanding.

The Ancona, placed on the High Altar under the cupola where it could be seen from the front and from the rear, was painted, in order to meet this situation, on both sides: on the nave side with the Virgin among the hosts of heaven, and on the choir side with more than a score of episodes from the life and death of the Saviour. In addition, there were the usual predella and several other panels with Biblical scenes, inserted at various

* "Cronaca d'Anonimo." Quoted by Lisini, "Bull. Sen.," V, 22.

openings in the elaborate Gothic frame, for what Duccio presented to his native city was not only a painting but also a small masterpiece of wood-carving and of architecture. In the course of the wanderings, imposed by the intolerant taste of the Renaissance, the beautiful frame was destroyed, and the Ancona itself broken into convenient sections, with the result that the picture now offered to view, though in a not unsatisfactory state of preservation, is merely the *disjecta membra* of the elaborate composition mounted by the artist.

The body of the altar-piece represents the Virgin amidst the companies of heaven. She is seated on her throne with the divine Child before her, attended by a court of saints and angels in solemn, ordered rows. In the foreground on their knees are four members of the blessed troop particularly dear to Siena—our old friend, Sant' Ansano, of course, among them—begging her favor for the town which in the stormy period preceding Montaperti had proclaimed her liege and sovereign. Though it is immediately apparent that Duccio exhibited in this picture a knowledge of his craft which was nothing short of revolutionary, though the panel is touched with such rich splendor as to make it a sensuous delight, our deepest satisfaction in its presence springs not from these sources, but from the sincere and unmistakable revelation which it affords of the religious sentiment of the Middle Age. We are often told by critics of a scientific bent that he falls into egregious error who extracts other than æsthetic emotion from a work of art, and does not soberly confine his attention to such elements of technical skill as tone, color, line, and composition. Without embarking on a theoretical dis-

cussion which can have no place here, it may be catagor-
ically affirmed that followers of this unbending creed
will never establish a simple and cordial relation with
Duccio and his school. For, though a thing so subtle
as to defy analysis, the fact remains that the rarest
charm and most lasting distinction of Sienese painting
is the serene atmosphere of Christian sentiment in which
it is steeped. But let no one dream that Duccio's
merit is exhausted with this praise. His unreflecting
and instinctive relation to the gods of his home establishes chiefly his quality as a man; as an artist he commands a host of specifically artistic merits. What these
are can any one doubt who will surrender himself to the
impression of the great Ancona? Gazing with open
senses, can he fail to respond to the rich glow of color,
to the delicate details, and to the stately proportions of
the composition? Gold, a liquid gold, soft as evening
waters, fills the eye, for it lies upon the halos, the robes,
the background, touching everything with splendor;
the charming patterns, worked with the passion of the
miniaturist into mantles, throne, and shield-like aureoles
enforce the note of gaiety; and any loss of power and
simplicity threatened by the meticulous elaboration is
entirely overcome by the large, rhythmical swing of the
composition.

When we turn from Duccio's great panel of the enthroned Virgin to the scenes from the Passion of Christ
—originally the reredos of the great Madonna—we
perceive at a glance that his powers were not suited to
this particular task. No doubt these panels, too, possess the charm of surface which Duccio's brush gave to
everything it touched; nevertheless, they do not—to use

a term familiar to artists—carry. The painter who
could give us a vision of the Virgin and her company as
moving as a song, on turning to the dramatic episodes
recounted in the gospels, immediately lost his bear-
ings: he accumulates facts, he wanders among ac-
cessories, he babbles like a thought-free child. The
swift, clear seizure of all that was essential in a given
occurrence, in the kiss of Judas, in the scourging of
Christ, in every one of the familiar and always marvellous
scenes of the Passion, was denied him. So conspicuous
a failure in so sure a hand must plunge us into puzzled
reflection. Giotto, working at Florence, not forty miles
away, had, in a degree perhaps never matched in the
history of art, this very power of grasping with absolute
precision the significance of a human event and render-
ing it with the minimum of effort. Why Giotto's success and Duccio's failure? Without pretending to
solve unfathomable mysteries, we may point out that
the respective achievements of the two masters accurately
reflect their different inspiration and original proclivi-
ties. Duccio, looking back to the Byzantine mosaicists,
became a sumptuous decorator with no more than a
child's feeling for the sweet and terrible drama of existence, while Giotto, the naturalist, who moved familiarly
among men and steeped himself in all their grave concerns, achieved a gift of swift and simple statement
summoning our attention like a tocsin.

During the time Duccio was painting his altar-piece
for the cathedral the civil residence of the commune
was completed and the rulers, animated with the public
spirit with which we are now familiar, took up the matter of its ornamentation. The ideals of mediæval life

emanated so largely from the church that the pictorial imagery of a public hall no less than that of a house expressly built for worship would be determined by religion. When to Simone Martini, therefore, was committed a wall of the new chamber where the Great Council of the citizens was wont to meet, nothing was more natural than his presenting there, just as Duccio had done in the duomo, the liege Lady of Siena with her heavenly attendants. The Majestas, as the work is nobly called, done in fresco in the year 1315,* still survives, though considerably impaired by the ravages of time. Nevertheless, neither time nor the more wilful injuries of man have robbed it of its charm, a charm so delicate and imponderable that to express it in words seems like a vain beating of the air. Simone, it is plain, learned his art from Duccio, but by the force of genius was enabled to go far beyond his master. All that makes Duccio's cathedral panel memorable is here, too, but in every instance carried to a fuller, richer expression. Instead of Duccio's splendor, achieved by a profusion of gold-leaf, Simone gives us a harmony, different in kind but as effective as that of those masters of sensuous charm, the Venetians. For with the younger artist gold—a rich but barbaric medium, when all is said—is abandoned for color, which washes the draperies, throne, and faces with gay and delicate tints, mounting to a note of welcome austerity in the flat background, blue and cool and deep as an Italian night. In the composition, too, Duccio's rigorous symmetry has been replaced by a more flowing and resourceful treat-

* Owing to damage done by the humidity exuding from the neighboring government salt-stores, the fresco was in part renewed by Simone in 1321.

ment, revealed in a less mathematical grouping of the
saints and soldiery of heaven, and in such an expressive
detail as the long vertical lines of the poles which support
the canopy of the throne and endow the picture with its
agreeable effect of height.   But, elaborate as the composition is, it is dominated at every point by the Madonna herself.   To her, hieratic and remote, as tradition
would have her, but touched for the first time in Sienese
art with something of human grace, the eye returns
from every excursion as to its home and haven.   In
Simone we meet the art of the innovator Duccio carried
to its perfection.

And what the opposite wall of the same room dis-
closes will only confirm that impression.   There, some
years later (1328), Simone painted the equestrian
portrait of Guidoriccio da Fogliano, a professional
soldier frequently employed by the republic to command
its army in time of war.   Such a portrait signified a
departure from the tradition which favored the exclusive
presentation of religious themes, but which would
inevitably be subjected to change in measure as art
absorbed new elements of life.   Simone, though practising painting with characteristic Sienese reverence for
the past, was great enough to be afraid neither of new
ideas nor of new methods.   He shows us Guidoriccio
as he rides abroad before Montemassi, a Maremma
castle which had risen in revolt and which the Sienese
army had been sent to subdue.   The slight landscape,
showing the battlemented stronghold as well as the
camp of the Sienese, is treated as a pure accessory, and
all the emphasis is concentrated on the rider.   The rich
trappings, swathing both man and horse, display

Simone's fine sense of pattern, while the flowing movement of the wind-blown drapery lends, by that contrast
which only the greatest artists can employ successfully,
a wonderful impressiveness to the vertical rigidity of the
warrior.*

Adjoining the spacious hall of the Great Council was
the smaller and more intimate chamber of the Nine.
In the year 1337, nine years after Simone had limned the
portrait of Guidoriccio, its decoration was entrusted
to a man who had lately begun to attract attention,
Ambrogio Lorenzetti.   Ambrogio had an older brother,
Pietro, and the two, toward the middle of the fourteenth
century, and especially after Simone betook himself to
Avignon as painter to the pope, threw all their Sienese
rivals into the shade.   Although Ambrogio could boast
a much greater native endowment than Pietro, the two
brothers are logically associated together, owing to their
common departure from the artistic traditions of their
countrymen.   Of course both are profoundly Sienese,
but both none the less fell under the spell of Giotto's
naturalism. This larger range, coupled with their excellent color and grave types, may account for the wide
popularity they enjoyed throughout central Italy.   On
being entrusted with the chamber of the Nine, Ambrogio proceeded to prove his sympathy with the enlarged
ideals of painting by composing an allegory, called Good
and Bad Government.   It would be rash to say that he

* Simone worked much abroad; at Assisi he has left frescoes in the chapel
of Saint Martin, which for pure loveliness have rarely, if ever, been surpassed;
at Avignon, where he died in 1344, his work has been destroyed.   At Avignon
he met—a happy accident—the poet Petrarch, painted a portrait of Laura,
and was paid in poet's coin with two delicate sonnets (49 and 50 of Il Canzoniere).

achieved a great triumph. Allegory, with its tendency to impart information and inculcate a lesson, is always in danger of tiring its public, unless the artist sternly checks his garrulity by the exercise of dramatic brevity and self-restraint. These were not merits of Ambrogio or of his Sienese compatriots in general. Ambrogio, like Duccio in the case of the scenes from the Passion of Christ, found there was much to say and tried ramblingly to say it all. The result is that he came very near saying nothing. On the wall opposite the single window of the rectangular room in which he worked he presented his idea of the moral and political agents, Justice, Concord, Fortitude and so forth, which are the pillars of Good Government. On the neighboring wall he exhibited the images of Tyranny, Pride, Cruelty, and all the evils which in their sum signify Bad Government. Adjoining Good and Bad Government respectively are two further frescos which bring before our eyes the actual effects in a city and its district of the two systems. Two pictures of the four are, therefore, strictly speaking, allegorical, two are more particularly illustrative. The illustrative ones, as well as the allegory of Bad Government are almost ruined. What little can be still made out justifies us in saying that Bad Government, with a profusion of devils, monsters, and the like juvenile shapes of terror, is simple to the point of childishness, and that the expansive illustrations of the effects of Good and Bad Government are redundant to the point of weariness. Of course there are some exquisite details, especially, in the city blessed with a good government, a knight riding out to hunt and a group of girls executing the popular *ridda* or round dance. If Ambrogio had arrested his brush at this point he would have given us enough, but he chose to crush these modest flowers of his art under an overwhelming and meaningless machine.

There remains to be considered the allegory of Good Government, which, though injured, is far from a state of ruin and which represents the artist's highest achievement in the chamber of the Nine. Again the instructive element is too omnipresent to permit our spirit to take its ease, as it should in the presence of a work of art, but, our first distaste at this disproportion overcome, we encounter such an abundance of high, artistic charm, that it is impossible to resist the impression that Ambrogio, in spite of his scholastic aberrations, was a delicate and powerful genius. Good Government, conceived as a sovereign of grave and noble aspect, sits surrounded by a court of six ladies representing—as inscriptions inform us—Prudence, Fortitude, Peace, Magnanimity, Temperance, and Justice; at his feet, to his left, are his armed ministers who have brought in a group of evil-doers, bound and chained, while from his right, come to do him honor, approaches a company of citizens, all holding, in sign of civic union, by a cord committed to them by two women, seated apart and placarded, to help our understanding, as Concord and Justice. Nothing could be more effective than the ruler, looking out with level glance and planted, with his sceptre on his knee, firm as any tower; and nowhere can we hope to find so much grace, joined with so much dignity, as in the virtues seated at his side. Peace, robed in white, with a crown of olives in her hair, has always been singled out for praise. Prudence and

Magnanimity, to the sovereign's right and left, are hardly inferior to her. A very decorative touch, characteristically Sienese, is supplied by the long, massed lances of the armed men; in fact, wherever the eye falls, it encounters some feature of delight. The color is a chapter by itself; applied with the greatest delicacy, it acquires against a quiet background of deep blue a glow and fusion worthy of Simone.

The brothers Pietro and Ambrogio Lorenzetti, carried off their feet by the example of Giotto, and trying, with questionable success,* their hand at allegory and dramatic narrative, were unsurpassed in their day when they undertook altar-pieces in the meditative spirit and of the decorative quality traditional in their city. Pietro's triptych in the Opera del Duomo, representing the Birth of the Virgin, and the much suppler and gayer Ambrogio's many small madonnas—one at Sant' Eugenio outside Porta San Marco, another at San Francesco, a third in the Galleria, this last particularly fine with a bower of angels and four kneeling bishops— are wonderfully intimate revelations of fourteenth century feeling. A touch of naturalism, caught from Florence, gives these panels an unusual vivacity without impairing the charm of the hereditary and truly Sienese qualities of line and color.†

After the Lorenzetti came a period of stagnation. We have seen that Siena itself toward the middle of the century was touched with languor, and that its civic

* Look, for confirmation, at Pietro's work at Assisi. His scenes from the Passion are without a feature capable of communicating pleasure; they are chaos.

† Pietro and Ambrogio are lost track of toward the middle of the century; it has been surmised that they died in the great plague of the year 1348.

energy fell into decline.   Such a state of affairs was sure
to affect unfavorably the practice of painting, especially
as it coincided with a dearth of men on a level with the
creative geniuses of the last half century.   Even in the
Middle Age, though the nation influenced the production of the studios in a degree unknown to our time,
the arts had their ultimate root in the individual.   In
Florence, in the second half of the fourteenth century,
may be noticed an artistic decay as indisputable as the
contemporary failure of Siena, and in the case of
Florence, it is impossible to explain the phenomenon as
due to an enfeebled moral and economic condition.   If
painting in the Arno town declined, if it fell immediately
after its first brave flight to even a lower level than that
reached at Siena, the only satisfactory explanation is
that no individual appeared who was capable of turning
to account the magnificent inheritance of Giotto.   In
the upland city such men as Andrea Vanni (d. 1414)
and Taddeo Bartoli (d. 1422), though hardly more than
honest journeymen, showed at least that the spark
struck by Duccio was not extinguished.   To throw
a glance at Andrea's polytych in Santo Stefano, or at
Taddeo's scenes from the life of the Virgin in the
chapel of the Palazzo Pubblico, is to recognize the persistent vitality of a great tradition.   Florence has no
contemporary work of the same fibre, but Florence
presently achieved what was denied her rival—a second
period of creation more triumphant even than the first.
Were her slumbering energies revived because all
Florence—Florence considered as a people and a
nation—responded to the sharp stimulus of the Renaissance and expanded gratefully under the new influence,

or did her artistic energies owe their quickening rather
to leaders and geniuses like Masaccio and Donatello,
who freed the plodders in the *botteghe* from the chains
of old conventions and endowed them with new eyes
and a new understanding? Be the reason what it may,
Florentine art celebrated a glorious revival, expressive
of the young hopes which shed their light over mankind,
while in Siena, although there as elsewhere the Renaissance piped its alluring song, the painters contentedly
travelled the accustomed way, reproducing the forms and
sentiments with which they were familiar. We may
doubt whether even a succession of great leaders, had
they been granted to Siena instead of to Florence, could
have secured the victory of the Renaissance code of
life and art without the support of popular favor.
Indeed an earlier and a no less eloquent prophet of
the new time than Masaccio, Jacopo della Quercia,
was, by a strange caprice of nature, a son of provincial Siena, and during a score of years preached
the new gospel in his native city practically to deaf
ears.

In any case the fifteenth century broke over Siena
and produced, at least as far as painting is concerned,
no art specifically of the Renaissance. To be sure this
century witnessed the labors of a most fascinating group
of artists, who signify a second blossoming of the
Sienese genius; but the striking fact remains that they
hardly deign to take notice of the new movement of
civilization, and, except for the absorption of a few new
elements of skill, exhibit a devoted loyalty to the mediæval traditions of their home. Although the new
period decidedly merits a close and sympathetic study,

the scope of this sketch does not permit me to do more than to present its leading representatives under the form of a general characterization. The dominant figures of Sienese painting during its second period of bloom were Stefano di Giovanni, called Sassetta (1392–1447), Sano di Pietro (1406–81), Benvenuto di Giovanni (1436–1518 ?), Matteo di Giovanni (1435 ?–1495), Francesco di Giorgio (1439–1502), and Neroccio di Landi (1447–1500). One and all of these men exhibit, of course in varying combinations, the familiar Sienese tendencies and qualities. They seek a sumptuous effect, retaining for the purpose the use of gold long after it was abandoned elsewhere; they cling to a delicate and elaborate detail; they love the old generalized types better than the differentiated humanity of the new realism; they refuse to be betrayed by perspective, and light, and the other conquests of science into a surrender of their simple decorative principles; and, finally, they admirably produce the impression which is appropriate to their means and their intention. In this last feature lies the real test of all their qualities; by sending forth into the world, a whole century after the death of the Lorenzetti, and when secular influences were asserting their ascendency throughout Italy, religious pieces sincerely conceived and unerring in their effect, they establish their rank as true artists. However, let no one expect to encounter among their panels either the radiant, care-free figures of Simone's art, suggesting a distant world of blithe romance, or the robust saints of Ambrogio who seem to have stepped out of a meeting of dignified burghesses. In their passage through the minds of a weaker generation, the old types, though still recognizable, have undoubtedly lost something of their nobler nature and been brought nearer to our common human state of wistfulness and frailty. These fifteenth century masters, shut off from the fresh currents of thought and taking their pleasure in endlessly refining upon the old methods and the old sentiments, had necessarily to pay for their self-satisfaction with the loss of virility. They constitute an Indian summer, shedding a faint fragrance which, if sweet, suggests decay and a near end.

All these belated mediævalists, and more particularly Matteo di Giovanni and Neroccio, were endowed with great natural gifts and did not adopt their conservative creed purely from pride or indolence. They knew perfectly well what was going on at Florence and in the world around; they were acquainted with the work of Donatello, and admired Botticelli and his friends, going so far as to import occasionally a trait of one or another Florentine into their work; but from every excursion beyond the circle of their town they returned with spontaneous resolution to the tradition of their predecessors because these painters, and these alone, stirred the Sienese heart. There is something in such tenacious loyalty to home ideals which forces our respect, but the honor we gladly pay the Sienese quattrocentists should not lead us to overlook the fact that their attitude is the proof of a confirmed provincialism. Duccio and his followers, marching onward with the breath of the morning upon them, carried Siena into the van of Tuscan civilization; Sano, Neroccio, and Matteo were content to have her sit remote among her hills, spinning reminiscences like an ancient pensioner. Thus painting adds its bit of evidence touching the rapid exhaustion, under the conditions of the new age, of the once lusty commune.

The profusion with which pictorial decoration once colored the walls of municipal buildings and of churches is brought home with astonishment to any one who strolls through the rooms of the Palazzo Pubblico or along the choir of S. Francesco and the Servi. What is left, crumbling and growing fainter every day, constitutes a considerable production, but is a small fraction of the art which once made these places attractive and memorable. In the fourteenth century, not only every wall which in any sense belonged to the public glowed, like the rich page of a missal, with fair borders and grave saints, but the passion for decoration spread to personal and household articles as well, and painters, not excluding the greatest, gladly made a trial of their skill upon shields, coats-of-arms, banners, book-covers, and marriage chests. Only this general diffusion of the decorative taste can account for the immense number of painters who found employment in Siena in the fourteenth century.*

Everything affirms that the Sienese were a people who, among all the arts, felt most immediately drawn to the moving charm commanded by the art of painting. But, possessed with the desire to magnify life in every manner given to man, they gratefully accepted also such services as lay in the gift of sculpture and the artistic crafts. As early as the year 1266, while Duccio was still a boy, the operaio of the cathedral ordered the pulpit of Niccolò Pisano, which still stands in the shadow

---

* A list of them—more than two hundred names—in "Misc. Stor. Sen.," IV, p. 133.

of the cupola. If the beauty of this monument is not generally convincing, there can be no dispute as to its historical importance. The Gothic sculpture of all Tuscany may be properly said to have its roots in it. The sculptors of Siena, who, before the arrival of the Pisan master, are more correctly qualified as stone-cutters, now had a work set before them far beyond their scope. And to the inspiration of the pulpit was presently added the highly finished figure-work of Giovanni, Niccolò's son, technically as gifted as his father and endowed with much finer artistic perceptions. Giovanni, who, as we know, acted for many years as operaio of the cathedral, probably not only erected the first façade of that edifice—the façade which was afterward destroyed—but adorned its niches and taber-nacles with many statues. Although very few remains of Giovanni's work can be still identified in Siena, there is no doubt that he exercised a wide influence and became the real founder of the Sienese Gothic school. This school found occupation chiefly in connection with the stonework of the cathedral, where we can judge of its taste and skill in the capitals of nave and choir, and in the foliage and figure-work profusely scattered everywhere. The sculptors of the Sienese trecento also fashioned stone altars and tabernacles, and raised those curious sepulchral monuments which consist of sar-cophagi imbedded in the walls of churches, and which are still to be found in frequent examples throughout Tuscany. All things considered, the amount of their work which has come down to us is not great, and such as it is, stamped with the mark of the shop and never of the individual, gives us no reason to regret that its

bulk is small. With the temperamental bent of the
Sienese toward color, we need hardly wonder that
sculpture did not acquire the magic touch of contemporary painting and never rose above the level of an honest
mediocrity. A far more favorable opinion of the local
school would be forced upon us if it could be proved
that Sienese sculptors moulded the reliefs upon the
façade of the cathedral of Orvieto. These, the most
delicate creations in stone of the Gothic period to be
found in Central Italy, immediately communicate by
their delicate forms and expressive movements that
feeling of intensified existence which is the best return
man has from art. Very probably these reliefs were
executed by Sienese masters under the general direction
of the architect of the façade, Lorenzo di Maitano, who,
it is certain, was a native of Siena; but even if the Orvieto work is Sienese, the fact remains that to the city
of the Virgin accrued no recognizable benefit from the
skill of its sons.

Just as sculpture was falling into a languor that promised a complete demise, it received a new impulse from
one of the forerunners of the Renaissance, Jacopo della
Quercia (1374-1428). Although Jacopo's mind and
hand never entirely ceased to declare his mediæval
origin, he turned with bold initiative from the exhausted
conventions of the past in order to refresh his art by
direct study of the forms of nature. He was the first
and almost the only Sienese realist, but his realism, in
distinction from that of his Florentine contemporaries,
was held in restraint by a sense of form so purely classical
that we do not encounter its like again till the days of
Michael Angelo. His main work in Siena is the Fonte

Gaia, of which I have already spoken in another place,
but his name is also connected with the beautiful font
of the Baptistery, for which he drew the general plan
and contributed the bronze relief representing the
expulsion of Zaccharias.   However, though his countrymen admired, they did not comprehend.   Jacopo's
work was in effect an attempt to throw open the doors
and windows of the Sienese mind to new light and
understanding; but, smiling pleasantly, without a sign
of rancor, the people of the hill-city rejected the proffered salvation.   The realist creed did in the course of
time make headway in the Elsa valley and, wedded to
the decorative taste native to this region, produced a
local school of Renaissance sculpture, the work of which
we may sincerely admire in delicately ornate doors, in
shapely friezes, and in occasional statuary.   Federighi
(d. 1490), if not the most capable, was certainly the
most active of this group, and in work where he could
legitimately indulge his love for smoothness and finish,
as, for example, in the frieze of the chapel of the Campo
or in that of the Palazzo dei Diavoli outside Porta
Camollia, proved that the old Sienese refinement still
survived.   But energy and force, the virtues of the conqueror, neither he nor his contemporaries possessed,
wherefore their work fades to a shadow when confronted
with the impetuous creations of such fifteenth century
Florentines as Pollaiuolo and Verocchio.*

The Age of the Communes, which saw the revival of

* I may be permitted to remind the reader who observes my failure even
to mention artists like Vecchietta and Marrina, that I am as little engaged in
writing a history of sculpture as of painting.   My sole object is to convey by
the method of an historical review a general idea of the quality of Sienese
work in stone and color.

the democratic spirit of republican Rome and, rooted
in the general awakening of man's slumbering energies,
a new bloom of the Fine Arts, naturally witnessed also
an interesting development of the artistic crafts. We
have found that the men who painted the pictures and
carved the images of stone and marble received their
commission from the great corporations of the church
and commune. As soon as their products involved any
considerable outlay of money, the humbler workers in
wood and metal were obliged to resort to the same powerful patrons. The truth is that wealth, far from being in
any considerable quantity in private hands, was a corpor-
ate possession and was employed to serve the purpose and
flatter the taste of the ruling bodies of church and state.
The metal and wood workers of Siena, therefore, chiefly
produced in their shops, as the highest expression of their
skill, crucifixes, reliquaries, chalices, choir-stalls, and
other articles, serving to decorate the places of worship
and to ennoble the service of the Mass. Among the
various classes of craftsmen traceable in the Siena of
the trecento, the goldsmiths more particularly seem to
have enjoyed a great reputation, and one of them,
Lando di Pietro, who, after the manner of his time, was
also an architect and in this capacity drew the bold
plan for the uncompleted "duomo nuovo," was chosen to
fashion the crown used for the coronation of Dante's
hero, Henry VII. This crown, as well as Lando's
other works, are lost or, what is more likely, were, by an
age devoted to another style in jewel ornaments, returned to the crucible, unless it be that the exquisitely
worked reliquary of San Galgano, preserved by the nuns
of the Santuccio near Porta Romana, is of his hand.

Bronze Banner-holder
By Cozzarelli (attached to the Palazzo del Magnifico)

However, as this work has been also claimed for
Ugolino di Vieri, we must, waiving the question of attri-
bution, be content to receive it as an earnest of fourteenth
century skill and taste. The mediæval records prove
that republican Siena harbored within her walls, in
addition to goldsmiths, numerous workers in wood,
iron, and stained glass, but when we search for the surviving evidence of their handiwork, we find that it
reduces itself to a few scattered articles. True, after
time and man have for centuries done their worst to
disperse the artistic treasures of Siena, the town is still
remarkably rich in the product of the crafts, but an
examination will show that this product belongs, in its
bulk, either to the period of transition or to the full
Renaissance. As characteristic examples of this work,
conceived in the forms popularized by the new civilization, I may refer to the delicately ornate iron screen
of the inner chapel of the Palazzo Pubblico, to the
admirable bronze banner-holders of Cozzarelli on the
façade of the palace of Pandolfo Petrucci, and to the
exquisite wood pilasters carved for the same patron
by Barili. All these creations of the wood and metal
crafts breathe that quality of aristocratic refinement
which is met in all things Sienese in the last period of
life of the republic.

Therewith I have again reached the Renaissance and
the utmost chronological boundary of this book.
Casting our eye backward over the path we have
travelled, we are made aware that the art by which the
Sienese, in the period of their fullest development,
most significantly expressed their character and ideals
is the art of painting. In this field, in the course of

the trecento when youth and hope made their dwelling in the city, the people of the Virgin created radiant works, the effects of which were felt far beyond the narrow pale of home. Duccio and the Lorenzetti, but, above all, the magician Simone, showed, in their feeling for line and color and in the beauty of their decorative effects, a subtle refinement which, since the nation realized its noblest possibilities in these great sons, we may receive as the special message of this people; but thus delicately endowed, instead of shrinking from the world, Simone and his peers confronted it with the enterprise of fresh and elastic personalities. A hundred years after, in the Indian summer of Sienese art marked by such names as Neroccio and Matteo, the enterprise had vanished, but the refinement, coupled with the old sincerity of feeling, still remained. We are aware that in the period of these quattrocentists the whole public life of Siena began to exhibit ominous signs of collapse. The coincidence leads us back to the reflection which I set down at the head of this chapter: though in our day the arts, having, to a certain extent at least, become denationalized, do not always serve as a secure index of the life of a given people, in mediæval Siena the artists afford us without any doubt the most precious information which we have touching the civilization of the city of their birth. Happy in their communal setting and saturated with its special quality, these men unconsciously gave expression to the mute hopes and longings of their fellow-citizens. That is the reason why the art of Siena, as much as any art of any period of history, possesses a national and democratic character.

CHAPTER XII

MANNERS AND PASTIMES; LITERARY AND INTELLECTUAL ACTIVITY

BY the struggle of the young commune against the feudal system, by its gradual political organization, by its wars with its neighbors, by the arts which it cultivated—by such broad avenues as these the historian is most likely to arrive at what is significant in Sienese civilization; nevertheless an immense amount of curious information, occasionally adding an effective stroke to the picture, is afforded by investigating the more secret and unfamiliar paths which introduce us to the amusements of the people, to the forms of intercourse, and to the many homely aspects of daily living. In order that, for a moment at least in our long journey, we may feel upon us the breath of common day, I now plan to pass in review some of the more ephemeral aspects of street and square, although the pressure of space obliges me to be satisfied with an ideal sadly short of completeness. At the same time I shall define briefly the attitude of the Sienese toward the things of the mind by reviewing their relation to literature and science.

No lover of sport will neglect to inquire into the games of a nation which has engaged his notice, and games, it may be asserted without fear of contradiction, are a not

unimportant index of civilization. That the Greeks
celebrated their Olympic games with a healthy and
cheerful competition among men and horses, while the
Romans sought an outlet for their animal spirits in the
brutal spectacle of a gladiatorial show—do not these
contrasting scenes present effectively the whole startling
difference between Hellenic and Latin culture? And
letting our glance travel to the age which followed the
fall of Rome, is there anything which reveals the character of feudal society more successfully than the
jousts of steel-clad warriors, varied with the gentler
though still vigorous pursuits of hunting and hawking?
In examining the earliest games of which there is record
among the mediæval Sienese, we observe that our town,
or at least the dominant class of our town, was devoted
to the same amusements as those which enjoyed the
favor of the baronial element throughout Europe. In
the year 1222, to give a relatively late example, we hear
that *una bella e nobile giostra* was held in the meadow
outside Porta Camollia, and, further, that the first prize,
consisting "of an exceeding swift horse with housings
of silk together with a fine suit of armor," was awarded
to a certain Buonsignore of Arezzo.* Although the
dugento brought the political defeat of the nobility, the
great families, in part at least, survived, and with them
continued to flourish for some generations to come a
preference for the rude exercise of the lists. Even in
the trecento, therefore, when a group of purse-proud
merchants governed the city, tournaments were no
infrequent feature of Sienese life; nay, they must have
been looked upon with favor, for we find that they were

* Muratori, Vol. XV, "Cronica Sanese." Note under year 1222.

permitted in the Campo itself, in spite of the interruption of business occasioned thereby. The fact was that the city was keenly interested to possess among its citizens men capable of employing arms, and, in sign of being favorably disposed to martial exercises, even went so far as to extend its protection to that characteristic product of feudal society, the institution of knighthood.

A mediæval knight, it is well known, was not born but made. A necessary condition, indeed, especially in the north of Europe, where the institution had a much more exclusive character than among the city-democracies of Italy, was that the candidate for knighthood be of good family, but good and even noble birth alone did not suffice to secure the chivalric honors. Before a young gentleman might aspire to such a distinction he was required to give proof of his readiness and ability to do a warrior's service in some noble and unselfish cause. Then he was struck knight by the emperor or some great prince, and with significant ceremonies was received into the brotherhood of chivalry. It was a sign of the healthy self-esteem developed by the Italian republics that they soon assumed in this matter the prerogatives of feudal sovereignty, and freely created knights among those of their citizens who served in the communal army in the capacity of *milites*. In Siena candidates for the coveted honor were by formal statute permitted to erect a pavilion in the central square, and there, with all the world looking on, for the space of some two weeks, they feasted friends, gave and received presents, and offered proof of their prowess.* That jousting was slow to lose its popularity is proved

* Falletti-Fossati, "Costumi Senesi," pp. 219-21.

by one of the most picturesque of the sonnets addressed by Folgore da San Gimignano "unto the blithe and lordly Fellowship" of Sienese nobles, the famous *brigata spendereccia*. Let the reader imagine as scene of the events described the great Campo with its Palazzo Pubblico and girdle of Gothic palaces, and unless in reading Folgore's poem he realize with intensity one phase of mediæval sport and pageantry, rhyme may be declared to have no power over him:

> I give you horses for your games in May,
>   And all of them well-train'd unto the course—
>   Each docile, swift, erect, a goodly horse;
> With armor on their chests, and bells at play
> Between their brows, and pennons fair and gay;
>   Fine nets, and housings meet for warriors,
>   Emblazoned with the shields ye claim for yours,
> Gules, argent, or, all dizzy at noonday.
> And spears shall split, and fruit go flying up
> In merry counterchange for wreaths that drop
>   From balconies and casements far above;
> And tender damsels with young men and youths
> Shall kiss together on the cheeks and mouths;
>   And every day be glad with joyful love.*

Meanwhile the popular forces triumphed throughout Tuscany, and feudalism with its honors, feasts, and games sloped to its setting.† As jousting owed its

---

* Translated by D. G. Rossetti in his "Early Italian Poets." Nothing is known of Folgore. From evidence supplied by his poems we are made aware that he was a contemporary of Dante, and that the above sonnet describes or idealizes a Sienese scene of the early fourteenth century.

† By the end of the fourteenth century tournaments, looked on as hopelessly out of date, had become a subject of mockery. Their revival under the Renaissance tyrannies was strictly artificial, and served no other end but that of pomp.

existence to the need felt by the cavaliers for constant
practice in their chosen arms, so an exercise was certain
to be evolved which would enable the bulk of the communal army, composed of foot-soldiers, to prepare
itself in time of peace for the stern discipline of war.
Such pedestrian exercises, in distinction from the splendid and ceremonial combats of the upper class, would
naturally have a rude and democratic character. In
some form or other, under the generic name of *battaglie*,
they may be encountered in every city of Tuscany. In
these mimic battles bands of city youths would meet
from time to time in some open square, and using
stones or staves as weapons, would attempt to gain a
victory over one another. The oldest form of battaglia
known to Sienese annals, was, from the helmets
worn by the players, called *elmora*. Mr. Heywood, who
has treated of Tuscan sports in his usual penetrat-
ing fashion, informs us that besides the helmet—for
which a protection of basket-work might be substituted
—the player wore a breastplate, cuisses, and greaves.
A wooden staff and shield for thrust and ward completed
his regular equipment, but stone-throwing, resorted to in
the heat of the encounter, was a common feature of the
combat.* Under these circumstances elmora was not
likely to prove very different from a real battle, and indeed so numerous were the casualties usually associated
with it that efforts were made at a relatively early period
to effect a reform. Beginning in 1263 with the abolition
of stone-throwing, the whole game was presently put
under the ban.† But in spite of solemn ordinances the

* Heywood, "Palio and Ponte," pp. 179–80.
† "Il Constituto di Siena di 1262," Dist. V, 33 and 194.

sport continued to be followed until a peculiarly savage contest, which almost set the city topsy-turvy, rang its passing-bell.   The chronicler describes the event, which befell in the year 1291, in the following terms:

"In Siena there was a great battle of elmora after this manner, that the terzo of San Martino and the terzo of Camollia fought with the terzo of Città on such wise that the terzo of Città was driven back even to the chiasso delle Mora.   And there did they receive succor from the casato, and from the piazza Manetti, and from the Scotti and the Forteguerri.   Then began they to cast stones, and afterward they fought hand to hand with great assault of battle.   And thither came well-nigh all Siena, either to join in the fray or to interpose to separate the combatants.   But so great was the confusion and shouting that no man might hear himself speak; neither were they able to stop the battle.   Whereby it befel that there were slain ten gentlemen besides many of the baser sort; and many were wounded until at last the terzo of Città was victorious, and drove back the terzo of San Martino and that of Camollia, thrusting them forth from the Campo.   And in good sooth, if Messer Pino, the potestà, had not forced his way into the mêlée with his folk and compelled those men to lay down their arms, there would have been even greater slaughter.   And by reason of this battle it was ordained that thenceforth the game should not be played with staves and stones, but that they who joined therein should use their fists alone."*

This prohibition of the use of staves and stones no more than reënacted an old law, which from this time on, however, seems to have been fairly well respected.   To salve the feeling of the citizens, the edict, while abolishing elmora, expressly authorized a combat of another kind, the battaglia of fists, called *pugna*.

---

* Muratori, Vol. XV, "Cronica Sanese," 42.   I have used the translation of Heywood, "Palio and Ponte," p. 181.

Some writers maintain that now only did pugna come into existence, but Mr. Heywood adduces plentiful proof that as a relatively innocent variant of elmora it had enjoyed the favor of the Sienese throughout the dugento. When played, according to the rules, with fists alone, pugna, though still strenuous, ·was hardly likely to lead to serious accidents; in the heat of passion, however, the temptation would arise to seize other weapons, thus effecting a more or less complete resurrection of the proscribed elmora. Of this circumstance a pugna of 1324, when the Nine were in their glory, gives ample proof.

" On the Sunday before carnival, the same being the third day of February, a game of pugna was played in Siena. Those of the terzo of San Martino with those of the terzo of Camollia numbered six hundred each; and there came against them the terzo of Città. Whereby it befel that there was in the piazza of Siena much folk stripped to their doublets, with caps of cloth upon their heads furnished with cheek-pieces for the protection of the face and head. Also they wrapped handkerchiefs around their hands according to custom. And playing at the pugna on this wise, the two terzi cast out the terzo of Città from the Campo. And they commenced to throw stones, and certain persons took staves; and so they fought on. Thereafter they armed themselves with shields and helmets and with lances, swords, and spears; and so great was the uproar in the Campo that all the world seemed upside down for the multitude of folk that was therein. And all the soldiers of the commune came armed into the Campo, and likewise the potestà with his attendants. And the Signori Nove made proclamation that the battle should cease. . . . And ever there came more people into the Campo by all the ways that led thereto, with crossbows and with axes and with bills. And the battle ever increased, and neither the Signori nor any others that were there were able to remedy so great ruin. Wherefore the bishop of Siena, with the

priests and friars of all the orders, came into the Campo in procession, bearing the cross before them. And they commenced
to pass through the battle . . . until at last they who fought were
separated by reason of the prayers of the said bishop and of all
the priests and friars. . . . Now, therefore, when the tumult was
over, the Signori Nove took counsel concerning the said battle and
slaughter and arson . . . and it was resolved that henceforth
they should play no more at the pugna."*

A courageous resolution, but without other than
temporary effect! These hand-to-hand struggles not
only suited the vigorous temper of the time, but were
favored and perpetuated by the strong sectional feeling
among the city wards or terzi. Hence pugna remained
a national diversion far into the Renaissance, and when
during the siege of 1555 the citizens wished to honor
the representative whom the French king had sent
among them to strengthen them in their resistance,
they introduced the magnanimous Sieur de Monluc to
an exhibition of their ancient pastime.†

Elmora and pugna do not complete the tale of Sienese
national games. Because of the relative infrequency
with which it was played I pass over *pallone*, one of the
many variants of mediæval foot-ball, in order to fix my
attention on horse-racing, a sport deeply rooted in
popular devotion. Throughout Italy horse-races were
commonly designated as *palii* from the rectangular piece
of silk, brocade, or other material (*palio*) which was
given to the winner as a prize. Of the existence of a
Sienese palio there is record as early as the year 1238,
and characteristically enough the first known palio was

* The above translation is from Heywood, "Palio and Ponte," p 186. The
original is in "Misc. Stor. Sen.," V, 174.
† Sozzini, "Diario Delle Cose Avvenute," p. 354.

run in connection with the festival of August, held in
honor of the Virgin Mary.* This latter circumstance
should be noticed, for it brings to our attention that the
palio was never merely a horse-race—a secular sporting
fixture—but a feature in a great religious celebration
as well. In the course of the trecento not only did the
August race become annual, but, owing to the growing
popularity of this form of sport with all classes of the
population, additional palii were gradually instituted
by the commune. In the later period of the republic
as many as four palii, all like their prototype of Mid-
August religio-secular events, were run annually under
the auspices of the government.†

These races, open to all comers, were run by the best
horses and jockeys which Italy commanded. For this
reason they were run *alla lunga*, that is, on a straight-
away course as far as the circumstances permitted.
In the early period the highway outside the Porta
Camollia seems to have enjoyed a preference, but, later
on, probably owing to the desire to let as large a number
of people as possible share in the spectacle, a city course
was mapped out, extending from Porta Romana to the
cathedral square and marked by not a few dangerous
slopes and turns. In the days of their splendor the
palii were held in such high honor that the greatest
lords of Italy were proud to compete in them, and surviving records apprise us that such men as Pietro

---

* Heywood, "Palio and Ponte," p. 62.
† The four palii of the last phase of the republic were: The palio of the
Blessed Ambrogio Sansedoni on the 30th of March; the palio of Saint Mary
Magdalene on the 22nd of July; the palio of Our Lady of Mid-August; and
the palio of San Pietro Alessandrino on the 26th of November. Heywood,
"Palio and Ponte," p. 89.

Gambacorti of Pisa, Lorenzo de' Medici, and Cæsar
Borgia sent the best blood of their stables to capture the
coveted banner. Thus matters stood till the fall of the
republic (1555), when with the decay of the national
spirit the palii fell into gradual disuse and were abandoned, all except the original palio, the palio of Mid-
August. Owing to its connection with the annual
ceremonies conducted in honor of the liege-lady of the
town, it managed to survive, dragging on an increasingly
unnoticed existence till far into the nineteenth century
when by general consent it was quietly suppressed.*

"The palio of Mid-August suppressed?" I hear an
exasperated reader remarking who may have seen it
with his own eyes no later than last summer. It is even
as I say: the palio *alla lunga*, dating back to the thirteenth century and run with high-bred horses in order to
test their speed and endurance, is now no more. There
is indeed still a palio of Mid-August, one of the brightest
spectacles withal the summer sun looks down upon in
its circuit of the glad earth, but except for a few points
of external resemblance, it is not related to the palio of
the Middle Age. The modern race, run on August
16th, the day after the Feast of the Assumption, was
instituted not earlier than the seventeenth century by
the ward or district societies of Siena called *contrade*.†
Of these societies there are seventeen, and for over two
hundred years they have, with very few interruptions,

---

* Heywood, "Palio and Ponte," pp. 89–90.
† The attempt has been made to identify the contrade with the ancient
military companies of the dugento. Signor Lisini has successfully exploded
this view ("Misc. Stor. Sen.," I, 26; IV, 67–69). The contrade are societies
formed in the fifteenth century—they are first mentioned in 1482—for the
purpose of sharing in and increasing the splendor of public festivals.

conducted this contest of August 16th, as well as a similar one on July 2nd, the day of the Visitation of the
Blessed Virgin.   The two modern palii, as not concerned
with the matter of this book, I shall not undertake to
describe further than to point out how they differ from
the similarly named events of an earlier period.   To
begin with they are not primarily horse-races at all.
Horses indeed contest in them—and for the prize of a
banner—but every ancient cab-horse tottering on the
verge of the boneyard is considered good enough for the
event, and blooded stock is on no account brought to the
starting-post.   The fact that the race is run not *alla
lunga*, but *alla tonda*, that is, around the irregular and
sloping course of the ancient Campo, should suffice to
prove that the promoting contrade are not aiming at a
horse-race of the type of those which flourish at Epsom
or Latonia.   What the contrade had in mind from the
moment of the inception of the modern palio was a
pageant, which was to be made as splendid as possible
with music, banners, floats, and richly costumed companies; and with this spectacle they planned should be
associated, as an additional touch of vivacity, a com-
petitive struggle among the seventeen rival societies.
It is this latter circumstance, which, by having become
through long established habit part of the blood and
marrow of every born Sienese, contributes the real
flavor to the events of July 2nd and August 16th; it
and it alone explains why the modern palii continue to
thrive lustily in a time inwardly hostile to the ceremonial
inheritance of the past.*

---

* I am the more ready to deny myself the pleasure of entering upon the
story and description of the modern palio as this theme has inspired the pens

Thus we see that while tournaments were often celebrated on the Campo, the original horse-races were run
elsewhere. Still the life of the mediæval town was to an
extraordinary extent concentrated in the ample square.
Every week of the year market was held there, market
for vegetables, fish, and for a long time even for cattle,
while a good part of the space was permanently leased
out at a stipulated sum per square yard (*a misura di
braccia*) to bakers, cobblers, coopers, and other shop-
keepers and artisans.* Considering the unsatisfactory
sanitary conditions of the average mediæval town, we
shall doubtless be disposed to hold that whatever
picturesqueness was gained by this crowding of business
at a central point was heavily paid for with the accumulation of every variety of filth. In fact, on the side of
cleanliness, the piazza for a long time left much to be
desired, as we may convincingly gather from a document of 1296, which makes clear that the work of re-
moving the market-waste was chiefly performed by a
troop of roaming hogs.† None the less, higher standards of municipal decency began to impose themselves,
with the result that before the fourteenth century had
run its course, all the squares and streets of the city were
paved with brick or stone, and were kept tolerably
clean by ordinances which laid the obligation of remov-
ing the dust and dirt before each house upon the owner.

A citizen of the twentieth century, however, if he

of two of the most attractive writers on matters Sienese. No visitor of Siena
should fail to read Signor Riccardo Brogi's amusing "Il Palio di Siena" and
Mr. Heywood's "Our Lady of August and the Palio of Siena," revised and
reprinted as a section of a more recent book, "Palio and Ponte."

* Zdekauer, "La Vita Pubblica nel Dugento," p, 113 (Conferenza di 1897).
† The document mentions unam troiam et quattuor porcellos. See
Appendice VI of Zdekauer's Conferenza of 1897.

could have visited the Campo of the trecento, would
have had his curiosity aroused by nothing so much as
by a sort of stockade roofed over with canvas, which
any native would have told him was the *baratteria*—the
public gambling den.   A gambling establishment conceded for a stipulated sum to a group of promoters
may come with the shock of surprise to those of us who
habitually see the Middle Age adorned with a halo of
righteousness.   And yet, though modern opinion would
not hesitate to declare the improvised structure of the
Campo a house of evil manners, historical investigation
has established that the licensed baratteria represents
a distinct improvement over the rough and ready
practices of earlier times.

The morality of the Middle Age was not opposed to
gambling.   Saint Thomas Aquinas, the highest theological authority of the age, expressly declared that games
of chance were not in themselves bad, but that they were
made so through certain circumstances (*accidentiæ*)
attending them, such as fraud and blasphemy.*   Accordingly the earliest Sienese statutes which have
reached us authorize gambling, provided it takes place
at daytime and in the city streets (*in viis publicis et
palam*).†   Under conditions of publicity, it was probably imagined that fraud and blasphemy, the really
objectionable features, would be eliminated, or at least
reduced to a minimum.   These tolerant views enabled
gamblers in Siena and elsewhere to organize as a regular

---

* Zdekauer, "Il Giuoco in Italia nei secoli XIII e XIV." Arch, Stor. It.
Tomo, XVIII. Anno 1886, pp. 21, 49.   This effective article has established
our knowledge of mediæval gambling on new and solid foundations.

† *Ibid.*, p. 23.   Another paragraph inveighs against playing *nocturno
tempo*.

guild or corporation, which, in view of the vile riff-raff
composing it, was naturally held in general contempt.
Such was the status in Siena of games of chance until
we reach the end of the thirteenth century. Owing to
the gradual enlightenment of public opinion, the
restrictions upon gambling had been growing more and
more numerous until in 1295, in an access of virtue, the
practice was entirely forbidden by a sweeping municipal
ordinance. When this action was promptly rescinded,
because it was found to do no more than to drive the
games and those who lived upon them underground, the
commune reauthorized the current vice, but, in the hope
of better regulation, concentrated it, as far as possible,
at a single point. Out of these circumstances and
considerations arose that curious institution, the baratteria of Siena, which, if we will imagine ourselves to be
strolling around the Campo of the fourteenth century
with the holiday crowd come to attend the August fair,
we should come upon, conspicuous with awning and
banner and surrounded by an excited multitude, not far
from the central position occupied by Fonte Gaia.

Much matter which the student of manners is likely to
find highly entertaining has recently been collected on
mediæval games of chance. Suffice it to say here that
such games fall into two main groups, the first played
with dice alone, the second with figures or *men*.* In a
period when, as we have just seen, there was no
objection in principle to dicing, and when, further,
young and old habitually gave vent to their emotions with a fervor which no exercise of reason
checked, the crush and excitement around the Sienese

* Zdekauer, "Il Ginoco" etc. p. 7.

gambling booth must have been constant and considerable. At Grosseto, Magliano, Montalcino, and a dozen other places of the contado, similar scenes took place, for each dependent town had a baratteria on the Sienese model conducted by some lessee who bought the privilege from the republic. Add that at Florence, Lucca, Pistoia, and other centres of Tuscany, the same gambling frenzy had led to the same arrangements, and we can appreciate to how common an experience Dante appealed when he described the press of the shades in purgatory around himself by casting up a marvellously vivid picture of *il giuoco della zara*.* Zara, a game of dice, the key to which we no longer possess,† seems to have wrought immense havoc among the young and spendthrift, and in the period when restrictions began, was put under special disabilities in favor of games with some intellectual content, such as chess and backgammon. But although games with men were encouraged by the government and were, indeed, extremely popular, the wild passion for dice persisted even among the upper classes, as is plentifully attested by fourteenth century literature.‡

It is interesting to speculate whether the official gambling booth in the Campo was permitted to drive its unpleasant trade all the year round, spreading its lure

* "Purgatorio," VI, p. 1.

† For some account of Zara see Zdekauer, pp. 7–8. The game has given us our word hazard.

‡ To let one instance serve for many, see the gay picture of the Mercato Vecchio developed by the Florentine poet, Pucci (died about 1373). He sings of the beauty of the old piazza on an autumn day:

"Quando de' tordi son, sempre n'è piena
La bella piazza, e *molti gentilotti*
Co' *dadi in man*, fan desinare e cena."

even during the *sacre rappresentazioni*, which, in Easter
week or on other Christian holidays, were occasionally
given in the piazza. There is nothing in mediæval
morals which would have caused any one to be particularly shocked by such an association. At any rate,
whether to the accompaniment of the rattle of dice or
not, following a very prevalent custom of the age, re-
ligous plays were given from time to time on a temporary
stage erected on the Campo. At first these representa-
tions took the form of simple scenes, such as Christ's
Birth or Resurrection, selected with reference to the
season of the year; later, whole miracle plays were
produced, enriched with song and dialogue, and representing a dramatic version of some impressive Bible
story.* But nowhere in Italy, and certainly not in
Siena, did these enjoy the favor and exhibit the vitality
which in northern Europe enabled them to serve as
the nucleus of one of the most wonderful forms of
modern artistic expression, the drama. The feebleness
of the Italian drama during the Renaissance, a feebleness which is the more astonishing in the light of the
brilliant contribution made by the people of the peninsula to every other department of art, is explained
by the failure of the nation to develop the opportunity
extended by the miracles and moralities of the ecclesiastical stage.

For some unfathomable reason the sacre rappresentazioni of the trecento did not appeal to the Sienese
imagination, and tended to become less and less frequent.† In consequence Siena produced no drama

* Falletti-Fossati, "Costumi Senesi," p. 195 *ff.*
† Lisini shows ("Misc. Stor. Sen.," V, 23) that miracle plays continued

worth mentioning—an accident, we might be inclined
to argue, if we did not have to acknowledge that, in
spite of its many gifts, this people was never strongly
drawn to any form of literature whatsoever, and that it
failed to produce a single poet or writer rising above the
common stature.   A review of Sienese literature, therefore, is neither a heavy nor a very inspiring task.   In
connection with certain aspects of Sienese knighthood,
I mentioned Dante's contemporary, the poet Folgore
from San Gimignano.   He will be found of exceeding
interest in affording glimpses of Sienese life, but in view
of his origin he can not fairly be assigned a place among
purely Sienese authors.   This is not the case with
Cecco Angiolieri (died 1312 ?), another contemporary
of the great Florentine.   Cecco was a Sienese born and
bred, and contributed in his sole person a considerable
section of what there is to the literature of his native
town.   In sharp contrast with Folgore, who dwelt among
the lofty concepts of chivalry and composed his sonnets
under the spell of the troubadours and trouvères and
their Italian imitators, Cecco sounded the realistic
note of the rising middle classes, curiously modified by
an element of individual lawlessness and literary bohe-
mianism.   Rossetti, for whom he is "the scamp of
Dante's circle," speaks, not without admiration, of
"his natural bent to ruin."   In fact it is the utterly
frank disclosure of his wild passions which recommends
him to us of a later time as the singer of certain true,
though by no means admirable, emotions of the human

to be given in the quattrocento, but in a closed room and before a small
audience.   All this proves that they failed to take root in popular favor—the
capital difference between them and the same variety of amusement among
the transalpine nations.

breast.   To read him in company with his contemporaries is to grow aware that he is, within the small and
sinister circle of his thoughts, more direct and vivid
than any poet of his age with the notable exception, of
course, of the incomparable Florentine.   In the spirit
of the boastful tavern brawler Cecco ventured to
resent a real or fancied slur addressed to him by Dante,
and did not scruple to revenge himself upon the great
Ghibelline with some impertinent verses.   He sang with
frank indelicacy the material charms of the pretty
Becchina; he gambled, got drunk and was arrested;
he venomously defamed his father and mother; he
showed his fangs to Dante—such was Cecco Angiolieri,
decidedly something of a jail-bird, but also, by reason of
his strict avoidance of the romantic make-believe which
was the stock-in-trade of so many contemporary poet-
asters, an authentic son of the muse.*

In Cecco's generation, a generation which has the

* In order that the reader may have a taste of Cecco's peculiar quality,
made up in about equal proportions of swagger, cynicism, and genuine humor,
I quote one of his sonnets in Rossetti's exquisitely delicate translation:

"If I were fire, I'd burn the world away;
    If I were wind, I'd turn my storms thereon;
    If I were water, I'd soon let it drown;
If I were God, I'd sink it from the day;
If I were Pope, I'd never feel quite gay
    Until there was no peace beneath the sun;
    If I were Emperor, what would I have done?—
I'd lop men's heads all round in my own way.
If I were Death, I'd look my father up;
    If I were Life, I'd run away from him;
    And treat my mother to like calls and runs.
If I were Cecco (and that's all my hope),
    I'd pick the nicest girls to suit my whim,
    And other folk should get the ugly ones."

The best edition to consult is I Sonetti di Cecco Angiolieri . . . per cura
di A. F. Massèra.   Rossetti has translated twenty-one sonnets, of which it is
not too much to say that they do not fall below the original.

distinction not only of having produced some of the
greatest poetry of all time, but also of having given the
Italian language its literary form, other poets, as, for
instance, Bindo Bonichi (*d.* 1337), flourished in Siena,
but little from their hand has come down to us.   Undeniably the share of Siena in Italian verse is small.
Presently Italian prose began its career, and in this
department the Sienese contribution, if not widely significant, is at least not without a considerable local interest.
Starting with private letters and tongue-tied chronicles
—from many of these belonging to a later period of relatively high expressiveness I have had occasion to
quote—Sienese prose reached its culmination, as far as
the Middle Age is concerned, in the Letters of Saint
Catherine (1347–80),* the "Assempri" of Fra Filippo
Agazzari (1339–1422),† and the sermons of San Bernardino Albizzeschi (1380–1444).‡   All of these have
an immense philological importance as *testi di lingua;*
all of them are invaluable to the student of manners by
reason of the lifelike glimpses they afford of a fascinating period; but they have not, with the possible exception of Saint Catherine's Letters, a place in that realm
of pure literature which lives for its own sake and
embraces the best of what has been thought and written
in all ages.   This subtraction made, the fact remains
that the investigator, engaged in establishing the ways
in which men lived in the trecento and early quattro-

* On Saint Catherine see chap. 9.
† The "Assempri" are popular sermons, composed largely of tales and
anecdotes pointing a lesson.   They were published in 1864 by C. F. Carpellini.   Some of them have been translated and ably commented by Heywood
in his The "Ensamples" of Fra Filippo.
‡ On him and his sermons see chap. 14.

cento, can not do better than to give the closest possible
study to the works of the above-named religious ex-
horters and critics.*

Meanwhile Boccaccio, down at Florence, which in
matters literary set the tone for all Italy, had popularized the *novella*. As this form of expression rapidly
took possession of the general fancy, it was only natural
that an occasional Sienese should try his skill at the
production of short tales. About the year 1425 Gentile
Sermini composed his forty stories,† while to the same
general period belongs Æneas Silvius Piccolomini's
(Pope Pius II) *Storia di due amanti*.‡ If these works,
as regards their moral tone, are not precisely edifying,
they are decency itself compared with the productions
of such later *novellieri* as Giustiniano Nelli and Pietro
Fortini, who illustrate the unbridled license, as well as
the essential hollowness, of the full Renaissance. In
this field, quite as much as in the field of the Christian
moralists, the productions which have reached us furnish
an interesting comment on Sienese life, but it would be
absurd to judge them as worthy, on the literary and
æsthetic side, of being classed with the Decameron.§

* Whoever desires to know what place these writers hold in the literary
history of Italy may consult Bartoli, "Storia della Letteratura Italiana," or
Gaspary, "Geschichte der Ital. Literatur."

† "Le Novelle di Gentile Sermini ora per la prima volta," etc., Livorno,
1874.

‡ Written originally in Latin. Æneas, the humanist, held Italian to be an
inferior literary medium.

§ Following literature, a people usually develops scholarship—a thing like
literature and yet distinct from it. But the history of Sienese scholarship
would lead me too far. Suffice it to say that the Renaissance produced the
first serious students of history in Sigismondo Tizio (*d.* 1528), Orlando
Malavolti (1515–96), and Giugurta Tommasi (*d.* 1620). Each of these men
produced a history of Siena of a high order of thoroughness, if not of literary
skill.

Perhaps one reason for the relatively low level maintained by Sienese literature is that this lively and sensuous people had neither the patience nor the inclination
for that mental discipline which can be acquired only
by means of hard, desperate, and persistent labor.
This opinion of the small enthusiasm of the Sienese
for matters intellectual would appear to be borne out
by the story of the local university, *lo studio di Siena*.
Before the year 1250 we have notice of masters employed
by the republic to give instruction in grammar (Latin),
medicine, and law, and from that early period the state
was at some pains to develop a seat of learning in its
midst which should rival the universities of Bologna
and Padua. But though by no means despicable the
studio never exercised much influence beyond the
circuit of the walls, and, even within this narrow range,
it served frankly the primary end of supplying the town
with lawyers and doctors.* When, in the fifteenth century, the new learning began to flourish, the Sienese
teaching was necessarily influenced by it, but the chief
effect from the presence in the town of an occasional
humanist like Filelfo would appear to have been an increased laxity of morals. At any rate the designation
"Soft Siena" (*molles Senæ*) owes both its currency and
justification to this time. The learned Sienese, Pope
Pius II, acquired his really admirable culture more by
reason of travel than by his steady attendance upon the
lectures at the university of his native town, but it is
perhaps no more than fair to admit that he may have re-

---

* On the studio see Zdekauer, "Sulle Origini dello Studio di Siena" and
"Lo Studio di Siena nel Rinascimento"; also, Sanesi, "Documenti per la
storia della R. Università di Siena." Arch., Stor. It. Tomo. XXVII, 1901.

ceived his first scholarly impulses from the local masters.
Making all possible allowances, we can not but find the
story of the studio decidedly meagre. Admitting that
it satisfied the narrow purpose of turning out a body of
reasonably trained professional men, the fact remains
that it did not in any notable way advance the intellectual life of contemporary Italy.

Consideration of such matters as these will always
bring us back to a previous reflection: the gifts of the
Sienese were not eminently intellectual. As soon as
Siena fell behind in the economic and political race
among the Italian states, her mental fibre was exposed
to decay from lack of hardy exercise. Perhaps this is
the chief reason for the slow pulse-beat of Sienese
thought. With the inclination to inertia once established, a dozen other influences, above all, the highly
conservative influence of the church, came to the support of the original tendency. We noticed in treating
of Sienese art that a curious self-satisfaction on the part
of the artists induced them to adopt an unfriendly attitude toward the new ideals of the Renaissance, and that
by virtue of their quattrocento contributions to the
realm of painting the Sienese proclaimed themselves
essentially a provincial folk. Nothing brings this fact
out more clearly than a story which is related by the
Florentine Ghiberti and which, as a most delightfully
apposite characterization of the mercurial temper and
mental philistinism of the Sienese, I set down here as
my final word on the subject.

Lorenzo Ghiberti, the Florentine sculptor of the famous bronze gates of his native Baptistery, wrote before
his death some very interesting Commentaries upon art,

in the course of which he narrates that, once on a visit
to Siena, he was shown a beautiful drawing from the
hand of Ambrogio Lorenzetti of a Greek statue existent
in Ambrogio's day and afterward destroyed. His infor-
mant told him that the statue had been accidentally dug
up in Siena a hundred years before, and had aroused
tremendous enthusiasm, not only among the painters
and goldsmiths of the town, but also among the common people. Amidst universal rejoicing it had been escorted to the Campo, and there set up over the new
fountain, the Fonte Gaia, which had just been inaugurated and which lacked as yet the monumental setting
created by Jacopo della Quercia. On the strength of
the drawing put into his hands, Ghiberti assigned the
original to Lysippus, one of the most distinguished names
of Greek art, and from the description which he adds
we are led to surmise that the statue represented the
goddess Aphrodite rising from the sea. For some years
the recovered wonder of antiquity continued to crown
the Fonte Gaia, smilingly prophesying to those who
could understand its mysterious language the coming of
a new age, when a succession of misfortunes, bringing
famine and pestilence in their wake, roused to life the
ever latent forces of mediæval superstition. In a
session of the council a citizen arose and spoke—I use
Ghiberti's own words—as follows: "'Gentlemen. Considering that ever since we have set up this statue we
have encountered nothing but ill-luck, and, considering
further, that idolatry is totally forbidden by our religion,
we are obliged to believe that our adversities have been
sent us by God in punishment for our sins. As a matter
of plain fact no one will deny that ever since we have

done honor to the said statue, matters have steadily gone with us from bad to worse. My fixed opinion is that as long as we keep it on our soil misfortunes will continue to befall us. Wherefore I move that it be taken down and broken and the remnants carried away to be buried in the territory of the Florentines.'" And Ghiberti concludes his tale by dryly adding that "the council unanimously supported the motion, which was accordingly put into execution by burying the statue in our territory."

Very possibly the last amusing touch about the final disposal of the idolatrous statue is an invention of Ghiberti's Florentine malice, but the incident itself is a certain fact of history, having befallen, as the documents prove, in the year 1357.*

Thus perished what was apparently a priceless monument of ancient art, sacrificed to the fickle temper of a peopie, splendidly capable of occasional bursts of creative enthusiasm, but not given to apply itself with steady intensity to a moral and intellectual task which nothing short of the continued devotion of many generations of men can carry to a triumphant maturity. The noble statue of Lysippus, emotionally received and just as emotionally rejected, is more than an incident: it is a symbol—a symbol which speaks eloquently to us both of the qualities and the defects of the lovable but undisciplined sons and daughters of the Virgin.

* On the whole incident of the statue see "Misc. Stor. Sen.," V, 175.

CHAPTER XIII

SAN GALGANO: THE STORY OF A CISTERCIAN ABBEY OF THE SIENESE CONTADO

IN speaking in an earlier chapter of the Sienese
church, I took account of the important share
which the monasteries had in the official organization of religion. I referred the monastic movement to
its origin in the ascetic spirit of Christianity, and spoke
of the successive waves in which the movement would
rise from time to time to a climax, and leave its mark on
all the countries of Europe in the shape of a new series
of splendid edifices devoted to the service of God.
Because the story of a monastery affords a peculiarly
significant glimpse of the Middle Age, I purpose now to
follow such an institution in detail; and further, because
no monastery of the Sienese territory maintained more
intimate relations with the city of Siena than the abbey
of San Galgano, and since no other surpasses it in fairness of site or can compare with it in beauty of architecture, from the long list of Sienese foundations, which
includes such famous names as San Salvatore on Monte
Amiata, Sant' Antimo near Montalcino, Lecceto, lying
a short journey outside the gate of Fonte Branda, and
Monte Oliveto near Buonconvento, I shall select San
Galgano in order to show by a specific example how a
monastery came into being, how it grew in usefulness

361

and honors, and how with the sapping of its spirit in the period of the Renaissance, it settled into irretrievable decline.

For the student of monasticism no order of the twelfth century can vie in importance with that of the Cistercians. Founded at Citeaux in Burgundy as a reformed offshoot of the Benedictines, they immediately achieved great honor through one of their early leaders, Saint Bernard, who not only personally called into being the great abbey of Clairvaux, but who, by reason of his wide reputation for wisdom and holiness, popularized the order throughout Europe. Monks from Citeaux, Clairvaux, and other French foundations penetrated into the neighboring countries, and were received with such favor that before the new movement celebrated its centenary it could boast a roster of eight hundred rich and flourishing abbeys. In Italy successful houses already existed at Fossanova, Casamari, and other places, when a peculiarly inviting set of circumstances secured to the brothers a foothold in Southern Tuscany.

In the wooded upland country, in which the Merse river begins its winding course, lies the little town of Chiusdino, crowning a hill, which is remarkable, like almost all the dwelling-places of mediæval men, by reason of its wide survey and splendid inaccessibility. In the twelfth century, when our story begins, Chiusdino with the neighboring hills and valleys belonged to the diocese of the bishop of Volterra, who, under the added title of count of the empire, exercised also civil authority in this region. Here, shortly after the year 1180, tidings of strange and miraculous import began to pass from mouth to mouth. The simple peasant folk told one

The ruined Abbey Church of S. Galgano

another as they sat before their doors at eventide or
paced the road together to the neighboring market, that
a knight, Galgano by name and a citizen of Chiusdino,
forswearing the delights of the flesh, had abandoned
family and friends, that he had gone to dwell as an
anchorite in the forest solitudes around his home, and
that when, after a year of unexampled hardships, he
had died and been buried, immediately, in sign of the
favor which he enjoyed with the Lord, wonderful
cures began to be effected at his tomb.   Presently, a
pious stream of pilgrimage began to flow toward Monte
Siepi, as the wooded hill was called which was the
scene of the good man's rigorous self-discipline, as well
as the place of his burial.*   This spontaneous veneration, which has numerous counterparts throughout
Europe and brings home to us the passionate attachment of mediæval folk to all the material manifestations
of holiness, not only met with no opposition on the part
of the church, but presently received the highest possible
endorsement through an act of the pope—probably of the
year 1185—elevating the Chiusdino knight and hermit to
the ranks of the saints.   Naturally the reputation of the
newly canonized Galgano was sedulously nursed by the
leading dignitary of the region, the bishop of Volterra,
who, beginning with the erection of a simple shrine over
the grave of his late subject, gradually formed the ambitious plan of making the new cult serve as the basis for a
great monastic foundation.   He communicated with the
Cistercian brothers, always eager to extend the influence
of their order, with the result that a few monks, appar-

* On the story of San Galgano, see Rondoni, "Tradizioni popolari e leggende di un Comune medioevale," p. 110 ff.

ently Frenchmen hailing from Clairvaux itself, settled
in the unpeopled solitudes of Monte Siepi. Thus the
first step was taken in the creation of the abbey of San
Galgano.

A *cartularium*, preserved in the archives of Florence
and containing the privileges conceded to the new foundation by temporal and spiritual rulers, supplemented
by abundant material to be found in the Archivio di
Stato of Siena, makes it possible to develop an accurate
picture of the growth of the settlement on Monte
Siepi.* The oldest existing document is of the year
1191; it was issued from the chancellery of Emperor
Henry VI, and declared that the sovereign, probably
at the instigation of Hildebrand, bishop of Volterra,
who signed as a witness, took the monks of San Galgano
hailing from Clairvaux under his high protection. He
added the gift of a field *juxta Abbatiam* and solemnly
warned all neighbors not to "violate our munificence
with temerarious audacity."† The imperial shelter,
good so far as it went, needed to be supplemented by the
more valuable, because more constant, protection of the
local lord. That was the bishop of Volterra, who, as
inaugurator of the settlement, was not likely to withhold
a liberal support. Accordingly, in the year 1201,
Bishop Hildebrand, recapitulating, we are led to surmise, a number of earlier grants, issued a comprehensive
privilege, in which, after enumerating a long list of
fields and forests made over by him to a certain Bono

---

* The Sienese material is in three large folio volumes, called *caleffi*, and
consists of about 2,250 documents. This material, together with the cartularium at Florence, has been consulted and, in part, published by Canestrelli in
his excellent "L'Abbazia di San Galgano," to which I am deeply indebted.

† Canestrelli, "Documento V."

and a band of monks, he not only took the brothers under
his protection, but promised them complete liberty in
their internal affairs together with freedom from taxation.* Evidently the foundation, favored and enriched
by the bishop, assured of a friendly interest by the emperor, was advancing rapidly. To complete its legal
safeguarding nothing was lacking, according to mediæval ideas, except the word of the pope. It was not till
the year 1206, fifteen years after the emperor had spoken
in the matter and five after the deed of Bishop Hildebrand, that Pope Innocent III issued a bull, declaring
his good-will toward the enterprise in the remote hills
of the upper Merse. Innocent III, it may be remembered, was the pontiff of fiery, uncompromising temper,
under whom the pretensions of the papacy to universal
rule were stretched to the utmost. The increase of
monasteries, representing each one the lighting of a new
hearth of religious and, more particularly, of papal
influence, must have been deeply to his liking. When
he spoke, therefore, though he spoke tardily, he poured
out for the monks of San Galgano a veritable cornucopia
of bounties. In the first place, the head of the monastery—apparently Bono, the earliest leader of the
Cistercian enterprise of whom there is record, had by
this time passed away—was no longer designated as
priest or prior or by some other title indicative of small
beginnings, but as abbot, the dignity reserved for the
chief official of a perfected and influential organization.
Proceeding, Innocent confirmed all the possessions of
the monks; reiterated their freedom from taxation and
immunity from sentences, pronounced in the courts of a

* Canestrelli, "Documento II."

bishop or any lay lord whatsoever; and proclaimed their
right to elect their own abbot and to govern themselves,
practically as a sovereign body.* The new monastic
venture, dedicated to the high task of spreading civilization through the sparsely settled wilds of the upper
Merse, was now as secure as the formal authorities of
feudal society could make it.

However, no amount of official sanction could contribute greatly to the development of a monastery, if the
institution did not perform effective service in the
society in which it was situated, or if it failed to enlist the
sympathies and support of all classes of the population.
Only if these conditions were satisfied could San Galgano hope to arouse the pride and become identified
with the patriotism of the neighborhood, thus winning
recruits for its ranks and stimulating the stream of
private contributions necessary for the realization of its
Christian programme. Following the Cistercian ideal
this programme consisted not only in the creation of a
retreat for holy men, but also in genuine pioneer labors,
such as the clearing of forests and the bringing of unbroken land under the plough. In all these respects
the success of our monastery in the first flush of its
hopeful youth was conspicuous. The sons of the neighborhood came in such numbers to knock for admission
at the portals of the house of peace that whatever slight
French character the personnel of the first group of
monks may have had was presently lost to make room
for a genuine Tuscan foundation. Admitted within the
walls, the fugitives from a world of empty honors were,
after due probation, apportioned to one of two classes:

* Canestrelli, "Documento XII."

either they became spiritual brothers who, as priests, served the mass and attended to the duties pertaining to religion, or they joined the *conversi* or lay brothers, who tilled the fields and performed the various kinds of manual labor required in connection with the operation of a busy farmstead,

In a society where men gladly give their lives to a cause conceived as worthy, they hesitate even less in offering of their plenty. Gifts of land, bounties of all kinds, of which the record still exists, were showered upon the abbey. While these benefactions testify to the profound conviction of the Middle Age regarding the usefulness of an institution which no longer awakens our enthusiasm, their form betrays the peculiar and, to our taste, somewhat unctuous piety of the period. According to mediæval theology, a gift to the church was a good work, especially remarked by God and sure to be taken into account on the day of reckoning. For this reason the clergy could, with perfectly good conscience moreover, stimulate the charitable instincts of the laity. Something of this desire to acquire credit with the Lord, palliated by a child-like candor, reaches us from the old deeds of hand. In the year 1196, for instance, Matilda, described as daughter of the departed Ugolinus and derelict of Guidaldonius, and the first private donor of whom there is record, presents the monks with a farmland, because "whoever shall contribute to sacred and venerable places shall receive a hundredfold and have eternal life"; on which exordium she adds, with simple-hearted readiness to lay bare every fold of her heart, that she hopes by means of her gift to save her soul and that of her relatives, doubtless the

departed Ugolinus and Guidaldonius aforesaid.* Many
bequests came to the brothers from neighboring Siena
and her prosperous merchants. We hear of one commercial citizen, a certain Andrea di Giacomo, who left
as much as a thousand lire (*libræ*), a very considerable
sum, for the purchase of a farm with the direction that
the product thereof be distributed among the poor.
If this is charity at all times and the world over, Andrea
clearly sounds the note of his age when he adds a bequest of eight hundred lire for the purchase of a second
farm to be given to the monks on the condition that they
daily recite a mass for the repose of his soul.† Let one
more example suffice to depict both the gifts and the
givers. In the year 1287, a citizen of Massa, after
leaving twelve hundred lire to San Galgano, adds a gift
of four hundred lire "for the construction of an altar
in the said church in honor of the blessed Virgin Mary
and the saints James, Christopher, and Nicholas, near
which altar let my name be written in *patentibus licteris*
(in large letters!), in order that all the priests who cele-
brate mass at that altar may be reminded to pray for my
soul and to make mention of my name in the service."‡
Although a charity, associated with such intense spiritual
profit-seeking, may kindle an amused smile upon our lips,
it furnishes no occasion to treat it with contempt. When
all is said the fact remains that the habit of giving of one's
substance for an unselfish end was widespread, and that
it testifies to the success with which the church infused
the spirit of idealism into a dull and brutalized society.

---

* Canestrelli, "Documento I."
† Canestrelli, p. 72.   The bequest is of the year 1274.
‡ Canestrelli, p, 73.

We have seen that Bono and his small Cistercian band made their home near the grave of San Galgano on Monte Siepi. They built there the circular chapel which still stands, and added a dormitory and other quarters, parts of which survive in the two wings leaning upon the chapel like awkward buttresses. Presently the donations of which we have taken note began to pour in, and the brothers saw an opportunity for enlarging the circle of their activity. Dissatisfied with their narrow and primitive quarters on Monte Siepi, they resolved to descend from their wooded spur to the broad meadow immediately at its foot, and to commence a second structure on a scale which more adequately represented the accumulated means and golden prospects of the monastery. The information on this removal afforded by the documents is unfortunately slight, but by piecing together various items we arrive at the conclusion that the new edifices were begun about the year 1224,* while still existing walls and lines of masonry enable us to affirm that they included, besides the great abbey church, a dormitory, a cloister, a refectory, barns, stables, and all the various offices of a corporation which, if primarily a religious retreat, had also something of the character of a library, a school, and a great agricultural establishment. By accidents and changes, to which I shall return in due time, most of the accessory structures have been swept away, but the great abbey church still stands, desolate and in ruins, it is true, but touched with such enduring beauty that it may be called without hesitation one of the most exquisite churches of Tuscany and even of all Italy. Built in slow stages, as suited the

* Canestrelli, pp. 69–75.

gradually accumulating means of the brothers, it was probably not finished till the end of the century which saw the laying of the corner-stone. In the place of ascertained facts, enabling us to compose a secure narrative of the construction of the famous church, we must content ourselves with conjecture, and conjecture, too, supplies the only answer to our eager question concerning the names of the great artists who drew the plans for it. Without doubt they were Cistercian monks, for the Cistercians, apart from their jealous desire to keep their buildings in their own hands, were recognized as the architectural leaders and innovators of their day. However, when we appeal to the documents for the names of the individual monks who distinguished themselves in this great enterprise, we are denied an answer, and must content ourselves with the general conclusion that the order built the abbey church of San Galgano. Considering the nature of the order, and remembering that men entered it to lose their personality in the hope of finding it again in the Lord, we can hardly quarrel with the accident which produced a result so fully in accord with the profound spirit of the institution.*

On one very fascinating matter, included in the dark chapter of construction and involving the much-mooted question of the style of the great abbey church, it is possible to speak with precision, for the building being still in existence, at least as regards its structural lines, furnishes all the material necessary for an intelligent opinion. No student of art standing before these re-

---

* Canestrelli, pp. 77–78, names some of the builders (*operai*), who not improbably figured also in the capacity of architects.

mains will fail to be struck by the fact that here is an edifice of such pure northern Gothic as is not to be found again in all Tuscany. Indeed these lithe and graceful forms would not be held to be out of place if one came upon them suddenly on a tour through northern France. Were the architects, whom we have agreed to be Cistercians, also Frenchmen, imported when the resolution was first taken to begin the edifice? The general plan, as well as the grouped piers and the ribbed vaults, point to that conclusion, although Canestrelli, patriotically eager to vindicate the monument for his own people, affirms with some show of proof that Italian architects were quite capable of this quality of work. That Italian influences are perceptible here and there is undeniable, but the structural skeleton with its harmonious system of concentrated strains and balanced thrusts is so emphatically French that we are forced to conclude that, if men of French blood did not build this church, the Italian monks, entrusted with the work, must have received their architectural training in France, if not directly by residence in the Burgundian houses of their order, at least indirectly through the agency of the traditions accumulated in the earlier Cistercian foundations in Italy, such as Fossanova and Casamari.

During the thirteenth century, while the monks were engaged upon the reconstruction of the abbey on a monumental scale, they remained a vigorous and growing organization. It is an old observation that an ideal, devotedly pursued, almost magically creates the energies necessary for its fulfilment. The thirteenth century, therefore, constitutes the abbey's heyday, marked not only by the loud and steady ring of hammer and chisel, which came across the meadow of the Merse and sounded through the encircling woods, but also by the quality of the converts attracted by the cloistered life. Nothing is more erroneous than the common notion that it was the broken and unfit, the sad company of life's derelict, who were drawn to the mediæval monasteries. Undeniably this defeated section of society might be found in large numbers in a given institution in the period of decay, but in the flourishing time, which was, of course, the time of youth, the monastic programme, universal enough to reach the operative as well as the reflective temperament, laid a spell upon the best minds of the day. Turn as one may there is no way of accounting for the part played by the monasteries in mediæval civilization, save on the ground that their ranks constituted a representative expression of the intelligence and energy of society. San Galgano bears out this assertion at every point. We have already seen that when the monks undertook to build themselves an abbey, which still, though in ruins, communicates the most delicate spirit of beauty, they did not have to go for help outside their own cowled brotherhood. By the side of the architects, and wearing like them the yoke of monastic obedience were to be found trained lawyers and notaries. With its varied business the monastery could turn them to good use and was at pains to assemble for their behoof a considerable law library.* Physicians and surgeons, who in their youth had trudged on foot to the schools of Salerno and Montpellier, paced the quiet garden walks with ordained priests, expert in

* Canestrelli, "Documento XVIII."

the lore of Saint Thomas Aquinas and the Schoolmen. With such elements represented in the remote community, we can hardly go wrong in assuming that its intellectual level rose far above that of contemporary lay society. How else shall we account for the fact that the neighboring city of Siena frequently requested the aid of the monastery in purely civic affairs? With the commune's growth the office of treasurer acquired an increasing importance, and when the citizens wanted a thoroughly capable and reliable man to put in charge of their moneys, whither did they turn but to the abbot of San Galgano? They asked for the loan of one of his monks, for the first time, it would seem, in the year 1257, and were so satisfied with the service they received that they kept up the practice for almost a hundred years.* Then they resorted to a layman, indicating in plain terms that it was not until the democratic government had been established for some generations that the average citizen acquired those moral and mental qualities which put him on a level with the monks. I pointed out in a former chapter that a quaint memorial of these comptroller-monks, called *camarlinghi di Biccherna*, is carefully preserved in the archives of Siena. On certain of the painted covers of the account books which they kept in their time will be found the solemn countenance of a cowled brother, who thus still seems to guard from his grave the treasure entrusted to his care while living. Nor was the treasurership the only tribute which Siena paid to the high character of the Galgano fraternity. In the thirteenth century the chief public

---

* Canestrelli, "Documento XX," gives a list of the *camarlinghi* from S. Galgano.

enterprise in which she was engaged was her cathedral,
for great buildings, both for civil and ecclesiastical uses,
were one of the passions of the age.   Encouraged probably by the splendid success with which the monks were
raising their own abbey, the municipality entrusted the
erection of the duomo to their tried and skilful hands.
Through the second half of the thirteenth century Fra
Vernaccio, Fra Melano, Fra Villa and other brothers—
empty, featureless names furnished by the stolid records
—were at the head of the works, and during their incumbency the magnificent pile was, in all essential
respects, given the form which still meets the eye.*

Such services rendered by San Galgano to the commune of Siena indicate that the shuttle was flying back
and forth, weaving a mutually profitable intimacy between the abbey and the city.   In view of the general
political situation of Tuscany in the thirteenth century
this development was inevitable.   The monks were
men of peace; their object in the world, the works of
peace.   We have seen that in settling on the upper
Merse they needed and had sought the protection of the
established powers, the pope, the emperor, and the
bishop of Volterra.   But with the death, in the year
1250, of Frederick II, the last great Hohenstaufen, the
empire, long threatened with decay, was definitely reduced to impotence, and though the pope tried to seize
his rival's heritage, he failed, in Tuscany at least, because the cities of that province were resolute to appropriate for themselves whatever benefits resulted from
the decay of the federal power.   The bishop of Volterra,

---

* Canestrelli, "Documento XXI," gives the full list of monks who served as
operai.

indeed, continued to play the part of a local sovereign, theoretically of considerable sway, but his glory waned as soon as he ceased to draw light and power from his feudal master. Thus Siena came to dominate in Southern Tuscany over a region which included the Merse valley and therewith the abbey of San Galgano. Abbey and city did not fail to see the mutual advantage of a close political alliance. Siena, and Siena alone, could in the changed political circumstances of Italy offer to the abbey an adequate guarantee against violence and spoliation, and the abbey would give to the city an increased security on its southern frontier, in addition to conferring on it the honor which in a religious age attached to the patronage of a great ecclesiastical establishment.

Thus, under the pressure of time and change, San Galgano replaced the patronage of its earliest protectors for that of the neighboring commune, That great treasury of fact, the Constitution of 1262, upon which I have so often levied, proclaims the relation in terms indicative of the large confidence of the young commonwealth. On entering upon his office the potestà of Siena was obliged to swear that he would diligently watch over the monastery of San Galgano and all its possessions, and, continuing, he was made to say that " at the demand of my lord abbot I shall give notice by messenger and letter to the lords and people of the region, near which the possessions of the abbey are situated, that the said abbey and its goods are under the protection of the commune of Siena; and I shall extend the affectionate request to them that they inflict no injury upon it or any of its goods, seeing that we of Siena are held to aid the monks and to defend them from wrong as if they were our fellow-citizens."* And this promise of protection was anything but hollow. The lords of the neighborhood, as well as such small but often violent communities as Chiusdino and Grosseto, wisely kept their hands off the abbot's possessions, and the abbey continued to flourish till the arrival of its evil day.

The thirteenth century, I have already said, was the prosperous period of the Cistercian order in Italy, and, particularly, of its offspring near the grave of San Galgano. Then gradually signs of decay appeared. The phenomenon has its parallel in the story of every spiritual institution evolved by the children of men. The monks raised by wealth above the necessity of effort, became estranged from their own ideals and gave themselves to idleness and vice. Just as the Cistercians themselves originated in a protest against the decay of the older Benedictines, so a passionate revolt was certain to direct itself against Cistercian self-satisfaction, and to gather the most promising and candid spirits of the age in new affiliations. This is the meaning of the rise of the begging friars. The noble orders founded by Saint Francis and Saint Dominic did not at once affect San Galgano, owing to the great and merited prestige which it enjoyed in its immediate neighborhood. But slowly, if imperceptibly, they exercised a disturbing influence on what we may call the recruiting market of our monastery, for, in entering the field to bid against the older institutions, they appealed with irresistible force to all the more strenuous spirits by virtue of their youthfulness and fire. Early in the fourteenth century,

* "Il Constituto di Siena dell' anno di 1262," I, 103.

about the time the new abbey in the meadow under
Monte Siepi celebrated its first centenary, one catches
signs suggesting that its moral tone has suffered. For
one thing Siena ceased to look to it for architects and
camarlinghi. That may have been, as I have already
hinted, because lay society had at last advanced to the
point where it could trust itself for these services, but,
on the other hand, the suspicion cannot be dismissed
that the services could no longer be rendered. In any
case the usefulness of the institution decreased, and
with the usefulness the efficiency of the residents. An
ominous silence gathered around San Galgano, the
silence descending upon a society which has outlived
its time, and when it is broken by confused sounds of
war and panic, drawing our attention once more to
the upper Merse, we are brought face to face with
disaster.

In the second half of the fourteenth century Italy was
visited by one of the most abominable social plagues
with which the much tormented peninsula was vexed
during the long agony of feudalism. It consisted in the
so-called Companies of Adventure. Since the central
authority, still nominally represented by the emperor
across the Alps, was destroyed, and ambitious local
powers, lords and cities, quarrelled fiercely for dominion,
a chaotic condition was created, marked by almost
uninterrupted petty warfare and furnishing lucrative
employment for large bands of mercenary soldiers.
The leaders of these bands were not slow to see that with
the decay of the various city militias, a decay which was
in full swing by the middle of the fourteenth century,
they really held Italian society at their mercy. I spoke

in another place * of this cruel phenomenon, showing
how the lawless freebooters, representing the dregs of
all Europe, ravaged the Sienese country around the
walls and squeezed incalculable sums out of the frightened burghers. Of course the rich abbey lands of San
Galgano fell a helpless prey to the adventurers, who
again and again spread over them in insolent ease, not
unlike a devastating cloud of locusts. The chroniclers
assure us that the worst of the plunderers of the beautiful Cistercian settlement was the Englishman, Sir
John Hawkwood, nothing more than a successful
brigand according to our mild standards, but rewarded
with royal honors in an age when he and his like commanded the most powerful armed forces of society.
Hawkwood, employed by Florence to do the fighting,
for which the burghers, with their attention concentrated
on trade and profits, had lost the taste, was cheered as
if he were the shepherd David by the Florentine populace, and when he died received the extraordinary honor
of being painted on horseback over the inner portal of
the Florentine cathedral. There he still rides exalted
over the worshippers, clamorously preaching in the impressive silence of Christ's temple the world-old doctrine
of the mailed fist. Hawkwood, under engagement to
Florence, was of course free to harry the territory of
Siena. His practice, as well as that of other *condottieri*
who visited the Merse valley, was to establish himself
with head-quarters at San Galgano, and then burn, rob,
and devastate within a radius of many miles.† The
scenes which occurred everywhere in the Middle Age

* Chapter 8.
† Muratori, Vol. XV, "Cronica Sanese," pp. 187, 189.

when a lawless horde burst upon a defenceless population, put a tax upon the imagination of a humanitarian
age like ours. Hawkwood's first visit to San Galgano
befell in the year 1363, and many visits by him and
others of his kind followed in the succeeding generation.
When the pest of the adventurous companies was at last
eradicated and better times dawned, the monastery
was in a state of complete disorganization. In 1397
the then abbot, one Lodovico di Tano, was constrained
to sell a piece of land in order to pay a papal imposition.
He found a purchaser, but could not meet the legal requirements for perfecting the bargain, because the
monks, whose consent was indispensable, were all dis-
persed. The abbot dwelt alone in the deserted halls of
the great monastery.*

With the return of tranquillity in the fifteenth century
San Galgano experienced a revival. Enough monks
returned to form a new nucleus, the offices were chanted
as of old, and the damage done by the Companies of
Adventure was gradually repaired. But the former
splendor never returned. The melancholy story of the
decline to the point of abandonment and ruin that now
, meets the eye is written legibly enough in the records,
but can only be briefly indicated here. Before the new
and vital interests, which the Renaissance, now mounting to its meridian, popularized throughout Italy, the
monastic idea began to pale. San Galgano, buried
among thick woods in a remote valley, did not bulk so
large as in a simpler age. Its revenues were still considerable, but its ranks represented a descending curve
of efficiency and were no longer crowded with cheerful

* Canestrelli, p. 21.

and self-sacrificing volunteers. The abbey worried along, however, as vested interests will, until presently it fell a victim to one of the growing diseases of the Roman system, the canker of prelacy. With the passion for a princely scale of living, which the Renaissance fastened upon the Roman pontiffs, went the need of a court, of gorgeous palaces, and of a numerous retinue of sycophants to shine as minor lights around the central sun. To meet the multifarious demands upon their budget the popes were driven to tap such questionable sources of income as the sale of indulgences, while to satisfy the covetous and luxurious prelates they were constrained to assign to them the revenues of fat bishoprics and abbacies. Every one will remember how powerfully this reckless exploitation contributed to the reform movement which swept over northern Europe in the sixteenth century. San Galgano, a rich benefice close at hand, was not likely to escape the general fate. In the year 1503 Pope Julius II, one of the most imposing personalities of the whole line of popes, but, as ill-luck would have it, always desperately in need of cash, gave the abbey *in commendam* to one of his cardinals. On the surface the transaction signified no more than that the abbey was "commended" to the cardinal's paternal care; in reality it appropriated the entire revenue to his personal use. The keeping up of the abbey depended henceforth on the distant commendatary's charity, supplemented by the begging talents of the monks. Some monks of an adventurous temper might still be inclined to take their chances with the institution under the nefarious absentee system, but they had no legal claim to anything. Their money flowed to Rome, and once at Rome was past reclaiming.

There is no reason for following closely the miserable tale of decay under the successive commendataries, though the story is not without its element of pathos. In the year 1576 a papal inspector, sent on a tour through Tuscany, found a single monk acting as caretaker of the vast establishment, reflecting in his rags the crying destitution of the monastery.* The inspector reported to Rome that the refectory was without a roof, that many chapels were in decay, that of the four bells three could not be rung, and that through the broken windows the birds entered and made their nests in the church. In the year 1632 the pope, himself scandalized at the results of a prolonged exploitation but incapable of devising an effective policy of reform, reduced the dishonored monastery from its dignity of abbey, and, twenty years after, secularized it by organizing it as a simple benefice. The benefice, however, embracing the many estates which San Galgano had accumulated through the ages, produced an undiminished revenue, and this revenue continued to flow into the hands of a commendatary, who, in return for an unmerited bounty, assumed the meagre obligation of maintaining Christian worship in the abbey church and of making a few repairs at his discretion. The Cistercian order now definitely left the place which was associated with a not inglorious chapter of its past. The commendatary, looking for cheap labor, sent first some Vallombrosans, and later, occasional Franciscans to act as custodians of the edifice, but these uninterested guardians, drawing an infinitesimal wage,

* Canestrelli, "Documento XXVIII."

were glad if they could eke out a living without giving a
thought to the maintenance of the splendid monument,
in whose ample enclosure they must have rattled around
like peas in a bushel.

And so we arrive through the long and painful stages
of neglect at the last phase, the chapter of total abandonment. On the 22nd of January, 1786, a congregation
of perhaps fifty peasants was gathered in the sacristy
before the only altar which seems to have been kept in
sufficient repair for the celebration of the mass. The
rest of the edifice, we are informed, had become fright-
fully damp and unwholesome, owing to the fact that
whenever it rained the water poured through the roof
like a sieve. Suddenly on that January day, "all' atto
della consecrazione,"* at the moment when the Franciscan caretaker and priest consecrated the bread,
there came a tremendous roar, followed by a shock
which threw the terrified worshippers upon their knees.
The bell tower, which rose just behind the sacristy and,
as was usual in Italy, stood free of the church, had given
way and crashed to the ground. It must have seemed
to the witnesses like a divine intervention that, instead
of burying them under its ruins in the sacristy, it had
measured its length upon the open field behind the
choir. After this catastrophe neither peasants nor
caretaker would trust themselves in the dilapidated
edifice. They got leave to transfer the worship, maintained in the crumbling abbey for the convenience of the
scattered peasants of the neighborhood, to Monte
Siepi; and the venerable though neglected round chapel
which marked the grave of San Galgano and had served

* Canestrelli, p. 61.

as the original settlement of the Cistercians, was once
more supplied with an altar and rang with the solemn
music of the liturgy. To this day, on Sundays and other
Christian festivals, it is visited by a thin congregation of
silent, stoical-looking peasants, attended by their wives
and children. With the withdrawal of the priest and
his flock a formal deconsecration was required by the
regulations of the Catholic church, in sign that the great
abbey was left to perish in peace. The Bishop of Volterra, in whose diocese the abbey lay, in due time
published the necessary decree, and on August 10, 1789,
the pertinent ceremony was gone through with by two
commissioners, accompanied by a notary to make the
necessary legal attestation. It is interesting to observe
that just six days before, some hundreds of miles away
across the snow-capped barrier of the Alps, a body of
Frenchmen, calling themselves the National Assembly,
had swept the remnants of feudalism out of existence
and inaugurated for Europe a new age, founded upon
the bold belief, no less than blasphemous to the mediæval mind, of the ability of reason to effect the salvation
of the human race. The chronological coincidence,
linking the far-sounding pronouncement made on the
Parisian stage with the abandonment unwept, unsung,
of a monument which had its root in the warm heart of
the Middle Age, touches the imagination. *Sunt lachry-
mæ rerum.*

Neglected since the days of the Renaissance by greedy
and conscienceless commendataries, the doomed abbey
was from the moment of deconsecration left unguarded
and untenanted, a prey to the conquering elements.
Not long before the tower came down in the manner

we have seen, a cardinal commendatary, Feroni by name, had managed to persuade the pope to transfer the whole property of San Galgano as a private estate to his family, with the sole obligation of contributing to the maintenance of religious worship in the abbey. When the tower fell, the family, in return for fitting up the chapel on Monte Siepi, got the maintenance clause abolished. The disavowal of the edifice was now complete; as far as the law was concerned, the owners were free to look upon the ancient monument as a useless encumbrance amidst their pleasant fields and meadows, and nothing hindered them from destroying it at pleasure. While balking at this extreme step, they freely resorted to it as a quarry, and the peasants, following the example of their enlightened masters, plundered it at will for such building material as their need required. Whenever a vault fell in, bullock carts rolled lumberingly to the scene to appropriate the fine blocks of travertine which littered the ground, and a heap of indistinguishable rubbish might be the only evidence of the existence of the abbey at this day, if the Italian government, sluggishly responding to the indignant appeal of a devoted lover of his country's history and art, had not, in the year 1894, stayed further demolition by declaring the ruin a national monument and by making meagre provision for its preservation.

Hardly a building, testifying to the character and splendor of the Italian past, is more worthy of a visit than the ruined abbey of San Galgano. Unvisited by the casual tourist by reason of its remoteness from the common highways of travel, utterly untouched by the many vulgar influences of modern life, it has gathered

Interior view of San Galgano

about itself the atmosphere of silence which settles upon all noble works. On an afternoon in June, abandoning the hot and dusty highway which I had followed for some hours, I mounted a grassy bank, and across a sun-lit meadow saw it lying, white and glittering like the gates of pearl. Around the level field, from whose thick clover came the riotous song of summer mounting to its acme, stood the wooded hills, grave and watchful. To the west, its defiant outline almost obliterated by the strong light, rose the cliff of Chiusdino. Fronting the lofty citadel and close at hand, lay gently-sloping Monte Siepi with the purple roof of the old round chapel just visible above the tree-tops. Here at last in the silence of the white summer afternoon, broken only by the voices in the grass and the faint, clear call of the cuckoo, the long story of the monastery became perfectly intelligible by being lifted out of the conditions of material fact into the realm of beauty. To the wakeful inner vision will always come a moment when things, born in time, assume the aspect of eternity. From that westward rock, its sharp lines dissolving in the sun, had the knight Galgano ridden forth upon his quest of God, his golden hair, of which the legend tells, waving in the wind; in these peaceful hills had he wandered, carrying his heart in his hands like a sacrifice; and here, on brooding Monte Siepi, earth had gathered the exhausted body like a leaf of the dead year. Presently over the grave had risen the round chapel of the Cistercian brotherhood, and, in the due course of time, built of the prayers of men, the abbey yonder, lifting a pure front above the meadow. Even so. The crickets rehearse the tale to the cicadas shrilling in the hedges, the thrush and cuckoo inform the hills, which, when evening falls, will hold silent conference with the marching stars.

Just before sunset I entered the portal and stood in the deserted nave. The vaults had fallen in, disclosing the blue sky covered with a web of delicate rose vapor. A few blocks of weathered travertine, which had lately given way, littered the grassy floor. At the entrance to the transept a brilliant patch of yellow marked a bed of buttercups, graciously planted by some wandering wind. At either hand the eye followed the rows of piers till it rested upon the marred choir wall with its ghostly apertures. Finer clustered columns one may not hope to find, each one composed of perfectly articulated members, simple, serviceable, and beautiful. Equally simple, with an added grace of subtle rhythm, are the triforium and clerestory. If this was Italian workmanship it was at least directed by the delicate Gothic spirit which emanated from the Isle de France. In the days when the ribbed vault terminated the nave and aisles, the church must have produced an effect as rounded and complete as a sonata by some great master. But if completeness has been lost, its absence is not noticed by reason of a quality much more moving to us in our character of men, a quality which Wordsworth has called "the unimaginable touch of time." Daily as the light fails from the sky and dusk gathers within the spacious enclosure, time, and its kindred spirit, beauty, circle like great birds above the deserted home of men.

CHAPTER XIV

THE TWILIGHT OF SIENA

WE are nearing the end of our journey. The mediæval commune, the history of which I set out to trace, perished with the spread of the new civilization bearing the name of the Renaissance. In a formal sense, indeed, the republic of Siena lived far into the new period, but it led a maimed existence, at the mercy of circumstances, and without that splendid vigor which distinguished it in those strictly mediæval centuries, called by the Italians the dugento and trecento. It was precisely because the town in its creative period exhibited an irrepressible activity and developed an attractive and original civilization that we of another age are content to follow its fortunes and to linger over its works. For the same reason the Age of the Renaissance, a period of unarrested decline, has but a weak claim upon our interest. Still, whoever has followed with sympathy the rise and culmination of this original and perplexing people will not rest until he has given himself the melancholy satisfaction of viewing also the end.

We dropped the thread of Sienese political development at the close of the fourteenth century, when the town stood face to face with a score of difficulties which seemed on the point of overwhelming and destroying it.

We noted the domestic turmoil of the monti, the industrial and financial depression, the prowling Companies of Adventure, the rebellious nobility—surely a formidable array of evils. But these troubles were not all, for at the moment of this domestic crisis the whole Italian peninsula was swept by a political revolution, the effects of which Siena, remote and provincial though she was, could not hope to escape.

In the course of the fourteenth century a movement of concentration had affirmed itself, by reason of which the numerous republics and lordships of the peninsula began to disappear in order to make room for more ample and powerful political aggregations. Five states had pushed their way to the front—Venice and Milan in the north, Florence between the Apennines and the sea, the States of the Church embracing the central Apennines, and Naples to the south. Milan was held by the Visconti, who had raised their tyrannical régime on the ruins of the democratic commune; Venice was an oligarchy of rich merchants; Naples was a feudal kingdom—in fact each of the five states had a political organization peculiar to itself. Widely differing in constitutional forms, they resembled one another, however, in that they all alike strove ceaselessly, by means fair or foul, to enlarge their boundaries by absorbing their weaker neighbors. Out of this general greed grew ever fresh wars which, by the side of the radiant and cloud-capped Italy of the Renaissance evoked by the humanists and artists, set a material Italy which was a very lazar-house of sorrow and disease.

In these Italian wars Siena had no other interest than that of self-preservation. She was perpetually between hammer and anvil and obliged to take desperate chances to escape from each new predicament. Florence was as always the chief source of alarm. In the face of this situation the natural policy of the smaller city was to secure itself against subjection to the Arno town by avoiding scrupulously to give offence, and Florence for her part was magnanimously content to be friendly, pending the arrival of the favorable moment when she could safely show her fangs and seize her prey. Patriotic historians of Siena speak indignantly of the Florentine policy of this period, charging it, as in the past, with faithlessness and violence. These offensive traits, indeed, undeniably characterize the conduct of the Arno merchants, but beneath such baser qualities, it is only fair to Florence to insist, stirred an entirely healthy desire of expansion, fed by the dim but unerring perception that a more effective organization of Italy was inevitable in an age which was pushing its galleys into unknown seas beyond the Mediterranean, and girding its loins for the conquest of new continents.

A single glance at the geographical position of Florence will convince us that her most immediate ambition was the control of the Arno valley. It was therefore a signal satisfaction to the republic when in the year 1384 she raised her banner over Arezzo. This success, carrying Florentine influence far inland, must have encouraged the government to think that the time had come for a renewed grappling with Siena. Ever since the Montaperti period, when Siena had become Guelph, that is, for more than a hundred years, the relations of the two neighbors had been fairly satisfactory, but now plainly Florence felt strong enough to resume offensive operations. In pursuit of this policy she conducted a secret intrigue with the Sienese dependency of Montepulciano till that town revolted and put itself under her protection. This breach of a long established amity occurred in the year 1387. The Sienese sent an embassy to Florence to lodge a complaint; pursued patient negotiations, marked, on the part of the Arno city, by deceit and subterfuge; and presently, in alarm lest worse follow, sought the alliance of Gian Galeazzo Visconti, lord of Milan. Gian Galeazzo is a highly remarkable example of that new order of political being, the tyrant, brought forth by the wild confusion of the peninsula. Too much has been written about the personal aspect of the tyrant, about his ambition, his violence, his disregard of the laws of God and man, and too little about the political purposes which he served. Gian Galeazzo had a clearer understanding of the necessity of uniting Italy than any statesman the peninsula produced down to the time of Macchiavelli. An illuminating glimpse of his policy is afforded by a declaration which he once launched to the effect "that Tuscany and Lombardy must become one and inseparable."* What a statesmanlike vision that simple utterance proves him to have possessed, but what a storm of protest it was sure to raise in an age of small and infinitesimal corporations, profoundly persuaded that they existed by reason of a divine mandate!

By the force of genius Gian Galeazzo had already imposed his authority on the valley of the Po, when he received the proffer of an alliance from the Sienese

---

* "Quod Tuscia cum Lumbardia fiet unum et idem." Quoted by Professione "Siena e le Compagnie di Ventura," p. 160.

which would secure him a welcome foothold in Tuscany.
The treaty was signed in the year 1389 and was to last
ten years. Even before its arrangements were perfected
war with Florence over Montepulciano had broken out,
the usual ferocious war waged with mercenaries, and
marked by the harrying of the open country, by plunder
and arson. If Siena, soon reduced to pitiful straits, at
least preserved her independence, she owed that boon
to the political support of the Milanese duke. Occasional efforts to bring about peace proved vain. Not
only did Florence refuse to give up Montepulciano, but
her stubborn rancor even made the Sienese tremble for
the safety of their own city. Rather than fall into the
hands of their archenemies, in the year 1399, at the
expiration of the ten years' treaty, they offered the sovereignty of their city to Gian Galeazzo. The step won
them a respite, and the Milanese duke, by scrupulously
avoiding interference in local affairs, proved that his
supremacy was perfectly consistent with the essentials
of self-government.* Victory after victory had carried
the duke by this time far toward the realization of his
plans. The year before the acquisition of Siena, he had
raised his banner, bearing the famous writhing viper
of the Visconti, over Pisa. Perugia, Assisi, and proud
Bologna were presently added to his dominions. It was
whispered that he was on the point of making a frank
avowal of his hopes by crowning himself king of Italy,
when he was taken with fever and died (1402). Immediately his dominions melted away, and Siena, find-

---

* See the admirable regulations by which he circumscribed the powers of
his personal representative in the city. Malavolti, "Storia di Siena," terza
parte, p. 189.

ing no security in a continued submission to a weak
successor, reasserted her independence (1404). The
Visconti episode was closed, but it brought into clear
relief two things: first, that Siena had little good to
expect from Florence, and, second, that she could meet
a persistent onslaught from the Arno city only with the
aid of a protector.

I do not plan to follow the fortunes of Siena in the
new century with any detail. Although the disturbances of Italy continued, the agitated peninsula being
unable to find peace in her system of small states, Siena
for a long time enjoyed a relative quiet, as Florence
temporarily turned her energy in other directions. In
the year 1406 she acquired Pisa, and therewith free
access to the open sea; and in 1430 she tried to throw
her net about Lucca. This rapid development alarmed
Siena, and in the latter case led to her taking up arms
in behalf of the threatened city on the Serchio, but
apart from flurries of this nature, no notable event, defining the relation of Siena to her neighbors, took place
until we reach the pontificate of Pius II, inaugurated
in the year 1458. Pius II, whose family name was
Æneas Silvius Piccolomini, was an offspring of one of
the oldest houses of Siena, and was a famous scholar and
traveller. As he was attached with passionate intensity
to his home, Siena during his rule (1458–1464) was as
effectually under the protection of the papacy as she
had once been under that of Milan. Accordingly,
neither Florence nor any other power threatened her
territory, which happy circumstance Pius, during frequent prolonged stays in Siena, tried with noble inspiration to turn to account by effecting a permanent cure

of the secular divisions of his fellow-townsmen. The
local situation, therefore, as it presented itself to the
eyes of Pius, and as it developed under his personal
pressure, invites our attention.

The system of the monti, hereditary parties which
struggled for the possession of the power and honors,
was a device apparently invented for the express purpose of perpetuating domestic disorder. We are already
aware that to this political system was largely attribu-
table the steady decline of the town. We have followed
the story of the monti to the revolution of 1385 when the
Riformatori were overthrown and the monte del Popolo,
the fifth and the last of these cantankerous castes, came
into being. The victory of that year gave the sovereignty to the Noveschi, the Dodicini, and the Popolari (as
the members of the monte del Popolo were called), the
now time-honored exclusion of the nobles or Gentiluomini from the signiory being, of course, maintained.
Presently, in a most unusual access of magnanimity, a
concession* was made to the Riformatori with the result
that the four peoples' parties seemed to have been
reduced to an apparent harmony. But the old rancor
glowed beneath the ashes. In 1403 the Dodicini,
whom we know from of old as tireless sowers of dissen-
sion, entered into a conspiracy with some of the nobles
to overthrow the government, and on being discovered
were *ammoniti in perpetuo*—excluded forever from the
signiory. The government thus devolved on the three
monti of the Noveschi, the Riformatori, and the Popolari, and remained with them without any substantial
change till the time of Pius II, that is, for half a century.

* In 1387 and again in 1398.

This long period of inner quiet was made possible
by an unusual understanding among the three ruling
groups, aided by their sharp repression of every hostile
demonstration on the part of the excluded orders of the
Gentiluomini and the Dodicini. To keep these domestic enemies in the proper degree of submission their
leaders were from time to time, without even the sem-
blance of legal procedure, packed out of the town and
banished. San Bernardino (1380–1444), saint and
orator, who acquired an added authority among his
countrymen from being a Sienese born and bred, pleaded
in public addresses, attended by vast crowds of male
and female auditors, for a civil peace founded on
justice for all, but his eloquence entered the ears and
did not penetrate the hearts.* The city fathers were
satisfied that they had done their whole duty when they
yielded so far to the saint's persuasions as to fix the
monogram of Christ, surrounded, in sign of universal
love, by the rays of the sun, to the front of the palazzo.
Upon this monogram, San Bernardino, so to speak,
founded his ministry. Carrying it with him whenever
he mounted the pulpit, he urged upon his hearers that
they adopt it in place of the worldly devices and coats-
of-arms which their provocative zeal led them to attach
to the house-fronts. Like the magistracy, the citizens
generally, as Sienese walls still testify, complied with
the saint's demand. Professions but no deeds, lip-
worship but no conversion! Long habit inclined the
citizens to turn periodically to the excitement of street

---

* The addresses, gratefully free from the bombast of the humanists and
delivered in the honest dialect of shop and market, afford admirable glimpses
of the time. The series delivered in 1427 has been luckily preserved for us.
Banchi, "Le Prediche Volgari di S. Bernardino."

San Bernardino Preaching in the Campo
By Sano di Pietro (in the Sala del Capitolo of the Cathedral)

brawls as drunkards do to the bottle.   How else are we
to interpret the remarkable notice reported by the
historian Malavolti for the year 1439 ?   The young men
of the town, we hear, made restless by the *otio continuo*,
the long years of domestic peace, formed themselves into
two bands under the names of *Chiassa* and *Graffio*
(Noise and Scratch!), and engaged in street-fighting
which would have set the town topsy-turvy if the government had not ended the mischief with rigorous penalties.
As Chiassa and Graffio had nothing to do with politics,
nor stood even remotely for any programme of govern-
mental action, we may accept them as the naïve expression of an inborn and ineradicable contentiousness.
I have tried to be just to the great and impersonal
forces which determined the course of Sienese history,
but let us not forget that the national temper counts for
something, nay, counts for much in the general result.
Whoever wants further proof need but give attention
to the reception extended by the Sienese to the reform
plans of Pope Pius II.

The family of Pius, the Piccolomini, belonged to the
grandi, who, at the time of Pius's accession to the chair
of Saint Peter, had been excluded from the signiory
for almost two hundred years.   To curry favor with
the new pope, the male members of his family residing in Siena were made eligible to all honors as
soon as the news of Pius's election was reported at home.
The pope was a man of too elevated a character to be
caught with such small bait.   He asked for the re-
habilitation of all the nobles, and did not hesitate to
come in person to Siena to plead with the magistrates
to bury the past and inaugurate an era of concord.

Tardily, and with every sign of discontent, the government yielded; but when Pius now demanded the same favor for the Dodicini, in order that the whole citizen body might be at last embraced in a single union of hearts, he met with obdurate resistance. It was the last and the best chance the Sienese ever had of putting their government on a foundation of true democratic justice. Their rejection of Pius's proposals, made with the love of a citizen and the authority of a pontiff, showed an attachment to their hereditary rancors which had become an element of the blood. They were enamored of their differences and did not want to be cured of them! Pius was no sooner cold in his grave than, with a meanness which is as ludicrous as it is melancholy, they even withdrew the rights that they had granted to the nobility.

As we approach the end of the fifteenth century a new factor, passing almost unnoticed at first, made itself felt in the politics of Italy. Foreign powers, and, more particularly, France and Spain, began to throw covetous glances in the direction of the peninsula. If there had been a grain of true statesmanship among the princes, or a spark of patriotism among the people, the peril to the national liberties resulting from the incursion of overwhelmingly powerful foreign states, would have made all discord cease. Instead, the Italian governments, without a thought or a scruple, continued to pursue each other's destruction: now it was Venice leagued with the pope against Milan, now Naples with Milan against Florence, and again some other combination of partners, as if politics were a drawing-room amusement on the level of a quadrille. Siena counted

for little or nothing in these combinations and would
have preferred to observe a strict neutrality.   However,
that was not always possible.   In the year 1477 the pope
and the king of Naples planned a war against Florence,
Milan, and Venice, and as they could most conveniently
reach their northern enemies, and more particularly,
Florence, through the territory of Siena, they obliged
that government to enter into alliance with them.   In
the struggle that followed Florence suffered some heavy
losses,* resulting in an ephemeral occupation of some
of her territory by the elated Sienese.   This short-lived
triumph almost cost the sons of the Virgin their political existence, for the leader of the victorious allies,
the Duke of Calabria, on being admitted into Siena with
an armed host, showed a strong disposition to remain.
As soon as the war with Florence was terminated with
a general peace (1480), he engaged in intrigues with a
group of local supporters—chiefly of the Noveschi—to
play the town into his hands.   Success was as good as
assured when an accident intervened.   The Turks disembarked on the Neapolitan coast, and the Duke of
Calabria was hurriedly recalled to protect his own state
and people.   The incident deserves a place in this rapid
story of Siena's fall, first, because it proved that the
government of the town could be disturbed by any
adventurer who came on horseback at the head of an
armed force, and second, because the treason of the
Noveschi precipitated an era of disturbances which
grew into a political bedlam beyond anything recorded

* Above all, a signal defeat at Poggio Imperiale (1479) in the Elsa Valley.
The Sienese signiory ordered a pictorial representation of the victory to be
made for the palazzo. The poor fresco may still be seen adjoining the
splendid Madonna of Simone Martini.

in the annals even of Italy, and which lasted till the end of the republic.

Into the story of this last mad chapter of Sienese political history it is entirely unprofitable to enter except to rescue from oblivion two important episodes, the one connected with the name of Pandolfo Petrucci, the other with Siena's siege and heroic end.

I have already spoken in general terms of that interesting phenomenon of Italian history, the tyrant. He is the strong man who, when the confusion in the city republics became intolerable, seized the government and reorganized it around himself as master. That Siena with its plots, street-fights, and banishments was sedulously preparing the way for such an end of its liberties must be clear as day to whomsoever has attentively followed the vicissitudes of the town. Here lies the significance of Pandolfo Petrucci,* the story of whose rise bears a striking resemblance to that of Cosimo, founder of the Medicean fortunes in neighboring Florence.

Pandolfo and his family belonged to the Noveschi, who, we have just seen, were involved in the intrigues woven around the person of the Duke of Calabria. When the intrigues came to naught the intriguers found themselves hoist by their own petard. In consequence of popular commotions many leading Noveschi, among them the Petrucci family, were banished, and the whole monte was presently declared excluded forever from the

---

* For Petrucci consult Pecci, "Memorie Storico-critiche della Città di Siena," Vol. I. To correct Pecci, the panegyrist, read Mondolfo, "Pandolfo Petrucci, Signore di Siena." The political duel between Petrucci and Cæsar Borgia is treated by Lisini, "Bull. Sen.," VI—a splendid episode worthy of close study on the part of every critic of the Renaissance.

government (1483). The decree had been in force four years when the Noveschi, who were rich merchants with powerful connections, overthrew their adversaries. In the early morning hours of July 22, 1487, Pandolfo and his friends scaled the wall at Fonte Branda, took possession of the Campo, drove the rulers from the palace, and reformed—that was the euphonious expression hallowed by usage—the government. The changes which followed during the next years need not engross our attention further than to take note that the influence of the Noveschi kept constantly growing, and that *pari passu* increased the family power of the Petrucci, represented by Pandolfo and his brother Jacopo. When Jacopo—he, too, a clever politician—died in 1497, Pandolfo added his brother's authority to his own. In the same year the Consiglio Generale practically resigned the responsibilities of government for a term of five years into the hands of a committee or Balìa,* in which the partisans of Pandolfo had a clear preponderance. Such a step, concentrating the authority in a few hands, was an open avowal that the old democratic

---

* For the evolution of the magistracy of the Balìa see Paoli's monograph, "Del Magistrato della Balìa nella Repubblica di Siena," published in the "Atti e Memorie della Accademia dei Rozzi (1879)." I called attention in chap. 5 to the early habit of appointing Balìe or special committees, and showed how some of them became permanent magistracies. All through the period of the republic such Balìe continued to be appointed to wrestle with difficulties arising in connection with finance, administration, and so forth. Beginning with 1455 we note a change. Owing to the need, in a grave crisis of that year, of secrecy and dispatch which could not be secured by the ordinary channels of government, the Consiglio Generale gave full powers to a special Balìa "qui congregentur de per se et habeant eandem auctoritatem quam nunc habent Magnifici Domini, Capitaneus Populi, etc." This Balìa was manifestly a kind of dictatorship for a limited period. The growing difficulties favored a more and more frequent resort to it, until, in the time of Pandolfo, it quietly made itself permanent.

constitution was no longer practicable. Whenever the
Balìa approached the end of its term, its authority was
renewed, and thus the same group continued in power,
serving as the convenient mantle beneath which a
private citizen concealed his autocratic rule. Cosimo
de' Medici, a half hundred years before, had established the same kind of latent tyranny in Florence,
maintaining it by means of a ring of political friends
who shared the offices and honors. In Florence and
Siena, which did not keep standing armies, but only
engaged foreign soldiery as the need arose, a prospective
master was obliged to have recourse not to force,
frankly and openly asserted, but to the prudential combinations and subterranean methods of the professional
politician.

Pandolfo had to present a bold front in two directions,
first, against the domestic enemies, ambitious men of
his own temper who enjoyed the advantage of being able
to rally the people by the cry of liberty, and, second,
against Siena's foreign foes, chief of whom was, now as
always, Florence. The local enemies he got rid of by
the means, usual among the Italian city tyrants,
of banishment and assassination. Some sixty men,
it has been calculated, paid for their opposition to
his supremacy with their lives, among them some
of his earliest friends and nearest relatives. In that
famous manual for despots, "The Prince" of Macchiavelli, we can read in words which have a glint
like steel, how a man new to power must never let his
hand be stayed by weakness or pity. When Pandolfo's
own father-in-law, Niccolò Borghesi, persisted in crossing his plans, the tyrant plotted his destruction. On

June 19, 1500, as Niccolò was returning home from the
duomo, he was struck down by hired assassins.   Apart
from such domestic incidents, we must recognize, if we
wish to be fair to the general character of Pandolfo's
rule, that Siena was tranquil under him as hardly ever
in her history, that trade flourished, and that the unscrupulous tyrant enjoyed great popularity not only
among the men of his own monte, but among the people
in general.   Macchiavelli, the all-observing Florentine,
has expressed the opinion * that Pandolfo's power had
its root in the little armed force of three hundred men
which the city took into its employ to maintain order,
and of which he had the captaincy.   Of course
Pandolfo was only too ready to confirm his position
with the aid of soldiers, if necessary, but the fact
remains, reflecting considerable credit on the deftness
and effectiveness of his system, that he maintained
himself among so restless a people as the Sienese
largely by the sole weight of his masterful personality.

In Pandolfo's day occurred the successive invasions
of Italy by France and Spain which prepared the en-
slavement of the peninsula.   In the presence of the two
western giants even Milan, Florence, and their peers
counted for little, and a state of the slender resources of
Siena became, of course, almost negligible.   Critics of
Pandolfo's foreign policy fluently charge him with timid-
ity, coupled with a flagrant lack of creative leadership.
As if Siena would have made herself other than ridicu-
lous by a swash-buckler attitude!   The best thing a
small state in love with life could hope, in the terrible
trial through which the peninsula was passing, was to

* "Discorsi sopra la Prima Deca di Tito Livio," C. VI, del l. 3.

keep from under the wheels of the Juggernaut. That is
what Siena accomplished under Pandolfo's leadership;
not much, if you will, but the utmost possible under the
circumstances. Neighboring Florence, it is true, went
through a crisis which offered a rare opportunity for
aggression and seemed to superficial observers to herald
the demise of the merchant city. Pisa revolted, while
Montepulciano and Arezzo soon followed the bold
example. Many Tuscans thought and declared that
with a little determination the Red Lily might be hum-
bled in the dust. But Pandolfo knew better. Taking
cool inventory of the resources of the Florentines and
the value of their tried alliance with the King of France,
he moved among the pitfalls of contending factions with
extreme caution. Of course he hated Florence as a
good Sienese must, and in his heart wished all enemies
of the Arno city well, not scrupling to lend them secret
help whenever he could in the form of money and supplies, but, when asked to join openly and without
reserve the movement against Florence, he always drew
back. Some modern scholars have declared their horror
of this system of lying professions of friendship for
Florence, coupled with secret machinations with all her
enemies; they have declared Pandolfo a person of mean
stature without talent and sincerity.* Sincerity in the
age of Cæsar Borgia! A person so afflicted would have
done well to get himself a suit of motley at once. I say
again that Pandolfo's diplomacy was anything but edifying; that its note was prudence, a prudence imposed
upon it by the feebleness of the Sienese state; and,

* This is the view of Burckhardt, " Cultur der Renaissance," I, chap. 4.
Even Mondolfo in his careful sketch of Pandolfo's policy inclines to this view.

finally, I assert that as its aim was and could be nothing higher than the conservation of the independence of Siena, we can not refuse some credit to Pandolfo for having weathered a storm which wrought the ruin of Milan and Naples, not to mention a half-score of lesser Italian states.

A close examination of Pandolfo's career will disclose that he did not differ essentially from the other tyrants of his day. His secretary, Antonio da Venafro, was once asked by Pope Alexander VI how his master kept the turbulent Sienese under control. "By lies, Your Holiness," was Antonio's prompt reply—*colle bugie!* That was the system of every tyrant of Italy, to which the more desperate sort, like the Baglioni of Perugia and the Bentivogli of Bologna, added indiscriminate slaughter, and an occasional genius, like Cæsar Borgia, military skill and an unlimited enterprise. The active will, at least in the form of that colossal daring which we encounter in the adventures of Cæsar, was not among the qualities with which nature had endowed Pandolfo for better and worse. A single glance at his portrait,* showing a lean man with high philosophical forehead and watchful eyes beneath, will confirm the impression conveyed by his acts, that we are face to face with the manipulator of men, the sleepless planner, the politician. A heavy and protruding underlip is a blot in a countenance not without distinction and suggests periods of misanthropic gloom and sudden lapses into vulgarity. And of episodes illustrating the latter tendency his life was certainly not free. He was already an invalid on

---

* An engraving from a portrait said to be by Peruzzi will be found as frontispiece to Pecci, "Memorie," etc.

the verge of the grave when he became enamored of a woman of the people, Caterina from the Salicotto region, a filthy quarter where the poor were herded. The Sienese smiled maliciously at their lord's infatuation for the smith's daughter and saddler's wife, whose height and general bulk had won for her the amusing sobriquet of the Two-handed Sword. But Caterina's buxom charms did not restore Pandolfo to gaiety and health. In the spring of the year 1512 he tried the baths of San Filippo, whence, finding no relief, he started back for Siena. But death was in pursuit and overtook him on the way. On May 21, at the little town of San Quirico, he breathed his last.

While Pandolfo's career offers a resemblance in many points to that of Cosimo de' Medici, the fortunes of their respective descendants differ widely. Cosimo, by the lucky circumstance of a capable family succession, founded a dynasty, whereas Pandolfo's heirs, as vicious as they were incompetent, frittered away, in a surprisingly short time, the hard-won prestige of their father. Four years after Pandolfo's death, his son and successor, Borghese Petrucci, had to flee from Siena for his life. For a number of years (1516-22) Borghese's cousin, Raffaele, who enjoyed the powerful support of the Medicean pope, Leo X, held sway, and on his death, Fabio, a younger son of Pandolfo's, was called to the supreme position in the state. When Fabio, a thought-free youth, more occupied with love than with affairs of state, was banished in 1524, the Petrucci chapter of Sienese history came to an abrupt close.

Having rid themselves of a threatening dynasty the Sienese were again masters of their own fortunes. The

Noveschi, the monte from which Pandolfo issued and upon which he chiefly leaned, hoped to assume his inheritance, but a rising of the people under the leadership of the Libertini, the friends of liberty, overthrew them, and punished them with the usual measures of exclusion from the honors and banishment from the city. The news was highly distasteful to Pope Clement VII, with whom the Noveschi maintained a strict alliance. Clement resolved to interfere, animated, it would seem, by the secret reflection, natural enough in a born Florentine and a Medici, of making the opportunity serve to crush Siena once and for all, and to subject it to his house. He sent a papal army against Siena, supported by a considerable Florentine force. Then occurred wonders in the city which for over a century had exhibited so many ominous signs of decrepitude. Then was seen that one thing and only one could heal the bitter divisions of the townsmen: the fear and hatred of Florence. The approach of Clement's army lit a patriotic fire in every heart, and with spirits consecrated as in the days of Montaperti by a renewed offering of the city to Madonna, the Sienese prepared to meet the foe. On July 25, 1526, the citizen levies fell unexpectedly on the hostile forces camped outside of Porta Camollia, and drove them from the field. In the sheer explosive energy of a consuming passion the victory of Camollia may fairly be coupled with the stroke which gave the Arbia a place in the immortal verse of Dante. The angered Clement became involved at this juncture in a war with Emperor Charles V and saw ruin descend on himself and Rome in the form of Bourbon's army. In place of plundering Siena, the pope's own sacred seat was put to a terrible sack (1527). Siena, rescued from danger, sought the alliance of the mighty Charles, whose protection seemed to promise ample immunity against the further ill-will of the pope.

But the protector, once admitted within the gates, himself began to play the part of master. Charles, it must be acknowledged, had some justification for his encroachments. He began by condescending to play, from his lofty eminence, the part of friend and moderator. Again and again he counselled the Sienese to end their local quarrels, readmit their proscribed citizens, and live in peace. In the year 1536 he came in person and gravely repeated his advice. Not only, in spite of these exhortations, did murder and violence continue to reign within the walls, but, owing to the weakness of the government, law and order ceased also to be enforced in the countryside. By virtue of a treaty of the year 1530, Charles, in order the better to protect Siena, had put a Spanish garrison in the town. Imperceptibly his representative increased the scope of his powers, until he gave advice to the magistrates on all affairs of importance, assumed the policing of the territory, and made himself virtual governor of the state. Finally, in the year 1547, he took a step in which the Sienese unanimously recognized the end of those liberties which, though they consistently abused, they nevertheless loved instinctively and deeply. He began the construction of a fortress on the hill of San Prospero, the public garden of the present day, from which he could easily dominate the city with his artillery. Repeatedly the Sienese sent ambassadors to Charles to beseech him to respect the independence of the republic; again, as in other grave crises of the state, they went in solemn procession to the cathedral to invoke the protection of the Virgin.* By the side of these peaceful measures, however, they did fail to take more practical steps by opening secret negotiations with the agents of the French king, in the assurance that that sovereign was always eagerly ready to encourage any opposition which might manifest itself against his rival of Spain. In accordance with carefully laid plans the Sienese rebellion broke out in the summer of the year 1552. The Spaniards, taken by surprise, were obliged, after a brief resistance, to abandon both the city and the fortress. A treaty secured them an unmolested retreat (August 5th). As they filed out of the fortress between dense masses of exultant citizens, some Sienese youths addressed a polite greeting to the commander, Don Franzese, whose gracious manners had secured him the personal attachment of a large circle. "I thank you for your good-will," answered that gentleman; then bowing a dignified farewell to the company he added significantly: "You Sienese have done a handsome stroke, but bear yourselves discreetly in the future, for you have offended too great a man."†

The revolt of Siena from Emperor Charles V was one

---

* It may be noted at this point that Siena dedicated itself five times to the Virgin, in 1260, in 1483, in 1526, in 1550, and in 1555. A brief record of the special circumstances connected with each case will be found in Heywood "Palio and Ponte," p. 40 ff.

† Sozzini, p. 88. I refer to his "Diario delle Cose Avenute in Siena da 20 Luglio 1550 al 28 Giugno 1555," published in "Arch. Stor. It.," II (1842). For the siege consult the above vivid book of Sozzini, an eye-witness; also Montalvo, "Relazione della Guerra di Siena" (ed. by Ricomanni and Grottanelli, 1863), Monluc, "Commentaires et lettres" (ed. by Alphonse de Ruble, 1864). Very important, as a means of controlling Monluc, is Courteault, "Blaise de Monluc Historien," Paris, 1908.

of a series of actions in Italy and Germany which
inaugurated a new general war between that sovereign
and his rival of France In the world-game played by
the two rulers in the sixteenth century Siena had, by the
accident of geographical position, become a point possessed of a certain strategical advantage, and each
would attempt to hold it against the other. To such
a pass had the new political organization of Europe
brought the ancient commune. She could maintain
herself only by leaning on one or the other: Spanish
yesterday, she might be French to-day and Spanish
again to-morrow, but she could never more belong to
herself alone. Strange to say neither the people nor
their leaders saw this simple fact, which, to our perception, looms as palpable as a mountain. They
actually believed they were defending their liberties—
a term on which the history of the town throws a lurid
light—and hugged to their breasts the ignorant hope of
being able to treat as equals with France and Spain.
If this was an illusion, it is at least to be said for the
Sienese that they gave themselves to it with such sincerity that they reached in this, the final chapter of their
history as a free republic, a level of heroism rarely attained by any people, great or small, ancient or modern;
for heroism is independent of reason and success, and
often puts forth its fairest flower in the niggard soil
of lost hopes and desperate causes.

In January, 1553, Charles made his first attempt to
recover the town. His army, moving northward from
Naples, presently spread through the Val di Chiana,
with the end in view of establishing a military base in
Sienese territory. The Spanish commander had not

yet completed this action, the necessary preliminary to the contemplated siege, when he was recalled by the necessity of defending Naples against the Turkish fleet, sent westward by the sultan in aid of his ally, the French king. Siena celebrated the withdrawal in the usual way with a religious procession, followed by bonfires and brazen fanfares from the battlements, but the relief was only temporary. In January, 1554, the Spaniards returned, in close alliance this time with Cosimo, Duke of Florence—a most ominous circumstance in the eyes of every thinking Sienese. The great Charles alone was an enemy of weight, but Charles in alliance with the hereditary foe of Siena might well fill the mind with evil prognostications. The commander-in-chief of the Imperialist forces was the Marquis of Marignano, who began hostilities by boldly pitching his camp before the Porta Camollia along the northern or Florentine road.

Henry II, King of France, was prepared to be at considerable pains to preserve a town in his obedience which afforded his army its only foothold in central Italy. In the very month, therefore, in which Marignano reopened the hostilities, he sent one of his marshals, Piero Strozzi, to act as his vicar-general for Italy, and, more particularly, to conduct a vigorous defence of Siena against the Spaniards. Strozzi, the head of an ancient Florentine family which had gone into exile rather than suffer the tyranny of Duke Cosimo, could be counted on to carry a fiery and venomous zeal into the struggle. His military talents, too, were of no mean order. Commanding a small French troop, which he hoped to enlarge presently by well-equipped reinforcements from

the north, and supported by the ardent citizen levies of
Siena, he faced with confidence the problem of defending
the town. It is indicative of the regeneration of the
inhabitants effected by the inspiring occasion, that
though they had long ago permitted their ancient military organization to fall into complete decay, they now
gladly presented themselves to serve with spade, panier,
pike, arquebus, or whatever arm the defence of their
beloved country seemed to require.

Both Marignano and Strozzi were hampered for a
time in the execution of their plans by the insufficient
number of their troops. Any offensive action, on the
part of Strozzi, was out of the question till the arrival
of succor, while Marignano with his thin line of besiegers could not effectually blockade the city. In
April, however, the Imperialists scored a notable success by seizing the lofty villa, Belcaro, and the ancient
Munistero, both crowning hills outside Porta San
Marco and commanding the important Maremma road.
Summer was on hand before Strozzi got assurance of the
dispatch from the north of the longed-for reinforcements. At the word he undertook the execution of a
plan which was surely not lacking in imaginative daring.

The French were to come in two divisions by routes
carefully kept secret, one force, composed of Swiss,
across the Apennines to Lucca, the other, made up of
Gascons and Germans, by sea from the ports of France
to Viareggio. On June 11, 1554, with the fall of night,
Strozzi slipped out of Siena, leaving a garrison sufficient
to man the walls; made his way westward by a circuitous route; crossed the Arno at Pontedera; and
successfully established a junction with the Swiss at

the appointed place of meeting. As soon as the fleet
had disembarked the other auxilliaries, with an army
which, for the moment, would completely outnumber
that of Marignano, he intended to swoop down on
undefended Florence. It was a plan worthy of his
hatred of the Medicean tyrant of his native city, but
dependent on the coöperation of too many individual wills. The French admiral failed to put in a prompt
appearance—in resentment, it was said, of the royal
order which subordinated him to Strozzi's command—
and Strozzi, after a few days of waiting near Lucca, had
to give up his enterprise. He recrossed the Arno in
order to be within reach of Siena, and at last received
the news that the French fleet had appeared off the coast
of the Maremma, several weeks behind the appointed
time. Recovering from his profound disappointment,
he met the new arrivals, and then led his united troops
back to Siena, quickly prepared, after the fashion of
sanguine men, to work out another plan.

On July 15, the French army entered the city which
it had come to save with all the pomp and circumstance
of war. Alessandro Sozzini, one of the cheering citizens, tells us how the parti-colored raiment of the German arquebusiers and the gallant bearing of the French
pikemen delighted a people who fed greedily on every
spectacle.* Of greater moment, however, to us of a
later age is that among the new arrivals was a man who
could wield a pen. I refer to Monsieur Blaise de
Monluc, appointed by Henry II at Strozzi's own request
to serve as governor of the town. A poor Gascon
gentleman by birth, who had entered the royal service

* Sozzini, p. 264.

as soon as he could swing a sword, he had been advanced in honor for the sole reason of merit until he ranked with the best soldiers of his day. Loyal to his king with every drop of his blood and full of frank admiration for brave men, fair women, good wine, and all similar bounties of a generous earth, he was just the man to appreciate the exalted mood of the Sienese. Late in life, during a period of leisure forced upon him by a bullet wound, he sat down to write his autobiography—an amazing book, which Henry IV called the "Soldier's Bible," and which treats of the Sienese siege with a vividness obliterating all the intervening years.

Strozzi's new plan, the second string to his bow, was as follows: Departing from Siena with the bulk of his troops, he would establish a base in the rich Chiana valley to the east, whence he could provision Siena at pleasure in case Marignano continued the siege. If Marignano, on the other hand, abandoning Siena, fastened upon his heels, he would, under favoring circumstances, put everything upon the arbitrament of a battle. The second eventuality came to pass. Strozzi had hardly left Siena (July 17) when the Imperialists made ready to follow. Some days of manœuvring in the Chiana region followed, reaching a fitting climax in a great shock of arms on August 2, 1554, at the castle of Marciano. Through a series of mishaps, among which, according to Sienese tradition, treason had a part, Strozzi was not only defeated but overwhelmed. Some of his men, casting away their armor and weapons, made their way back to Siena; Strozzi himself with the remnant of his horse escaped to friendly Montalcino.

Siena, breathless for news of the host manœuvring to

the east, heard only too soon of the events of that August day of fierce sunshine. Toward evening the first stragglers appeared, bleeding, covered with dust and sweat, and dropping from sheer exhaustion in the streets. "Never did spectacle so claim compassion as this of the poor wounded, and especially the plight of the French and Germans, who uttered sobbing cries and held out their hands, asking for water and a bit of salt for their wounds; so that men and women brought them salt, bread, and wine, and aided them as best they could. And I swear that I saw more than a hundred men lean against a wall, unable to restrain their tears for pity of these poor soldiers reduced to the last extremity."*

The destruction of Strozzi's field army sounded the doom of Siena. The victorious Imperialists could now return, complete the blockade without hindrance, and starve the town into surrender. Cold reason might urge the citizens to end the struggle, but patriotism had been fanned to a consuming flame, and patriotism whispered to die rather than yield. This resolution, taken by the rulers, was in harmony with the set determination of the citizen body; needless to say it had the enthusiastic approval of the buoyant and grandiloquent commander, Blaise de Monluc.

Shortly after the battle of August 2, the blockade of Siena, maintained in a loose way since January, became close and complete. And immediately prices rose and a shortage announced itself in all articles of food. Loyal peasants who tried to drive cattle or carry vegetables to market were seized by the Spaniards, plun-

* Sozzini, p. 272.

dered of their goods, and hanged up by the roadside as
a warning to their fellows.   All around the city the oaks
bore among the acorns of that autumn this horrible
human fruit.   Strozzi, off at Montalcino, transmitted
hopeful messages of stores upon the way, to be followed
by a new French army sent to his good Sienese by their
beneficent protector, Henry II, but apart from a few
pack-asses who occasionally broke through the Spanish
lines under cover of night, nothing happened to lighten
the growing burden of starvation.   With Strozzi indeed
rests no blame.   He did what he could by sending stirring
appeals to the French court, but was unable to rouse the
distant government from the apathy which had overtaken it with regard to all things Italian.

The siege in this final phase lasted eight terrible
months.   On Christmas eve, Marignano, stirred by an
impatient message from Duke Cosimo at Florence, resolved to bring matters to a conclusion by a general
assault.   His preparations were carefully made, but
were not kept so secret as to escape detection.   Two
hours past midnight the great bell of the Mangia tower
boomed forth the news to the sleeping city; the citizens
and soldiers, springing from their beds, ran to their appointed posts; and the attack was victoriously repelled.
Thenceforth Marignano contented himself with the
slower methods of starvation.   The soldiers taunted
one another from behind trench or bulwark; occasionally
cavalry bands, supported by arquebusiers on foot, skir-
mished in the valley below Porta San Marco; or again
Marignano enlivened the tedium of camp life by dropping a few canon balls into the town—such incidents as
these afforded food for daily gossip but did not incline

Siena During the Siege

From an Old Print in the Uffizi at Florence

the balance one way or another. The real work of the siege was done by hunger and disease. Cattle soon ceased to be brought to market, and asses, dogs, cats, and rats were greedily devoured.* If a peasant got through the lines with a basket of figs or nuts, he was surrounded in a moment by a shouting and gesticulating crowd, wildly outbidding one another for his dainties. The poor picked the weeds from the crevices of damp walls and made them into a soup. The magistracy, which, for the purpose of a better control, had confiscated all grain and flour within the walls, saw with anxiety the shrinkage of supplies, and repeatedly cut down the weight of the daily loaf allotted to each soldier and citizen. Finally, desperately resolved to leave no stone unturned, the defenders decided to get rid of the *bocce disutili*—the useless mouths which had to be fed, but did not strengthen the resistance. The wonderfully expressive phrase illustrates the viewpoint of a grim and patriotic people brought face to face with disaster. As early as September the expulsions began, involving sometimes the peasants who had fled from their homes before the harrying Spaniards, sometimes the serving classes who waited upon the well-to-do, and at last, the very orphans of the hospital. Occasional bands of these expelled wretches the Imperialists charitably let pass their lines; others they sternly thrust back toward the walls and trenches, where, equally rejected by both sides, they were left to wander, like the wailing souls of Limbo, till death brought relief.

* Monluc, II, p. 89. "Les chatz se vendoinct trois et quatre escuz, et le rat ung escu"—at least those are the figures Monluc remembered fifteen years after the event.

It was on October 5 that two hundred and fifty children from the famous hospital of the Scala, ranging from
six to ten years of age, were led to the gate of Fonte
Branda. Accompanied by a group of men and women
who desired to improve the opportunity to effect their
own escape, they set out with the fall of night, carrying
their slender effects in bundles or thrown across the
backs of asses. They had not proceeded far upon their
way before they were challenged by a Spanish guard—
whereupon in the dark ensued a terrible scene of wanton
wickedness, and when the morning dawned the survivors
of that hapless caravan, sobbing, bleeding, robbed of
everything, were back at Fonte Branda gate. "The
spectacle would have made a Nero weep," says an eye-
witness, who adds that, unable to shake off the horrible
impression, he could neither eat nor drink for three
days.*

But let it not be imagined that the long and tragic
struggle spread an atmosphere of unbroken gloom over
the city. The natural gaiety and mercurial disposition
of the Sienese did not desert them in these days of trial,
and often filled the streets with laughter and amusement.
Monluc, who shared the faith that men were no worse
fighters for a little cheerfulness, saw many a sight which
stirred his pulse and filled him with admiration.† On
January 13, for instance, some youths improvised a
dance, *un ballo tondo*, in the Campo. Then with

---

* Sozzini, p. 307.

† His admiration for the women of Siena, who, from the lowest to the
highest classes, presented themselves to work with the men at the trenches
and bastions, led him to compose one of the most charming passages of his
book. "Il ne sera jamais, dames siennoises, que je n'immortalize vostre
nom, tant que le livre de Monluc vivra: car, à la vérité, vous estes dignes
d'immortelle louange si jamais femmes le feurent." Then he relates how at the

mounting zest they played at *pallone* * with half the
city looking on amidst applause; and finally, at a
trumpet signal, they divided as of old into three bands
according to terzi, and played with unabated passion at
the rude and vigorous game of *pugna*. The French
commander, surrounded by a group of his transalpine
officers, looked on at the wild frolic, and was so amazed
at the unquenchable vivacity which could shake off the
sadness of the time, that a wave of emotion passed over
him and filled his eyes with tears. Hardly was the
game ended when the cry arose from all sides: *alle
guardie, alle guardie.* "And in a flash they rushed from
the piazza to get their weapons and present themselves
at their appointed posts."†

At last when spring came and no French army was
on the way for their relief, the famished burghers saw
that they had no alternative but to surrender. They
opened reluctant negotiations with Charles—his ally,
Duke Cosimo, playing the part of mediator—and after
long discussions, on April 17, 1555, a treaty was drawn
up which, if saving appearances for the besieged, none
the less signified subjection.‡ The French garrison
was to march out with the honors of war, but Siena had
to accept the protection of the emperor, who received
the right to change the government and to occupy the

beginning of the siege the noble and well-to-do ladies divided themselves into
three companies with leaders, banners, and appropriate and beautiful cos-
tumes, and how, company-wise, they marched each day to their work, singing
a song in honor of France as they fared along. And, says the emphatic
soldier, "I would give my best horse if I could remember that song to quote
it here." Monluc, II, pp. 55–56.

* A variety of foot-ball.
† Sozzini, p. 354.
‡ The treaty will be found in Pecci, "Memorie," etc., IV, 218 *ff.*

town with his troops. Under the circumstances an
additional article, declaring that the republic retained
its liberties, was, of course, meaningless. And that
was the view of a group of patriots who in literal truth
preferred exile and death to living in subjection. When,
therefore, on April 21, the gates were thrown open and
Monluc, preceded by his arquebusiers and pikemen,
marched out with drums and banners like a conqueror,
there went with him a company of eight hundred
Sienese, who turned their steps toward Montalcino,
resolved to live out their days on earth in the little
mountain town as freemen wearing no lord's livery.
Monluc has left a moving picture of these heroic
victims on the march, showing us the old women and
infants seated on sumpter mules amidst the wreck of
their belongings, while the rest plodded along on foot,
many an old man leading his wife by one hand and his
daughter by the other.* Arrived at Montalcino, which,
with some of the neighboring points of Southern Tuscany, was still occupied by the French and not included in the capitulation, they set up what in a spirit
of stubborn pride they called "The Sienese Republic
in Montalcino." The republic, according to their view,
was to be found wherever there were unconquered
Sienese.

A few hundred feet from the Roman gate, by which
he issued forth, Monluc was met by his opponent,
Marignano, who had won the reputation during the
siege of being both an efficient and a courteous commander. Leaning from their horses they embraced
effusively, and fared along together for a space, discuss-

* Monluc, II, p. 102.

ing with the easy comradery of men-at-arms the incidents of the late campaign. The occasion was of the
sort to draw out all of the Gascon's native talent for
dramatic display. He tells us that he condescended to
point out to Marignano some of the mistakes which that
general had made in the conduct of the siege. "Un'
altra volta sarò piu savio," quietly responded the well-
bred Italian, showing thereby that he could use his
tongue quite as effectively as his sword.* On taking
leave of one another, Marignano rode back to lead his
Spaniards into the conquered town, and presently the
ringing of bells and the roar of artillery declared that
Siena had again passed under the dominion of the
emperor.

The aging Charles did not enjoy the recovery of
Siena long. In the very year of the surrender, broken
by the burden of life, he began to relinquish his honors
and possessions to his son Philip, and Philip, hard-
pressed like his father by the King of France, soon discovered that his position in Italy required close and
unrelaxing vigilance. In order to keep the valuable
friendship of Duke Cosimo of Florence, he was presently
obliged to cede to that sovereign Siena and all her territory (July 3, 1557). It is only too plain that Cosimo,
who was one of the subtlest of diplomats, had been
working steadily toward this end ever since he offered
to help Charles subdue the recalcitrant city. Naturally
he was not minded to let Montalcino and the southern
rim of the Sienese contado escape his grasp. Following
his custom, he watchfully bided his time, and when, in
the year 1559, in the treaty of Cateau-Cambrésis, Henry

* Monluc, II, p. 104.

II agreed to hand over the last French outpost in Tuscany to Philip, Cosimo was on hand to remind his
Spanish friend that Montalcino was indubitably implied
in the cession of 1557. Thus "the Sienese Republic in
Montalcino," after four years of undaunted struggle
against the fates, came to an end, and over the undivided
territory of Siena reigned the House of Medici.* The
state was not fused with the Florentine state, for it
maintained a separate administrative existence, but
henceforth it shared with Florence a common sovereign
and a common destiny. In this limited sense Siena
had, after a stubborn resistance prolonged through four
centuries, been at last subjected to the rule of the rival
commonwealth. Perhaps it would correspond more
nearly with the facts to declare that both cities had
alike fallen victims to the guile and vigor of the Medicean tyrant.

The reader who has followed with sympathy the long
story of the commonwealth of Siena will not refuse to
share the grief of the citizens over its end. And yet, if
he listens to the voice of reason, he will be forced to
acknowledge that the end was prepared by ineluctable
necessity, and came in the fulness of time. To every
thing under the heavens there is a season. Thus for
the free communes there was a season which opened
to them an escape out of the prison of feudalism, and
which endowed man with a new conception of his
powers and purposes. The communes have the immense merit of having created a new civilization, a

* For these last events and arrangements consult Pecci, "Memorie,"
etc., IV.

civilization, in fact, with the elaboration of which the world has been occupied down to our own day. In the glory of the city republics of Italy, in the immortal achievements of Venice, Milan, Florence, and the rest, Siena has a small but assured share. But time revolved and the season came for political organizations of an ampler sort. Then it was that Siena began to show signs of gathering perplexity and insufficiency. She could not solve the problem of a stable government; she could not protect from robbery and violence the country population committed to her care; she could not maintain her independence except by binding herself, at the sacrifice of dignity, to a protector. It was as right as it was inevitable that she should terminate her career by being gathered under a government representing all Tuscany, regrettable though it was that Tuscany in its turn was not gathered under a government which embodied the unity of the Italian people. Against that natural consummation of the impressive development which had given the inhabitants of the peninsula a common speech, common interests, and a common culture, fate had, for the present at least, set its face. None the less, if Italian unity was delayed, its coming was certain, and, as a measure of preparation, the disappearance of the Sienese republic imposed itself by the logic inherent in events.

Thus, coolly, the historian, occupied with the objective study of man in society, records a political catastrophe, but even as he writes he is reminded by his quickened pulses that the heart has a share in human events which is beyond the control of reason. No argument of science can rob death of its sting, and no overthrow of a heroic people will fail to stir our regret; for, says the poet, contemplating the end of the last of the Italian communes—the end of Venice,

"Men are we, and must grieve when even the shade
Of that which once was great has passed away."

COMPLETE LIST OF PRINTED WORKS REFERRED TO IN THE TEXT AND FOOTNOTES

"Archivio Storico Italiano" (since 1842). Vieusseux. Firenze.

Arias, G. "Itrattati commerciali della repubblica fiorentina." Le Monnier. Firenze, 1901.

Ashley, W. J. "Introduction to English Economic History and Theory." 2 vols. New York, 1892.

"Atti e Memorie . . . della R. Accademia dei Rozzi." 3 vols. Siena, 1870–88.

Banchi, L. "Le prediche volgari di S. Bernardino. 3 vols. Siena, 1880.

Banchi, L. "Statuti volgari de lo spedale di Santa Maria Vergine di Siena, scritti l'anno MCCCV." Siena, 1864.

Banchi, L. "I Posti della Maremma durante la Repubblica." Firenze, 1871.

Bargagli-Petrucci, F. "Le Fonti di Siena." 2 vols. Olschki, 1906.

Bartoli, A. "Storia della letteratura italiana." 8 vols. Sansoni. Firenze, 1878.

Bartoli, A. "Della Vita di Dante" (section of same author's "Storia della letteratura italiana).

Berenson, B. "The Central Italian Painters of the Renaissance." Putnam. New York, 1897.

Berlinghieri, R. "Notizie degli Aldobrandeschi." Porri. Siena, 1842.

Bernardino, San. "Le prediche volgari," etc. Edited by Banchi. 3 vols. Siena, 1880.

Blashfield, E. H. and E. W. "Italian Cities." 2 vols. Scribner. New York, 1901.

Boccaccio. "Il Decamerone."

Bonichi, Bindo. "Rime." Romagnoli. Bologne, 1867.

Borghesi and Banchi. "Nuovi documenti per la storia dell' arte senese." Torrini. Siena, 1898.

Brogi, R. "Il Palio di Siena." Torrini. Siena, 1894.

"Bulletino Senese di storia patria." (Since 1894.) Sordomuti di L. Lazzeri. Siena.

Burckhardt, J. "Die Cultur der Renaissance in Italien." 2 vols. Seemann. Leipzig, 1885.

Burckhardt, J. "Der Cicerone." 9 te Auflage. Seemann. Leipzig, 1904.

Caggese, R. "Un comune libero alle porte di Firenze nel secolo XIII." Seeber. Firenze, 1905.

Canestrelli, A. "L'abbazia di San Galgano." Alinari. Firenze, 1896.

Capecelatro, A. "Storia di Santa Caterina da Siena e del papato del suo tempo. Siena, 1878.

Cappelletti. "Le chiese d' Italia." 30 vols. Venezia, 1862 +.

Carpellini, D. C. F. "Gli Assempri di Fra Filippo." Gati. Siena, 1864.

Catherine, Saint. "Opere." Published bv G. Gigli. 4 vols. Siena and Lucca, 1707 +.

Catherine, Saint. "Epistole della serafica Vergine S. Caterina da Siena." With notes by P. F. Burlamacchi. 4 vols. Milan, 1842.

"Conferenze." Published by the Commissione Senese di Storia Patria. 3 vols. Siena, 1895–97. Nuova serie (2 vols. 1900–1).

"Constituto (il) del comune di Siena dell' anno 1262." Edited by L. Zdekauer. Hoepli. Milan, 1897.

"Constituto (il) del comune di Siena, volgarizzato nel MCCCCIX–MCCCX." Siena, 1903.

Coulton, G. G. "From St. Francis to Dante: A Translation of all that is of Primary Interest in the Chronicle of Salimbene." David Nutt. London, 1906.

Courteault. "Blaise de Monluc, Historien." Paris, 1908.

Dante Alighieri. "La Divina Commedia."

Davidsohn, R. "Geschichte von Florenz." 2 vols (to 1908). Mittler. Berlin, 1896, 1908.

Davidsohn. "Forschungen zur Geschichte von Florenz." 3 vols. Mittler. Berlin, 1896–1901.

Douglas, Langton. "A History of Siena." Murray. London, 1902.

Drane, A. T. "The History of Saint Catherine of Siena." 2 vols. Longmans. London, 1899.

Falletti-Fossati, C. "Costumi senesi," etc. Siena, 1882.

Ficker, J. "Forschungen zur Reichs und Rechtsgeschichte Italiens." 4 vols. Wagner. Innsbruck, 1874.

Fioretti di S. Francesco d'Assisi. "Per cura di Mons." Leopoldo Arnoni. Roma, 1889.

Folgore da S. Gimignano. "Rime." Romagnoli. Bologna, 1880.

Gardner, E. G. "Saint Catherine of Siena." London (Dent) and New York (Dutton), 1907.

Gaspary, A. "Geschichte der Italienischen Literatur." 2 vols. Berlin, 1885.

Gigli, G. "Diario Sanese." 2 vols. Siena, 1854.

Gregorovius, F. "Geschichte der Stadt Rom im Mittelalter." 7 vols. 4 te Auflage. Cotta. Stuttgart, 1889 +.

Hartwig, O. "Quellen und Forschungen zur Geschichte der Stadt Florenz." Elwert. Marburg, 1875.

Hegel, Karl. "Geschichte der Städteverfassung von Italien." Leipzig, 1847.

Heinemann, Lothar von. "Zur Entstehung der Stodtverfassung in Italien." Leipzig, 1896.

Hewlett, M. "The Road in Tuscany." 2 vols. Macmillan. London and New York, 1904.

Heywood, W. "Our Lady of August and the Palio of Siena." Torrini. Siena, 1899.

Heywood, W. "The 'Ensamples' of Fra Filippo." Torrini. Siena, 1901.

Heywood, W. "A Pictorial Chronicle of Siena." Torrini. Siena, 1902.

Heywood, W. "Palio and Ponte." An Account of the Sports of Central Italy from the Age of Dante to the 20th Century. Methuen. London, 1904.

Heywood, W., and Olcott, L. "Guide to Siena." Torrini. Siena, 1903.

Hodgkin, T. "Italy and Her Invaders." 8 vols. Clarendon Press. Oxford, 1885 +.

"Libri dell' entrata e dell' uscita della repubblica di Siena." Published by the Commissione Senese di Storia Patria. 2 + vols. Siena, 1903 +.

Lisini, A. "Provvedimenti economici della repubblica di Siena nel 1382." Torrini. Siena, 1885.

PRINTED WORKS REFERRED TO 425

Lisini, A. "Le tavolette dipinte di Biccherna e di Gabella." Olschki. Firenze, 1902.
Luchaire, G. "Le statut des Neuf Gouverneurs et Défenseurs de la commune de Sienne." Extrait des *Mélanges d'Archéologie et d'Histoire* publiés par l'Ecole française de Rome. Tome XXI. Rome, 1901.
Luchaire, G. "Documenti per la storia dei rivolgimenti politici del comune di Siena dal 1354 al 1369." Lyon and Paris, 1906.
Malavolti, O. "Historia de' batti e guerre de' Senesi." Venezia, 1599.
Marenduzzo, A. "Gli Assempri di Fra Filippo da Siena." Nava. Siena, 1899.
Massèra, A. F. "I Sonnetti di Cecco Angiolieri." Zanichelli. Bologna, 1906.
Mengozzi, N. "Il Monte dei Paschi di Siena e le aziende in esso riunite." 6 vols. Lazzeri. Siena, 1891 +.
Milanesi, G. "Documenti per la storia dell' art esenese." Porri, Siena, 1856.
"Miscellanea Storica Sanese." Edited by O. Porri. 1844.
"Miscellanea Storica Senese." Published at Siena. 5 vols (1893–99).
Molmenti, P. "Venice: Its Individual Growth," etc. Translated by Horatio Brown. 6 vols. McClurg. Chicago, 1906 +.
Mondolfo, U. G. "Pandolfo Petrucci, Signore di Siena." Siena, 1899.
Monluc, Blaise de. "Commentaires et lettres." Edited by Alphonse de Ruble. 5 vols. Paris, 1864 +.
Montalvo, A. "Relazione della guerra di Siena." Edited by Ricomanni and Grottanelli. Torino, 1863.
"Monte (Il) dei Paschi di Siena," etc. See Mengozzi.
"Monumenta Germaniæ Historica." Hanover, 1826 +.
Muratori, L. A. "Rerum Italicarum Scriptores." 25 vols. Mediolani, 1723–51.
Muratori, L. A. "Antiquitates Italicæ medii ævi." 6 vols. Mediolani, 1738–42.
Norton, C. E. "Historical Studies of Church-building in the Middle Ages." London, 1881.
"Ordo officiorum ecclesiæ senensis." Bologna, 1766.
Paoli, C. "La battaglia di Montaperti" (in vol. II of "Bulletino della società senese di storia patria." Siena, 1869).
Paoli, C. "Il Libro di Montaperti." Vieusseux. Firenze, 1899 (vol. IX of "Documenti di Storia Italiana").
Paoli C. "Siena alle fiere di Sciampagna." In Conferenze della commissione senese di storia patria. Siena, 1898.
Paoli, C. "I Monti o fazioni della Repubblica di Siena" (In "Nuova Antologia," August, 1891).
Paoli and Piccolomini. "Lettere volgari del secolo XIII." Romagnoli. Bologna, 1871.
Pasqui, U. "Documenti per la storia della città di Arezzo." Vieusseux. Firenze, 1899 (vol. XI of "Documenti di Storia Italiana").
Pecci, G. A. "Storia del vescovado di Siena." Lucca, 1748.
Pecci, G. A. "Memorie Storico-critiche della città di Siena." 4 vols. Siena, 1755.
"Periodico di Numismatica." (Since 1868.)
Petrarca. "Il Canzoniere."
Piccolomini, Æneas Silvius (Pope Pius II). "La storia di due amanti." Milano, 1864.
Pliny. "Natural History" ("Historia Naturalis").
Polidori, F. L., and Banchi, L. "Statuti Senesi. 3 vols. Romagnoli." Bologna. 1863–77.

Professione, A. "Siena e le compagnie di ventura." Civitanova-Marche, 1898.

Ptolemy. "Geography."

Repetti, E. "Dizionario geografico fisico-storico della Toscana." 5 vols. Firenze, 1833–45.

Richter, L. "Siena." Seemann. Leipzig, 1901.

Rondoni, G. "Sena Vetus." Fratelli Bocca. Torino, 1892.

Rondoni, G. "Tradizioni popolari e leggende di un comune medioevale e del sur contado." Firenze, 1886.

Rossetti, D. G. "Early Italian Poets." Dent. London, 1904.

Salvemini, G. "Magnati e Popolani in Firenze dal 1280 al 1295." Firenze, 1899.

Santini, P. "Contado e politica esteriore del secolo XII" ("Estratto dall' Archivio Stor. It.," Serie V, Tomi XXV, XXVI, anno 1900).

Savigny, F. C. "Geschichte des Römischen Rechts im Mittelalter." 7 vols. Heidelberg, 1834.

Schneider, G. "Die finanziellen Beziehungen der Florentinischen Bankiers zur Kirche." Leipzig, 1899.

Scudder, Vida. "Saint Catherine of Siena as Seen in Her Letters." Dutton. London and New York, 1906.

Sermini, G. "Novelle." Vigo. Livorno, 1874.

Sozzini, A. "Diario delle cose avvenute in Siena dal 20 Luglio 1550 al 28 Giugno 1555." (Tomo II of "Archivio Stor. It.," 1842.)

"Studi Giurdici dedicati a F. Schupfer." Bocca. Torino, 1898.

"Studi Senesi nel Circolo Giuridico." 20 + volumes. Siena.

Tacitus. "Historiæ."

Thureau-Dangin, P. "S. Bernardino da Siena." (This Italian edition is fuller than the original French.) Siena, 1897.

Tocco. "L'eresia nel medio evo." Firenze, 1884.

Tommasi, G. "Dell' Historie di Siena." Venezia, 1625.

Toti, A. "Atti di votazione della città di Siena." Siena, 1870.

Ugurgieri, A. "Le pompe senesi." 2 vols. Pistoia, 1649.

Vasari, G. "Le Vite de' più eccellenti pittori," etc. Edited by G. Milanesi. 9 vols. Sansoni. Firenze, 1880 +.

Villani, G. "Croniche." Edited by F. G. Dragomanni. 4 vols. Firenze. 1844.

Villari, P. " I primi due secoli della storia di Firenze." 2 vols. Sansoni. Firenze, 1893.

Zdekauer, L. "Il constituto dei consoli del placito del comune di Siena." Torrini. Siena, 1890.

Zdekauer, L. "Il constituto del comune di Siena dell' anno 1262." Hoepli. Milan, 1897.

Zdekauer. "Lo studio di Siena nel Rinascimento." Hoepli. Milan, 1894.

Zdekauer. "Sulle origini dello studio di Siena." Siena, 1896.

Zdekauer, L. "La vita privata nel dugento." "La vita publica nel dugento." Two lectures published with documents. Siena, 1896–7.

Zdekauer, L. "Sugli Statuti del Monte Amiata" (see "Studi Giuridici dedicati a F. Schupfer").

"Zeitschrift für Geschichtswissenschaft."

"Zeitschrift für Handelsrecht."

INDEX

ADEODATUS, bishop of Siena, 24, 27.
Agniolo di Tura, 211.
Alaric, 12, 13.
Aldobrandeschi, 40, 65; as lords of Grosseto, 122; at Montaperti, 178, 180; and the Nine, 203-4; slow decay of, 231-2.
Alexander VI (Pope), 403.
Alleluia (The) of, 1233, 251.
Ambrogio (The Blessed) of Siena, 255.
Andrea Dei, 198, 205.
Ansano, Sant', Sienese protomartyr, 11, 22, 28, 85, 183, 317.
Antimo, Sant', 41.
Aquinas (Saint Thomas), on gambling, 349.
Arbia, 176, 179, 182.
Ardengeschi, 40, 61, 62, 65.
Arezzo, quarrel with Siena over eighteen parishes, 22-4, 52, 76; bishop of acquires immunities, 42; divides body of Sant' Ansano with Siena, 85; is subjected to Florence, 389.
Army, composition of in cities, 164-6; army of Siena, 281.
Arti. See guilds.
Asciano, 157, 161.
Augustus, founder of Roman Siena, 9.

BABYLONISH Captivity, terminated, 270.
Balestre (cross-bows), 166-7.
Balià, 128, 129, 130; as governing committee, 399-400.
Banking companies of Siena, 99, 109; their connection with the papacy, 110-12; the Buonsignori 112-3; signs of decay of, 225; acquire castles in the *contado*, 236-7.
Baratteria. See gambling.
Barili, 335.
Bartoli (Taddeo), 326.
Battaglie. See games.
Bells (of Siena), 296-8.
Beneventum (Battle of), 187.

Benincasa, Jacopo and Lapa, parents of Saint Catherine, 259.
Benvenuto di Giovanni, 328.
Bernardino (San), 355; sermons of, 394.
Bernardo (The Blessed), 255.
Biccherna, 144-6; housed on Campo, 296.
Bishop of Siena, acquires immunities, 42-4; receives submissions of nobles, 63; himself subjected to Siena, 63; review of his position, 72.
Black Death. See *grande mortalità*.
Boccaccio, 211, 241; popularizes the *novella*, 356.
Bolgano (the Sienese mint), 147; on Campo, 294.
Boni homines, 49-50.
Borghesi (Niccolò), assassinated, 400-1.
Borgia (Cæsar), 402, 403.
Breve consulum, 54, 128.
Buonconvento, 201.
Buonsignori (The), 112-3.
Byzantine art, 311-2.

CACCIACONTI, 40, 61, 62 (note), 65, 157, 230.
Calabria (Duke of), in Siena, 397.
Camarlingo (The), 145, 373.
Camollia (*terzo*). See *terzi* and *porta*.
Campo, 212; its position, 276; government buildings erected on, 294; form of, 301; fountain on, 304; jousting on, 339-40; life on, 348-52; games on during siege (1555), 416-7.
Caorsini, 101.
Capella di piazza, 299.
Capitano di guerra, 204.
Capocchio, 257.
Captain (The) of the People, 134, 142.
Carroccio, 78, 167-8.
Castellano, 235.
Castel Vecchio (*castellum vetus*), 8, 43, 276.

427